SO-BRH-665

AN
INTRODUCTION
TO
NEW
TESTAMENT
LITERATURE

AN INTRODUCTION TO NEW TESTAMENT LITERATURE

DONALD JUEL
WITH JAMES S. ACKERMAN
& THAYER S. WARSHAW

Abingdon
Nashville

AN INTRODUCTION TO NEW TESTAMENT LITERATURE

Copyright © 1978 by Donald Juel
Second Printing 1980

All rights reserved.

No part of this book may be reproduced in any manner whatsoever without written permission of the publisher except brief quotations embodied in critical articles or reviews. For information address Abingdon, Nashville, Tennessee

Library of Congress Cataloging in Publication Data

Juel, Donald.
    An introduction to New Testament literature.

    Bibliography: p.
    Includes index.
    1. Bible. N.T.—Criticism, interpretation, etc. 2. Bible as literature. I. Ackerman, James S., joint author. II. Warshaw, Thayer S., 1915– joint author. III. Title.
BS2361.2.J83   225.6   77-18036

ISBN 0-687-01360-7
ISBN 0–687–01361-5 pbk.

Scripture quotations in this publication unless otherwise noted are from the Revised Standard Version Common Bible, copyrighted © 1973 by the Division of Christian Education of the National Council of the Churches of Christ in the U.S.A., and are used by permission.

Scripture quotations noted NEB are from The New English Bible © the Delegates of the Oxford University Press and the Syndics of the Cambridge University Press 1961, 1970. Reprinted by permission.

Scripture quotations noted JB are from The Jerusalem Bible, copyright © 1966 by Darton, Longman & Todd, Ltd. and Doubleday & Company, Inc. Used by permission of the publisher.

MANUFACTURED BY THE PARTHENON PRESS AT
NASHVILLE, TENNESSEE, UNITED STATES OF AMERICA

CONTENTS

PART III The Individual Evangelists

CONTENTS

FOREWORD

This book is addressed to beginning students and general readers who are interested in the Bible and in literature. It tries to balance the concerns of biblical scholarship and literary criticism. As Donald Juel points out in his Introduction, scholars in both fields have begun to work together, to their great satisfaction and mutual advantage. We are fortunate to have as our author one of the new generation of biblical scholars who have taken an interest in the Bible as literature.

The book is organized in four parts. *Part I* (chapters 1 and 2) presents backgrounds for approaching the literature of the New Testament: its historical setting and some highlights of recent critical scholarship, using an illustration from the Gospel of Mark.

Part II (chapters 3 through 7) examines representative teachings and major events in the life of Jesus. It compares the differing accounts of certain key episodes in the four Gospels, especially the synoptics—Matthew, Mark, and Luke.

Part III (chapters 8 through 11) considers each of the Gospels as a separate whole. (It assumes that the book of Acts is the second chapter of Luke's history of Jesus and the early church.) Part III focuses on each evangelist's special preoccupations and characteristic modes of expression.

Part IV (chapters 12 and 13) looks at other New Testament genres: two representative letters (Galatians and I Corinthians) and an apocalypse (Revelation). We give less space to the Epistles because of our feeling that they have more value as theology than as objects of literary analysis.

Thus, one textual passage may be approached from different perspectives: as illustrative of the synoptic problem, as one of several slightly different accounts of the same episode, and as a segment of an integrated story by one evangelist. Repetition, though unavoidable in such an exercise, is kept to a minimum.

This method of organizing our introduction to New Testament literature is supplemented by chapter summaries, a fairly detailed table of contents, and an index of scriptural references. Together, they should be helpful for the reader who wants to refer to a specific passage or a particular aspect of New Testament literature.

It may seem only natural to start with the Gospels and to emphasize them, both from the order of the New Testament canon and the centrality of the life and ministry of Jesus. Yet the choice represents another decision in balancing the concerns of literary analysis.

On the one hand, one might well start with Paul's Letters. Most critical scholars think that they were written before the Gospels. Paul was a central figure in interpreting Christianity to the early church, which he greatly helped to found. If, as is further believed by critical scholars, the Gospels grew out of the early church and were influenced by its struggles, then one should read Paul first for those influences on the Gospel writers.

On the other hand, to understand Paul, one should be familiar with the story and message of Jesus, which were the inspiration for Paul's own life and teachings. The Gospels are as much background for the Epistles as the Epistles are for the Gospels. We start with the Gospels; but in doing so, we constantly refer to their setting in the early church.

In writing about the Bible in a pluralistic society, one is obliged to take into account a range of reader attitudes toward scripture, from fundamentalism to humanism. This book emphasizes the approach of critical scholarship: it attempts to present the consensus of modern critical theory. At the same time, we respect the alternatives offered by religious tradition.

Thus, we have tried to reconcile competing interests in several areas: (a) both literary and biblical concerns, (b) three alternate approaches to the Gospels, (c) the interacting stories of both Jesus and the early church, and (d) possibly conflicting critical and confessional predispositions of readers.

We have learned about these problems and have arrived at the compromises embodied in this book from our valuable contact with teachers of English (and teachers of teachers) who attended our Indiana University Institute on Teaching the Bible in Literature Courses in its first seven years. With each new group of participants we tried a different textbook for the New Testament, until we were forced into producing our own, as a companion to our *Teaching the Old Testament in English Classes* (Indiana University Press, 1973).

We dedicate this book affectionately to the hundreds of institute graduates who hounded us for years for such a volume. We hope it meets their expectations.

James S. Ackerman
Bloomington, Indiana

Thayer S. Warshaw
Andover, Massachusetts

INTRODUCTION

Study of the literature of the New Testament needs no defense. Even apart from their religious significance, stories of Jesus and letters of Paul have had a far-reaching impact on literature, music, and art in Western culture. They are part of our heritage.

Studying books of the New Testament as works of literary art may require some defense, however. People have always read the Bible in bits and pieces, confident that the fragments were part of a single whole. Folk tradition imposes a unity that tends to ignore the variety of perspectives in the New Testament. Oversimplifying, readers harmonize material drawn from several books.

Even biblical scholarship in the last century has largely neglected the artistic integrity and craftsmanship of the individual books, while it focused on preliterary stages in the history of traditions. Scholars have dismantled the New Testament narratives and teachings, but until recently have done little to reassemble them into works of literature.

The past decade or two has seen a shift in biblical studies. Biblical scholars have become interested in literary criticism. Both the traditional methods of examining the esthetic surface of a piece of literature and the new developments in structuralism seem to offer rewarding ways of understanding the Bible. Conversely, students of secular literature increasingly venture into literary analysis of the New Testament. They are finding the "good book" to be good literature as well.

These two complementary trends have brought new perspectives to the New Testament writings, uncovering dimensions that, if not altogether overlooked by earlier readers, certainly have never been fully appreciated.

This book is designed principally for students and teachers

of literature—as an introduction to the *literature* of the New Testament. It focuses on the four Gospels and Acts, which lend themselves more readily to literary analysis than do Paul's letters, whose greatest interest is for students of theology and church history. Nevertheless, to give a rounded picture of the literary genres in the New Testament, a chapter each is given to examples of the letters and of apocalyptic literature.

Background of the New Testament and history of biblical scholarship have been furnished to the extent thought useful for students and teachers of literature. For an exhaustive introduction to scholarly consensus in matters of the authorship, situation, and purpose of all the New Testament writings, including those not examined here, we recommend the many excellent books listed in the bibliography.

Thanks are due to many people involved in this project. First, I extend my appreciation to the Lilly Endowment, whose funding made publication of the volume possible. Next, Indiana University and Princeton Seminary have given me encouragement and support. Also I want to give particular credit to Esther Elizabeth Johnson for preparing the annotated bibliography and to Judy Lange for her near-flawless typing. But my special gratitude must go to James S. Ackerman and Thayer S. Warshaw for asking me to write this book for their series, for spending so many hours reading and editing, for providing stimulating suggestions at every stage of the work, and for preparing the chapter summaries.

CHAPTER ONE

❦

THE HISTORICAL CONTEXT OF EARLY CHRISTIANITY

Christianity began not as a new religion but as a sectarian movement within Judaism. Jesus was a Jew, born and raised in a Jewish family. Although the New Testament tells us little about Jesus' life prior to his public ministry, it does identify him as a Galilean, since his early years were spent in the town of Nazareth in northern Palestine. When he began his public ministry, he gathered about him followers who were Jews, and he worked almost exclusively among Jews. The few exceptions are noted as such (e.g., the stories of the Canaanite woman in Matt. 15:21-28 and of the Roman centurion's servant in Luke 7:1-10).

Those around Jesus perceived his ministry in accordance with concepts and precepts from the Jewish Bible and Jewish tradition;[1] he himself spoke of the kingdom of God that was about to dawn—a kingdom for which the whole history of Israel had been the prelude. When his followers tried to characterize Jesus, they took the terms from their Bible: Messiah, Son of God, the prophet, Elijah (see Matt. 16:13-16). Jesus and his followers participated in Temple worship, attended synagogue services, followed the Law of Moses, and considered the Jewish Scripture their Bible. When Jesus criticized the religious practices of his countrymen, he did so as a Jewish reformer, in the name of the God of Abraham, Isaac, and Jacob.

Even after Jesus' death, it was some time before his followers began to include Gentiles, or non-Jews, within their circle. For Israelites, non-Jews were outside God's covenant. The New Testament contains considerable evidence that the proposed inclusion of Gentiles within the early Christian community occasioned bitter controversy. As an ardent inclusionist, the apostle Paul was at the heart of the controversy, and it was, in all probability, disputes over the status of Gentiles in the church that led to his arrest in Jerusalem and eventually to his death. Paul's letters indicate how difficult it was for the first followers of Jesus to move beyond a conception of themselves as Jews—Jews who accepted Jesus as the Messiah of Israel. But Gentiles soon did gain entrance into the fellowship of believers, and by the second century C.E., the movement had become predominantly non-Jewish.

Sometime before the turn of the first century the break within the Jewish community between the small minority who believed that Jesus was the long-expected Messiah and the majority who did not became decisive. The precise circumstances that produced the crisis are unclear, although the exclusion of Jews who accepted Jesus from synagogues evidently was part of a broader purge within the Jewish community.[2] Whatever the circumstances, by the end of the first century C.E., the separation had been completed. Followers of Jesus came to view themselves as members of a separate religion, indicated by their acceptance of the name "Christians" (from the Greek *Christos,* the translation of the Hebrew word for "Messiah"). That sect name is used only three times in the New Testament (Acts 11:26, 26:28; I Pet. 4:16), and according to Acts, it originated outside of Palestine among Gentile followers of Jesus. Both groups continued to confess allegiance to the same God, to view the same books as sacred Scripture, and to consider themselves the true heirs of Jewish tradition. Yet by the second century, followers of Jesus the Christ were calling themselves Christians to distinguish themselves from Jews.

In general, the literature of the New Testament developed prior to the complete break between Christians and Jews. Thus, in the New Testament, the question of what it meant to be a follower of Jesus is still bound up with what it meant to be a Jew. To understand the character of Christian writings—the outlook, the biases, and the problems reflected in the literature—the reader must know something about what it did mean to be a Jew in the first century, something quite different from what it had meant to be a Jew in ancient Israel. Profound changes had taken place through the centuries. What follows,

then, is a brief review of Israel's more recent history as well as
a sketch of Judaism in the era when Christianity arose.

I. Historical Survey:
587 B.C.E. to 132 C.E., Exile to Expulsion

A. Postexilic Foreign Domination

In 587 B.C.E., the Babylonians destroyed the southern
kingdom of Judah, thus marking the end of the Davidic
Empire. The Babylonians were themselves conquered in 539
B.C.E. by the Persians, and the following year, Cyrus, as head
of the Persian confederation, issued an edict permitting the
many Jews who had been deported to Babylonia to return to
Jerusalem. The circumstances of those resettled Palestinian
Jews, however, had been significantly altered. The Exile
proved to be a watershed in the history of Israel. God's
Temple had been destroyed, and the promised land
conquered by foreigners. Most Jews now spoke Aramaic not
Hebrew. New institutions like the synagogue were evolving,
and the political situation in Palestine was radically changed.
Israel was no longer an independent kingdom; the government was headed by a high priest who owed his authority to
the Persian king. The conquest of Palestine by Alexander the
Great in 333 B.C.E. brought little change; Israel simply
became subject to a different imperial power.

After the death of Alexander in 323 B.C.E., his kingdom was
divided among his generals. Judea became part of the
kingdom of the Ptolemies, a Macedonian dynasty that located
its capital in Alexandria, Egypt. Ptolemaic rule permitted
Jews considerable independence in running internal affairs
and in practicing their religion, as they had done under the
Persians. Although the Ptolemies continued to rule Egypt
until its Roman subjugation, in 198 B.C.E. Judea came under
the domination of the Syrian monarchs known as the
Seleucids, another of the Hellenistic dynasties that succeeded
Alexander. The Seleucids proved to be far less tolerant
masters. They greatly increased the burden of taxation, and
one of their rulers, Antiochus IV Epiphanes, harshly
persecuted many Jews.

Palestine had gradually become Hellenized during the reign of the Ptolemies. To many Jews, as to others throughout the former Greek empire, Greek culture appeared extremely attractive. To other Jews, however, the new language and the novel religious and cultural patterns were a threat to their own biblical faith. A dangerous rift developed within the Jewish community, and Antiochus IV, an ardent proponent of Hellenistic culture and an even more devoted follower of Zeus, exploited the rift to further the Hellenization of Judea and to initiate the worship of Zeus among Jews. In the process, he deposed the current high priest in Jerusalem, replacing him with his own candidate—in return for a sizable bribe.

When civil war finally broke out, Syrian forces brutally suppressed the revolt, and troops were stationed in Jerusalem. Judaism became an outlawed religion; circumsion of infants was made a capital offense; Torah scrolls were burned; and, as the ultimate insult, swine were sacrificed on an altar to Zeus erected in the Temple. It was probably during these difficult times that the book of Daniel assumed its final form.

B. Rise and Fall of the Hasmoneans

Due to the intransigence of religious Jews and to problems within the Seleucid Empire, Jews under the leadership of Judas Maccabeus ("the Hammerer") were able to carry out a moderately successful revolt, and in 165 B.C.E., the Temple was reconsecrated. Although it remained within the Seleucid Empire, Judea experienced a measure of autonomy and status among the small group of nations in Palestine for the next century.

Descendants of the Maccabees, the Hasmoneans, reinstituted the office of kingship; they expanded the borders of the kingdom considerably; and the country enjoyed a degree of prosperity. Yet, as external circumstances improved, internal affairs in the Hasmonean kingdom worsened. Because the Hasmonean line could boast no Davidic ancestry, many people considered its rulers to be usurpers. Some of them proved to be tyrants. Growing disenchantment within the

religious community spawned a number of dissident movements that were to be of profound importance in Jewish
history. Among these were the Pharisees and the Essenes,
who will be discussed later.

In 63 B.C.E., the rule of the Hasmoneans ended. Two royal
brothers, Hyrcanus II and Aristobulus II, were competing for
power, and in the course of their struggle, each appealed to
the Romans for help. Apparently, segments within the Jewish
community also sent a deputation to Rome, insisting that they
would prefer Roman rule to that of either brother. After some
indecision, Pompey chose to occupy Jerusalem himself. His
troops marched into the city, where they encountered
resistance from Aristobulus' supporters, who eventually
barricaded themselves in the Temple. With the aid of
Hyrcanus, the Roman legions finally breached the wall and
slaughtered the remaining defenders. Pompey then
confirmed Hyrcanus as high priest, although depriving him of
the title of king. As head of the Jerusalem government,
Hyrcanus continued to rule Judea, but the boundaries of the
province were drastically reduced.

By 57 B.C.E., Hyrcanus lost all of his political power, and his
adviser, an Idumean named Antipater, emerged as the real
leader. After the defeat of Pompey by Julius Caesar,
Antipater was able to render military and diplomatic service
to the Romans in their Egyptian campaign. In return,
Antipater was named procurator, the chief provincial official,
of Judea in 47 B.C.E.

C. Herod the Great

Any hopes the Hasmonean family had of returning to
power were finally crushed by Antipater's son Herod.
Through his father's influence, Herod was given charge of
affairs in Galilee, where he proved to be an able fighter and a
strong, if ruthless, ruler. After surviving first a confrontation
with the Jewish government in Jerusalem, then the war
between Cassius and Mark Antony and Octavian, and later
the battle between Antony and Octavian, Herod was named
king of Judea by Octavian, better known as Caesar Augustus.
In 37 B.C.E., Herod put down, with Roman assistance, a revolt

in Jerusalem; thereafter, he was in complete control of
Palestine. By 25 B.C.E., he had destroyed the last of the
Hasmoneans (including his wife, Mariamne, a princess of the
Hasmonean line, and his own children by her), thus
eliminating any serious rivals for the throne from within the
Jewish community.

Herod was not a popular ruler. The Jewish community
never considered him to be a real Jew, and he further incensed
the religious community by assuming the right to appoint the
high priest. His brutality was notorious. According to
Matthew, Herod the Great ordered the slaughter of all male
children under three years old in and around the town of
Bethlehem because he was told that a young king had been
born (Matt. 2:1-18). Although there is no corroboration
outside the New Testament for the slaughter, Matthew's
account is an appropriate reflection of the king's character as
it is described in other sources.

A typical Hellenistic ruler and an ardent devotee of the
Roman emperor, Herod undertook ambitious building
projects, erecting magnificent cities. The cities were built in
proper Hellenistic fashion, including stadia, gymnasia, and
theaters. These projects must have required massive funding,
all of which came from taxes collected in Palestine; even
Herod's magnificent restoration of the Temple in Jerusalem
did little to win the favor of the religious community. Begun in
20 B.C.E., this grand project was not completed during his
lifetime. His death in 4 B.C.E. caused little mourning among
Jews.

D. Direct Roman Rule and the Zealots

The Romans divided Herod's territory among his three
sons, Herod Antipas, Philip, and Archelaus. Archelaus,
whose territory included Judea, Idumea, and Samaria, was
particularly incompetent and tyrannical, and in 6 C.E., the
Romans replaced him with a Roman procurator, Coponius.
Judea was now under direct Roman rule. One of Coponius'
first acts was the redistricting of the province for the purpose
of taxation, now a direct responsibility of the Romans rather
than the Herodians. This was a source of bitter resentment

among segments of the Jewish community for whom payment of taxes to Caesar represented acknowledgment of Caesar's lordship in a land whose citizens could acknowledge only one Lord. In 6 C.E., Quirinius, the Roman legate of Syria under whose jurisdiction the procurator of Judea fell, ordered a census to aid in the redistricting process. According to Josephus, the Jewish historian writing under the patronage of the Roman court two generations later, this census led to the rise of a Galilean revolutionary named Judas and to the formation of a revolutionary movement within the Jewish community:

> The territory of Archelaus was now reduced to a province, and Coponius, a Roman of the equestrian order, was sent out as a procurator, entrusted by Augustus with full powers, including the infliction of capital punishment. Under his administration, a Galilean, named Judas, incited his countrymen to revolt, upbraiding them as cowards for consenting to pay tribute to the Romans and tolerating mortal masters, after having God for their lord.[3]

The coming of the Roman procurators marked the beginning of a period of revolutionary fervor in Palestine. A loosely organized group known as the Zealots was formed; the group was composed of Jews who insisted that compromise with the Roman government violated the lordship of God. Some of the more radical elements of Jewish society formed small groups of assassins, carrying out executions of Romans and Roman sympathizers. A number of religious leaders also appeared, claiming to have been appointed by God to bring about the liberation for which everyone longed:

> Besides these there arose another body of villains, with purer hands but more impious intentions, who no less than the assassins ruined the peace of the city. Deceivers and imposters, under the pretense of divine inspiration fostering revolutionary changes, they persuaded the multitude to act like madmen, and led them out into the desert under the belief that God would there give them tokens of deliverance. Against them Felix, regarding this as but the preliminary to insurrection, sent a body of cavalry and heavy-armed infantry, and put a large number to the sword.[4]

E. Pilate

Revolutionary zeal among Jews continued during the time of Pontius Pilate, procurator from 26 to 36 C.E., and the man who tried and crucified Jesus as a threat to the peace. According to Josephus, Pilate was notorious both for his dislike of Jews and for his brutal methods of enforcing his rule. One of his most provocative acts apparently involved financing the construction of an aqueduct for Jerusalem with money taken from the Temple treasury. When people gathered to protest this violation of the sacred treasury, Pilate scattered soldiers disguised as protestors through the crowd. At his signal, the soldiers began to beat the protesters with clubs, killing or seriously injuring many Jews in the ensuing stampede.

The incident leading to Pilate's recall by Rome was equally characteristic of his brutality. A group of Samaritans had gathered at Mount Gerizim, their sacred mountain, at the instigation of a prophet who promised that he would uncover sacred vessels buried by Moses on the mountain. Pilate learned of the gathering and, interpreting it as seditious, dispatched his soldiers to disperse the mob. The result was a slaughter. The Samaritans lodged a protest with the governor of Syria, who had Pilate removed from office in 36 C.E.

F. End of the Jewish Homeland

Subsequent officials appointed by the Roman government to oversee the affairs in Judea were either unable or unwilling to forestall revolution. Despite the efforts of the religious leaders in Jerusalem and groups like the Pharisees, who realized that war with Rome would prove disastrous, advocates of revolt finally seized control of the Jewish government in 66 C.E., and declared independence from Rome. Internal power struggles destroyed what little chance the rebels had against the Roman forces. The Romans recaptured Jerusalem in 70 C.E. and burned the Temple; by 73 they had taken the remaining rebel outposts.[5] The Temple, the second in Israel's history, was never again rebuilt.

Yet the fires of revolution had not been quenched. Under a

powerful leader named Simon bar Kosebah, revolt broke out once again in 132 C.E. Simon was hailed by Rabbi Akiba, one of the leading authorities in the religious community, as the long-awaited Messiah who would deliver Israel. Simon bar Kosebah came to be known as Bar Kochbah ("son of the star"), identifying him as the star that was "come forth out of Jacob," according to Numbers 24:17—a passage that at the time was considered to be a prophecy of the coming of the Messiah. The Jewish forces put up stiff resistance, but the Roman legions crushed them within three years. The results of this conflict were disastrous. A Roman historian reported that 985 villages were destroyed and five hundred and eighty thousand Jews killed.[6] Even allowing for exaggeration, this final struggle still marked the end of Jewish life in Judea and of Jerusalem as the focal point of Judaism. The Roman emperor Hadrian passed a law making it a capital offense for Jews to be found in the environs of the city, and he built a temple to Jupiter in the holy city. The influence of Palestinian Jews continued to wane until finally Babylonia became the cultural and intellectual center of Jews throughout the world.

II. The Jews During the First Century of the Common Era

Following the destruction of the monarchy and the Babylonian exile of 587 B.C.E., there were always more Jews living outside the land of Israel than within, even during the reign of the Hasmoneans, which was the era of greatest power and prosperity in Jewish Palestine. By the first century of the common era, Jewish communities existed in most of the major cities of the Roman Empire, including Rome itself. Alexandria, the great Hellenistic city in Egypt, had a Jewish population of considerable size and importance. Jews in Babylonia eventually assumed religious and intellectual leadership among Jews everywhere.

The differences between Palestinian and Diaspora (a Greek term meaning "scattered") Judaism have been exaggerated unduly by earlier scholars but are significant enough to warrant the separate consideration of each tradition. Both are important to a complete understanding of the New

Testament. Although Jesus and his earliest followers were Palestinian Jews, succeeding generations of early Christians (among them the apostle Paul) were familiar with the experience of Diaspora Jews born and raised outside the land of Israel.

A. Diaspora Judaism

Current knowledge of Judaism outside Palestine is based on a study of artifacts, synagogues, and art, plus a relatively small number of writings.[7] One of the more important literary sources is the vast corpus of writings produced by Philo, an Alexandrian Jew born *ca.* 20 B.C.E. Philo attempted a synthesis of Hellenistic thought and Jewish tradition. As one thoroughly enamored of Greek culture and philosophy, Philo was hardly typical of Diaspora Jews, but his work does indicate the extent to which Jews living outside Israel had been able to digest other cultural and intellectual traditions and to create a new synthesis.

The end of the Davidic kingdom marked a new stage in relations between Jews and Gentiles. With the destruction of the first Temple, the loss of the land of Israel, and the elimination of kingship, all of the national symbols of Jewish identity were lost. Jews had to learn how to survive in communities where power resided with Gentiles. The experience of the Babylonian exile left an indelible mark on Judaism even after resettlement of Israel was permitted by the Persians.

The most obvious feature of Jewish life outside Israel was a tendency for Jews to live close together. Certainly many Jews followed the pattern of other subjected people and simply disappeared into non-Jewish society; Hellenistic culture held an almost irresistible attraction for cosmopolitan Jews living in major cultural centers. Other Jews, however, retained their sense of election, the conviction that they were called by God to remain distinctive. With the loss of national symbols and policy, Judaism became principally a way of life, holding the community together and providing the defense against assimilation. Jews ate only certain food; they practiced circumcision (an obvious mark of identification in the

Hellenistic world, where exercising and bathing in the nude were common); and they did no work on Saturday, their sabbath. For those Jews who believed that God was not yet finished with them and that they had been chosen to survive as Jews, the Law was as important as an external symbol of identity as of inner piety; it was a powerful social as well as religious force.

1. The Bible and Its Translations. The Jewish way of life was spelled out in legal traditions identified with Moses. (Some scholars suggest that it was probably during the Exile that these Mosaic traditions were edited in final form and that the actual books in the Pentateuch [Genesis through Deuteronomy] assumed their present form.) At the heart of sacred tradition was the written Torah (a transliteration of the Hebrew word for teaching), the first five books of Moses, whose authority was recognized by Jews everywhere. Because of the close tie between the sacred Torah and daily life, Scripture came to assume a prominent role among Jews. To understand Judaism, one must recognize that since the time of the Exile it has been a religion of the Book. When a Jew wished to know the will of God, he consulted those trained in the interpretation of Scripture.

It is in relation to the Jewish Bible that Hellenistic culture came to have a profound impact on Judaism. By the time of Ezra the Scribe (late fifth century B.C.E.), few Jews spoke Hebrew or could read the Bible in its native language. Instead, most spoke Aramaic, and eventually Jews read Aramaic translations *(targumim)* of the Hebrew texts at worship services. After the time of Alexander the Great, Greek became the universal language; consequently, scholars prepared Greek translations of the Jewish Bible, the most famous being the Septuagint. According to legend, this translation was prepared by seventy-two scholars at the request of Ptolemy II Philadelphus (ruler of Egypt in 285-46 B.C.E.).[8] Although the first translation probably came from Alexandria, a major center of Greek-speaking Jews, in reality the present Septuagint represents a conflation of numerous translations over a period of time.

Translation of the sacred writings into Greek had a significant effect on the evolution of Jewish thought. For the first time, Jewish sacred writings became accessible to all Greek-speaking people, including Gentiles, opening the Scriptures to a far broader range of interpretations. The translations themselves inevitably introduced Greek words and their related thought forms into Jewish tradition. The Bible used by the New Testament community was Greek, and with few exceptions, the quotations in the New Testament from the Jewish Bible come directly from Greek translations rather than from the original Hebrew.

2. The Synagogue. One of the most important institutional developments to evolve in the Diaspora was the synagogue (derived from the Greek term indicating a gathering place). The precise circumstances of its origin are unclear, but it probably emerged, at least in embryonic form, soon after the beginning of the Exile. By the first century C.E., it was a well-established feature of Jewish life throughout the world. In addition to serving as a place of worship on the Sabbath, it also provided a center for instruction and study and for social gatherings. Outside Israel it also apparently provided an opportunity for interested Gentiles to participate in a limited way in Jewish worship. There was a special category of Gentiles, known to the Jews as "God-fearers," who observed some of the dietary laws and participated in synagogue worship but who had not yet become full proselytes to Judaism. This category is of particular importance in the book of Acts, which will be examined in a later chapter.

The most striking feature of Diaspora Judaism is the extent to which Jews were able to digest new cultural, intellectual, and language patterns and still survive as Jews. Yet as recent studies have shown, the Hellenization of Judaism was by no means restricted to those Jewish communities established outside Palestine. Patterns that developed among Diaspora Jews had an impact on life in the land of Israel as well. The synagogue, for example, became a standard feature of life even in the city of Jerusalem. Although it originally served as a substitute for the Temple as a place of worship, the synagogue and Temple services coexisted in Palestine. After the destruction of the second Temple, the synagogue replaced it as the center of worship among Jews.

B. Palestinian Judaism

1. The Religious Establishment. The dominant factor in the life of the Palestinian Jew was the Temple in Jerusalem. According to tradition, God had chosen Mount Zion, the site of the Temple, as his "resting place for ever" (Ps. 132:14). Daily sacrifices were conducted, the most important of which were the burnt offerings twice a day. Once a year—on the solemn Day of Atonement—the high priest entered the Temple's holy of holies, a chamber in the sanctuary to which all access was forbidden except on this special day, to atone for the sins of Israel. Although two Jewish temples existed in Egypt at least partially concurrent with the Jerusalem cult, the Temple in the holy city was the primary symbol of Jewish identity for Diaspora and Palestinian Jews for as long as it stood. Most Jews throughout the world tried to make at least one pilgrimage to Jerusalem in their lifetime, and Palestinian Jews were expected to visit the city for the three annual pilgrimage festivals—Passover, the Feast of Weeks (Pentecost), and the Feast of Tabernacles (Sukkoth).

The Temple staff included not only priests but Levites, whose functions included providing musical accompaniment for services. This sizable staff was supported at a considerable expense. Part of the money came from individual gifts and part from an annual Temple tax expected of every Jewish male over twenty years of age.

At the head of the Jerusalem religious establishment was the high priest. Candidacy for this office was restricted to members of priestly families, whose lineage was scrupulously examined. In addition to his cultic responsibilities, the high priest also presided over the Sanhedrin, the Jewish high court that had the responsibility of adjudicating all matters of Jewish law. The Sanhedrin itself was composed of representatives from various segments of Jewish society: the chief priests, predominantly from aristocratic families; the scribes, professional legal scholars; and the elders, lay representatives from the community. The real power of the high court was in the hands of the wealthy, conservative members of Jerusalem society, and since there was no real distinction in Jewish law between secular and religious matters, the Sanhedrin's jurisdiction was far-reaching. Although there has been considerable debate about the precise legal authority of this body under the Roman procuratorship (in particular whether the high court could order and execute capital sentences for appropriate offenses in Jewish law), it is clear that the body was granted broad power by Rome.

2. *The Sadducees.* The Jewish religious community included a variety of sects, or parties, modeled after patterns familiar from philosophical movements in the Hellenistic world.[9] Although all were included within the one community of God's people, each sect was characterized by its particular views of what it meant to be a Jew and what should be considered authoritative for the community. Members of these groups composed only a small minority of the total Jewish population; the majority of the community apparently demonstrated a less than overwhelming interest in religious matters and were considered by members of the various sects to be nominal Jews—*'Am Ha' arez.* Though small in membership, these sects were extremely influential in the life of the community.

Prior to the destruction of the second Temple by the Romans in 70 C.E., the most powerful of these sects was the Sadducees. Their origin probably can be traced to the period of the Hasmoneans, and the name Sadducee apparently was a tribute to Zadok (Sadoc), the high priest under David. Composed principally of members of priestly families, those who controlled the Temple establishment in Jerusalem, the Sadduccees were characterized by their conservative religious attitudes. They were suspicious of innovation and assimilation of Hellenistic ideas. They insisted that the laws to be followed by Jews must come from the written Law; the Torah, Genesis through Deuteronomy, was the only real scriptural authority.

Profound changes in Jewish society had occurred since the Mosaic era, and many facets of daily life in postexilic times were simply unprovided for in the Law. All those aspects of life about which the Torah was silent were not matters of religious concern, and the Sadducees were free to develop their own rather worldly philosophy, a striking contrast with the more pietistic Pharisees. The Sadducees' conservative attitude toward tradition meant in practice, therefore, a real separation between the sacred and the secular.

A particularly important issue separating Sadducees from the rest of the Jewish community was their disbelief in the afterlife. By the first century C.E., most Jews had adopted the Hellenistic notions of resurrection after death and of the world to come. Nevertheless, since the Sadducees could find no mention of either in the written Law, the Torah, they refused to accept them. The short account of Jesus' confrontation with the Sadducees in Mark 12:18-27 is an excellent example of the attempt by the sect to ridicule belief in the resurrection. Jesus' response accurately reflects a Pharisaic view.

The Sadducees owed their influence not to the size of their membership or to the popularity of their beliefs but to the social and political status of their membership. The wealthy aristocratic families who were in charge of the Temple and who controlled the Sanhedrin were Sadducean in sympathy. With the destruction of the second Temple, however, the Sadducees' base of power disappeared; thus when the Jewish government was reestablished at Jabneh, scholars of Pharisaic persuasion assumed control and secured the support of the Roman government. Reduced to the status of a heretical sect, the Sadducees soon disappeared from the pages of history.

3. The Pharisees. The Pharisees are probably the most familiar of the Jewish sects and, as far as the later history of Judaism is concerned, the most important. The name probably comes from *parash,* a Hebrew word meaning separate. Although the precise origin of the movement is unclear, the "separate ones" apparently are related to the *hasidim,* the "pious ones" who steadfastly resisted Hellenization during the time of the Seleucid kingdom. The Pharisees emerged as an organized movement during the later stages of Hasmonean rule. Composed of Jews who disagreed with the policies of various Hasmonean rulers, the Pharisees at times participated in political intrigue and actively sought political power. By the first century C.E., however, the political ambitions of the sect had waned significantly—particularly after its unsuccessful conflict with Herod the Great. Instead, it had become a pietistic movement within the Jewish community, favoring toleration of Roman rule.[10]

In the New Testament, Pharisees are portrayed as being extremely scrupulous about dietary laws and laws of purification. They believed that laws in Scripture that were intended for those involved in Temple activities should be extended to every Jewish home. They insisted that food laws in the Mosaic Code be strictly observed and that food could be consumed only when all the proper religious taxes (portions of most foodstuff intended for the support of the Temple cult) had been paid. Their scrupulousness in observing laws of purification and in eating only with other Jews who shared their concerns for the Law was part of a genuine zeal for the Mosaic Law and a desire to extend religion to all facets of daily life.

In contrast to the Sadducees, the Pharisees believed in a much broader definition of normative tradition. They accepted all thirty-nine books presently included in the Jewish Bible as authoritative; in fact, one of the accomplishments of the Pharisaic community was the precise definition, sometime around 90 C.E. in Jabneh, of what was to be contained within the Jewish canon. Even more important, however, was their concept of oral law that, according to the Pharisees, had been handed down and accumulated from generation to generation since the time of Moses. This vast oral tradition had legal authority equal to the written Torah. Because the oral law was subject to continual development, it provided the real means of adapting the Law of Moses to new situations. In addition to making possible the evolution of new beliefs—such as belief in the world to come—it also provided the means for extending religion to all facets of life. Thus the Pharisees were far more religious than the Sadducees in their day-to-day lives and more progressive in their religion and in their humanitarian values.

The Pharisees appear as opponents of Jesus more often than any other group in the New Testament. This antagonism, recorded by New Testament writers, probably reflects the Pharisees' role in later Jewish society rather than their role during the time of Jesus. Prior to the destruction of the Temple, the Sadducees were firmly in control of the government, and the Pharisees seem to have been something less than final authorities even for the common people. Even though the Pharisaic party was firmly opposed to revolt against Rome, it still was not powerful enough to dissuade the populace from war in 66 C.E.

The real importance of the Pharisees stems from their position subsequent to the destruction of Jerusalem. A small community of Pharisaic scholars, under the leadership of Johanan ben Zakkai, organized a provincial government in a city called Jabneh (also spelled Yabneh or Jamnia). Shortly after, Jabneh was granted permission by the Romans to serve as the indigenous government for the Jews in Palestine, and the Jewish community henceforth was headed by scholars, rabbis of Pharisaic persuasion. The new establishment managed to survive the disastrous Bar Kochbah revolt of 132 C.E., which the majority of Pharisees apparently opposed even though such prominent men as Rabbi Akibah supported it. Within three centuries Judaism had been thoroughly rabbinized. Pharisaic beliefs came to be synonymous with orthodoxy. The Pharisees' interpretation of the Law is dominant in all rabbinic literature: in the Midrashim (commentaries on biblical works), in the Mishnah (compilation of the Law, arranged by subject matter), in the Gemara (commentary on the Mishnah), and in other works. (The Mishnah and Gemara together constitute the Talmud.)

It is highly probable that Jesus and his first followers came into conflict with the Pharisees. Jesus' claims to personal authority instead of appealing to tradition, as well as his willingness to include in his circle Jews whose lives indicated little respect for the Law, must have struck Pharisees as strange, if not offensive, behavior for a religious leader. Yet Jesus' attitude seems to have been close to that of the Pharisees on numerous issues; indeed, those participating in his death were not the Pharisees, but the Sadducees, the representatives of the Jerusalem establishment.

Why then do the Pharisees appear in the New Testament as the typical adversaries of Jesus? The reason, as suggested above, is the prominent role they assumed in later Jewish society, when the New Testament was being written. There is general agreement among critical scholars that the Gospels, while incorporating traditions originating with Jesus himself, were not composed until decades after his death; the earliest may not have been composed until after the destruction of Jerusalem in 70 C.E.[11] Those Jews with whom later generations of Christians came in contact— those Jews who finally excluded Christian Jews from synagogues—were Pharisees; therefore, it is not surprising that in such a situation Christian narrators would select stories portraying the Pharisees as opponents. Later generations of Christians probably had little conception of the Sadducees, and although the Sadducees had far more involvement in Jesus' death, they are not even mentioned in some Christian writings, such as the Gospel of John.

  4. The Essenes and the Dead Sea Scrolls. A third important sect within the Jewish community was the Essenes. Little was known about them prior to the discovery, in 1947, of the now-famous Dead Sea Scrolls, believed to have been produced by a monastic community of Essenes located at Qumran in the barren region near the Dead Sea. The attention the sect has received is probably out of proportion to the impact it actually made on Jewish society during the time of its existence. Nevertheless, scholars are in the extraordinarily fortunate position of possessing much of the community's literature, as well as considerable archaeological evidence from an area near the site where the scrolls were discovered. The account of the discovery and of the subsequent detective work is one of the most exciting chapters in the history of scholarship.[12]

  Like the Sadducees, the Essenes had a decidedly priestly stamp and apparently also originated in controversies during the time of the Hasmoneans. A particular group of priests evidently became convinced that those in charge of the Temple cult were basing their rituals on improper interpretation of Scripture and on an improper calendar (lunar instead of solar). The faulty interpretations rendered the whole Temple cult corrupt and its sacrifices invalid in the eyes of these Essene sectarians. They eventually broke off all ties with the Temple and the controlling priesthood, the majority withdrawing—in all probability under duress—to the wilderness where they lived a Spartan life of worship and study.

The Qumran sectarians believed that God would soon intervene in history to restore the fortunes of his elect. They considered themselves to be the true representatives of Israel, the remnant of the elect from which God would staff the cult in Jerusalem when the kingdom of the last days arrived; and they spent their time preserving their purity, studying Scripture, and preparing for the great battle soon to take place between the "sons of light" and the "sons of darkness."

Like the Pharisees, the Essenes were preoccupied with matters of ritual purity, and even in the arid surroundings at Qumran, ritual bathing was an important facet of community life. They were also intensely interested in study of the written Law. Also like the Pharisees, the sectarians included virtually the entire thirty-nine books of the present Jewish Bible within their collection of sacred writings, and much of their energy seems to have been invested in producing commentaries, only a few of which survive.

When the war against Rome broke in 66 C.E., the Essenes apparently believed that the great war of the last days had begun. They joined the revolt, with disastrous results for their community. The site was captured by the Romans and was never resettled. Fortunately for history, members of the community were able to conceal their sacred writings in caves near their settlement, and the scrolls remained in those caves until they were discovered by a Bedouin in 1947.

There is a vast quantity of literature about the Qumran Scrolls. A few early scholars believed that a source of profound influence on the early Christian movement had been discovered. Some suggested that John the Baptist and perhaps even Jesus himself had at one time been members of the sect. Today scholars are generally convinced that there was little direct influence from the Dead Sea sectarians on early Christianity.

Regardless of the degree of actual Essene influence on Christianity, the scrolls are invaluable sources for students of the New Testament, for they provide information about a little-known period in the history of Judaism. The only other sources available for reconstructing a picture of Judaism prior to 70 C.E. are the works included in the so-called Old Testament Apocrypha and Pseudepigrapha and the writings of Josephus.[13] Although the literature produced by the rabbis after 70 C.E. certainly contains material from earlier times, that literature is extremely tendentious, presenting only one facet of what surely was a complex Jewish community. The Qumran writings, hidden in caves following the war with Rome, remained uncensored by rabbinic scholars and thus offer an extraordinary addition to knowledge of Judaism prior to 70.

The Qumran literature provides a particularly interesting comparison with the New Testament. Knowledge of both the social character of sectarian life at Qumran and the history of the movement leads to a comparison of the Essene reinterpretation of Jewish Scripture and tradition with that of the early followers of Jesus. Each group was convinced that the story that began with Abraham, Isaac, and Jacob had come to something of a climax in its own community and during its own history. Although their versions and interpretations of the sacred story were strikingly different, the two groups were remarkably similar in one respect—both viewed the prophetic writings as oracles, predicting what was to happen at the end of time. Each group considered its own time to be the one in which many of the prophecies had been fulfilled. For each, interpretation of these oracles was not simply a scholarly task but actually was reserved for "inspired interpreters" who had been given "eyes to see" the hidden meaning of the text. This is precisely what the apostle Paul meant when he told the church at Corinth that those who did not believe in Jesus had a "veil" over their eyes when they read the Bible (II Cor. 3:14-16). Each group believed that its members alone had been given the ability to see the real meaning of Scripture. Each was confident that its beliefs and its history represented the fulfillment of promises made by God in former times.

5. The Jewish Context of Early Christianity. Not only Diaspora Judaism but also Palestinian Judaism had been thoroughly Hellenized. The extent of the impact that Hellenistic civilization had on Jewish life is becoming ever more apparent through the efforts of recent scholarship.[14] The various sects within the Jewish community seemed to have modeled themselves on philosophical schools prevalent in Greco-Roman society. The popular ethical advice of the rabbinic sages, the literary forms used in Jewish writings, the veneration of tradition, and the very pattern of rabbinic Judaism as a community of sages were all familiar Greco-Roman phenomena. And perhaps most interesting of all, the rules established by leading rabbinic authorities for the interpretation of the Jewish Bible were almost without exception derived from Greek principles of interpretation.

Christianity began as a Jewish sectarian movement in Palestine; by the end of the first century, it had become a movement that attracted primarily people with no background in Judaism. The message of Jesus the Messiah, therefore, had to be translated into a new language and recast into new thought forms. In their search for categories of thought appropriate for Gentiles living in a Hellenized world, Christians undoubtedly found in Judaism a ready-made synthesis of inestimable importance, and much of the impact made on early Christianity by non-Jewish religious, intellectual, and cultural traditions was mediated through Hellenized Judaism.

Summary

To understand the New Testament, one must know something of the historical and religious background of the Palestinian Judaism in which it arose. Jesus and his earliest followers were Jews and remained within the faith throughout their lives. The decisive break between Jews and Christians did not come about until the latter part of the first century, when the split was part of a restructuring within Judaism caused by the Roman destruction of Jerusalem. The New Testament, formulated prior to and during this schism, reflects both ancient Jewish traditions and the changing contemporary situation in its perceptions of Jesus.

Ever since their return to Palestine after the Babylonian Exile in the sixth century B.C.E., Jews had lived under a succession of foreign rulers: Persian, Greek, Egyptian, and finally Syrian. As loyal subjects, Jews in Palestine were allowed considerable autonomy in government and religious practices. Nevertheless, around 175 B.C.E. a Syrian ruler tried to unify his empire by imposing Hellenistic culture; he saw the unique features of Jewish religion as impediments to his program. Harsh persecution sparked a successful revolt led by the Maccabees, and Jews achieved a century of relative political independence.

Jewish self-rule ended in 63 B.C.E. when Roman intervention in a controversy among the descendants of the Maccabees led to Roman rule, enforced first by an ambitious local representative, Antipater, and then by his son Herod. Shortly after Herod's death in 4 B.C.E., Rome took direct control. Palestine's Jews reacted variously. Zealots demanded "freedom now." Others (called Herodians in the Gospels), who had become part of the Roman power structure, prospered. Between these extremes were other unhappy dissidents. Every move of the harsh and arbitrary Roman rulers to squelch revolt further fanned the flames. Finally, two widespread and disastrous rebellions (66–70 C.E. and 132–135 C.E.) destroyed the Jerusalem community and drove virtually all Jews out of Palestine. The execution of Jesus by the Romans as a would-be king of the Jews was only one chapter in these oppressive and turbulent times.

Most Jews had lived outside of Palestine ever since the Babylonian Exile, interacting with foreign mannerisms and thought forms while still retaining the ongoing traditions of Mosaic Law. The synagogue emerged as the focal point for each community to maintain its solidarity through worship and the study of Scripture. By the first century B.C.E., the language of Diaspora Judaism was Aramaic, a Babylonian heritage; its culture was Hellenistic; its way of life was Jewish.

In Palestine, the Temple cult had revived. Its high priest presided over the Sanhedrin—reponsible for Jewish law. A variety of religious parties arose:

1. The *Sadducees* were from the most powerful families, members of the priesthood and aristocracy. They took a conservative approach to Scripture, maintaining that only the written Torah was binding. Many changes in the Jewish situation were not covered by the Mosaic Law, so that a broad secular area of life appeared. Since the power of the Sadducees was tied to Temple worship and to collaboration with the Romans, their influence waned rapidly after the

destruction of the Temple and the dispersion of the Jews in 70 C.E.

2. The *Pharisees* were interested in extending Judaism to every aspect of life so that one could be holy and humane in all things. After 70 C.E. they unified and rebuilt Judaism. They cherished their traditions and would have been offended by Jesus, who spoke on his own authority and associated with those who led impure lives. But Jesus and the Pharisees shared many viewpoints (e.g., belief in the resurrection of the dead). The Pharisees are portrayed as Jesus' chief opponents in the New Testament largely because the stories of Jesus were being crystalized by Christians at the time after 70 C.E., when Jews (now led by Pharisees) and Christians were dividing into two mutually hostile religious groups.

3. The *Essenes* were probably responsible for producing the Dead Sea Scrolls. Earlier a part of the Jerusalem priesthood, they withdrew to found a community in the wilderness where they could prepare for the kingdom of God. The relationship between the Essenes, who perished during the first Jewish revolt against Rome in 66–70 C.E., and the early Christians is still debated by scholars.

CHAPTER TWO

❦

THE CRITICAL SCHOLAR LOOKS AT THE GOSPELS

The Gospels should appeal to readers with a sense of curiosity, since so much vital information is left to conjecture. The books say virtually nothing about themselves: why they were written, who wrote them, what circumstances surrounded the writing, how they are to be understood. Although each book now bears a title, "The Gospel According to—," it raises more questions than it answers. How and when were the titles added and the authors identified? Within the text none of the works identifies its author by name.

Even the label "gospel" is enigmatic. It certainly did not originate with the works, and it appears as a quasi-title only in Mark—not at all in Luke and John. The Greek word literally means "good news," and the apostle Paul regularly used it for the message Christian missionaries preached—not for a literary work of any sort.

It is true that few literary works begin with a careful statement of purpose or with a list of rules of interpretation; that omission usually does not trouble readers. Nor does the precise source of a story seem to be of real concern to scholars who study the mythologies of the Greeks and Romans. But the lack of such information assumes importance in the minds of readers of the Gospels, for the New Testament seems to invite an interpretative framework different from most other works of literature. The reason is certainly the immense significance the Gospels have assumed in Christian circles as scriptural texts. Because the Gospels came to be regarded as symbols of orthodoxy at a time when other books were competing with them for acceptance, questions about authorship and historical reliability were extremely important to interpreters. Since the second century of the common era, the classic defense of the authority of the four canonical

Gospels has been that they derive from apostles, members of Jesus' inner circle who presumably had access to information not available to others.

Interest in the Gospels as literature was almost completely absent from the immense corpus of commentaries written prior to the eighteenth century. The only literary questions in which there was any interest were those dealing with authorship. In the third century, Dionysius, bishop in Alexandria, Egypt, did a stylistic analysis of the Apocalypse of John in order to determine whether the author was the same John to whom the Fourth Gospel was attributed.[1] Augustine (354–430 C.E.) wrote an essay entitled "The Harmony of the Gospels," in which he raised some interesting questions about the relationship of Matthew, Mark, and Luke to one another.[2] But the few attempts at critical study of the New Testament were always related to doctrinal matters, and as the Gospels came to be accepted by all Christians as canonical, interest even in such marginally literary questions virtually disappeared.

I. Source Analysis: The Synoptic Problem

Study of the Gospels as literature did not begin until the Age of Enlightenment. To be more precise, what actually began toward the end of the seventeenth century was critical study of the biblical literature. Literary criticism, the term frequently used to describe this early stage in biblical studies, should more accurately have been called source analysis, for the first step toward reading the Gospels as works of literature was an observation about sources.

The relationship among the first three Gospels has consistently engaged students of the New Testament, perhaps more than any other question. Their language is remarkably similar at various points in the story. Augustine had proposed that Mark used Matthew as his source, that he was Matthew's "epitomizer."[3] But a new era in the study of the problem began with J. J. Griesbach, who contended that to make any truly scientific examination of the relationships among Matthew, Mark, and Luke, it was necessary to view them together. He suggested that the best means for such study was a synopsis (from the Greek "see together"), an arrangement in parallel columns of the three Synoptic Gospels. He published his synopsis in 1776, and its importance has been inestimable. Similarities in wording among the three Gospels are obvious even in a casual sequential reading. The real extent, precise character, and patterns of agreement, however, most clearly appear when the works are lined up in parallel columns on the same page.

The best way to understand the synoptic problem, as the relationship among the first three Gospels has been called, is in terms of specific examples. Four examples of the synoptic problem are included as an appendix to this chapter, and should be referred to during the following discussions of the four types of patterns observable among the Gospels.

First, some passages reveal extensive identity of wording in Mark and Luke but with no parallel in Matthew. An example of this first pattern is the story of an exorcism in the synagogue at Capernaum, an incident that Matthew does not mention. In Mark and Luke it occurs at roughly the same point in Jesus' ministry and is followed by the healing of Peter's mother-in-law. The significance is not simply that Mark and Luke tell the same story, but that they do so using such similar language. Beginning with "What have you to do with us," three sentences in the two Gospels are the same. Numerous small differences between the two accounts make those three consecutive identical sentences all the more noteworthy. Apparently there is some relationship between Mark and Luke not shared with Matthew. Either one author depended directly on the other, or they used a common source.

The second selection reveals a different pattern—extensive parallels between Matthew and Mark, with no corresponding material in Luke. In the example taken from the passion story, the wording in both Gospels is almost the same, beginning with the mention of the two robbers; it is completely identical from "And those who passed by" through "save yourself," with the single exception of "Aha!" in Mark. This passage suggests a relationship between Matthew and Mark not shared with Luke, or perhaps a source common to both but unavailable to Luke.

In the story of the rich young man a third pattern emerges: in some places all three Gospels use the same wording, even entire phrases and clauses. "All these I have observed" and "sell . . . to the poor, and you will have treasure in heaven; and come, follow me" are two such examples. The patterns of relationship in this particular story are especially unpredictable. At times all three Gospels have identical language. Elsewhere parallels occur only between Matthew and Mark or only between Luke and Mark. In a very few cases, Matthew and Luke agree but Mark diverges. And finally, in some wordings all the Gospels differ.

The fourth pattern—extended passages in which Matthew and Luke exhibit identical wording with no parallel in Mark—is exemplified in passages from Matthew's famous Sermon on the Mount. With few exceptions, they are sayings of Jesus. Luke's Gospel describes no Sermon on the Mount as such; instead, several of the sayings that Matthew includes in the sermon are scattered throughout Luke's Gospel. A particularly intriguing point is that several of the almost identical sayings occur at radically different places in the Gospels of Matthew and Luke. Since this relationship between Matthew and Luke relates almost exclusively to sayings of Jesus, it is reasonable to assume that the two authors made use of a source composed of Jesus' sayings, to which Mark did not have access.

A. Source Theory: Markan Priority

Scholarship in the last century and a half has tended to confirm Augustine's view that at least one of the three Gospels was used as a source by the other two. Some such explanation would seem to be demanded by the identity in wording among the three books. Jesus and his earliest followers undoubtedly spoke Aramaic, and the possibility that three separate individuals would have translated random Aramaic phrases into identical Greek is remote. Even taking into account the tendency in many of the Greek manuscripts to harmonize readings from all the Gospels, most scholars believe that some source relationship existed among Matthew, Mark, and Luke.[4] The majority of scholars today believe that Mark was the earliest of the Gospels; that his work was used independently by both Matthew and Luke; and that Matthew and Luke shared a second source, comprised almost exclusively of Jesus' sayings, called "Q" (from the German *Quelle* meaning "source") that was not available to Mark. The arguments adduced in support of this hypothesis may be summarized as follows.

The most extensive agreement among the three Gospels occurs in the narrative portions. Matthew, Mark, and Luke all follow a similar outline of Jesus' ministry, an outline that differs considerably from that in the Fourth Gospel. Little of Mark's Gospel is unique: about 97 percent of the verses in Mark can be found in Matthew or Luke; yet a good deal of material is unique to Matthew and Luke. Three inferences are possible:

1. Matthew and Luke both used Mark as a source, each separately and selectively, and each supplemented Mark from other sources;
2. Mark used Matthew (and Luke) selectively;
3. Matthew, Mark, and Luke each independently used a common source, which must be presumed lost.

There is strong evidence against the second conclusion. First, when Matthew and Luke agree with each other in narrative sequence, they also agree with Mark; further, when they differ from Mark, they also differ from each other. Second, in several of the stories common to the three Gospels, Mark's version is by far the longest, and his stories are stylistically closest to popular forms of storytelling. (A typical example [Mark 5:35-43 and parallels] is included in the appendix.) It is reasonable to explain the abbreviated and more literary versions in Matthew and Luke as alterations and polishing of Mark, rather than as Mark's changing a literary version to a more popular form.

The third conclusion is also unlikely, because there is little reason to postulate a source common to Matthew, Mark, and Luke. Matthew and Luke may have decided not to use the six stories unique to Mark: the parable of the seed growing secretly (Mark 4:26-29), the healing of the deaf mute

(7:31-37), the healing of the blind man from Beth-saida (8:22-26), the relatives' regarding Jesus as beside himself (3:20-35), the strange saying about being salted with fire. (9:49), and the cryptic remark about the youth who flees naked as Jesus is arrested (14:51). The omission of most of these by both Matthew and Luke can be explained without great difficulty: the two healings both mention the means of the cure, means that to early Christians might have seemed too close to stories about magicians; the statements about Jesus' relatives are offensive; the saying about salting with fire is unintelligible; and the remark about the young man who runs away naked may well have had meaning only for a particular group. That leaves only one parable—the seed growing secretly—whose omission by Matthew and Luke is unclear. While the arguments against this inference are not conclusive, it does seem that any hypothetical common source used by all three Gospels would look so much like the present Gospel of Mark that it is an unnecessary complication.[5]

B. Outside Sources: "Q"

The extensive and exclusive parallels between Matthew and Luke in the sayings of Jesus suggest that, in addition to the Gospel of Mark, the two authors shared another source composed almost exclusively of Jesus' teachings. This source would account for almost one-third of Matthew and one-fourth of Luke, portions of the two Gospels without parallel in Mark. The radically different locations of many of the sayings in the two Gospels imply that such a collection of sayings was not part of any consecutively arranged narrative of Jesus' ministry that would tell when he gave each lesson. Nevertheless, the identity in wording makes such a written source probable. This source—referred to as "Q"—has never been found, and it remains a hypothetical entity.

A work entitled "The Gospel of Thomas," a gospel composed entirely of sayings of Jesus, was discovered in 1945 in Egypt.[6] It is presumed to derive from a collection of Jesus' sayings in Greek, dating perhaps from around the turn of the first century. The Gospel of Thomas contains many of the parables of Jesus found in the Synoptic Gospels, but both the additional sayings and the radically different form of many sayings make it unlikely either that the author used the canonical Gospels as a source or vice versa. Although the Gospel of Thomas is not the hypothetical "Q," the discovery of this written collection of Jesus' sayings at least provides some evidence that a work like "Q" could indeed have existed.

In the Gospels of Matthew and Luke, much material that is not found in Mark is also unique to each. Hypotheses about the nature and origin of these passages are the least secure, since presently there is no reliable way to test the various theories. In the last decades, however, scholars have tended to view this material as having derived from oral tradition rather than from any written document. This view reflects a more basic picture of early Christianity in which all the first stories about Jesus were handed down orally rather than in writing.

C. Characteristic Differences

Additional support for Markan priority has resulted from the recent careful scrutiny of the minute differences among the Gospels. If Mark was used as a source by Matthew and Luke, it should be possible to explain the changes in one Gospel made by the other writers in light of individual and characteristic interests and tendencies that are observable elsewhere in each writer's Gospel. Scholars have had considerably greater success in interpreting these differences among the Gospels as purposive alterations made by Matthew and Luke than by Mark.

For example, the literary quality of the Greek in Matthew and Luke is often superior to that of Mark, a fact that is easier to explain as a later polishing of Mark's text than otherwise. The story of the rich young man (included in the appendix) illustrates the differences between Matthew and Mark in several cases. Jesus' question in Mark, "Why do you call me good?" might well have struck early Christians as strange, since to them Jesus obviously was good. The form of the question in Matthew, "Why do you ask me about what is good?" would guard against possible sacrilegious misunderstanding.

The commandments also take different forms: Matthew reads "You shall not—," while Mark and Luke read "Do not—." In the Septuagint, the Greek translation of the Jewish Bible used by early Christians, the form of the commandments is "You shall not—." It is easier to understand why Matthew would have altered the form to fit this biblical pattern than to understand why Mark would have modified the biblical pattern found in his source.

This kind of evidence is cumulative; each small argument is not convincing by itself. But their overall weight does tend to support the hypothesis that Mark was the first Gospel to be written and that Matthew and Luke used it. This conclusion does not answer all the problems for historians of early Christianity. But it does raise some fascinating questions for students of literature. Why did Matthew and Luke write their Gospels? How did the respective authors use their sources? What unique purposes and interests directed the way each author chose to retell Jesus' story?

The fact that two authors found it necessary to retell a story that already appeared in Mark makes the existence of separate versions more intriguing. Yet there was remarkably little interest in the question of each writer's purposes and interests among students of the Gospels until the last decade and a half. One reason is that until recently the Gospels have been studied by Christian believers for whom the books are sacred and authoritative. In scholarly circles, interest focused not on Matthew and Luke but on Mark, since this work was viewed as a primary source, a closer avenue to the events in the life of Jesus and to the historical Jesus himself. To understand the more recent stage of biblical scholarship, we need to begin with some observations about the Gospel of Mark.

D. Some Characteristics of Mark

Ironically, the Gospel of Mark became most interesting to students of biblical literature because of those characteristics that are least literary. Even a novice can appreciate the aesthetic shortcomings of the work. Mark's Greek is popular as opposed to literary; the sentence structure is simple to the point of being elementary; the author relies on a relatively small number of transitions in the narrative, the most common of which is "and immediately" (the "immediately" often having no adverbial function at all). The story is episodic and often disjointed, showing little effort to narrate it as an integrated whole. Close scrutiny of these features of Mark, however, reveals a great deal about the character of the composition and the nature of the author's sources. Many scholars began to theorize that Mark did indeed use sources in the composition of his work and that these sources were oral, not written.

Two observations make this proposal attractive. The first is that the outline of Jesus' ministry in Mark is extremely vague. Jesus spends the first part of his ministry in the north (Mark 1–8); he proposes to travel to Jerusalem (10:32-34); and he arrives in Jerusalem, where the final drama is enacted (11–16). Apart from this general movement in the story, the Gospel exhibits little geographical or temporal structure or specificity. Mark introduces individual incidents with general terms such as "one sabbath" (2:23) or "again" (3:1, 20; 4:1). Scenes are set "beside the sea" or "in the synagogue." Few episodes have any causal relationship to one another. Singly or in groups, they are united to form a story in an unsophisticated way; whole incidents may be removed from their context with little effect either on the meaning of the incident or on the progress of the narrative. The stories seem to be tied together by similarity in kind: Jesus' conflict with scribes and Pharisees (2–3:6), parables (chap. 4), miracles (5–8:29). The structure of the Gospel, in other words, seems to have been imposed on material that had already circulated independently, most likely orally. Mark gives no evidence of an earlier written biography of Jesus that began with his baptism and ended with his resurrection.

Another observation about the Gospel of Mark is that many of the individual stories in Mark (and in the other Gospels as well) follow a limited number of formal patterns—parables, miracle stories, and so forth. The pronouncement story, for example, begins with a brief mention of the setting ("Once while Jesus was walking through the grainfields with his disciples," or "Once when Jesus was eating with tax collectors and sinners"). Then a short narrative leads up to the striking pronouncement, with which the episode concludes. The story is little more than a narrative framework for the saying, with no attempt to link the incident to whatever follows. Miracle stories similarly have a formal pattern: a hopeless situation, a wonderful cure, and comment from witnesses.

II. Form Criticism and Redaction Criticism

Around the turn of this century, students of the Bible became interested in narrative patterns in the Gospels that could be found in other literature. Here two miracle stories from non-Christian sources either prior to, or contemporary with, the literature of early Christianity will be compared with Mark's story of the raising of Jairus' daughter (included in the appendix).

1. An inscription found at the temple of Aesclepius, a Greek god of healing, at Epidaurus in Greece:

> A man came as a suppliant to the god. He was so blind that of one of his eyes he had only the eyelids left—within them was nothing, but they were entirely empty. Some of those in the temple laughed at his silliness to think that he could recover his sight when one of his eyes had not even a trace of the ball, but only the socket. As he slept a vision appeared to him. It seemed to him that the god prepared some drug, then, opening his eyelids, poured it into them. When day came he departed with the sight of both eyes restored.[7]

2. A story about Apollonius of Tyana in Philostratus' *Life of Apollonius:*

> Here too is a miracle which Apollonius worked: A girl had died just in the hour of her marriage, and the bridegroom was following her bier lamenting as was natural his marriage left unfulfilled, and the whole of Rome was mourning with him, for the maiden belonged to a consular family. Apollonius then

witnessing their grief, said: "Put down the bier, for I will stay the tears that you are shedding for this maiden." And withal he asked what was her name. The crowd accordingly thought that he was about to deliver such an oration as is commonly delivered as much to grace the funeral as to stir up lamentation; but he did nothing of the kind, but merely touching her and whispering in secret some spell over her, at once woke up the maiden from her seeming death; and the girl spoke out loud, and returned to her father's house, just as Alcestis did when she was brought back to life by Hercules. And the relations of the maiden wanted to present him with the sum of 150,000 sesterces, but he said that he would freely present the money to the young lady by way of a dowry. Now whether he detected some spark of life in her, which those who were nursing her had not noticed,—for it is said that although it was raining at the time, a vapour went up from her face—or whether life was really extinct, and he restored it by the warmth of his touch, is a mysterious problem which neither I myself nor those who were present could decide.[8]

Despite obvious differences, a comparison of these two miracle stories with Mark's story of Jarius' daughter reveals striking similarities in pattern. First, each begins with an introduction of the person to be healed, usually with a comment that shows the seriousness of the illness or the hopelessness of the victim. In Mark, mourners are already present when Jesus arrives, indicating that he is too late; in the Aesclepius story, witnesses at the temple laugh at the foolishness of the man who is seeking the cure; and, in Philostratus' tale, the funeral procession has already begun. Second, in each story the hero accomplishes what must be viewed as an impossible task—a miracle. Finally, such episodes usually end with an appropriate expression of astonishment on the part of the witnesses.

The effect of the miracle story is to awaken in the reader (or listener) respect for the hero—recognizing him as divine (Aesclepius), as one who possesses divine power (Jesus), or as a man of overwhelming wisdom (Apollonius). These miracle stories told by different groups about very different heroes exhibit notable similarity in form. Even Philostratus' attempt to rationalize the miracle does not obscure the features of popular story forms. Such observations have given rise to one of the most influential movements in biblical scholarship—form criticism.[9]

The nineteenth century witnessed a remarkable interest in folk tradition in Europe, particularly among German and Scandinavian scholars, typified by the brothers Grimm. Biblical critics trained in the study of this folk literature recognized signs of oral tradition and of the various genres of folk stories in the formal story patterns evident in the Gospels. These form critics applied the methods of study originally developed for other oral and literary folk tradition to the gospel tradition. Their rather startling conclusion was that what preceded the Gospel of Mark was not a coherent biography of Jesus or a number of sermons by Peter but rather popular stories about Jesus set into forms similar to those of stories told about other heroes. Anonymous storytellers, therefore, achieved prominence as the bearers of sacred tradition, and form critics studied stories in Mark as much for what they reflected about the purpose of the early storytellers as for what they said about the historical events they recounted. Study of the forms or genres of tradition suggested that the purpose of stories about Jesus was not primarily to preserve information but to impress, reprove, or convince their audiences; they were intended to inculcate sound morality or solve problems more than to give facts.

Many religious people have unfairly characterized form criticism as an attack on the veracity of the Gospels. Actually, the movement began as an attempt to account for certain literary peculiarities—stylistic and structural—of the Gospels of the sort noted above. While some form critics have been extremely sceptical about the historical reliability of the stories, others are equally convinced that many stories in the Gospels are historically accurate. Study of story patterns and comparison of biblical with nonbiblical material serves as another tool for interpreting the gospel tradition.

The results of form criticism can be relevant to students of literature as well as to historians. The various forms can suggest questions appropriate to the material. What is the point of a pronouncement story, a miracle story, or a parable? Further, although form criticism is interested principally in the oral stage of the gospel tradition, it raises questions about the written Gospels themselves. If the early Christian movement handed on stories about Jesus and sayings of Jesus to instruct converts, settle important matters of church policy, or to engender piety, why were oral traditions no longer sufficient? Why was it necessary to assemble them in the form of a written story? Students of early Christianity who used the tool of form criticism seem to have been so fascinated by the preliterary period in the gospel tradition that they ignored the end product—the Gospels themselves. How and why were the Gospels composed, each drawing from these oral and written sources in its own way?

Within the last two decades, biblical scholars have developed a general interest in the literary and artistic aspects of the New Testament—the final, written stage of oral tradition. One of the results of this interest has been the realization that the Gospels actually are far more than just collections of material.[10] The works reflect creative personalities; they exhibit important differences in theme, emphasis, and point of view.

Yet, students trained to view the Gospels as collections of traditions have had a difficult time viewing the works as unified compositions—a difficulty that may seem puzzling to those who have been trained to study secular literature. Even those who are interested in the interpretation of a whole Gospel—redaction critics, as they have come to be called—approach their task by looking for original sources. Redaction critics view biblical writers as editors or redactors, and the critics focus their study on the process of editing. They are interested in such questions as: How did the writer combine various oral traditions? Are there indications of modification? Has a particular unit of tradition been given an interpretation by its placement within the narrative context or by the addition of a phrase, and if so, why?

Redaction criticism is quite functional in Matthew and Luke, since their sources can be identified with at least some degree of certainty, and one can examine how each writer used those sources. The Gospel of Mark poses far greater difficulties to the scholar, although it still is possible to differentiate many sources because of the rather transparent methods of composition used by the author. Those who employ such methods of study assume that, by reconstructing the editing process, an interpreter should be able to detect both the direction of the composition and the Gospel's point of view.

The story of the raising of Jairus' daughter in Mark 5 will serve to demonstrate this approach. It is a miracle story, a form whose function is clear. Mark ends the story peculiarly, however. The stage has been set for a dramatic conclusion. Jesus arrives, only to find the mourners already present. When he suggests that the little girl is only asleep, he provokes ridicule. Nevertheless, he enters the house, leaving the scoffers outside. He performs the miracle, and those few witnesses who are present are appropriately astonished. The little girl is given something to eat, perhaps to prove that she is not a spirit. But the last verse includes a strange command: "And he strictly charged them that no one should know this" (Mark 5:43).

The injunction is totally unexpected. The reader anticipates some comment to the effect that those waiting to see Jesus proved the fool were astonished and ashamed of their earlier ridicule. Instead, Jesus tells the small group of witnesses not to tell anyone what happened. The command is not even reasonable. How can the parents keep the resurrection a secret? Are they to keep their daughter hidden? Are Jesus and his disciples to slip out the back door? What of all the people waiting outside?

Those who view Mark as an editor of traditional material find this injunction particularly significant. It seems to conflict with the obvious function and traditional pattern of a miracle story and may well represent an attempt by the editor to interpret his material. More evidence is needed to justify such a conclusion, however. It must be shown that this half verse is Markan rather than traditional by examining vocabulary and style and by determining whether the injunction fits a pattern of modifications discernible elsewhere in Mark's Gospel. Furthermore, if it can be demonstrated that the injunction is the work of the final editor, then the student must ask what it reveals about the work as a whole. Scholars have in fact satisfied all these requirements, the final step being Mark's overall preoccupation with his theme of the hidden Messiah, as we shall see later.

Redaction criticism, the study of the process of redaction or editing, is an approach to the study of the Gospels that has dominated New Testament scholarship to an extraordinary degree in the last decade. Redaction critics have made numerous important and fascinating observations about the nature of the Gospels. Here, at last, biblical scholars have begun to approach the New Testament as one approaches other literature, asking questions about the finished product to help the reader appreciate both the distinctiveness and the artistry of the work. Such an approach, however, usually has not been supplemented by other methods of study used by students in the critical analysis of almost all other types of literature. Even redaction critics have tended to view the Gospels as literature only in a narrow sense.

III. Literary Criticism and Esthetic Artistry

The Gospels may rank low on a scale of values as finished works of art, but they are, in fact, unified compositions, whatever the process by which they have assumed their present form. They ought to be studied, therefore, as one customarily studies a piece of literature. Recently the rather parochial character of biblical studies has been breaking down, and biblical scholars have begun to explore the possibilities of using the critical tools of literary scholars in studying the New Testament. Perhaps even more important, some extremely talented students of secular literature are beginning to devote some attention to the literature of the Bible.[11] Let us examine an outstanding example.

In *Mimesis,* Eric Auerbach's brief study of the Gospel of Mark provides eloquent testimony to the possibilities of studying the Bible as an artistic work.[12] In this monumental survey of Western literature, Auerbach also includes material from the Hebrew Scriptures as well as from the New

Testament. He came to the material with neither a particular interest in religious questions nor with a desire to determine the historical reliability of the narratives. Instead, he observed the way the author of the Gospel of Mark interpreted reality as he represented, or imitated, it in literary form and how this compared with other mimetic traditions among Mark's contemporaries. It is interesting that Auerbach chose to study Mark, which traditionally has been viewed as the least literary of all the Gospels.

The outstanding feature of Mark's style, as noted earlier, is its lack of any real transition from one scene to another. He provides little background information; he does little to place scenes in context, to explain how they are related to what has preceded and to what follows. In many instances he fails to provide even information that would seem essential to the story. The Gospel ends, for example, with frightened women who are too terrified to say anything to anyone about what they have seen.[13] Mark gives no account of an appearance by the risen Jesus; he makes no attempt to explain how, or even whether, the disciples learned about Jesus' resurrection. Mark's abruptness and omissions have frequently been cited by students of the New Testament as evidence of his modest abilities and rather slavish dependence on the incomplete oral traditions available to him. These breaks in the narrative seemed to reflect fragmentary sources.

To Auerbach, however, these same features of Mark's Gospel were signals of a special approach to the telling of a story. Mark's lack of coherence and choppiness, and the absence of information that readers might consider essential, indicate that the author is not primarily interested in recreating a complete picture of Jesus' ministry. He is not attempting to write a biography or an objective listing. Auerbach concluded that Mark's story is more than one-dimensional, that there are other, deeper levels within the Gospel, and that it is these ulterior levels to which the author intended to direct the reader's attention.

Auerbach's example is the account of Peter's denial of Jesus in Mark 14:54, 66-72.[14] There is a great deal, he observes, that the author fails to tell the reader. Peter's denial is played out against the backdrop of Jesus' trial. At the same time that Jesus is interrogated, found guilty of a capital crime, and beaten, Peter denies even knowing him. But the incident ends abruptly with no indication of what happens to this Peter who, as Mark's reader would have been expected to know, became one of the giants in the Christian movement. Why was Peter not arrested? How did he make his escape? According to Mark, Peter broke down and wept. Did this indicate repentance for what he had done? Was he forgiven? How was he accepted back into the ranks of the disciples? Mark answers none of these important questions. He reports only the statement made by the "young man" at the tomb that the women are to tell "the disciples and Peter" that Jesus is going before them to Galilee (Mark 16:7). But the women disobey the command, and the reader never learns whether the disciples ever went to Galilee.

To those who view the account as a piece of historical writing in which the intent is to describe events accurately and fully, Mark's work obviously must appear deficient. Auerbach, on the other hand, contends that these "inadequacies" actually reveal another outlook entirely. In fact, if a student views Mark from this different perspective, signs of real artistry begin to appear.

The story of Peter's denial is divided into two parts. In 14:53-54, the reader learns that while Jesus is being arraigned before the high court, Peter is waiting out in the courtyard. At this point the story moves from Peter to the drama being enacted inside, one of the climactic points in the main story. In this last great confrontation between Jesus and the Jewish religious establishment, Jesus, for the first time in the story, openly acknowledges his identity (verses 61-62) and is condemned to death. At the conclusion of the trial he is mocked and beaten by his adversaries, and the scene then shifts immediately back to the courtyard, where Peter is still waiting. The reader is expected to understand the simultaneity and the counterpoint: while Jesus faces his judges boldly and truthfully, Peter is denying that he even knows Jesus. It is not accidental that at the same time Jesus acknowledges his identity before the high priest, Peter denies Jesus to a female servant of the high priest. The irony is obvious; Peter's "trial" is a parody of Jesus' trial. Peter serves as a foil.

Further, Mark may be using the scene to demonstrate dramatically a statement made by Jesus early in the story: "I came not to call the righteous, but sinners" (2:17). Peter, the most prominent among Jesus' followers, is still a sinner for whom Jesus has mercy; Peter is one of those for whom the Son of man has come "to give his life as a ransom" (10:45).

The intertwining of the two scenes yields yet another meaning—perhaps its most important one. Mark's study of Peter's denial concludes rather abruptly with a reference to Jesus' earlier prediction that Peter would betray him: "And immediately the cock crowed a second time. And Peter remembered how Jesus had said to him, 'Before the cock crows twice, you will deny me three times'" (14:72). The mention of the cock crowing twice occurs only in Mark, but it is hardly incidental to his story. It emphasizes the absolute accuracy of Jesus' prediction (verses 28-30). What he told Peter about his denial has been fulfilled to the letter.

Mark provides a striking relationship between the denial scene and the mockery scene with which the trial concludes: "And some began to spit on him, and to cover his face, and to strike him, saying to him, 'Prophesy!'" (verse 65). In the trial Jesus makes at least one prediction. He tells his accusers that they will see the Son of man sitting at the right hand of Power (God) and coming with the clouds of heaven (verse 62). The court views this prediction as ridiculous—indeed, so outrageous that it is blasphemous. But at the precise moment Jesus is being ridiculed and abused as a prophet, his prophecy about Peter is being accurately fulfilled. The juxtaposition of the two incidents is a veiled promise that the prophecy about the Son of man will indeed be fulfilled. He will be seated at God's right hand, and he will (soon) return.

When studied as a piece of literature, the Gospel of Mark provides evidence of careful artistry. The work is tied together by themes; scenes serve a particular function in their context. The task of the critic is to unveil the artistry, to ask the questions that are appropriate to the particular work. For those unaccustomed to viewing the Gospels as literature, such study surely produces some surprises.

IV. Appendix: Examples of the Synoptic Problem

The Authority of Christ
Matt. 7:28-29

28 And when Jesus finished these sayings, the crowds were astonished at his teaching, 29 for he taught them as one who had authority, and not as their scribes.

Mark 1:21-28

21 And they went into Capernaum; and immediately on the sabbath he entered the synagogue and taught. 22 And they were astonished at his teaching, for he taught them as one who had authority, and not as the scribes.

23 And immediately there was in their synagogue a man with an unclean spirit; 24 and he cried out, "What have you to do with us, Jesus of Nazareth? Have you come to destroy us? I know who you are, the Holy One of God." 25 But Jesus rebuked him, saying, "Be silent, and come out of

Luke 4:31-37

31 And he went down to Capernaum, a city of Galilee. And he was teaching them on the sabbath; 32 and they were astonished at his teaching, for his word was with authority.

33 And in the synagogue there was a man who had the spirit of an unclean demon; and he cried out with a loud voice, 34 "Ah! What have you to do with us, Jesus of Nazareth? Have you come to destroy us? I know who you are, the Holy One of God." 35 But Jesus rebuked him, saying, "Be

And the unclean spirit, convulsing him and crying with a loud voice, came out of him. 27 And they were all amazed, so that they questioned among themselves, saying, "What is this? A new teaching! With authority he commands even the unclean spirits, and they obey him." 28 And at once his fame spread everywhere throughout all the surrounding region of Galilee.

silent, and come out of him!" And when the demon had thrown him down in the midst, he came out of him, having done him no harm. 36 And they were all amazed and said to one another, "What is this word? For with authority and power he commands the unclean spirits, and they come out." 37 And reports of him went out into every place in the surrounding region.

The Crucifixion

Matt. 27:33-44

33 And when they came to a place called Golgotha, (which means the place of a skull), 34 they offered him wine to drink,

Mark 15:22-32

22 And they brought him to the place called Golgotha (which means the place of a skull). 23 And they offered him wine min-

Luke 23:33-43

33 And when they came to the place which is called The Skull,

there they crucified him, and the criminals, one on the right and one on the left. 34 And Jesus said, "Father, forgive them; for they know not what they do." And they cast lots to divide his garments. 35 And the people stood by watching;

[See v. 38]

[See vv. 32, 33]

[See v. 37]

mingled with gall; but when he tasted it, he would not drink it. 35 And when they had crucified him,

[See v. 38]

gled with myrrh; but he did not take it. 24 And they crucified him,

[See v. 27]

they divided his garments among them by casting lots; 36 then they sat down and kept watch over him there. 37 And over his head they put the charge against him, which read, "This is Jesus the King of the Jews." 38 Then two robbers were crucified with him, one on the right and one on the left. 39 And those who passed by derided him, wagging their heads 40 and saying, "You who would destroy the temple and build it in three

and divided his garments among them, casting lots for them, to decide what each should take. 25 And it was the third hour when they crucified him. 26 And the inscription of the charge against him read, "The King of the Jews." 27 And with him they crucified two robbers, one on his right and one on his left. 29 And those who passed by derided him, wagging their heads, and saying, "Aha! You who would destroy the temple and build it in three but the rulers scoffed at him saying, "He saved others; let him save himself, if he is the Christ of God, his Chosen One!"

36 The soldiers also mocked him, coming up and offering him vinegar, 37 and saying, "If you are the King of the Jews, save yourself!" 38 There was also an inscription over him, "This is the King of the Jews."

days, 30 save yourself, and come down from the cross!" 31 So also the chief priests mocked him to one another with the scribes, saying,

"He saved others; he cannot save himself. 32 Let the Christ, the King of Israel, come down now from the cross, that we may see and believe."

[See v. 36]

[See v. 30]

[See v. 26]

days, save yourself! If you are the Son of God, come down from the cross." 41 So also the chief priests, with the scribes and elders, mocked him, saying, 42 "He saved others; he cannot save himself. He is the King of Israel; let him come down now from the cross, and we will believe in him. 43 He trusts in God; let God deliver him now, if he desires him; for he said, 'I am the Son of God.'"

[See v. 48]

[See v. 40]

[See v. 37]

The Rich Young Man

Matt. 19:16-30

16 And behold, one came up to him, saying, "Teacher, what good deed must I do, to have eternal life?" 17 And he said to him, "Why do you ask me about what is good? One there is who is good. If you would enter life, keep the commandments." 18 He said to him, "Which?" And Jesus said to him, "You shall not kill, You shall not commit adultery, You shall not steal, You shall not bear false witness, 19 Honor your father and mother, and, You

Mark 10:17-31

17 And as he was setting out on his journey, a man ran up and knelt before him, and asked him, "Good Teacher, what must I do to inherit eternal life?" 18 And Jesus said to him, "Why do you call me good? No one is good but God alone. 19 You know the commandments: 'Do not kill, Do not commit adultery, Do not steal, Do not bear false witness, Do not defraud, Honor your father and mother.'"

Luke 18:18-30

18 And a ruler asked him, "Good Teacher, what shall I do to inherit eternal life?" 19 And Jesus said to him, "Why do you call me good? No one is good but God alone. 20 You know the commandments: 'Do not commit adultery, Do not kill, Do not steal, Do not bear false witness, Honor your father and mother.'" And he said, "All these I have observed from my youth." 22

shall love your neighbor as yourself." 20 The young man said to him, "All these I have observed; what do I still lack?" 21 Jesus said to him, "If you would be perfect, go, sell what you possess and give to the poor, and you will have treasure in heaven; and come follow me." 22 When the young man heard this he went away sorrowful; for he had great possessions. 23 And Jesus said to his disciples, "Truly, I say to you, it will be hard for a rich man to enter the kingdom of heaven.

20 And he said to him, "Teacher, all these I have observed from my youth." 21 And Jesus looking upon him loved him, and said to him, "You lack one thing; go, sell what you have, and give to the poor, and you will have treasure in heaven; and come, follow me." 22 At that saying his countenance fell, and he went away sorrowful, for he had great possessions. 23 And Jesus looked around and said to his disciples, "How hard it will be for those who have riches to enter the kingdom of God!" 24 And the disciples were amazed at his words.

And when Jesus heard it, he said to him, "One thing you still lack. Sell all that you have and distribute to the poor, and you will have treasure in heaven; and come, follow me." 23 But when he heard this he became sad, for he was very rich. 24 Jesus looking at him said, "how hard it is for those who have riches to enter the kingdom of God!"

The Lamp and the Eye
Matt. 6:22-23

22 "The eye is the lamp of the body. So, if your eye is sound, your whole body will be full of light; 23 but if your eye is not sound, your whole body will be full of darkness. If then the light in you is darkness, how great is the darkness!"

Luke 11:34-36

34 "Your eye is the lamp of your body; when your eye is sound, your whole body is full of light; but when it is not sound, your body is full of darkness. 35 Therefore be careful lest the light in you be darkness. 36 If then your whole body is full of light, having no part dark, it will be wholly bright, as when a lamp with its rays gives you light."

God and Mammon
Matt. 6:24

24 "No one can serve two masters; for either he will hate the one and love the other, or he will be devoted to the one and despise the other. You cannot serve God and mammon."

Luke 16:13

13 "No servant can serve two masters; for either he will hate the one and love the other, or he will be devoted to the one and despise the other. You cannot serve God and mammon."

"Do Not Be Anxious"
Matt. 6:25-32

25 "Therefore I tell you, do not be anxious about your life, what you shall eat or what you shall drink, nor about your body, what you shall put on. Is not life more

Luke 12:22-30

22 And he said to his disciples, "Therefore I tell you, do not be anxious about your life, what you shall eat, nor about your body, what you shall put on. 23 For life is

than food, and the body more than clothing? 26 Look at the birds of the air: they neither sow nor reap nor gather into barns, and yet your heavenly Father feeds them. Are you not of more value than they? 27 And which of you by being anxious can add one cubit to his span of life? 28 And why are you anxious about clothing?

Consider the lilies of the field, how they grow; they neither toil nor spin; 29 yet I tell you, even Solomon in all his glory was not arrayed like one of these. 30 But if God so clothes the grass of the field, which today is alive and tomorrow is thrown into the oven, will he not much more clothe you, O men of little faith? 31 Therefore do not be anxious, saying, 'What shall we eat?' or 'What shall we drink?' or 'What shall we wear?' 32 For the Gentiles seek all these things; and your heavenly Father knows that you need them all.''

more than food, and the body more than clothing. 24 Consider the ravens: they neither sow nor reap, they have neither storehouse nor barn, and yet God feeds them. Of how much more value are you than the birds! 25 And which of you by being anxious can add a cubit to his span of life? 26 If then you are not able to do as small a thing as that, why are you anxious about the rest? 27 Consider the lilies, how they grow; they neither toil nor spin; yet I tell you, even Solomon in all his glory was not arrayed like one of these. 28 But if God so clothes the grass which is alive in the field today and tomorrow is thrown into the oven, how much more will he clothe you, O men of little faith! 29 And do not seek what you are to eat and what you are to drink, nor be of anxious mind. 30 For all the nations of the world seek these things; and your Father knows that you need them.''

The Daughter of Jairus Raised
Matt. 9:18-26

18 While he was thus speaking to them, behold, a ruler came in and knelt before him, saying, "My daughter has just died; but come and lay your hand on her, and she will live." 19 And Jesus rose and followed him, with his disciples.

20 And behold, a woman who had suffered from a hemorrhage for twelve years

Mark 5:21-43

21 And when Jesus had crossed again in the boat to the other side, a great crowd gathered about him; and he was beside the sea. 22 Then came one of the rulers of the synagogue, Jairus by name; and seeing him, he fell at his feet, 23 and besought him, saying, "My little daughter is at the point of death. Come and lay your hands on her, so that she may be made well, and live." 24 And he went with him. And a great crowd followed him and pressed round him.

25 And there was a woman who had had a flow of blood for twelve years, 26 and who had suffered much under many physicians, and had spent all that she had, and was no better but rather grew

Luke 8:40-56

40 Now when Jesus returned, the crowd welcomed him, for they were all waiting for him. 41 And there came a man named Jairus, who was a ruler of the synagogue; and falling at Jesus' feet he besought him to come to his house, 42 for he had an only daughter, about twelve years of age, and she was dying.

As he went, the people pressed round him.

43 And a woman who had had a flow of blood for twelve years and could not be healed by any one,

came up behind him and touched the fringe of his garment. 21 For she said to herself, "If I only touch his garment, I shall be made well."

worse. 27 She had heard the reports about Jesus, and came up behind him in the crowd and touched his garment. 28 For she said, "If I touch even his garments, I shall be made well." 29 And immediately the hemorrhage ceased; and she felt in her body that she was healed of her disease. 30 And Jesus, perceiving in himself that power had gone forth from him, immediately turned about in the crowd, and said, "Who touched my garments?" 31 And his disciples said to him, "You see the crowd pressing around you, and yet you say, 'Who touched me?'" 32 And he looked around to see who had done it.

33 But the woman, knowing what had been done to her, came

44 came up behind him, and touched the fringe of his garment; and immediately her flow of blood ceased. 45 And Jesus said, "Who was it that touched me?" When all denied it, Peter said, "Master, the multitudes surround you and press upon you!" 46 But Jesus said, "Some one touched me; for I perceive that power has gone forth from me."

47 And when the woman saw that she was not hidden, she came

in fear and trembling and fell down before him, and told him the whole truth.

22 Jesus turned, and seeing her he said, "Take heart, daughter; your faith has made you well." And instantly the woman was made well.

trembling, and falling down before him declared in the presence of all the people why she had touched him, and how she had been immediately healed. 48 And he said to her, "Daughter, your faith has made you well; go in peace."

34 And he said to her, "Daughter, your faith has made you well; go in peace, and be healed of your disease."

35 While he was still speaking, there came from the ruler's house some who said, "Your daughter is dead. Why trouble the Teacher any further?" 36 But ignoring what they said, Jesus said to the ruler of the synagogue, "Do not fear, only believe." 37 And he allowed no one to follow him except Peter and James and John the brother of James. 38 When they came to the house of the

49 While he was still speaking, a man from the ruler's house came and said, "Your daughter is dead; do not trouble the Teacher any more." 50 But Jesus on hearing this answered him, "Do not fear; only believe, and she shall be well." 51 And when he came to the house, he permitted no one to enter with him, except Peter and John and James, and the father and mother of the

23 And when Jesus came to the ruler's house, and saw the flute players, and the crowd making a tumult, 24 he said, "Depart; for the girl is not dead but sleeping." And they laughed at him. 25 But when the crowd had been put outside, he went in and took her by the hand, and the girl arose.

ruler of the synagogue, he saw a tumult, and people weeping and wailing loudly. 39 And when he had entered, he said to them, "Why do you make a tumult and weep? The child is not dead but sleeping." 40 And they laughed at him. But he put them all outside, and took the child's father and mother and those who were with him, and went in where the child was. 41 Taking her by the hand he said to her, "Talitha cumi"; which means, "Little girl, I say to you, arise." 42 And immediately the girl got up and walked; for she was twelve years old. And immediately they were overcome with amazement. 43 And he strictly charged them that no one should know this, and told them to give her something to eat.

child. 52 And all were weeping and bewailing her; but he said, "Do not weep; for she is not dead but sleeping." 53 And they laughed at him, knowing that she was dead. 54 But taking her by the hand he called, saying, "Child, arise." 55 And her spirit returned, and she got up at once; and he directed that something should be given her to eat. 56 And her parents were amazed; but he charged them to tell no one what had happened.

Summary

Although several early Christian theologians raised interesting questions about the authorship of the four Gospels and their interrelationships, critical study of the Gospels did not begin until the Enlightenment of the eighteenth century. The first three Gospels were obviously different in many respects from the fourth and were similar enough to one another to permit putting them into parallel columns to be viewed together, whereupon they were called the Synoptic Gospels.

Their similarities and differences led scholars to deal with the synoptic problem—what were their sources and how were they related? Scholars engaged in what they called literary criticism, by which they meant source analysis. The Gospels seen in parallel immediately revealed that most of what is in Mark is also found in Matthew and Luke, that some things in Matthew and Luke are the same but are not found in Mark, that all three shared some passages, and that each of the three has material not found in any of the other two. Much of the common material uses the same Greek wording, and where identical passages suddenly differ, the differences are often characteristic of the particular writer.

Critical scholars have examined these data and arrived at a broad consensus: Mark is the earliest Gospel and was used as a source in the composition of Matthew and Luke. The language is often identical; changes from Mark being for stylistic or theological reasons. Even the order of stories is generally the same, with only six Markan passages not appearing in Matthew or Luke. Mark's stories contain more detail, so one cannot argue that Mark is an abridgment of Matthew or Luke. Yet Matthew and Luke contain identical material not found in Mark. This is accounted for by a hypothetical "Q" (the first letter of the German word *Quelle,* or "source") which is thought to have contained many of Jesus' teachings. Finally, stories found only in Matthew or in Luke are thought to be derived from independent sources to which the other synoptic writers did not have access.

The next stage in biblical scholarship arose in the early twentieth century, largely as a result of methods used in identifying forms and genres of folklore. Form criticism recognizes that the stories about Jesus were circulated by word of mouth for at least a generation before being written down and that oral literature is transmitted in certain easily identifiable genres. There are many signs that the genres in Mark (e.g., pronouncement stories, miracle stories, parables) derive from oral tradition and that their primary purpose is not to preserve information but to impress and convince the hearers with certain truths. It is interesting and informative to note how the gospel writers adapt and rework genres common to the Greco-Roman world.

A still more recent interest of biblical scholars is redaction criticism, which focuses on the final shaping of each Gospel. How did the writer combine his sources, what changes did he make, and why? How does the context created by the ordering uncover thematic developments that help to interpret each story? Answering these questions helps to detect a unique point of view for each gospel writer.

Finally, scholars are now exploring the literary artistry of the New Testament. Eric Auerbach, for example, analyzes the story of Peter's denial in the Gospel of Mark. Peter's "trial" before the maidservant is seen as a foil for the trial of Jesus taking place in the room above. Jesus is being mocked and asked to prophesy just as his prophecy regarding the crowing of the cock is fulfilled—which sets his trial statement about his imminent return at the right hand of God in a new light. We see that Mark is not as interested in a coherent biography as he is in pointing out other levels of meaning.

CHAPTER THREE

BEGINNINGS

Almost everyone is familiar with the Christmas story: Jesus was born in a manger in a stable because there was no room for his parents in the inn at Bethlehem. Shepherds from nearby fields who were told by an angel of Jesus' birth left their flocks to see the babe in the manger. Three wise men came from the East bearing gifts to the newborn King of the Jews. Jesus' parents fled with their son to Egypt to escape the slaughter of male children by wicked King Herod.

It will probably come as a surprise to many people that none of the Gospels begins its story of Jesus with this familiar Christmas story. Rather, the birth story as just summarized actually is a composite, a mosaic of bits and pieces taken from two different Gospels—Mark and John provide no account of Jesus' birth at all. Each of the four Gospels begins the story of Jesus in its own particular way. Interpreters must take the differences seriously, for it is in the opening that each narrator introduced major themes that will run through the story, helping the reader to understand the unique portrait of Jesus that will emerge in each Gospel.

Because each of the Gospels begins quite differently, a synthesis is of little use; each must be studied individually.

I. Mark

Jesus' life prior to his public ministry is omitted from the opening of Mark: nothing about the circumstances of his birth, where he was from, or even what led him to seek out John the Baptist. Only later do we learn in passing the names of his mother and his brothers (Mark 6:3), that he was a carpenter by trade (6:3), and that he was raised in a city called Nazareth (1:9; Jesus is called "Jesus of Nazareth" in 1:24, 10:47, and 16:6).

The Gospel is about Jesus (1:1), but it starts with John the Baptist, who is introduced as the biblical preparer of "the way of the Lord" (verses 2-3). Jesus' first act in Mark is to submit to John's baptism of repentance. Questions arise, but are left unanswered: Where did Jesus come from? Why was he baptized? In what way is this ritual action an appropriate beginning of Jesus' story? By not answering those questions, the narrator complicates the task of his reader. This lack of information and the mystery attached to the person of Jesus are typical of Mark's Gospel.

Mark makes no secret about the identity of his main character, however. The superscription reads: "The beginning of the gospel of Jesus Christ, the Son of God" (1:1). The story is about someone of quite extraordinary religious significance—the Messiah, God's Son. But there is no evidence that these honorific titles accompany a particularly unusual birth or childhood. Did Mark know stories about Jesus' birth? If not, why not? If he did, his failure to include any birth stories in his narrative may indicate that he considered them unimportant or perhaps that he presumed his readers already were familiar with them. Because the Gospel of Mark makes no attempt to trace the development of the main character from childhood to the conclusion of his ministry, it obviously should not be classified as biography.

II. Matthew

Matthew devotes about fifty verses to introducing the main character prior to his baptism by John. Presumably, Jesus' lineage is important to the story; he is identified both genealogically and theologically in the very first verse: "The book of the genealogy [or genesis] of Jesus Christ, the Son of David, the son of Abraham." As is frequently the case in the Bible, this kind of information signals an important religious interest. Jesus is introduced as the Christ, that is, the Messiah. But this religious claim is then substantiated by tracing Jesus' lineage back to King David and to Abraham, two of the most important figures in Israel's history. Abraham was the traditional father of the nation of Israel; David was the king from whose line the Messiah was expected.

Any student who reads the narrative carefully will immediately discover a discrepancy: Jesus' genealogy is traced through Joseph; yet Matthew says Jesus was born of a virgin and that Joseph had no part in the conception of his son. Why are these seemingly contradictory facts both included in the story? Why no attempt to smooth out the inconsistencies? One can only speculate, for the Gospel of Matthew gives no indication that the discrepancy poses any problem. Some have suggested that the list of ancestors really applies to Jesus' mother; in Jewish society one's lineage is traced through the mother. In Matthew and Luke, however, Joseph is the one identified as a member of the Davidic family. The author seems to view Jesus as Joseph's adopted son. Sonship was as much a legal as a biological concept; adoption of sons and conferral on them of full familial status was a frequent practice, for example, among the Roman emperors. But that explanation would still leave the question of Jesus' blood line unresolved, and such a question was important in Jewish society. Did Matthew inherit two separate traditions from his predecessors and simply reproduce them without perceiving the contradiction? Or did he feel that both traditions were important enough to include in spite of the contradiction? These questions cannot be answered today with certainty.

Another feature of Matthew's opening verse is of some interest. The word that is translated "genealogy" is actually the Greek word *genesis*. Although the translation "genealogy" is appropriate, the Greek word may have been carefully chosen because of other associations. It appeared as a title to the first book in the Jewish Bible in the Greek translation: "The Genesis of the World."[1] Perhaps Matthew was portraying the story of Jesus as a new genesis, a new beginning.

Both Matthew and Luke recount the story of Jesus' birth in Bethlehem, and in both Gospels, Jesus is born of a young woman who is still a virgin. Yet the birth story is told quite differently in the two books. Matthew's narrative focuses on Joseph—a young Jew who has just learned that his wife-to-be is pregnant. To marry such a woman would be out of the question in Jewish society. Nevertheless, Joseph is a considerate man; he wants to cause Mary as little embarrassment as possible. Before he can act to resolve his dilemma, however, he learns in a dream that the child has been conceived by supernatural means—in fact, by God's own Spirit. It is Joseph's response to the situation that interests Matthew—in sharp contrast to Luke, who accords Mary the prominent role.

Elsewhere in the story of Jesus' birth, Matthew seems far more interested in the significance of events than in their human dimensions. The precise circumstances of Jesus' birth and his mother's reaction to the extraordinary event are unimportant. The significance of the virgin birth lies in its fulfillment of a scriptural prophecy that Matthew quotes from Isaiah: "Behold, a virgin shall conceive and bear a son, and his name shall be called Emmanuel" (Matt. 1:23).

Since the second century, biblical interpreters have argued the validity of Matthew's interpretation of Isaiah's prophecy (Isa. 7:14); and in most of the recent English translations of the Old Testament the term is "young woman" instead of "virgin." A few comments might be helpful. First, Matthew's quotation agrees with the Septuagint, the Greek version of the Old Testament, whose translators rendered the Hebrew term *almah* as "virgin" in the Greek. Second, the way the Isaiah text was read within the Jewish community during the first century of the Christian era and the rules by which texts were interpreted, both by Jews and by Christians, differ considerably from modern critical approaches to literature. Whatever the author of Isaiah 7:14 might have meant, Matthew understood the passage as a prediction of the virgin birth of the Messiah.[2]

The narrator obviously views the birth of Jesus as the fulfillment of the prophecy from Isaiah. In fact, interest in prophetic fulfillment is not confined to this one portion of the Gospel; Matthew characterizes almost every incident he relates as a fulfillment of a specific biblical prophecy. He uses formal expressions, such as "this was to fulfill what the Lord had spoken by the prophet," five times in the first two chapters. Jesus' virgin birth fulfills Isaiah 7:14; the location of Jesus' birth as Bethlehem, Micah 5:2; the flight to Egypt by Jesus' family and their subsequent return, Hosea 11:1; and Herod's slaughter of the male children, Jeremiah 31:15. Even the comment that Jesus and his family settled in Nazareth has been foretold, although in this case the precise text Matthew refers to is uncertain.[3]

Connecting these events in Jesus' life to foreshadowings that Matthew sees in the Jewish Bible suggests that the story of Jesus is to be read within a particular context. The narrator does not view Jesus as an isolated phenomenon; he has been foreseen and presumably awaited. Therefore, Jesus' life is something of a consummation, completing another story that has until this moment been unfinished.

Matthew's concern for detail and his great care in correlating each incident to a particular prophetic text, however, may suggest that the claims to be made for Jesus were not universally accepted. The reader senses that Matthew is presenting a case and that he or she will be expected to take sides in a dispute about Jesus.

The longest episode in these opening chapters is the visit of the magi to Jesus' birth site. The term *magi* does not mean "wise men" but, as the context suggests, something more like "astrologers." Matthew does not say that these visitors were three in number or that they were kings. That tradition developed early in the second century as Christians extended their attempt to interpret Jesus' story in the light of their sacred scriptures. The identification of the magi as kings probably derived from Isaiah 60:1-6:

> Arise, shine; for your light has come
>   and the glory of the LORD has risen upon you.
> For behold, darkness shall cover the earth,
>   and thick darkness the people;
> but the LORD will arise upon you
>   and his glory will be seen upon you.
> And nations [or Gentiles] shall come to your light,
>   and kings to the brightness of your rising. . . .
> A multitude of camels shall cover you,
>   the young camels of Midian and Ephah;
>   all those from Sheba shall come.
> They shall bring gold and frankincense,
>   and shall proclaim the praise of the LORD.

Some commentators have suggested that the reference in Matthew to a rising star has something to do with Numbers

24:17, a passage that, in the course of time, came to be regarded as a messianic prophecy:

> A star shall come forth out of Jacob,
> and a scepter shall rise out of Israel.

No unambiguous evidence, however, directly relates the star seen by the astrologers in Matthew to the metaphoric star referred to in Numbers. As noted in chapter 1, this text was also applied to Simon Bar Kochbah, the messianic figure who led the second uprising against Rome in 132 C.E. Stars that herald important events are hardly unique to the Gospel of Matthew or even to Christian literature.

Even apart from such traditional associations, the thrust of Matthew's story is quite clear. It provides striking testimony to the importance of the hero. His birth has been heralded by the heavens as an event of cosmic importance. The magi seek out Jesus, worship him, and offer gifts appropriate for royalty. (See Isa. 60:6 and Song of Sol. 3:6-7.) Jesus is genealogically related to David, from whose line the Messiah was expected; he is born in the city that, according to scripture, is to be the birthplace of the Messiah; and he is hailed as King of the Jews by astrologers who have seen his star.

The visit of the wise men also introduces a note of foreboding. The birth of the Messiah-King does not cause rejoicing in everyone. When King Herod hears the news, he is troubled, "and all Jerusalem with him" (Matt. 2:3). Through the intervention of God, the young King escapes the resulting slaughter of innocent children ordered by King Herod. The circumstances surrounding Jesus' birth as they appear in the episode of the wise men's visit foreshadow the end of Jesus' life. The next time the title "King of the Jews" occurs, it is used by Pilate, who condemns Jesus to death. The young child, as the readers eventually learn, will grow up to be the one who is crucified as King of the Jews. He is the King who reigns from a tree, the King who has come to die.

One last feature of the opening section of Matthew deserves some comment. The book begins with the allusive title, "The book of the genesis of Jesus Christ." May we see other allusions to motifs or patterns familiar to the reader who knows Israel's story? Parallels between the birth of Jesus and the birth of Moses come to mind. Both infants are miraculously delivered from the hand of a wicked king who has decreed the death of all male children within the community. Jesus, like Moses, comes out of Egypt. ("Out of Egypt have I called my son," Matthew quotes from Hosea.) It is possible that Matthew meant the flight to Egypt by Jesus' parents to be seen as an ironic contrast to Moses and the Israelites: while Moses led the Israelites out of Egypt from slavery and death toward the promised land, Jesus' parents are forced to flee Israel to Egypt for safety.

Jesus as a new Moses—or a new Adam or a new David—is a familiar theme in Christian writings. Matthew does not develop the parallels, however; he is far more concerned with the image of Jesus as messianic King than as a new Moses. Yet it is possible that there are allusions in Matthew to Mosaic images that become all the more interesting when Jesus provides an extended exposition of God's will from a mountain (chaps. 5–7).

III. Luke

Although there are no extensive verbal parallels between Matthew and Luke in the material preceding the account of John the Baptist's ministry, there are obviously related interests. Both writers recount circumstances of Jesus' birth, agreeing on certain basic facts: Jesus was born in Bethlehem (Luke 2:4-7), although he later lived in Nazareth; Jesus was conceived by the intervention of God's Spirit while his mother was still a virgin (1:31-35); at the time Mary was betrothed to a man named Joseph, a descendent of David (verse 27); Jesus was related to David through Joseph (3:23-38). Yet the two accounts vary, even with regard to basic facts:

1. According to Luke, Jesus' home was in Nazareth because that was where his parents had always lived (2:4). They were never residents of Bethlehem, but they traveled to the village only because of a census ordered by the Roman government (verses 1-5). In Matthew, Jesus' family moves to Nazareth only after Herod's death.

2. Mary and Joseph stayed in Bethlehem less than six weeks, according to Luke. Although he is not precise, Luke reports that Mary and Joseph traveled to Jerusalem to offer the sacrifice for purification prescribed in Leviticus 12:2-8. According to Jewish law, the sacrifice was to be offered at the end of the period of ritual uncleanness, presumed to last about thirty-three days after the child had been circumcised. According to Luke, after the sacrifice, "they returned into Galilee, to their own city, Nazareth" (2:39). No time is allowed for a visit by the magi to Bethlehem or for a flight to Egypt, both of which Matthew describes.

3. In Luke, Mary, rather than Joseph, receives the announcement of the supernatural origin of Jesus (1:26-36).

4. The young child is visited not by Matthew's prestigious magi but by shepherds—a despised class in Jewish society.

The two birth stories have different emphases. Whereas for Matthew the virgin birth is particularly important because it fulfills a prophecy, for Luke it is significant for what it indicates about the nature of the child: "The Holy Spirit will come upon you, and the power of the Most High will overshadow you; therefore the child to be born will be called holy, the Son of God [*alternative translation:* the holy child to be born will be called Son of God]" (1:35).

According to Luke, the manner of Jesus' birth indicates why he is called God's Son; God has, in fact, fathered the child through his Spirit. The idea of half-divine beings born of the union between a god and a mortal woman is hardly unique to Luke: Perseus and Hercules are two of the more prominent examples from classical mythology. Although Luke does not describe God in anthropomorphic terms and although his account of the supernatural conception of Jesus is restrained, his story is not far from popular ideas about supernatural births found through antiquity.

In Matthew, Mary has only a minor role, but in Luke she is a principal character. The angel appears to Mary and greets her as the "favored one" (1:28). In her modest response to the angel and in her acceptance of her incredible destiny, she becomes a model for all believers. Her response to the angel contrasts strikingly with that of John's father, Zechariah. Zechariah—a male and a priest—initially doubts: "How shall I know this?" (verse 18). Mary shows trust: "Behold, I am the handmaid of the Lord; let it be to me according to your word" (verse 38). Her Magnificat (verses 46-55) is one of the most beautiful compositions in the entire Gospel. In both language and form it is reminiscent of the hymn sung by Hannah, the mother of Samuel, at his dedication at the sanctuary (I Sam. 2:1-10). Mary, like Hannah, is one of the relatively few important women in the Bible; their prominence in the birth stories of their sons is similar in many respects.

Mary's Magnificat is more than a simple expression of piety. The hymn—sung by a woman, a member of a devalued class—emphasizes God's concern for the poor and the weak, a characteristic of Luke's birth story and of his Gospel as a whole:

> And his mercy is on those who fear him
> from generation to generation.
> He has shown strength with his arm,
> he has scattered the proud in the imagination of their hearts,
> he has put down the mighty from their thrones,
> and exalted those of low degree;
> he has filled the hungry with good things,
> and the rich he has sent empty away. (1:50-53)

Only Luke reports that Jesus was born in a stable. Those who visit the child are not exotic magi from the East bringing expensive gifts but simple shepherds from nearby fields. In Luke, Jesus' birth is an occasion of rejoicing for the poor and humble; the rich and mighty take no note of it. No new king threatens King Herod. At the Temple in Jerusalem, Mary and Joseph sacrifice "a pair of turtledoves, or two young pigeons" (2:24), the offering prescribed in Leviticus 12:8 for the poor who cannot afford a lamb.

To an even greater extent than in Matthew, the birth narratives in Luke emphasize the significance of the story that will follow. When John's mother sees Mary, now pregnant with Jesus, Elizabeth's babe leaped in her womb, and, filled with the Holy Spirit, Elizabeth exclaims, "Blessed are you

among women, and blessed is the fruit of your womb!" (1:42).
The coming births of both John and Jesus are announced in
advance by angels; John's father Zechariah is struck dumb by
the vision. At the birth of John, Zechariah, his tongue
suddenly loosed, blesses God. The astonished neighbors are
filled with fear, and a note of expectancy resounds throughout
the hill country of Judea: "What then will this child be?"
(verse 66).

The careers of these two extraordinary children are
anticipated in the hymnic passages in the first two chapters.
The angel tells Zechariah that John will be a great prophet.
The words come from Malachi 4:5-6, which speaks about the
coming of Elijah before the "great and terrible day of the
LORD."

> And he will turn many of the sons of Israel to the Lord their
>   God,
> and he will go before him in the spirit and power of Elijah,
> to turn the hearts of the fathers to the children,
> and the disobedient to the wisdom of the just,
> to make ready for the Lord a people prepared. (1:16-17)

In his own hymn, Zechariah calls his son the "prophet of the
Most High," whose role is to "go before the Lord to prepare
his ways" (verse 76).

According to the angel, John is to be great, but his ministry
anticipates something greater, the ministry of Jesus, the Son
of David and Son of God. The angel tells Mary that Jesus will
be a king:

> He will be great, and will be called the Son of the Most High;
> and the Lord God will give to him the throne of his father David,
> and he will reign over the house of Jacob for ever;
> and of his kingdom there will be no end. (1:32-33)

Zechariah, under the influence of the Holy Spirit,
prophesies that God has

> visited and redeemed his people,
> and has raised up a horn of salvation for us
> in the house of servant David,
> as he spoke by the mouth of his holy prophets from of old,
> that we should be saved from our enemies,
> and from the hand of all who hate us. (1:68-71)

Although Jesus' actual birth is announced only to shepherds, the angel punctuates his message with exalted titles: Jesus is "Savior," "Christ," and even "Lord." His birth is an occasion for a song by the heavenly host. When Simeon, a devout Jerusalemite "waiting for the consolation of Israel," sees Jesus in the Temple at Jerusalem, he realizes that God's promise to him has been fulfilled: he has seen "the Lord's Christ" (2:26). The sight of the child inspires still another hymnic outburst:

> Lord, now lettest thou thy servant depart in peace,
> according to thy word;
> for mine eyes have seen thy salvation
> which thou hast prepared in the presence of all peoples,
> a light for revelation to the Gentiles,
> and for glory to thy people Israel. (2:29-32)

What is beginning with the child Jesus will eventually affect all peoples. Yet amid all the auspicious signs, Luke, like Matthew, interjects a note of warning. Jesus' parents are told that Jesus is destined "for a sign that is spoken against," and that "a sword will pierce through your own soul also" (2:34-35). There will be opposition and pain. But in these early chapters, hopeful anticipation predominates. The chapters end, appropriately, with the young man Jesus in the Temple, his "father's house," discussing religious matters with the leaders of the people.

If these early chapters in Luke emphasize what is to come, they also look back, though less specifically than those in Matthew. Again and again, the events taking place are described as answering the hopes of previous generations, as Mary says:

> He has helped his servant Israel,
> in remembrance of his mercy,
> as he spoke to our fathers,
> to Abraham and to his posterity for ever. (1:54-55)

Simeon is looking for the "consolation of Israel" (2:25). The prophetess Anna speaks to those who are "looking for the redemption of Jerusalem" (verse 38). Later John the Baptist will, in his ministry, fulfill prophecies made by Malachi, and

Luke will portray Jesus as the long-awaited Messiah-King. Jesus' story is continuous with the story of Israel; in fact, it represents the decisive movement toward which all of history has been moving. Although Luke includes few specific quotes from the prophetic writings, he is no less interested than Matthew in tying the story of Jesus to the story of Israel; and Luke's birth stories introduce that theme.

One final comment on Luke's opening chapters to reinforce the concept of continuity: All the characters associated with the birth of Jesus (except Herod) are explicitly portrayed as pious Jews, zealous in keeping the Law of Moses:

Zechariah and Elizabeth. The first people introduced are identified as a priest and his wife who is also of priestly lineage. John's parents are further characterized as "right-eous before God, walking in all the commandments and ordinances of the Lord blameless" (1:6). They have their son circumcised on the eighth day, in accordance with the Law of Moses (verse 59).

Mary and Joseph. Jesus' parents are described as even more zealous Jews. They too have their son circumcised on the eighth day (2:21). They travel to Jerusalem to offer sacrifices for purification and to dedicate their son, once again fulfilling requirements of the Mosaic Law (verses 22-24). They leave Jerusalem, the narrator tells us, only "when they had performed everything according to the law of the Lord" (verse 39). In a later parenthetical remark, one learns that Jesus' parents were accustomed to going to Jerusalem to celebrate Passover, again fulfilling their obligations as devout Jews (verses 41-42).

Simeon. "There was a man in Jerusalem, whose name was Simeon, and this man was righteous and devout, looking for the consolation of Israel" (2:25).

Anna. "There was a prophetess, Anna, the daughter of Phanuel, of the tribe of Asher; she was of great age, having lived with her husband seven years from her virginity, and as a widow till she was eighty-four. She did not depart from the temple, worshiping with fasting and prayer night and day" (2:36-37).

The frequency of such descriptions suggests that the Jewishness of the principal characters in the story is of more than historical interest. These comments seem to be part of an apologetic tone, to which this study will return in chapter 10.

IV. John

The Fourth Gospel contains no story of Jesus' birth. The book begins with a prologue that is as distinctive as the rest of the Gospel. Because of the special character of that prologue and its place in the thematic structure of the Gospel, examination of these opening verses will be postponed until chapter 11, which is devoted to the Fourth Gospel.

Summary

The introduction to the story of Jesus is unique in each Gospel. These openings are especially important because each narrator introduces the major themes that will be developed further in the course of his story—shaping the unique portrait of Jesus that will emerge in each Gospel.

There are no birth stories in Mark and John. The Gospel of Mark begins with a superscription announcing that the story will be about Jesus—the Messiah who is the Son of God. Yet the opening scenes focus on John the Baptist. Jesus appears and is baptized, but the reader is not told whence he came or why he was baptized. An air of mystery pervades the introduction of this hero who, the reader is told, will fulfill a unique and supernatural role. The Gospel of John begins with a prologue so distinctive that it cannot be discussed with the others and is left for a future chapter that deals with the Gospel as a whole.

Matthew and Luke contain birth stories that together form the traditional Christmas story. The Gospel of Matthew emphasizes the influence of the past and the concept of royalty. It begins with a genealogy that relates Jesus, through Joseph, his earthly father, to King David (father of the messianic line) and Abraham (father of Israel). The writer apparently feels no contradiction between this tradition and his account of the virgin birth. Matthew focuses on Joseph, whose actions are determined by special dreams and angelic commands. The interest is more in the significance of events as fulfilling scripture than on depicting human responses. By calling his Gospel "the book of the genesis of Jesus Christ," by the genealogy, by the parallels with the Moses birth story, and by his family's coming up out of Egypt after their flight, Matthew is tying the story of this child into the traditions and expectations that had developed within ancient Israel.

From the genealogy and the visit of the star-guided magi, Jesus is heralded as king. His birth is portrayed as a long foreseen and awaited event of cosmic significance. Nevertheless, a note of foreboding is introduced: Herod fears this child called "King of the Jews," and the slaughter of the innocents in Bethlehem foreshadows the opposition Jesus will later encounter, culminating in his being crucified as King of the Jews.

Although Luke's Gospel shares basic parallels with Matthew, there are differences in both detail and emphasis that reflect divergent thematic concerns: the Gospel emphasizes both the future and the concept of lowliness. Differing details: in Matthew, Jesus' family moves to Nazareth after the wise men's visit and the flight to Egypt. In Luke, they had always lived in Nazareth, to which they return after the visit from the shepherds and after Mary completes her days of purification. Differing emphases: for Luke, the virgin birth shows Jesus as the Son of God, whereas the stress in Matthew is on the birth as the fulfillment of biblical prophecy. The announcement of the birth is made to Mary in Luke, where her response of faith is juxtaposed with the doubting response of Zechariah, John's father, when the angel appears to him. Mary's Magnificat shows a strong concern for the poor and weak.

Like Matthew, Luke is interested in relating the story of Jesus to Jewish tradition, but he does so in more general terms. Luke does not use scriptural quotations, but there is a biblical air permeating the hymns that run through these early chapters. They refer to the two children, John and Jesus, as accomplishing the long-awaited hope of Israel. Further, the tie to Israel's tradition is strengthened by the fact that each of Luke's broad cast of characters is a righteous and observant Jew.

CHAPTER FOUR

JESUS' TEACHING MINISTRY

The portrait of Jesus as teacher is one of the most predominant in the Gospels: he has great wisdom; brilliant in debate, he is capable of answering difficult or sensitive questions and of silencing opponents. Many of his sayings are formulated as aphorisms, resembling those of other renowned sages of antiquity. Disciples frequently call Jesus "Teacher," even in Mark, a Gospel that includes remarkably few formal teachings.

I. The Parables

Perhaps the best place to begin a study of Jesus' teaching is with his parables.[1] The form itself is not unique to Jesus or to early Christian literature. Parables are common in rabbinic literature. In the Gospels, however, this particular form of teaching—probably Jesus' most characteristic method—appears to a degree unparalleled in other literature of antiquity. The parable itself is a popular as opposed to a scholarly form. Its principal purpose is to interpret abstract teachings by means of concrete analogy. Jesus' parables vary in length from a sentence to a brief narrative, but in most the simile is concise, pointed, and simple. Generally they have one major point. They reveal a great deal about the character of his ministry, the themes of his preaching, his audience, and their response. For example, the imagery comes largely from agricultural life appropriate to northern Palestine, suggesting that most of them were intended for peasants.

The parables serve a variety of functions. Some explain such abstractions as the kingdom of God or forgiveness. The kingdom of God may be compared to a farmer or to a mustard seed. When asked about forgiveness, Jesus tells a story about a servant whose ten million dollar debt has been forgiven yet who refuses to excise a debt of twenty dollars owed to him

(Matt. 18:23-35). Proper obedience to the Law is illustrated by the story of a Samaritan (Luke 10:29-37).

Parables also serve as warnings. Jesus encourages listeners to count the cost before beginning an important project; they should not end up like the man who laid the foundation of a tower only to discover that he had insufficient funds to complete it (Luke 14:28-30). The danger of riches is exemplified in the stories of the rich fool (Luke 12:13-21) and of the rich man and Lazarus (Luke 16:19-31).

Many parables respond to criticisms by religious Jews about Jesus' followers or about his own behavior. He explains his actions by comparing them to those of a farmer (Mark 4:1-9) or of a woman who has lost a coin (Luke 15:8-10). Disapproving Pharisees and scribes are bewildered by Jesus' association with tax collectors and sinners; they are compared to an elder brother who is so bound up with a son's obligations that he cannot share his father's joy at the return of his profligate younger brother (Luke 15:11-32).

The present form of the parables reveals much about the early Christians who continued to tell them long after the end of Jesus' ministry. The parables were changed during the process of transmission, according to scholars, a process that may be observed by comparing versions of the same parables included in the three Synoptic Gospels. Although some differences are minor, others seem clearly to indicate that the parables have been edited, embellished, even reinterpreted. Some of the reinterpreting may be attributed to the writers of the Gospels. Scholars find some evidence, however, that encourages them to trace a gradual transformation of at least some of Jesus' parables back into the preliterary period of tradition. For the modern student, this situation provides a number of levels at which to study parables.

One of the most obvious ways the writers of the Gospels have influenced the interpretation of the parables is by providing a literary setting for them. By substituting a different audience one clearly alters interpretation.

For example, the parable of the lost sheep is found in virtually identical form in Matthew and Luke. In Luke 15:1-10, the parable is a response to criticisms leveled at Jesus by representatives of the Pharisaic community, the "religious" Jews: "Now the tax collectors and sinners were all drawing near to hear him. And the Pharisees and the scribes murmured, saying, 'This man receives sinners and eats with them.' So he told them this parable" (Luke 15:1-2). The little parable is the first in a series of three that emphasize God's love for the outcast and the lost. Jesus explains his behavior by comparing himself to a shepherd who discovers that one of his sheep is lost. He immediately leaves the rest of the flock to search for the one sheep—not because he is unconcerned about the flock, but because an individual sheep is in desperate need. In Luke, the purpose of the parable is to show that God is most concerned about those who most need help.

Matthew gives the parable a very different setting. It is included within a series of instructions Jesus gives his disciples just before he leaves Galilee (Matt. 18:1-35). The example of the shepherd is given as an illustration of behavior for Jesus' followers, who are enjoined to exercise concern about fellow believers. Matthew continues with instructions for bringing an errant member of the community back into the fold.

The different endings of the parable in Luke and Matthew illustrate their special emphases:

> Just so, I tell you, there will be more joy in heaven over one sinner who repents than over ninety-nine righteous persons who need no repentance. (Luke 15:7)

> So it is not the will of my Father who is in heaven that one of these little ones should perish. (Matt. 18:14)

In Luke, the point is that of bringing into the flock those who do not obviously belong. In Matthew, the image is rather preserving the flock, keeping it intact. Luke speaks about repentance, Matthew about sustaining concern. Change of audience helps give the parable a very different meaning.

A. The Parable of the Sower

Agricultural imagery for the kingdom of God is significant in the gospel tradition.[2] The sower in the field (Mark 4:1-20; Matt. 13:1-23; Luke 8:1-15) is one of the best-known parables. It presents an unusually vivid picture of the place of parables in the ministry of Jesus, as well as in the traditions of his followers. It is also one of the most interesting because of the variety of perspectives from which it can be studied.

Recounted and explained in detail by Matthew, Mark, and Luke, it provides a rare opportunity for scholars to compare the treatment and interpretation of the same parable in each Gospel. (For convenience, the three versions of the parable have been included as an appendix to this section.)

All three Gospels interpret the parable of the sower allegorically and in generally similar terms. Each identifies every component in the story: the seed is the Word, the various kinds of soil represent the listeners, the birds represent Satan (or the evil one, the devil), the sun stands for persecution, thorns symbolize the riches and pleasures of this world. The parable is more appropriately called the parable of the four kinds of soil, depicting various responses to the preaching of the Word. It serves as a warning for the faithful and encourages them to "hold it fast in an honest and good heart, and bring forth fruit with patience" (Luke 8:15).

Few of Jesus' other parables are interpreted; details are ordinarily ignored. Furthermore, they have a single, simple moral, and although that moral is often highlighted by exaggerated situations or surprise endings, the stories are usually clear and uncomplicated.

The parable of the sower, however, is offered as an allegory. An allegory is a cryptogram to be deciphered, a more or less thinly disguised story in which each element of plot, character, or setting represents someone or something outside the story. Most of Jesus' parables are not allegories in this sense. They are short, pointed anecdotes, usually taken from everyday situations; they need no deciphering because they have only one major thrust. Their effectiveness depends upon the ability of the speaker to engage his audience by describing realistic situations in which they can see themselves, to explain the obscure by the familiar.

Since the parables of Jesus in general are unaccompanied by allegorical explanations, scholars reason that interpretations such as the one tied to the parable of the sower have been appended during the history of their transmission. Such additions may be clues to the process of reinterpretation as the parables were handed on from generation to generation prior to their incorporation in the Gospels. A number of important studies of Jesus' parables from this perspective yield impressive results.[3] The parable of the sower is a convenient example for study, for the secondary interpretation is readily distinguished from the parable itself. The process of reinterpretation in other parables is far more subtle.

When one reads the parable of the sower apart from its explanation in each of the Gospels, new possibilities for understanding the story emerge. The parable ends with a bountiful harvest. The contrast is not among four equivalent situations but between the time of planting and the time of harvest. The major thrust of the parable is bound up with the contrast between these two scenes. In the first scene, the time of sowing, there is much wasted effort; seed falls among thorns, along the path, and on rocky soil, as well as on good ground. One would not expect the farmer to receive much reward for all his work. Yet he does. In fact, he enjoys an unusually spectacular harvest. In Palestine, a yield of tenfold was considered good, while a yield of seven and a half was about average; the greatly exaggerated figures mentioned in the parable create an impressive effect.

It may seem difficult today to believe that the story told by Jesus was drawn from real life. The behavior of the farmer seems almost irrational. Why sow everywhere—among stones and thorns, on paths? But in Palestine, the field was plowed after the seed had been sown, and paths and other areas would eventually have been included in the plowing—early audiences would have known this automatically. The plowing itself is not mentioned because the parable depicts as strikingly as possible the contrast between the appearance of the field at the time of sowing and at the time of harvest. Despite the signs of futility at the time of planting, the farmer knows what he is doing; there will be a rich harvest.

Is there a possible meaning of the parable apart from the appended allegorical interpretation? For what purpose might it originally have been told? To answer such questions, one needs to interpret the parable within the context of Jesus' ministry, to the extent that it can be reconstructed. This parable—minus the allegorical interpretation—fits well into the picture of Jesus' ministry and with the themes of his preaching that appear in the Gospels.

According to the Synoptic Gospels, the theme that

dominated Jesus' preaching was the coming of the kingdom of God. The great days God had promised his people were on the threshold of fulfillment. God's kingdom was about to break into history. Jesus' ministry was the announcement—or better—the inauguration of that kingdom. Although Jesus knew that he was ushering in God's kingdom, however, his contemporaries found it difficult to share that assurance.

Jews expected the coming of the kingdom of God to be a spectacular occasion. They could point to prophecies that God would destroy Israel's enemies, that the Messiah-King would "slay the wicked with the breath of his mouth," and that Jerusalem would become the center of worship for all nations. None of this seemed relevant to the ministry of the young man from Nazareth. Those who were attracted by his preaching were the undesirables in Jewish society—tax collectors, sinners, prostitutes—people with whom no respectable Jew would associate. Was this the awesome and glorious kingdom of God for which generations had waited? Even his disciples must have had difficulty understanding how this seemingly insignificant preaching tour could have anything to do with the coming of God's kingdom.

Many of Jesus' parables were addressed to such doubts, some of which can be heard throughout the stories. How can such a tiny, insignificant movement be related to the kingdom of God? The Kingdom is like a mustard seed. It is the smallest of all seeds, but after it has been planted, it grows into a treelike shrub that is large enough even for birds to build nests in the branches. If Jesus' ministry is really to be the inauguration of God's kingdom, then why isn't he rallying forces and preparing for battle? The Kingdom is like a field that has been planted. The seed grows in its own time, and until the appointed harvest time, the farmer must wait. What about all the hangers-on who are clearly uninterested in religion or who are hypocrites? The Kingdom is like a field in which weeds have been sown with the grain. To pull up the weeds before the harvest might damage the grain. But at the harvest, the weeds appropriately will be cast into the oven.

The parable of the sower properly belongs with the other parables of the Kingdom. It seems to reply to the criticism that Jesus' ministry was ineffectual, that much of his effort was fruitless, and that too many obstacles stood in his path. By comparing his efforts concerning the kingdom of God to those of a sower who has just begun to seed his field, the parable offers a concrete example for a difficult abstraction. The thorns, stones, and paths represent seemingly wasted efforts with no further significance. Although in the early stages of sowing much appears hopeless, the farmer knows he has done what is needed; at the time of harvest, there will be a bountiful crop. The same, Jesus tells his critics, is true of his own ministry. The emphasis in the parable is on the successful sowing, not on kinds of soil.

What, then, of the allegorical interpretation of the parable found in all three Synoptic Gospels? A plausible explanation is that it was added as the situation of Jesus' followers changed. They handed on Jesus' words not only because the revered Jesus said them but also because they were important to the life of the church. They served both to instruct and to exhort. But if the parables were to be relevant to changed situations, they frequently required at least minor reinterpretations. Shifting the audience is one way to effect such a reinterpretation. Allegorization is another. The less embellished form of the parable of the sower in Luke may be evidence that he accepted an earlier version—a stage in the process of transmission that culminated with the form of the parable in Matthew and Mark. In its final form, the parable of the sower would have been an appropriate form of exhortation for later generations of Jesus' followers. Numerous pitfalls await the believer, some of whom may even fall away. Those who persevere (whose soil nurtures the Word) will receive a rich reward, but reaching the goal requires more than mere good intentions.

B. Mark's Use of the Parable

The parable of the sower has not yet been studied from the perspective of its three literary settings. In each Gospel the parable serves as an exhortation, but each time it is narrated differently. For example, Luke cuts the parable and explanations to their essentials, whereas in Matthew, Jesus' answer to his disciples' question includes an extended quotation from Isaiah (Matt. 13:14-15). In Mark, Jesus tells his followers that he uses parables "so that" others will not understand (Mark 4:12), whereas in Matthew, it is "because" they cannot understand (Matt. 13:13). According to Matthew, Jesus chooses parables as a means of discourse because most of his listeners are dull and can only understand if appropriate teaching methods are used, whereas in Mark the point is almost the opposite. Thus, the setting of the parable is distinctive. To interpret the parable of the sower, one must read it in each of its three contexts. Mark's use of the parable will serve as an example.

A remarkable feature of Mark's Gospel is how little formal teaching it records, despite its numerous direct and indirect references to Jesus as a teacher. In Mark, the story of Jesus is not primarily that of a great teacher who instructs crowds about religion and morality. It is, rather, the story of the hidden Messiah, constantly plagued by others' misunderstanding and lack of insight and by controversy and opposition. It culminates not in the vindication of his teaching but in his arrest, trial, and death. He dies forsaken by his followers, misunderstood by Jews and Romans alike, ridiculed even by those with whom he is crucified. His last cry of anguish from the cross provides one more opportunity for misunderstanding. His resurrection merely frightens the women at the sepulcher.

Mark inserts the small collection of parables in chapter 4 after Jesus has begun to achieve some notoriety. His teaching has astonished the populace, "for he taught them as one who had authority, and not as the scribes" (Mark 1:22). Yet reaction to Jesus has not been uniform. Some take offense: religious leaders accuse Jesus of blasphemy (2:7) and argue that his ability to cast out demons comes from an alliance with the devil himself (3:22). His friends and relatives believe that he is "beside himself" and seek to take him home (3:21, 31-32). The only ones who truly recognize Jesus are demons, and they are enjoined by Jesus to remain silent (3:11). The first instances of his teaching serve only to heighten everyone's confusion about Jesus and his message.

The parables do little to enlighten the crowds; in fact, they only deepen the mystery. According to his disciples, the

parables with which he teaches the crowds are unintelligible
without some explanation:

> And when he was alone, those who were about him with the
> twelve asked him concerning the parables. And he said to them,
> "To you has been given the secret of the kingdom of God, but
> for those outside everything is in parables [riddles]." (4:10-11)

The Greek word *parabole* in this verse should be translated
as "riddle" rather than as "parable." The concept of the
parable as an intentionally obscure form of discourse certainly
conflicts with the use of the parable form in the rest of the New
Testament and in rabbinic literature. This difference suggests
that Mark is using Jesus' teaching material for his own
distinctive purposes. To Mark, understanding Jesus' parables—*real* hearing and seeing—is not a simple intellectual
act. Something more is involved, something that enables the
reader to penetrate the mystery and to understand it at
another level. Jesus' teaching is thus related to the great
theme in Mark's Gospel—the mystery of the kingdom of God
and the hidden Messiah.

Yet the parable of the sower is not simply an enigmatic
saying in Mark or merely an exhortation for those with ears to
hear. He includes the allegorization that foreshadows what is
to come in the story. Many followers will fall by the wayside;
many will fail to understand. Even those to whom the secret
has been given and to whom the parables have been explained
will fail at the moment of crisis. Numerous pitfalls await the
would-be disciple of Jesus; following the mysterious figure as
he moves inexorably toward his cross is an awesome task.

The parable also foreshadows events beyond the story of
Jesus as recorded in Mark. Almost without exception, the
parables in chapter 4 contrast two periods: the present, a time
of small beginnings, fruitless efforts, mystery, and misunderstandings; and the future, the time of bountiful harvest,
enlightenment, and revelations. In Mark, the parables are
followed by the story of Jesus' calming the sea. His stunned
and unperceiving disciples ask one another, "Who then is this,
that even the wind and sea obey him?" Something more is to
come; there will be a time of illumination and bounty. But for
the present the teacher and his teachings remain a mystery.

C. Appendix: The Parable of the Sower

Matt. 13:1-14; 18-23

1 That same day Jesus went out of the house and sat beside the sea. 2 And great crowds gathered about him, so that he got into a boat and sat there; and the whole crowd stood on the beach. 3 And he told them many things in parables, saying: "A sower went out to sow. 4 And as he sowed, some seeds fell along the path, and the birds came and devoured them. 5 Other seeds fell on rocky ground, where they had not much soil, and immediately they sprang up, since they had no depth of soil, 6 but when the sun rose they were scorched; and since they had no root they withered away.

Mark 4:1-20

1 Again he began to teach beside the sea. And a very large crowd gathered about him, so that he got into a boat and sat in it on the sea; and the whole crowd was beside the sea on the land. 2 And he taught them many things in parables, and in his teaching he said to them: 3 "Listen! A sower went out to sow. 4 And as he sowed, some seed fell along the path, and the birds came and devoured it. 5 Other seed fell on rocky ground, where it had not much soil, and immediately it sprang up, since it had no depth of soil; 6 and when the sun rose it was scorched, and since it had no root it withered away.

Luke 8:4-15

4 And when a great crowd came together and people from town after town came to him,

[See 5:1-3]

he said in a parable:

5 "A sower went out to sow his seed; and as he sowed, some fell along the path, and was trodden under foot, and the birds of the air devoured it. 6 And some fell on the rock; and as it grew up, it withered away, because it had no moisture.

7 Other seeds fell upon thorns, and the thorns grew up and choked them. 8 Other seeds fell on good soil and brought forth grain, some a hundredfold, some sixty, some thirty. 9 He who has ears, let him hear."

10 Then the disciples came and said to him, "Why do you speak to them in parables?" 11 And he answered them, "To you it has been given to know the secrets of the kingdom of heaven, but to them it has not been given. 12 "For to him who has will more be given, and he will have abundance; but from him who has not, even what he has will be taken away. 13 This is why I

---

7 Other seed fell among thorns and the thorns grew up and choked it, and it yielded no grain. 8 And other seeds fell into good soil and brought forth grain, growing up and increasing and yielding thirtyfold and sixtyfold and a hundredfold." 9 And he said, "He who has ears to hear, let him hear."

10 And when he was alone, those who were about him with the twelve asked him concerning the parables. 11 And he said to them, "To you has been given the secret of the kingdom of God,

[See 4:25]

but for those outside everything is

---

7 And some fell among thorns; and the thorns grew with it and choked it. 8 And some fell into good soil and grew and yielded a hundredfold." As he said this, he called out, "He who has ears to hear, let him hear."

9 And when his disciples asked him what this parable meant, 10 he said, "To you it has been given to know the secrets of the kingdom of God;

[See 8:18b]

but for others they are in parables, so that seeing they may not speak to them in parables, because seeing they do not see, and hearing they do not hear, nor do they understand. 14 "With them indeed is fulfilled the prophecy of Isaiah which says:

18 "Hear then the parable of the sower. 19 When any one hears the word of the kingdom and does not understand it, the evil one comes and snatches away what is sown in his heart; this is what was sown along the path. 20 As for what was sown on rocky ground, this is he who hears the word and immediately receives it with joy; 21 yet he has no root in himself, but endures for a while, and when tribulation or persecution arises on account of the word, immediately he falls away. 22 As for what was sown among

in parables; 12 so that they may indeed see but not perceive, and may indeed hear but not understand; lest they should turn again, and be forgiven."

13 And he said to them, "Do you not understand this parable? 14 The sower sows the word. 15 And these are the ones along the path, where the word is sown; when they hear, Satan immediately comes and takes away the word which is sown in them. 16 And these in like manner are the ones sown upon rocky ground, who, when they hear the word, immediately receive it with joy; 17 and they have no root in themselves, but endure for a while; then, when tribulation or persecution arises on account of the word,

see, and hearing they may not understand."

11 "Now the parable is this: The seed is the word of God. 12 The ones along the path are those who have heard; then the devil comes and takes away the word from their hearts, that they may not believe and be saved. 13 And the ones on the rock are those who, when they hear the word, receive it with joy; but these have no root, they believe for a while and in time of temptation fall away. 14 And as for what fell among the thorns, they are those who hear, but as they go on their way they are choked by the cares and

thorns, this is he who hears the word, but the cares of the world and the delight in riches choke the word, and it proves unfruitful. 23 As for what was sown on good soil, this is he who hears the word and understands it; he indeed bears fruit, and yields, in one case a hundredfold, in another sixty, and in another thirty."

immediately they fall away. 18 And others are the ones sown among thorns; they are those who hear the word, 19 but the cares of the world, and the delight in riches, and the desire for other things, enter in and choke the word, and it proves unfruitful. 20 But those that were sown upon the good soil are the ones who hear the word and accept it and bear fruit, thirtyfold and sixtyfold and a hundredfold."

riches and pleasures of life, and their fruit does not mature. 15 And as for that in the good soil, they are those who, hearing the word, hold it fast in an honest and good heart, and bring forth fruit with patience."

II. The Sermon on the Mount, Matthew 5–7

If the parables are the best-known individual examples of Jesus' teaching, then the Sermon on the Mount—which includes the Beatitudes, the Lord's Prayer, the injunction to love one's enemies and to turn the other cheek, and the Golden Rule—is the most familiar collection.[4] Students of the Bible have given these three chapters much attention, but disagree in assessing their role. For some, the sermon is the most sublime ethical statement of all time. Others say it is unrealistic, that if codified into law, it would lead to the disintegration of human society. Still others argue that Jesus did not intend to institute a universal ethic but that he was sketching a heroic life-style appropriate for his disciples to adopt during the short time left before the dawning of the kingdom of God.[5]

The sermon poses a number of problems for historians. Although it is included intact only in the Gospel of Matthew, most of its teachings appear with almost identical wording scattered throughout the Gospel of Luke. (Mark and John have no equivalent.) If, as many scholars currently believe, the sayings in Matthew and Luke derive from a common source, one must assume that the placement of the sayings in each Gospel reflects the redactive work of the respective writers. Examination of the way in which Matthew and Luke use source material elsewhere in their works has led many scholars to believe that Matthew has combined into one sermon sayings that he did not find so grouped in his source. In any case, whether Jesus actually delivered such a sermon—and Luke broke it into shorter sayings—cannot be determined from existing data.

A. The Literary Setting

If the composition of the Sermon on the Mount in Matthew does reflect editorial efforts, then it is even more important that these three chapters be studied in their literary context. Whatever the historical problems of ever tracing the sermon back to Jesus, today's interpreter of Matthew can establish with some assurance its meaning within the Gospel—its place in the thematic structure and its contribution to Matthew's portrait of Jesus.

The Sermon on the Mount appears soon after Jesus' formal ministry begins. He has been baptized by John. He has returned from a period of testing in the wilderness and has called his first disciples, the brothers Simon Peter and Andrew. The reader is given a summary of Jesus' early ministry: in Galilee his preaching and healing aroused enthusiasm, his fame spread "throughout all Syria," and "great crowds followed him from Galilee and the Decapolis and Jerusalem and Judea and from beyond the Jordan" (4:25). The sermon provides the first examples of this unusually moving and successful teaching. Its placement and its length—the longest of his teaching in the Gospel—indicate its importance.

The chapters have been called the Sermon on the Mount because of their brief preface: "Seeing the crowds, he went up on the mountain, and when he sat down his disciples came to him" (5:1).

Why the mountain? Does Jesus intend to escape the huge crowds? Or is the mountain considered a place from which to address a crowd? Luke mentions only a level place large enough to accommodate everyone. Apparently, the actual location (and topography) of the mountain is not important. The mountain itself may have only symbolic significance. For Matthew's audience, familiar with Jewish tradition, such a setting would certainly evoke the image of Sinai, the sacred mount from which Moses gave the definitive statement of God's will, the Torah. Is Jesus being depicted as the new Moses? The writer is clearly aware of the imagery. Surely, it is not accidental that the Gospel of Matthew concludes with Jesus once again on a mountain, this time instructing his followers to teach "all that I have commanded you" (28:20); at the end of the story of Moses, he is on Mount Nebo.

Whether Jesus is to be accepted as the new Moses or not, the mountain at least strengthens his image of authority. The sermon concludes appropriately: "And when Jesus finished these sayings, the crowds were astonished, for he taught them as one who had authority, and not as their scribes" (7:29). This verse includes a polemical note that runs throughout

Matthew's Gospel. Jesus' teaching is contrasted with something familiar to the audience: the teaching of the scribes, professional religious scholars, trained to interpret the sacred Law and tradition. The scribes appealed to Scripture and to earlier sages as their authority. Jesus, a nonprofessional, spoke on his own "authority."

Another, and ambiguous, aspect of the setting of the sermon is its audience—who heard him speak? When Jesus saw the crowds, according to Matthew, he went up to the mountain. But then Matthew notes that "his *disciples* came to him" and that he began to teach "them." Who are they? Nowhere else in Matthew's Gospel does the term "disciples" refer to the whole crowd, and yet it seems quite unlikely that Matthew wants the reader to view the sermon as delivered only to Jesus' inner circle of followers. Some scholars argue for this latter interpretation, but then the conclusion of the sermon makes little sense: "the crowds were astonished."[6] The narrator may be only calling attention to the presence of the disciples at this sermon because they will later be commissioned to teach "all that I have commanded you" (28:20).

B. Structure and Theme

The sermon itself is divisible into three sections: the body (5:17–7:12), framed by a series of future blessings for those who do what Jesus commands (5:2-16), and corresponding warnings and admonitions (7:13-26). The Beatitudes that introduce the sermon promise future blessings for those who meet God's requirements by serving as the "salt of the earth" and the "light of the world." The Beatitudes also characterize such disciples: they are "poor in spirit" (5:3); they "hunger and thirst after righteousness" (verse 6); they are peacemakers (verse 9); and they are willing to endure slander and even persecution because of their belief in Jesus (verses 11-12). Although their road will not be easy, these disciples have the promise of great rewards in the kingdom of heaven.

Balancing these introductory promises is a closing series of admonitions. Jesus exhorts followers to enter by the narrow gate and warns them about false prophets (7:13-20). Only those who obey the will of God will enter the Kingdom (verses 21-23). Nominal disciples will discover, to their dismay, that their lives have an insubstantial foundation, but by then it will be too late for them to escape ruin (verses 24-27).

The body of the sermon has no clear progression of ideas; its structure is largely formal. The first and longest section is a series of antitheses: "You have heard that it was said. . . . But I say to you" (5:21-48). The second section (6:1-18), which contains the Lord's Prayer, contrasts the proper manner of fulfilling religious obligations (giving alms, praying, fasting) with the false: When you do ____ do not do as the hypocrites. The final section (6:19–7:11) is a series of loosely connected injunctions, some greatly elaborated. The entire sermon is then summarized in 7:12: "So whatever you wish that men would do to you, do so to them; for this is the law and the prophets."

The unity of the sermon is largely thematic. It is about discipleship; Jesus sketches a portrait of an ideal follower, one who hopes to participate in the coming kingdom of heaven. In simplest terms, a disciple does what is righteous. The basic theme is clearly expressed in the opening lines of the body of the sermon: "For I tell you, unless your righteousness exceeds that of the scribes and Pharisees, you will never enter the kingdom of heaven" (5:20).

In Matthew, righteousness—uprightness, doing what God requires—is an important concept. It is more than that of the scribes and Pharisees, who are portrayed as the rigorous pietists within the Jewish society. Their way of life is insufficient for admittance into the kingdom of heaven. In his sermon, Jesus describes the higher righteousness expected of his followers.

C. The Antitheses

The demand for higher righteousness is particularly apparent in the series of antitheses (5:21-48). Jesus does not so much invalidate past behavioral expectations as pronounce them inadequate. He elucidates his understanding of God's will by contrasting it with former interpretation.[7] It was said to "men of old" that God forbids murder; according to Jesus,

eternal punishment awaits even those who hate their
brothers. It was said that adultery is wrong; according to
Jesus, the lustful thought is as serious as the act. More radical
commands follow, the most striking of which is that Jesus'
disciples love not only their neighbors, but also their enemies.
He rejects the *lex talionis,* the principle of measure for
measure, that imposed a limit on revenge, and he insists that
his followers forget revenge entirely, turn the other cheek,
and go a second mile. The series reaches a climax: "You,
therefore, must be perfect, as your heavenly father is
perfect."

It is not surprising that many have considered Jesus'
demands impossible. Within the context of Matthew's
Gospel, however, they are not considered impossible. The
word "perfect" does not mean the absence of imperfection or
an unblemished record; it means something more like
complete devotion, single-mindedness. God here is not a
remote, sinless being, but one totally—perfectly—concerned
with his creatures' well-being. (See 6:25-33.) This type of
perfection can be applied to the life of discipleship; elsewhere
in Matthew Jesus describes it as a realistic possibility (19:21).

The placement of the antitheses immediately after the
statement about a righteousness exceeding that of the scribes
and Pharisees suggests that the first half of each antithetical
statement is meant to represent Pharisaic views. Although the
last injunction (5:43) is the only one not based on scriptural
injunctions, rules from the Torah, undoubtedly it too was a
feature of traditional piety since it is treated in the same
manner as the others.

The reader may assume that the difference between Jesus
and the scribes and Pharisees lies in the authority to which
each appeals. Since the others ground their interpretation in
the Law of Moses, it appears at first glance that Jesus is
contrasting his view of God's will with that expressed in
Scripture. That is an erroneous understanding of the
relationship between the antitheses and the Law of Moses.
The whole sermon is introduced with a strongly worded
defense of the Mosaic Law:

> Think not that I have come to abolish the law and the prophets;
> I have come not to abolish them but to fulfill them. For truly, I

> say to you, till heaven and earth pass away, not an iota, not a
> dot, will pass from the law until all is accomplished. Whoever
> then relaxes one of the least of these commandments and
> teaches men so, shall be called least in the kingdom of heaven;
> but he who does them and teaches them shall be called great in
> the kingdom of heaven. (5:17-19)

No matter how radical Jesus' interpretations of the Law in
the antitheses may appear, they do not abrogate Scripture or
even contrast with it. According to Matthew's Gospel, Jesus
has come not to set aside the Law of Moses but to interpret it.
The individual commands are still to be obeyed as God's will.
Jesus, no less than the scribes and Pharisees, seeks to derive
the righteousness God requires from Scripture. It is their
interpretation of the Law, of righteousness, that is to be
contrasted with that of Jesus, both with respect to form and
content.

The first distinction between the scribes and Pharisees and
Jesus is their respective bases for scriptural interpretations.
Within the circles of the scribes, especially trained in the
sacred Law, interpretation followed carefully worked out
principles. One list of rules is attributed to Hillel the Elder, a
sage roughly contemporary with Jesus; a second, and longer
list, is attributed to Rabbi Ishmael.[8] In addition to these rules,
interpretation of the law depended heavily upon precedent,
upon the majority opinion in a particularly disputed issue, or
upon what some great sage of the past had said. A strong sense
of tradition runs throughout rabbinic literature. These
features are noticeably absent in Jesus' legal pronounce-
ments. Instead of relying on set principles of interpretation or
on precendents, Jesus speaks on his own authority: "You
have heard that it was said. . . . But I say to you."

The second point of contrast is the goal reflected in the
antitheses. Unlike those of the scribes and the Pharisees,
Jesus' interpretations are not case law. He is not applying
God's commandments to specific situations, taking into
account extenuating circumstances or new problems. Nor is
he presenting a definitive list of rules to be followed by one
who hopes to become righteous. Instead, his interpretations
are an absolute radicalization of the demands of the Law. The
examples Jesus uses are signs of a different attitude toward

the Law and toward obeying the Law. He is concerned with the basic intention behind each command; a person's sinful thought is as serious a violation of God's will as an overt act. Murder is wrong in God's eyes; but the command forbidding murder should not obscure the underlying opposition to hatred, whether toward a brother or an enemy. Illicit intercourse is wrong, but the prohibition of adultery does not excuse what is not expressly forbidden—lustful thoughts. The rather exaggerated series of interpretations of the Law, the following series of contrasts about religious duties, and the list of injunctions in the sermon direct attention to a more fundamental, totally committing view of discipleship that is essential to an understanding of the individual commands:

> So whatever you wish that men would do to you,
> do so to them; for this is the law and the prophets. (7:12)

D. The Pharisees

Although the Pharisees have this same desire to extend the Law to every facet of life, from Matthew's perspective their approach has become a way of evading God's absolute demands. Matthew portrays the Pharisees as legalists, as overzealous, scrupulous observers of minutiae who, in their concern for details, have missed the whole spirit of the Law and of true righteousness. To ask, "How many times shall I forgive my neighbor?" in itself implies a false approach to discipleship. In Matthew, the Pharisees represent an institutionalized religion that has lost all spirit, becoming a formality, a way of avoiding God. Jesus is the prophet, the leader of a pietistic reform movement within Judaism dedicated to recovering the real will of God, which has been obscured by tradition.

Were the historical Pharisees as bad as Matthew depicts them? Very probably not. Pharisaic rabbinic literature embodies most of the interpretations, precepts, and sentiments expressed in the Sermon on the Mount—even the antithetical arguments and the Golden Rule. Matthew's attitude toward the Pharisees, however, reflects his own perspective. To the Pharisees within such a tradition, as to people within any institution, ritual and concern for small details serve as signs of great piety and commitment. But to outsiders, represented by Matthew, the same practices can appear empty and formal. Matthew's Jesus is the leader of a dissident movement, members of which align themselves against tradition and traditional institutions.

One must remember, however, that the Pharisees were not the establishment in Jesus' day. They were not considered representatives of the Jewish religious institution until after the destruction of Jerusalem and the rise of the rabbinic academy in Jabneh. Scholars have suggested that Matthew's portrayal of the Pharisees as typical opponents of Jesus reflects the circumstances of the writer and his audience at the time the work was composed, after 70 C.E. This particular feature of Matthew's Gospel also occurs outside the Sermon on the Mount and will be considered more carefully in chapter 9.[9]

E. Jesus as Teacher and Messiah

A further aspect of the image of Jesus as teacher that emerges from the Sermon on the Mount becomes clear when Matthew is contrasted with the Gospel of Thomas, one of the noncanonical books about Jesus. This gospel, dating perhaps from the turn of the first century, is composed almost exclusively of Jesus' teachings. Its opening is particularly revealing:

> These are the secret words which the Living Jesus spoke and Didymos Judas Thomas wrote. And he said: Whoever finds the explanation of these words will not taste death.[10]

In the Gospel of Thomas, Jesus is a teacher and nothing more, although his teaching is of a particular sort: it is a revelation of the mysteries of life and death. Discipleship involves primarily studying these esoteric teachings to discover the hidden truth that promises life and is intended only for insiders.

In Matthew, on the other hand, Jesus is a very different kind of teacher. The Sermon on the Mount concerns practice not knowledge; it describes a way of life considered proper for those who are already disciples. The promise of admittance to the kingdom of heaven is not contingent on the ability of followers to interpret mysterious revelations; it depends on the closeness with which they follow the Teacher, who has been given "all authority on heaven and on earth." And what is perhaps most important, Jesus is not simply the teacher in Matthew. He is still first and foremost the Christ, the Son of God who died and was raised from the dead, the Son of man who came to give his life as a ransom.

III. Johannine Discourses

Thus far we have examined examples of teachings of Jesus from the Synoptic Gospels. When we turn to the Fourth Gospel, we are in another world of thought. The vocabulary and style are different; so is the content. John includes few of the events recorded in the Synoptic Gospels and none of the familiar parables or aphoristic sayings. Instead, carefully constructed discourses use elaborate symbolism and phrases with double meanings.

Even the themes in John are different from those in the Synoptic Gospels. Jesus speaks not about the kingdom of God but about himself—about his mission, his relationship to the Father who has sent him, and what he has been sent to accomplish. He describes himself as the "living water," the "bread from heaven," the "good shepherd," the "light of the world," the "true vine"—images that are found nowhere in the synoptic tradition. He says remarkably little about practical matters of discipleship.

The reader has seen how valuable, even necessary, it is to study the Sermon on the Mount and the parables of Jesus with full regard for the literary contexts of Jesus' teachings. Interpretation of the material is incomplete without noting its function within the Gospel and its relationship to the various motifs in the story. The Synoptic Gospels justify such studies even though Jesus' sayings in the three Gospels frequently are not completely integrated into the narrative.

That is much less true of the Fourth Gospel; it is far more difficult to isolate individual features of the story for interpretation. Close reading reveals that the discourses are carefully constructed, clearly related to one another, and usually integrated into the narratives of Jesus' miracles or signs. One suspects that even the apparent confusion and the contradictions in the narrative have some literary function.

A. Loaves and "Bread"

One of the most interesting examples of Jesus' teaching in John is the "bread from heaven" discourse in chapter 6. It closely follows the sign that is reported at the beginning of the chapter, the miraculous feeding of the five thousand (John 6:1-21). Although the simplest link between the sign and the discourse is its central image—both deal with bread—there are other less obvious links. The narrator's seemingly irrelevant comment that the feeding occurred at the time of Passover evokes traditions about Israel's exodus from Egypt and sojourn in the wilderness (verse 4). Passover is also called the "feast of unleavened bread." Further, the festival, as it was then celebrated, referred to bread from heaven —manna—that God had sent in the past and would send again in the future.[11] Pervading the Passover traditions was the figure of Moses, the prophet. When Jesus has miraculously fed the crowd, they agree that he must be "the prophet who is to come into the world" (verse 4). The allusions to manna and to Moses in the miracle resurface in the ensuing discourse on bread from heaven (verse 31) and provide the basis for Jesus' teaching.

At the conclusion of the miraculous feeding, Jesus flees the crowd because "they were about to come and take him by force to make him king" (6:15). Characteristically in John, the crowd has failed to understand the miracle as a sign. When on the following day he encounters the same crowd, Jesus chastens them for their lack of insight. Instead of looking for more free food, he says, they should seek food of another sort: "Do not labor for the food which perishes, but for the food which endures to eternal life, which the Son of man will give to you; for on him has God the Father set his seal" (verse 27).

Again the crowd understands little; they misconstrue his words. There follows a play on the Greek word for labor or work. The crowd asks Jesus what work they should be doing

to do the work, or works, of God and eternal life. Jesus replies
that the work of God is to have faith in the one whom God has
sent (Jesus' frequent self-designation in John). The crowd
then demands from Jesus a work, a sign by which they will
know that he has been sent by God. The dialogue is ironic, for
on the previous day the crowd witnessed a sign that they failed
to understand. Yet now they request such a sign, the
multiplication of loaves, and as part of their challenge, they
quote to Jesus a passage from Scripture: "what work do you
perform? Our fathers ate manna in the wilderness; as it is
written, 'He gave them bread from heaven to eat'"
(6:30-31).[12]

Can he perform a work as great as that of Moses, the giant of
Jewish tradition who, according to Scripture, gave the
Israelites manna? The irony is heightened: just the day before
Jesus had provided a miraculous supply of bread; it was at
Passover time, and they had called him "the prophet who is to
come into the world." Now they ask for a sign like the bread
from heaven that Moses provided for "our fathers." How
could the crowd be so blind!

B. Jesus' Response to a Challenge

Their uncomprehending challenge forces Jesus to develop
his theme still further.

> Jesus then said to them, "Truly, truly, I say to you, it was not
> *Moses* who *gave* you the bread from heaven; *my Father gives* you
> the true bread from heaven. For the bread of God is that which
> [or the one who] comes down from heaven, and gives life to the
> world." (6:32-33)

The first half of Jesus' response is puzzling because of the
form of the statement rather than because of any deliberate
ambiguity, although the Fourth Gospel abounds in ambiguity.
Jesus actually is offering a commentary on the scriptural text
quoted by the crowd: "He gave them bread in the wilderness
to eat." In a kind of shorthand formula familiar to those
conversant with rabbinic literature, Jesus challenges the
crowd's interpretation of the quotation by questioning both its
subject and verb. According to the crowd, the "he" in the

quotation refers to Moses. This is the conventional sense of the passage: Moses gave the Israelites manna in the wilderness. But Jesus suggests a new referent for the "he" in the quotation: this "he" refers to God, "my Father."

Jesus' interpretation of the quotation also involves the tense of the verb "to give." Although the Gospel of John is in Greek, this debate about the tense of the verb stems from the original Hebrew text of the Old Testament. The Hebrew alphabet was composed exclusively of consonants; written words had no vowels, which were supplied automatically by readers who knew the sounds of the words. In many cases, however, the same sequence of consonants could have a number of meanings, depending on which vowels were supplied. If English were a Semitic language, the verb *knw* would follow the typical pattern. By changing vowels, one can read it as "know" or "knew." The vowel indicates the tense. In the crowd's quotation, the verb whose tense Jesus questions is the root *ntn*, "to give." When it has only these root letters, it can be read either as *natan*, "he gave" or *noten*, "he gives"; the context does not always clearly indicate which tense is meant.

According to Jesus, therefore, the passage the crowd has quoted to him as a challenge should not be read "*Moses gave them bread*" but rather "*my Father gives* bread." This kind of careful argumentation, using the biblical text as authority and examining the possible interpretations of the language, is common in rabbinic literature. It is a technique, however, whose setting is the school, the scholarly institution. Unlike the typical examples in the Synoptic Gospels of Jesus' teaching methods, John depicts Jesus as a sage, one capable of intricate interpretation of the sacred text in the manner of the rabbis.

The ambiguity in the first half of Jesus' response, as we have seen, is unintentional; it results from reinterpreting the words of Scripture. The ambiguity is deliberate in the second half of Jesus' response, when he speaks of the real nature of the bread from heaven: "For the bread of God is that which [or "the one who"—the Greek can mean either] comes down from heaven, and gives life to the world." Is the bread something or someone? The crowd, unable to see beneath the surface, accepts Jesus' statement literally—a promise that God will send them all the life-giving bread they will ever need. But as the reader knows, the statement really is meant to identify Jesus as the true bread from heaven: he is the one who comes down from heaven, giving everlasting life to the world. John's narrative, like Mark's, frequently operates on two levels: one at which the participants understand (usually misunderstand) the events and one at which the reader properly understands them. Jesus speaks metaphorically; the crowd, unable to rise above the mundane, takes him literally.

Thinking that Jesus has agreed to provide an endless supply of bread, they reply, "Lord, give us this bread always" (6:34). Jesus becomes more direct: "I am the bread of life; he who comes to me shall not hunger, and he who believes in me shall never thirst" (verse 35).

C. The Gulf Opens

The Fourth Gospel emphasizes that Jesus is the emissary sent from the Father to reveal his identity and to bring life to the world. For this purpose he has come "down from heaven." This theme is introduced in the prologue (1:1-14) and repeated throughout the Gospel. Yet, as the prologue indicates, "he came to his own home, and his own people received him not" (verse 11). As Jesus' "bread from heaven" discourse becomes more revelatory, the crowd moves farther and farther from real understanding:

> The Jews then murmured at him, because he said, "I am the bread which came down from heaven." They said, "Is not this Jesus, the son of Joseph, whose father and mother we know? How does he now say, 'I have come down from heaven'?" (John 6:41-42)

The crowd "murmured." The Septuagint uses the same verb to describe the response of the Israelites to Moses in the wilderness (Exod. 16:7, 8, 9, 12; 7:3). Jesus' audience considered Moses their teacher, the one who gave their fathers manna in the wilderness. Yet their fathers understood and trusted in Moses no more than they have understood Jesus. They also "murmur."

Next the discourse examines why the crowd, or "the Jews," cannot understand Jesus' response: they have not been taught by God.[13] Jesus tells them that "every one who has heard and learned from the Father comes to me" (John 6:45).

Those who accept his words have been taught by God; those who do not, whatever they may claim, do not know God's will. The scripture that Jesus' opponents used to challenge his claims actually affirms him, as those who have eyes to see can perceive. Ironically, Jesus' revelation of his identity and of God's message in this and other speeches also illuminates the character of his audience. By their responses, they reveal in what camp they belong, exposing a profound gulf between Jesus' followers and others in the crowds, and Jesus emphasizes that gulf.

This polemical note becomes evident in his reply to the murmuring. Returning to the crowd's initial challenge that he provide manna, as Moses did, Jesus again compares his own revelation with traditional Jewish teachings about Moses. No one has seen the Father, says Jesus, but the one who has come from the Father (6:46). He echoes the statement in 1:18, which contrasts Jesus and Moses: the only true revealer is Jesus, in apparent contradiction to traditional views of Moses as the revealer of God.[14]

> I am the bread of life. Your fathers ate the manna in the wilderness, and they died. This is the bread which comes down from heaven, that a man may eat of it and not die. I am the living bread which came down from heaven; if any one eats of this bread, he will live forever; and the bread which I shall give for the life of the world is my flesh. (6:48-51)

The crowd, of course, still does not understand; and his mention of "my flesh" at the end increases their antagonism: "The Jews then disputed among themselves, saying, 'How can this man give us his flesh to eat?'"

This is an invitation to cannibalism! The only thing more totally repugnant to his audience than cannibalism is the idea of drinking blood—which, indeed, they understand Jesus to advocate in the last portion of his discourse. Drinking even animal blood was strictly forbidden as far back as Noah. In the eyes of the crowd, therefore, Jesus not only has transgressed the bounds of decency, but he has actually placed himself completely outside Jewish tradition. The Greek verb in the verse above suggests a violent argument rather than the relatively innocuous dispute. The crowd that only the day before had been ready to make Jesus king is now thoroughly scandalized. Even his disciples find it difficult to accept his teaching: "Many of his disciples, when they heard it, said, 'This is a hard saying; who can listen to it?'"

In John, when the gulf separating Jesus from his audience is the widest, the ironic element in the speech is also most pronounced—as in the "cannibalistic" statements. The reference to eating his flesh and drinking his blood must certainly point to sacramental practices within the church in John's day. In the Synoptic Gospels and in First Corinthians, Jesus speaks of bread as "my body" and of wine as "my blood" or as "the new covenant in my blood" (Matt. 26:26-28 and parallels; I Cor. 11:23-26). Within the context of the sacred meal shared by Christians, the flesh and blood imagery express the most intimate relationship between Jesus and his followers, the point at which the gift of life is most tangible. Yet it is this profound symbol of God's graciousness that outsiders are least able to comprehend.

The discourse we have been examining is similar to the others in John's Gospel. They follow a pattern: greater and greater distance between Jesus and his audience, amplification of the speech in response to the crowd's misunderstandings, increasing use of irony and double meanings. The pattern of the discourses suggests something about their function. Unlike the parables or the Sermon on the Mount, the discourses do not teach the crowds; they are not enlightened but alienated by Jesus' teachings. The discourses develop themes introduced in the prologue, as we shall see more fully later, and they serve to interpret Jesus' signs. But they do so only for the reader. The closest approximation to this paradoxical form of teaching is Mark's use of the parable, which is also intended to inform Mark's reader rather than Jesus' audience.

The discourses are as important for what they reveal about the nature of the opposition to Jesus as for what they reveal about Jesus. In their response to Jesus and in their inability to

understand his message, people in the story are revealed for
what they are: children of darkness, outsiders, people whose
father was not Abraham but one "who was a murderer from
the beginning." The distinctive features of Jesus' discourses in
John will be studied in greater detail in chapter 11.

Summary

Three of the best-known forms by which the Gospels
preserve Jesus' teaching are the parables, the Sermon on the
Mount in Matthew, and the discourses in John.

The parable was Jesus' most characteristic teaching
method. He often draws the imagery from Galilean farm life
to communicate abstractions, such as forgiveness or the
kingdom of God, to unlearned peasants. Usually the parable
tries to make one point, and often that point is highlighted by
exaggerated situations and a surprise ending. It probably
arose within the context of dialogue, as a response to
questions or criticism.

Sometimes, when a parable appears in more than one
Gospel, one may note how it has been reinterpreted in the
course of transmission as one discovers distinctive settings or
slightly different versions of the teaching among the Gospels.
These differences often provide excellent clues for discovering
the particular themes and emphases of each gospel writer. As
in the story of the sower, a parable may develop into an
allegory, in which each element of the plot, character, or
setting represents someone or something outside the story.
Here, as elsewhere, the focus has shifted from Jesus'
immediate concern, the kingdom of God, to the concerns of
the early church.

The teachings in the Sermon on the Mount are scattered
throughout Luke, whereas they are grouped in Matthew 5–7.
Following his baptism, Jesus has spent forty days in the
wilderness. Now he gives his teachings from the mountain—all of which suggests that Matthew is portraying Jesus as
a new Moses.

In addition to this setting within the Gospel, the sermon
itself has a definite structure and central theme. The
Beatitudes (5:2-16) are a prologue that sketch out the

life-style of discipleship. The epilogue in 7:13-26 warns that
the gate is narrow—one cannot be a nominal believer. The
main body is characterized by antitheses—"You have
heard. . . . But I say to you"—and contrasts—"When you do
____ do not do as the hypocrites." Yet Jesùs is neither
challenging Mosaic Law nor applying it to specific situations.
Instead he is challenging some current interpretations of the
Law. His concern is that the Mosaic injunctions be pressed all
the way back to the feelings from which actions spring. The
would-be follower, then, is pointed to a single-minded
devotion beyond the extent of prohibited actions or
prescribed piety.

The Gospel of John gives Jesus' teaching in an entirely
different form and setting. There are no parables or
aphorisms, but carefully constructed discourses that follow
each sign he performs. Rather than focusing on the kingdom
of God, as in the Synoptics, the discourses speak about Jesus'
mission and his relationship to God. The discourses abound
with allusive symbolism and double meaning (e.g., manna
and the bread from heaven, John 6). The crowd usually fails to
understand Jesus' teachings, and as the dialogue continues
polarization grows. Irony becomes the dominant mode.
Jesus' discourses do not teach the crowds in John; they are
intended for the reader-believer. The growing misunderstanding of the crowds serves as a foil to highlight the proper
response of the believer.

CHAPTER FIVE

MIRACLE STORIES

I. The Synoptic Gospels

Jesus' ministry, as recorded in the Synoptic Gospels, emphasizes the working of miracles. He performs over twenty of them—not counting slightly differing versions of some stories and the numerous summaries of the multitudes whom he healed.

Although most of his miracles are healings or exorcisms, the stories appear in a variety of forms and serve many functions. Some contain little detail, the miraculous act serving only as an occasion for raising important, often controversial, questions. For example, in the story of his healing the man with a withered hand (Mark 3:1-6 and parallels), the miracle is subsidiary to the main issue: work on the sabbath. Other miracles serve primarily a didactic function, exemplifying the power of faith. Such stories are particularly common in Matthew—for example, healing the Canaanite woman's daughter (Matt. 15:21-28) and the two blind men (9:27-31). Sometimes the miracle story is a symbol or allegory within the narrative, as in cursing the fig tree (Mark 11:12-14, 20-21) and healing blind Bartimaeus (10:46-52).[1] Finally, an extended miracle story is told with an apparent relish for detail and serves almost exclusively as testimony to Jesus' power. Instances of this last type are raising Jairus' daughter (Mark 5:21-43) and healing the Gerasene demoniac (verses 1-20).

A. Jewish, Greco-Roman, and Christian Stories

Stories of the miraculous deeds of heroes and gods were not unique to Christianity. Classical Greek and Roman literature overflows with stories of the exploits of the gods. In Jewish tradition, however, present-day knowledge of earlier popular lore is limited by the nature of the literary sources. Information about first- and second-century Judaism is transmitted through writing produced by a scholarly community. Though stories told about rabbis for whom or by whom miracles were performed are often entertaining, they are almost exclusively intended to instruct. Rabbinic literature contains few of the other types of miracle story described earlier.

Comparison among Jewish, Greco-Roman, and Christian miracle stories may clarify the various story forms and their functions, while illuminating the distinctive features of each tradition.

1. *Jewish*

    a. R. Hanina entered his home and discovered his daughter in tears. By mistake she had poured vinegar into the lamp on Sabbath eve. He declared, "May He who commanded the oil to burn, command also the vinegar to burn." The vinegar burned until after Habdala [the end of the sabbath].[2]

    b. Joseph-who-honors-the-Sabbath had in his vicinity a certain Gentile who owned much property. Soothsayers told him, "Joseph-who-honors-the-Sabbath will consume all your property." So he went, sold all his property, and bought a precious stone with the proceeds, which he set in his turban. As he was crossing a bridge the wind blew if off and cast it into the water, [and] a fish swallowed it. [Subsequently] it [the fish] was hauled up and brought [to market] on the Sabbath eve towards sunset. "Who will buy now?" cried they. "Go and take them to Joseph-who-honors-the-Sabbath," they were told, "as he is accustomed to buy." So they took it to him. He bought it, opened it, found the jewel therein, and sold it for thirteen roomfuls of gold *denarii.* A certain old man met him [and] said, "He who lends to the Sabbath, the Sabbath repays him."[3]

    c. Our Rabbis taught: In a certain place there was once a lizard which used to injure people. They came and told R. Hanina b. Dosa. He said to them: Show me its hole. They showed him its hole, and he put his heel over the hole, and the lizard came out and bit him, and it died. He put it on his shoulder and brought it to the Beth-ha-Midrash and said to them: See, my sons, it is not the lizard that kills, it is sin that kills! On that occasion they said: Woe to the man whom a lizard meets, but woe to the lizard which R. Hanina b. Dosa meets![4]

2. *Greco-Roman*

    a. A man came as a suppliant to the god [Aesclepius]. He was so blind that of one of his eyes, he had only the eyelids left—within them was nothing, but they were entirely empty. Some of those in the temple laughed at his silliness to think that he could recover his sight when one of his eyes had not even a trace of the ball, but only the socket. As he slept a vision appeared to him. It seemed to him that the god prepared some drug, then, opening his eyelids, poured it into them. When day came he departed with the sight of both of his eyes restored.[5]

    b. Gorgias of Heracleia with pus. In a battle he had been wounded by an arrow in the lung and for a year and a half had suppurated so badly that he filled sixty-seven basins with pus. While sleeping in the temple he saw a vision. It seemed to him that the god [Aesclepius] extracted the arrow point from his lung. When day came he walked out well, holding the point of the arrow in his hands.[6]

    c. Here too is a miracle which Apollonius [of Tyana] worked: A woman had died just in the hour of her marriage, and the bridegroom was following her bier lamenting as was natural his marriage left unfulfilled; the whole of Rome was mourning with him, for the maiden belonged to a

consular family. Apollonius then witnessing their
grief, said: "Put down the bier, for I will stay the
tears that you are shedding for this maiden." And
withal he asked what was her name. The crowd
accordingly thought that he was about to deliver
such an oration as is commonly delivered as much
to grace the funeral as to stir up lamentation; but
he did nothing of the kind, but merely touching
her and whispering in secret some spell over her,
at once woke up the maiden from her seeming
death; and the woman spoke out loud, and
returned to her father's house, just as Alcestis did
when she was brought back to life by Hercules.
And the relations of the maiden wanted to
present him with the sum of 150,000 sesterces,
but he said that he would freely present the
money to the young lady by way of a dowry.[7]

3. *Christian*

They came to the other side of the sea, to the country of
the Gerasenes. And when he had come out of the boat,
there met him out of the tombs a man with an unclean
spirit, who lived among the tombs; and no one could bind
him any more, even with a chain; for he had often been
bound with fetters and chains, but the chains he
wrenched apart, and the fetters he broke in pieces; and
no one had the strength to subdue him. Night and day
among the tombs and on the mountains he was always
crying out, and bruising himself with stones. And when
he saw Jesus from afar, he ran and worshiped him; and
crying out with a loud voice, he said, "What have you to
do with me, Jesus, Son of the Most High God? I adjure
you by God, do not torment me." For he had said to him,
"Come out of the man, you unclean spirit!" And Jesus
asked him, "What is your name?" He replied, "My name
is Legion; for we are many." And he begged him eagerly
not to send them out of the country. Now a great herd of
swine was feeding there on the hillside; and they begged
him, "Send us to the swine, let us enter them." So he
gave them leave. And the unclean spirits came out, and
entered the swine; and the herd, numbering about two

thousand, rushed down the steep bank into the sea, and were drowned in the sea.

The herdsmen fled, and told it in the city and in the country. And people came to see what it was that had happened. And they came to Jesus, and saw the demoniac sitting there, clothed and in his right mind, the man who had had the legion; and they were afraid. And those who had seen it told what had happened to the demoniac and to the swine. And they began to beg Jesus to depart from their neighborhood. And as he was getting into the boat, the man who had been possessed with demons begged him that he might be with him. But he refused, and said to him, "Go home to your friends, and tell them how much the Lord has done for you, and how he has had mercy on you." And he went away and began to proclaim in the Decapolis how much Jesus had done for him; and all men marveled. (Mark 5:1-20)

Consider some obvious differences among the three groups of stories. Each of the Jewish tales deals with some aspect of piety. Even though the righteous Rabbi Hanina ben Dosa can make vinegar burn at his command, the miracle exemplifies his respect for the Sabbath rather than his abilities as a wonder-worker. The story of Joseph-who-honors-the-Sabbath also bears testimony to the power of piety. In addition it contains ethnic humor. The one who loses his property is wealthy and a Gentile; the winner is a Jew whose only strength apparently lies in his piety. The story adds to its lesson a bit of entertainment for an audience that more often than not may have been victimized by wealthy Gentiles. The story of Rabbi Hanina and the lizard, which may look like a pure miracle story because it has little moral build-up, is no less an illustration of piety: "See, my sons, it is not the lizard that kills, it is sin that kills."

The function of the Greco-Roman stories is very different, both from the Jewish stories and from each other. The first two tales are from inscriptions at the temple of Aesclepius in Epidaurus, an ancient city in southern Greece. The details chosen by the narrator highlight the extraordinary character of the miracle and extol the power of the god. Apart from the elaborate description of the malady, the narrative is terse and to the point. In the Aesclepius tales, the god customarily appears to the suppliant in a dream. They reveal little about the god except his ability to cure the sick.

Philostratus' stories about Apollonius, of which this is a typical example, reveal a good deal more about the wonder-worker. The stories have greater detail, often allowing Apollonius to deliver a brief oration. Although he does raise the dead and cast out demons, he is primarily a sage. Many of his miracles are attributed to his unsurpassed wisdom rather than to any supernatural powers he possesses. In contrast to the Jewish stories, both the Aesclepian and Apollonian stories emphasize the power of the one (whether god or man) who performs the miracle. The Apollonian stories celebrate the man's wisdom, whereas the Jewish stories emphasize piety and imply the power of God.

Since Christian storytellers had roots in Jewish tradition and in Greco-Roman culture, similarities can be discovered in patterns and themes among all three kinds of miracle stories. The common purpose of Jewish and of Christian stories was not simply to preserve interesting information about a revered figure out of the past; like Jewish miracle stories, those concerning Jesus were often told to inculcate morality or to portray piety. Distinctive Christian beliefs, however, led to different emphases. Like the Greco-Roman stories, Christian miracle stories also had intrinsic value as testimonies to Jesus' supernatural powers, especially over demons and disease.

B. The Gerasene Demoniac

The story of the Gerasene demoniac (Mark 5:1-20; Luke 8:26-39) merits closer examination. Many scholars view the story of the two demoniacs from the "country of the Gadarenes" in Matthew 8:28-34 as a variant of the story; if so, the shortened form is characteristic of Matthew's style.

As narrated in Mark, the story has a popular quality and a delight in detail unusual even in the longer miracle stories. The possessed man is absolutely uncontrollable; chains and fetters have proved useless. The man is pathetic: he lives among the tombs, apart from his fellows, unable to restrain himself even from abusing his own body. Mark's wealth of detail particularizes the man, invites sympathy, emphasizes the difficulty, and heightens the suspense. Only someone with extraordinary power could deal with such an extreme case. Will even Jesus be able to help such a man?

The interchange between Jesus and the demoniac is a bit puzzling. Only after the demon has recognized Jesus and begged to be left alone does the narrator say that Jesus has already been commanding the demon to come out. Have his commands so far been ineffective? Mark does not offer any explanation. The important point, however, is that the demon recognizes Jesus as a man with real power, to be feared.

The actual exorcism focuses on the name of the demon, another motif also found in non-Christian literature. Knowledge of the demon's name gives the exorcist power over him. To Jesus' question the demon answers that his name is Legion—for, as he reveals, "we are many." Either he is not powerful enough to resist Jesus or he has been tricked into making a foolish boast. The name "Legion" may quite possibly be a conscious allusion to Roman military terminology. The implicit link between Romans and demons would be obvious to a Jewish audience.

As soon as he has divulged his name, the demon seems to realize that his time is up; all he can hope for now is a concession from this man of superior power. The demon desires to remain in the neighborhood, evidently necessitating a new lodging. (Luke 8:31 says that the demons beg not to be sent into the abyss.) Jesus apparently permits Legion to enter a herd of swine feeding nearby. As soon as the demon enters the swine, however, the whole herd rushes headlong over the bank into the sea—dramatic testimony to the presence in them of the demon, as well as confirmation of the success of the exorcism. The loss of the herd would cause no concern to the Jewish audience because to them swine were unclean animals.

As noted earlier, the story has a popular quality unusual among the miracle stories in the Gospels. Here Jesus is the clever exorcist who uses familiar tricks of the trade instead of disposing of the demon with a single word, as he does in other miracle stories. The anecdote appears to have little didactic value. The writer includes no striking saying from Jesus nor does he derive any moral about the efficacy of faith or the power of prayer. The possessed person is important only as a witness who is to spread the news about what the Lord has done for him. The sole objective of the story seems to be to portray Jesus as a mighty exorcist.

Yet one must remember that the story appears in the context of the Gospels, and it does indeed serve their overall purpose—to bear witness to Jesus as the Messiah and Son of God. More specifically, in Mark the story provides an opportunity for a glimpse at Jesus' hidden identity, a continuing Markan theme. The demon's recognition of the exorcist is a familiar motif, but in this story, the demon identifies Jesus in a special way: "What have you to do with me, Jesus, Son of the Most High God?" (Mark 5:7; Luke 8:28).

The supreme confession in the Gospels is that Jesus is the Messiah, the Son of God. Yet in Mark and Luke, the only ones to make that confession are the demons. Presumably because they are supernatural beings, they recognize Jesus as the Son of God, something that Jesus' human audience does not. The demon's testimony is of considerable importance; it contrasts with the views of the religious leaders, some of whom insist (with dramatic irony) that Jesus' ability to cast out demons is only a sign that he himself is in their power: "And the scribes who came down from Jerusalem said, 'He is possessed by Beelzebul, and by the prince of demons he casts out the demons'" (Mark 3:22 and parallels).

Jesus counters that the prince of demons would hardly support warfare among members of his own household; on the contrary, his ability to cast out demons shows him to be on God's side and with considerable power. The demons themselves, through their submission and their words, reveal Jesus' hidden identity. As shall be seen, this feature of the miracle stories is particularly significant in Mark.

C. Miracles and the "Prophet"

One function of miracle stories is to contribute to the overall portrait of Jesus. He is a teacher, but he is also "a man attested to you by God with mighty works and wonders and signs which God did through him in your midst" (Acts 2:22). Jesus' power is a sign that God works with him and through him. The Fourth Gospel clearly depicts the miracles as signs that Jesus is God's authorized emissary, but that notion is implied in the Synoptic Gospels as well.

The miracle stories belong with a traditional constellation of ideas that are related to a specific figure in Jewish tradition. This is all the more significant if, as many scholars have proposed, there existed, prior to the written Gospels, collections of stories of Jesus' miracles.[8] A collection of Jesus' sayings might imply that many people viewed Jesus as a sage, familiar in the ancient world. But with what traditional figure did the New Testament writers and their audiences associate Jesus the "worker of wonders?"

One suggestion has already been proposed: in the story of the Gerasene demoniac, the demon recognized Jesus as "Son of the Most High God"; and the reader is told elsewhere that many demons recognized Jesus as the Son of God (Mark 3:11). Did the early Christians believe that the miracles attested to Jesus' special status as God's Son? This proposal finds little support in the conceptual world of which the New Testament was a part. Jewish tradition has little precedent for a miracle-worker known as the "Son of God." Although the miracle-worker is familiar in non-Jewish tradition, he is never identified as God's Son.

Luke provides another possible interpretation of the title, however: "And demons also came out of many, crying, 'You are the Son of God!' But he rebuked them, and would not allow them to speak, because they knew that he was the Christ" (Luke 4:41).

Here, "Son of God" and "Messiah" are fairly clearly synonymous. Despite the reluctance in later Jewish tradition to call any human (even the Messiah) God's Son, during the first Christian century, Jews did think of the Messiah-King as the Son of God, at least metaphorically. Calling the King God's Son is familiar from biblical traditions, the two most important of which are II Samuel 7:14 and Psalm 2:7. One can assume, therefore, that when the demons call Jesus "Son of God," one is to understand the phrase as a synonym for

Messiah. Yet there is still no evidence in Jewish tradition that the Messiah was expected to appear as a worker of miracles. He was to appear as a warrior/deliverer or simply as king.

The confessions of the demons occur only in a particular type of miracle story—exorcisms. The titles "Son of God" and "Messiah" are not responses of the crowds to Jesus' miracles. It is only the demons, the supernatural beings, who acknowledge him as Son of God. Their confessions are puzzling: they seem to have absolutely no impact on either Jesus' disciples or the crowds who witness the exorcisms. They are extremely important revelations, but only for the reader. The absence of the title "Son of God" from the majority of the miracle stories and from the evaluations of Jesus' ministry both by the crowds and by the disciples suggests that the miracles are not performed for the purpose of showing people that Jesus is the Son of God or Messiah. If the miracles are to be related to a figure in Jewish tradition, from the evidence of the Gospels, one must look elsewhere.

1. Elijah. The Gospels depict Jesus within the tradition of miracle-working prophets like Elijah, Elisha, and Moses. In Luke 7:11-15, Jesus raises from the dead the only son of a widow from a city called Nain. The story concludes with the crowd's response: "Fear seized them all; and they glorified God, saying, 'A great prophet has arisen among us!'" (7:16).

The account in Luke is clearly reminiscent of stories told about earlier prophets. One is found in I Kings:

> After this the son of the woman, the mistress of the house, became ill; and his illness was so severe that there was no breath left in him. And she said to Elijah, "What have you against me, O man of God? You have come to me to bring my sin to remembrance, and to cause the death of my son!" And he said to her, "Give me your son." And he took him from her bosom, and carried him up into the upper chamber, where he lodged, and laid him upon his own bed. . . . And the LORD hearkened to the voice of Elijah; and the soul of the child came into him again, and he revived. And Elijah took the child, and brought him down from the upper chamber into the house, and delivered him to his mother. (I Kings 17:17-23)

Both biblical and postbiblical Jewish traditions stressed the expectation of Elijah's return to earth. In the important summary passage, which precedes Peter's confession in all the Synoptic Gospels (Mark 8:27-28 and parallels), the disciples tell Jesus that many consider him to be Elijah, a belief that is linked to the miracle stories. Like Elijah, Jesus raised the dead. Like Elijah's successor, Elisha, Jesus miraculously fed a large number of people with very little food and even had some left over (II Kings 4:42-44).

By the standard of literary prophets like Isaiah and Jeremiah, Elijah's working of miracles is not typical of the prophetic office. But by the beginning of the Christian era, the concept of the prophet seems to have been heavily influenced by the Elijah stories. The reason for the interest in this enigmatic figure of the distant past is obvious: Elijah, according to the Bible, was taken up to heaven alive. Speculation about what plans God had for Elijah must have begun as soon as the stories about his ascension began to circulate. By the time of Malachi, the last of the canonical prophets, Elijah had become a fixture in pictures of the future:

Behold, I will send you Elijah the prophet before the great and terrible day of the LORD comes. And he will turn the hearts of fathers to their children and the hearts of children to their fathers, lest I come and smite the land with a curse. (Mal. 4:5-6)

The evolution of such traditions did not conclude with the book of Malachi. According to the Gospels, the scribes expected Elijah to prepare the way for the Messiah (Mark 9:11-13). Even today, when Jews celebrate Passover, they pour a special cup for Elijah at the conclusion of the meal in anticipation of his coming to herald the new age.

2. Moses. Elijah was not the only traditional prophetic figure whose return Jews awaited:

I will raise up for them a prophet like you [Moses] from among their brethren; and I will put my words in his mouth, and he shall speak to them all that I command him. And whoever will not give heed to my words which he shall speak in my name, I myself will require it of him. (Deut. 18:18-19)

Moses dominated not only traditions of Israel's past but also expectations for the future. By the first century, this prophet like Moses was eagerly awaited. To the Essenes at Qumran, for example, he was one of three figures who would appear at the "end of days." The image of the Mosaic prophet is important throughout the Gospel of John, and Jesus is explicitly identified as the prophet like Moses in Acts 3:22. According to Deuteronomy 18, the prophet is to appear as an authoritative teacher, and while one cannot possibly determine all the variations within popular tradition about this figure, it does seem clear that he too would perform miracles as well as teach. Deuteronomy 13 describes a prophet as someone who performs signs and wonders. This expression is almost a technical term in the Gospels. Acts 2:22 calls Jesus a "man attested to you by God with mighty works and wonders and signs"; in John the term "sign" is used to refer to all of Jesus' miracles; in Mark 13:22, Jesus warns his followers—much as Moses warned the Israelites—of false prophets who will "arise and show signs and wonders."

To summarize, there were at least two distinct prophetic figures in contemporary Jewish tradition whose appearance was expected—Elijah and Moses. Both would perform miracles, signs, and wonders, and their return (particularly that of Elijah) would signal the dawning of a new day. Because Jesus performed such signs and wonders, many of his contemporaries were convinced he was the long-awaited prophet. Certainly, his arrival suggested that something important was about to occur. According to the Gospels, Jesus' miracles are not simply revelations of his identity; they are also signs that the kingdom of God is at hand. God's rule is imminent; by implication, the rule of the "prince of demons" is at an end. It is logical that exorcisms should be a weapon of the one who preaches about the kingdom of God: "But if it is by the finger of God that I cast out demons, then the kingdom of God has come upon you" (Luke 11:20).

3. The Prophetic Motif in Mark. The miracle stories are part of a traditional constellation of ideas focusing on the coming of God's kingdom and the coming of the miracle-working prophet. This prophetic motif fits into the story of Jesus and contributes to the overall portrait of him in the Gospels.

Matthew says least about Jesus as prophet; Luke directly names Jesus the prophet like Moses. Further, this identification is extremely important within the thematic structure of Luke's Book of Acts. Yet for Luke, the image of Jesus as prophet is by no means exclusive: Jesus is also "Lord" and "Christ" and "Son of God." Luke makes no real attempt to integrate these ideas; he simply identifies Jesus with a variety of distinct figures in Jewish tradition.

Mark assimilates prophetic imagery more carefully into his story. Two stages in Jesus' career can be distinguished in Mark. They are separated by the passage containing Peter's confession (Mark 8:27-30) and the first prediction of Jesus' death (verses 31-33). The prophetic imagery belongs to the first stage in Jesus' ministry, and virtually all the miracle stories in Mark also fall within the first half of the Gospel. Those who have witnessed the miracles believe that Jesus is a prophet of some sort (6:14-15; 8:27-28).

The three miracle stories that occur in the second half of Mark function quite differently. They are clearly symbolic. Healing the young boy with a dumb spirit (9:14-29) provides a striking contrast to the transfiguration that immediately precedes it (verses 2-8). The inability of the disciples to perform the cure stands out: they have not yet understood what it means to follow Jesus or what resources are available to them. They have not yet glimpsed the possibilities that Jesus can make available to them, for they do not yet understand who he is. This miracle story includes no reference to the astonishment of the witnesses, typical of stories in the first half of the Gospel; that would detract from the real emphasis.

The second miracle in this half of the Gospel, the healing of blind Bartimaeus (10:46-52), is also symbolic: a blind man who "sees" that Jesus is the Son of David receives his sight immediately prior to Jesus' entrance to Jerusalem, where those who are not blind do not perceive that Jesus is the Messiah and deliver him up to die. The third, the cursing of the fig tree (11:20-25), symbolically frames the brief account of Jesus' cleansing of the Temple: the priestly establishment is punished for not "bearing fruit."

The stories in Mark that focus clearly on Jesus' role as

miracle-worker occur prior to chapter 8; among them are raising Jairus' daughter, healing the Gerasene demoniac, feeding the five thousand and the four thousand. At two places in this first half the narrator pauses to include evaluation of what has occurred. The first is in chapter 6:

> King Herod heard of it; for Jesus' name had become known. Some said, "John the baptizer has been raised from the dead; that is why these powers are at work in him." But others said, "It is Elijah." And others said, "It is a prophet, like one of the prophets of old." (6:14-15)

The second evaluation sums up the first stage, with the decisive confession of Peter; it marks the end of Jesus' public ministry in Galilee, after which everything moves toward Jerusalem.

> And Jesus went on with his disciples, to the villages of Caesarea Philippi; and on the way he asked his disciples, "Who do men say that I am?" And they told him, "John the Baptist; and others say, Elijah; and others one of the prophets." And he asked them, "But who do you say that I am?" Peter answered him, "You are the Christ." (8:27-29)

The three suggestions for Jesus' identity made in chapter 6 are repeated; in the estimation of some of his contemporaries, he is a prophet. These evaluations, however, are what men in general say about Jesus, in contrast to what the disciples themselves believe. When asked "But who do you say that I am?" Peter introduces what is a new concept in Mark (apart from the superscription): Jesus is the Messiah.

According to Matthew, Jesus tells Peter that "flesh and blood has not revealed this to you, but my Father who is in heaven" (Matt. 16:17). There is no indication, however, in Mark's Gospel of what has shown Peter (and the rest of the disciples) that Jesus is the Messiah. Jesus devotes much of his ministry to exorcisms and healing, signs that he is someone important. Some people in the crowds view them as indications that Jesus is a prophet, perhaps *the* prophet whose appearance has been long awaited. Mark does not suggest that these people are wrong but rather that their evaluation does not penetrate the real secret of Jesus' identity. Jesus is, as Mark tells the reader at the outset, "Christ, the Son of God." Somehow Peter glimpses the truth.

Yet even Peter does not see clearly. He believes Jesus to be the Messiah, but he is stunned when Jesus announces that he must die. As will be seen in chapter 8, Jesus is a Messiah of a unique sort, one who has come to die. The early miracles in Mark are part of a prophetic motif, identifying Jesus to contemporaries as a great prophet. The most revealing period in Jesus' ministry is yet to come. The real secret of his identity will be unveiled only through the events that will occur in Jerusalem.

II. The Man Born Blind, John 9

The miracle stories in the Fourth Gospel are as distinctive from those in the Synoptic Gospels as is the teaching material. Few of John's stories have parallels in another Gospel, and the miracles (or "signs" as he refers to them) seem carefully selected. They include:

1. Changing water into wine (2:1-11)
2. Curing the son of a royal official (4:46-54)
3. Curing the paralytic at the pool of Bethesda (5:1-15)
4. Multiplying the loaves in Galilee (6:1-15)
5. Walking on the sea (6:16-21)
6. Restoring sight to the man born blind (chap. 9)
7. Raising Lazarus from the dead (chap. 11)

Of these signs, only multiplying the loaves and walking on water are paralleled in the synoptic tradition. Healing the official's son (4:46-54) is similar to a story in Matthew and Luke, where the official is a Roman centurion. The stories of raising Lazarus, changing water to wine, curing the paralytic at the pool, and restoring the sight of the man born blind are unique to John.

John tells of no exorcisms, so characteristic of Jesus' ministry in Matthew, Mark, and Luke. The only mention of demons is in the repeated accusation that Jesus "has a demon." Further, John does not group the miracle stories or include summary statements about Jesus' accomplishments as a miracle-worker. Instead, John carefully arranges the individual miracle stories, integrating them into the narratives; they frequently introduce themes that are picked up in the discourse that follows them.

The miraculous signs in the Fourth Gospel are intended to do more than evoke a reader's sense of awe and wonder at Jesus' power. They have an important significance:

> Now Jesus did many other signs in the presence of the disciples, which are not written in this book; but these are written that you may believe that Jesus is the Christ, the Son of God, and that believing you may have life in his name. (20:30-31)

The signs Jesus performs are revelations of his identity, which is, to some extent, tied to prophetic imagery from Deuteronomy. Signs and wonders characterize the prophet, according to Deuteronomy 13, but the reference is ambiguous: false prophets also perform signs and wonders, and, according to Deuteronomy, false prophets are to be killed. This tradition gives a special meaning to the miracle stories in John; the question runs throughout the Gospel: Is Jesus the true prophet coming into the world from God (6:14) or a false prophet who must die? Jesus' signs occasion threats against his life in chapters 5 and 9, and the last sign, raising Lazarus, is tied directly to his arrest and death.

To appreciate the special artistry of the Fourth Gospel and the distinctive character of its miracle stories, the reader should consider an example: Jesus' healing a man born blind. In some respects this story is like the more popular and less artistic miracle stories in the Synoptic Gospels. A problem is posed (Jesus encounters a man who has been blind from birth). Witnesses are present. Jesus accomplishes the cure, and the man's neighbors attest to the miracle. Mention of the physical means of the cure—clay with which he anoints the man's eyes—is a bit unusual, but corresponding details appear in Mark's account of healing the deaf mute (Mark 7:31-36) and the blind man in Bethsaida (8:22-26).

The differences in John's story begin with its introduction; the miracle is motivated by the disciples' question about the relationship between misfortune and sin. One purpose of the preliminary exchange is to refute the popular notion that misfortune and disease are always punishment for sin.

According to Jesus, the man is blind not because of any sin, but "that the works of God might be made manifest in him." The short discourse that follows is also distinctive, and even more characteristic of John. Jesus begins to develop imagery taken from the miracle that will follow: "We must work the works of him who sent me, while it is day; night comes, when no one can work. As long as I am in the world, I am the light of the world" (John 9:4-5).

The imagery of light and enlightenment, found in the prologue to the entire Gospel, introduced a basic theme: "The true light that enlightens every man was coming into the world" (1:9). Its reappearance in the present discourse should alert the careful reader. The restoration of sight to a blind man appropriately follows this discussion of light/darkness, day/night. Linking the miracle to a major theme of the Gospel, however, is a clue that the sign has an important figurative meaning that must be discovered. Notice that Jesus says "we" must work. Do others do the "works of him who sent me"? If so, how does the miracle that follows typify the experience of these other workers with whom the audience is expected to identify?[10]

The most obviously distinctive formal characteristics of John's narrative method are evident after the healing. In the typical miracle story of the Synoptic Gospels, Jesus is the focal point from beginning to end. Biographical information about those who are healed is unimportant except where relevant to the miracle. The stories are revelations of Jesus' power; after the healing nothing more is heard about the one who has been cured. The narratives customarily conclude with only an expression of astonishment on the part of the witnesses.

In John, however, the miracle introduces the main lesson. In this example the cure is simply the first act in the drama of the man whose sight is restored. With the arrival of the blind man's neighbors, Jesus moves off stage and does not reappear until the little drama has been completed. The main action begins with a dispute among the neighbors of the blind man who has just received his sight: "The neighbors and those who had seen him before as a beggar, said, 'Is not this the man who used to sit and beg?' Some said, 'It is he'; others said, 'No, but he is like him.' He said, 'I am the man'" (9:8-9).

The difficulty the man's neighbors have in recognizing him provides testimony to the spectacular nature of the miracle. They find it impossible to believe that his sight has been restored. The man himself later agrees that the miracle is extraordinary, saying that there has never been a cure of someone born blind "since the world began" (9:32). The argument among the neighbors epitomizes a more important division among witnesses of Jesus' many signs: some accept them; some do not. The event is alarming enough to warrant consulting the religious scholars, the Pharisees. The crowd takes the blind man to the synagogue for the next scenes in the drama.

Before the interrogation begins, the reader learns something new: the healing took place on the sabbath. Consulting the religious authorities is indeed urgent: on the one hand, a marvelous cure has been accomplished; on the other hand, the strict prohibition against working on the sabbath has been violated. Once before in John, Jesus had healed someone on the sabbath, and the result was that Jews sought to "persecute Jesus" and even to kill him (5:15-18). This sign will be no less controversial.

The Pharisees begin questioning the man as the crowd did: How did he receive his sight? The man repeats his story: Jesus placed clay on his eyes, he washed, and his sight was restored. As with the crowd, a dispute arises among the scholars. For some, faithfulness to tradition is the infallible measure of religiosity; Jesus' breaking the sabbath law indicates that he cannot possibly be from God (9:16). Others are not so sure: "How can a man who is a sinner do such signs?" The Pharisees now confront a dilemma. Hoping to escape the dilemma, or perhaps looking for a scapegoat, they turn to the man: "So they again said to the blind man, 'What do you say about him, since he has opened your eyes?' He said, 'He is a prophet'" (verse 17).

This is not the first time in John's Gospel that such a confession has been encountered. It resonates throughout this story with the question, Is Jesus the prophet who is coming into the world to save it? The blind man has obviously understood something significant. Nevertheless, his perception does not impress the Pharisees. They are now forced to interpret the sign in the light of their own tradition. They must decide whether Jesus is "from God," whether he is the prophet.

Still they try to avoid that choice. Perhaps the whole episode is a fraud and the man was not born blind at all. They call his parents to testify:

> "Is this your son, who you say was born blind? How then does he now see?" His parents answered, "We know that this is our son, and that he was born blind; but how he now sees we do not know; nor do we know who opened his eyes. Ask him; he is of age, he will speak for himself." (9:19-21)

The proceedings take an ominous note. The parents appear unwilling to become involved, unloading the burden of responsibility onto their son. Why?

> His parents said this because they feared the Jews, for the Jews had already agreed that if any one should confess him to be the Christ, he was to be put out of the synagogue. Therefore, his parents said, "He is of age, ask him." (9:22-23)

His parents must have known who had restored their son's sight. But any acknowledgment of Jesus' power is dangerous, so they choose to plead ignorance. They do not want to risk expulsion from the synagogue, which means ostracism from the Jewish community.

The Pharisees have received little aid from the parents. They cannot escape the conclusion that Jesus has indeed restored sight to one born blind, but they still have hope: perhaps Jesus is a false prophet. They recall the man for further interrogation; now he finds himself defending Jesus and is subjected to a spirited attack: "So for the second time they called the man who had been blind, and said to him, 'Give God the praise; we know that this man is a sinner.'"

The council seems to believe that they can escape making the decision if they can convince the man to confess that Jesus is not from God, that he is outside the Law. The man does not understand the problem. After all, he is not a religious authority; he professes ignorance about such matters as Jesus' alleged sinfulness. One thing he does know: he was blind, but now with help from Jesus he sees. Once more the decision is thrown back to the Pharisees. Is Jesus from God? And once more they try to find some way of escaping the decision. Again they ask the blind man how Jesus opened his eyes. Was it a trick? Did he use magic? But the simple man only makes the question more pointed for his learned inquisitors: "I have told you already, and you would not listen. Why do you want to hear it again? Do you too want to become his disciples?" (9:27).

To the man who has received his sight, the miracle is a clear sign that Jesus is someone worth following. Why don't his interrogators accept his story? His answer now brings the contrast between disciples and opponents of Jesus to the fore. The Pharisees are finally forced to declare themselves: "And they reviled him, saying, 'You are his disciple, but we are disciples of Moses. We know that God has spoken to Moses, but as for this man, we do not know where he comes from'" (9:28-29).

Their appeal to Moses is ironic. Earlier in the Gospel, Jesus has told his opponents that the scriptures they seek to use against him actually point to his coming. John includes several carefully chosen proofs from Scripture as examples. Moses, Israel's traditional defense attorney in the heavenly court, will in the last judgment, according to Jesus, serve as chief witness against "the Jews" who have rejected Jesus (5:45).

Further, the strange statement about not knowing where Jesus is from is an antithetic parallel to an earlier declaration:

> Some of the people of Jerusalem therefore said, "Is not this the man whom they seek to kill? And here he is, speaking openly, and they say nothing to him! Can it be that the authorities really know that this is the Christ? Yet we know where this man is from; *and when the Christ appears, no one will know where he comes from.*" (7:25-27)

The Pharisees themselves furnish proof that Jesus is the Christ: they do not know where he comes from. Their inability to understand that Jesus is "from above" or "from the Father" reveals that indeed they are the ones who are blind; they, not Jesus, are not of the truth, are outsiders. The response of the cured blind man is a bitterly ironic pronouncement of judgment on his would-be judges:

> The man answered, "Why, this is a marvel! You do not know where he comes from, and yet he opened my eyes. We know that God does not listen to sinners, but if any one is a worshiper of God and does his will, God listens to him. Never since the world began has it been heard that any one opened the eyes of a man born blind. If this man were not from God, he could do nothing." They answered him, "You were born in utter sin, and would you teach us?" And they cast him out. (9:30-34)

The judges are judged; the religious scholars are given instruction in basic religious truth; the simple blind man sees what scholars with eyes cannot. The light of the world has enlightened one, but "his own people received him not."

This sign and the ensuing drama end in the excommunication of a member of a Jewish synagogue. They represent attempts to make sense out of an experience shared by many Jewish Christians at the time the Fourth Gospel was written. According to John's story, the Pharisees had already decided to exclude from the synagogue anyone who confessed Jesus to be the Christ. Such expulsions of Jewish Christians were discussed in the chapter on the historical background of the New Testament. John may have included this miracle story to provide some glimpse into the realities of the bitter conflict that developed between the Jews who believed Jesus to be the Messiah and those who did not. Whether this is the intent or not, the story does seem to dramatize what Jesus later predicts his followers can expect in the future:

> I have said all this to you to keep you from falling away. They will put you out of the synagogues; indeed, the hour is coming when whoever kills you will think he is offering service to God. And they will do this because they have not known the Father, nor me. But I have said these things to you, that when their hour comes you may remember that I told you of them. (16:1-4)

The miracle stories in the Gospel of John are carefully constructed narratives that are, in most cases, well integrated into the thematic structure of the work. That structure and the place of the signs within it will be studied in chapter 11.

Summary

The Synoptic Gospels describe Jesus performing more than twenty miracles, most of them healings and exorcisms. The miracle stories serve a variety of functions within these Gospels: some are addressed to controversial issues, such as work on the sabbath; others have a didactic purpose, pointing up the power of faith; others have a symbolic effect; others, relishing each detail, serve as testimonies to Jesus' power. These stories share with Greco-Roman miracle stories an interest in displaying the power of the wonder-worker and with Judaic miracle stories their didactic purpose.

For example, the story of the Gerasene demoniac in Mark shows Jesus' power against the demon(s); at the same time it discloses that only the supernatural powers recognize him as the Son of God. The story also teaches that Jesus is the long-awaited prophet, whether Elijah or one like Moses. Both the hidden identity of Jesus and the expected prophet motifs are basic in Mark. And exorcisms emphasize Mark's theme that the kingdom of God will replace the reign of demons.

The motif of Jesus as prophet is not developed within the Gospel of Matthew. It is used in the Gospel of Luke, along with other titles that identify Jesus with a variety of figures in Jewish tradition—Elijah, Elisha, and Moses. The motif has been carefully integrated into the Gospel of Mark, where the miracle stories dominate the first half of the story. The crowd perceives Jesus as the prophet preparing the way whereas, beginning with Peter's confession in 8:29, the reader is shown that Jesus is in fact the hidden Messiah.

Whereas the miracle stories in the Synoptic Gospels had focused on Jesus—as a revelation of his power and identification of his role—the Gospel of John shows more interest in the meaning of the miracle and the response of people to it. There are seven miracle stories in John, only two of which also occur in the Synoptics. All the stories are given as signs that identify Jesus as the true prophet. Rather than being grouped into one section in John, these signs become the frame around which the entire book is structured. The miracle is followed by a discourse in which Jesus explains its meaning. Often this meaning is challenged by a questioner or a group who, as the discussion progresses, are further alienated from Jesus. Irony dominates, as the real meaning of his words is missed. Thus a division develops in the discourses between those who see Jesus as the light and those who remain in darkness.

The story in the Fourth Gospel of the man born blind shows John's distinctive integration of miracles and teachings. From the prologue to the Gospel, this extended miracle story picks up the themes of light/enlightenment and Jesus' rejection by his own people. The miracle is a sign, a lesson: faith enlightens the simple person, but learned traditionalists and their followers reject the truth.

CHAPTER SIX

THE CRUCIFIED MESSIAH IN THE SYNOPTIC GOSPELS

In all four Gospels, Jesus' death dominates the story. Mark devotes more than one-third of his Gospel to the last week of Jesus' life, almost half of that to his trial and death. In each of the Synoptics, Jesus predicts his own death on three separate occasions. Although successful as a teacher and miracle worker and immensely popular with the common people, Jesus encounters opposition by religious Jews, the guardians of tradition, from the outset. Plots form against him almost at once. The hostility grows more and more intense until, during the festival of Passover in Jerusalem, it climaxes in Jesus' arrest, trial, and execution.

Increasing specificity in each of the four narratives also testifies to the centrality of Jesus' death. Earlier episodes in Jesus' life are usually vague in details; from the moment Jesus arrives in Jerusalem, however, people, places, and times become important and specific: "on the first day of Unleavened Bread," "as soon as it was morning," "they led him inside the place (that is, the praetorium)," "it was the third hour when they crucified him," "and when the sixth hour came." The high priest's servant whose ear is cut off when Jesus is arrested is identified as Malchus (John 18:10); the high priest is Caiaphas (Matt. 26:57; John 18:28); the man forced to carry Jesus' cross is Simon of Cyrene, the "father of Alexander and Rufus," who was conscripted while "coming in from the country" (Mark 15:21); the place Jesus is crucified is called "Golgotha (which means the place of a skull)" (verse 22).

The martyrdom of a hero was not a motif unique to the New Testament. There were stories about Jewish martyrs who had died at the hands of foreigners rather than forsake their faith, and perhaps the most famous martyrdom in antiquity was that of Socrates. The story of Jesus' trial and death, however, is distinctive in many respects. Paradoxically, his death is a triumph—not only for the truth, but for himself as well. Jesus "reigns from the tree"; his crucifixion, according to John, is a "lifting up"—both literally, his elevation on the cross, and figuratively, an exaltation. His death has a purpose: he dies to "give his life as a ransom for many" (Mark 10:45). In one of the oldest confessional summaries in the New Testament, believers are told that Jesus "died for our sins in accordance with the scriptures" (I Cor. 15:3). In this death that is more than a death, Christian storytellers understandably might have found it necessary to modify traditional literary models.

The passion story is also distinctive in its imagery. Here the Gospels portray Jesus as a king, the Messiah-King. His entry into Jerusalem has details from the book of Zechariah that describe the coming of the king ("humble and riding on an ass"); Jewish leaders try him as Christ, and Pilate tries him as King of the Jews; Roman soldiers mock him as king; he is ridiculed as "the Christ, the King of Israel"; and he dies on a cross, with the inscription of the charge against him, "King of the Jews." Yet specific messianic and royal images are almost totally absent from the accounts of Jesus' ministry in the Gospels. Only in John do the crowds believe Jesus to be a king (John 6:15). In the Synoptic Gospels, Peter and the other disciples call Jesus the Messiah, but they do not understand the true meaning of Jesus' Messiahship.

If the accounts of his trial and death portray Jesus as the Messiah-King, why is the messianic and royal imagery absent from the earlier portions of the story? Why should such imagery suddenly become prominent precisely at the stage in the story at which Jesus looks least like the traditional Messiah? His followers could have hailed him as a martyr for the cause of freedom—freedom from Rome or from the religious authorities sympathetic to Rome. They might even have venerated him as a prophet, another of God's many spokesmen who, according to the Gospels, had traditionally been opposed by the establishment (Matt. 23:29-36; Luke 11:47-48; Acts 7:51-53). The last thing Jews expected was that the foreign oppressors from whom he was to deliver them would execute the long-awaited Messiah in a most humiliating way. Yet in recounting his trial and death, the gospel writers make their greatest use of messianic imagery—Jesus is not just another martyr; he is the crucified Messiah.

In these last chapters of Jesus' life the narrators' hostility to Jews intensifies. According to Matthew, Jesus delivers his scathing indictment of the scribes and Pharisees during these last tumultuous days (Matt. 23). Jesus predicts that not one stone will be left upon another in Jerusalem (Mark 13 and parallels). In all four Gospels, Pilate, the Roman procurator, is an apologist for Jesus, a weak man who has Jesus executed only because of the persistence of the Jewish mob. Pilate "perceived it was out of envy that the chief priests had delivered him up" (Mark 15:10). When Pilate has washed his hands of the matter, the Jewish crowd shouts, "His blood be on us and on our children!" (Matt. 27:25). This frightening passage has, unfortunately, been used on numerous occasions in the history of Christianity to justify persecution of Jews.

Why this hostility toward Jews in the evangelists' story? According to all the Gospels, the final decision about Jesus' execution is made by Roman officials, and Jesus is executed on a Roman cross. Even Mark, who carefully describes a full-blown trial of Jesus before the Jewish court on religious charges, reports that Jesus was tried before Pilate on political charges and was executed as a political criminal—no effort is made to relate the two trials. This hostility toward Jews is another of the many details in the narrative that requires some explanation.

The passion stories should be examined from two perspectives. First, by focusing on Mark's account, one may identify some of the major themes and distinctive literary characteristics of the passion traditions common to all the Gospels. Then a brief look at the historical background of the passion tradition attempts to account for some of these themes and characteristics.

I. Jesus' Trial and Death in the Gospel of Mark

In Mark, Jesus' story moves inexorably toward the cross. Significantly, Jesus' ministry begins at the moment of the arrest of John the Baptist, a prophetic figure with whom Jesus has been confused (Mark 6:14, 8:27-28). Plots against Jesus begin almost at once.

Although the denouement is expected, the reader may be surprised at how total the collapse of Jesus' movement, how complete the failure of his disciples, how utterly hopeless the last hours of the would-be King. The process of disintegration begins with Jesus' last meal with his followers, one of whom has already betrayed him. The three intimate friends (Peter, James, and John) whom Jesus takes with him to pray, cannot even keep their eyes open; the only observable response Jesus gets to his agonized prayer is sleeping disciples. The reaction of his faithful group—those who have been with him since the beginning of his ministry—to his arrest, is poignantly summarized: "And they all forsook him, and fled" (14:50). For a moment there is a flicker of hope: the stalwart Peter follows him to the house of the high priest. Perhaps Peter will remain faithful, perhaps he has understood after all. But Peter's abandonment is even worse than that of the others: he denies Jesus three times, even invoking a curse upon himself.

Now completely abandoned, Jesus is quickly found guilty of blasphemy by the leaders of the Jewish religious community. Directly thereafter, Pilate tries him and before the execution releases Barabbas, a convicted revolutionary, in his place. The Roman soldiers mock Jesus, beat him, and hang him on a cross—where he is mocked not only by those who witness the execution but even by the two men crucified with him. The crowd misunderstand his last cry of desperation, "My God, my God, why hast thou forsaken me?" They think that he is calling Elijah ("my God" and "Elijah" are similar in Aramaic and in Hebrew), and some decide to wait and see whether anything spectacular will happen. It does not. With one final cry, this King of the Jews dies. Even his premature death after only a relatively short time on the cross is a sign of weakness: "And Pilate wondered if he were already dead; and summoning the centurion, he asked him whether he was already dead. And when he learned from the centurion that he was dead, he granted the body to Joseph" (15:44-45). The career of the King of the Jews has come to an end.

Mark's story of Jesus' death seemingly has at least one element of Aristotelian tragedy (a heroic character brought down because of his fatal flaw, his *hubris*). Superficially one might infer that Jesus' flaw is his belief that he is more than a man—a belief that the guardians of the truth for the religious community consider blasphemous. In the end, Jesus, like all who consider themselves superhuman, must fail. Yet this pattern fits Mark as little as it does the other Gospels: from the onset of his ministry Jesus knew he would die. On three occasions, he has explicitly predicted his death and his resurrection in three days (8:31, 9:31, 10:33). Jesus' death is not the end of the story.

Mark's account of the actual death, however, gives little indication that more is to come. The tone of his passion story is surprisingly somber and more appropriate to a tragedy. In Matthew we learn that if he chose, Jesus could request from God twelve legions of angels (Matt. 26:53); in Luke, Jesus promises a criminal that "today you will be with me in Paradise" (Luke 23:43). In Mark, were it not for Jesus' earlier predictions, his resurrection would come as a genuine surprise. Little light penetrates the gloom of Mark's account of Jesus' last days; one might well ask how this can be the climax to the "gospel of Jesus Christ, the Son of God" (Mark 1:1).

A. Peter's Denial

There are indications that the story of Jesus' death has a second level of meaning and that the tragic note veils a deeper reality. Mark's account of Peter's denial has been glanced at in chapter 2; now it will be examined more carefully. Uniquely, Mark tells the story in two separate parts that bracket the account of the trial, a literary device that shows the simultaneity and close relationship of two events. After the arrest, Peter, who was warned earlier that he would betray Jesus, follows him as far as the courtyard of the high priest's house. The scene then shifts to the inside, where Jesus is on trial for his life before the Jewish authorities. At the climax of the trial, after consideration of other charges, the high priest asks Jesus the decisive question, "Are you the Christ, the Son of the Blessed?" For the first time in the Gospel, Jesus publicly reveals his identity. The revelation and the gratuitous prediction outrage the court. It finds Jesus guilty of blasphemy and condemns him as deserving death. The trial concludes with the prisoner's being beaten and mocked (14:65).

The scene shifts back to the courtyard. Peter is also being interrogated, but his "trial" is a parody of Jesus'. A female servant of the high priest takes her master's role. While Jesus openly acknowledges the truth about himself even though it means death, Peter, to escape death, denies that he knows Jesus—even invoking a curse upon himself. Peter's denial completes the collapse of Jesus' movement and fits the pattern of disintegration in the last chapters of Mark.

Mark's conclusion of the story is unique and a bit puzzling: "And immediately the cock crowed a second time. And Peter remembered how Jesus had said to him, 'Before the cock crows twice, you will deny me three times.' And he broke down and wept" (14:72). The story leaves many questions unanswered. How did Peter escape? Did he repent? How was he reunited with the rest of the disciples? And yet despite Mark's characteristic lack of interest in detail, the reader learns that the cock crows twice! The significance of this detail lies in its fulfillment of Jesus' earlier prediction: "And Jesus said to him, 'Truly, I say to you, this very night, before the cock crows twice, you will deny me three times'" (verse 30). But why is it important that Peter's denial end with the fulfillment of a prophecy of Jesus?

At that precise moment Jesus is being mocked—as a prophet: "And some began to spit on him, and to cover his face, and to strike him, saying to him, 'Prophesy!' And the guards received him with blows" (14:65). The characters in the story remind Jesus—and the reader—of something Jesus said at his trial: "Again the high priest asked him, 'Are you the Christ, the Son of the Blessed?' And Jesus said, 'I am; and you will see the Son of man sitting at the right hand of Power, and coming with the clouds of heaven'" (verses 61, 62).

Not only does Jesus confess to the Jewish authorities that he is the Messiah, Son of God, he also prophesies that his judges will see him in his triumphant glory. It is an incredible prediction, particularly coming from one as powerless as Jesus appears to be. At the conclusion of the trial, those who have been maltreating Jesus ridicule him further, inviting him to make another such prophecy. Yet unknown to everyone but the reader, at that very moment in the courtyard one of Jesus' earlier prophecies is already being fulfilled to the letter. Contrary to all appearances, everything is proceeding according to plan. Will Jesus take his place at God's right hand and return with the clouds after all? The reader knows that he will.

Viewed from this perspective, the passion narrative has two levels of meaning. The first level is the story of the false prophet and would-be Messiah; here the characters do not completely understand what is happening. Jesus does not fit their expectations of a Messiah. The Jewish leaders, guardians of tradition and harmony, consider Jesus a blasphemer and a dangerous imposter. For Pilate, Jesus is a threat to the peace, even if the charges do seem somewhat inappropriate. At the second level, the events have a truer significance that neither the Jewish leaders nor Pilate can appreciate. The reality behind the appearance is that Jesus is the Messiah-King and Son of God. Only the reader has access to this irony. Herein lies the literary artistry, directing the reader to the true interpretation of the story.

B. Jesus' Kingship

Ambiguity and misunderstanding apply especially to the notion of kingship, a motif that, as noted earlier, ties the passion narrative together. The Jewish court condemns him as the false Christ (the anointed Messiah-King). The term "King of the Jews" is used by Pilate three times (15:2, 9, 12), by the Roman garrison (verses 16-20), and in the inscription of the charge (verse 26); and, as he hangs on the cross, the chief priests and scribes mock him as "the Christ, the King of Israel" (verses 31-32). (Whereas Romans and other foreigners refer to "Jews" and give Jesus the derisive title "King of the Jews," "Israel" is in fact the designation for the sacred nation that Jews themselves would use.)

The language is appropriate in the political context. The Romans arrest Jesus as a would-be revolutionary. They cannot tolerate anyone claiming to be a king within Caesar's empire, particularly in Judea where only a spark might touch off revolution. The Gospel of Mark itself tells us that the kingship issue is political.

At the same time Mark indicates that the political charge against Jesus represents a fatal misunderstanding. English translations obscure the clear meaning of the Greek. Jesus protests to the arresting mob that a show of force is hardly necessary:

> And Jesus said to them, "Have you come out as against a robber, with swords and clubs to capture me? Day after day I was with you in the temple teaching, and you did not seize me. But let the scriptures be fulfilled." (14:48)

The term translated as *robber* would more accurately be rendered "brigand" or "revolutionary," as the context and the usual meaning of the Greek word require. Jesus protests that he is being treated not just as a common criminal but as a dangerous revolutionary. As he tells the mob, the public character of his ministry hardly justifies any impression that he is a secret insurrectionist plotting to overthrow the government.

The erroneous political nature of the charge against the King of the Jews is even clearer in the Barabbas episode. A condemned criminal is released in place of Jesus, who actually is innocent of any wrongdoing. The real irony, however, lies in the nature of Barabbas' crime: "And among the rebels in prison, who had committed murder in the insurrection, there was a man called Barabbas" (15:7).

Barabbas is a convicted revolutionary who has been arrested for participating in a bloody insurrection. He goes free, while Jesus, who has no interest in political powers, remains in custody as a threat to the state. The irony is complete when Jesus is executed, as King of the Jews, alongside of two "revolutionaries" (not *robbers* ; the Greek term is the same as in 14:48).

The kingship at issue in the passion story is more than just political, however. The Romans cannot be expected to appreciate the full implications of Jewish kingship; to them a king is one who has climbed to the top of the slippery pole of political power. For the Jewish religious leaders (and for the reader), however, the kingship is essentially religious. The

King of Israel is anointed by God himself (Messiah and Christ literally mean "anointed one"). The true issue is Messiahship. Jesus is alleged to be "the Christ, the King of Israel" or, equivalently, "the Christ, the Son of the Blessed." This religious claim, disputed by the Jewish leaders, is basic for Mark and his readers.

The recurrent motif of Messiahship provides for the reader ironic testimony to Jesus' real identity as first learned in the introductory superscription: "The beginning of the gospel of Jesus Christ [Messiah], the Son of God." Who in the story repeats this formula, this full confession of Jesus as the Christ and Son of God? It is the high priest, though he expresses it in the form of a question and does not know how accurate the designation is. Three times Pilate refers to Jesus as king—each time without understanding the sense in which the title is appropriate. The Roman soldiers carry out a mock investiture without knowing that they are indeed saluting an anointed king. When Mark reports that the chief priests mock Jesus on the cross as "the Christ, the King of Israel," their taunts provide further testimony to the real Messiah—but only for the reader, who has already noted Mark's confession in the opening verse of the Gospel.

C. Foreshadowings

1. Scripture Fulfilled. Mark's passion narrative contains other hints that all is occurring according to God's plan. At the last supper, Jesus tells his disciples that the "Son of man goes as it is written of him" (14:21). At his arrest, he says, "But let the scriptures be fulfilled" (verse 49). The narrative of the trial and crucifixion also includes several scriptural allusions:

14:62   "And you will see the Son of man seated at the right hand of Power, and coming with the clouds of heaven." (Ps. 110:1: "The LORD says to my lord: 'Sit at my right hand,'" and Dan. 7:13: "With the clouds of heaven there came one like a son of man.")

15:24   "And they crucified him, and divided his garments among them, casting lots for them, to decide what each should take." (Ps. 22:18: "They divide my garments among them, and for my raiment they cast lots.")

15:29 "And those who passed by derided him, wagging their heads." (Ps. 22:7: "All who see me mock at me . . . they wag their heads.")

15:34 "And at the ninth hour Jesus cried with a loud voice, 'E'lo-i, E'lo-i, la ma sabach-tha'ni?' which means, 'My God, my God, why hast thou forsaken me?" (Ps. 22:1: "My God, my God, why hast thou forsaken me?")

15:36 "And one ran and, filling a sponge full of vinegar, put it on a reed and gave it to him to drink." (Ps. 69:21: "They gave me poison for food, and for my thirst they gave me vinegar to drink.")

These parallels—allusions and quotations—reinforce what the reader already knows: all events take place according to scripture, according to God's plan.

2. The Centurion's Confession. At the moment of Jesus' death, two things happen: the veil of the Temple is torn from top to bottom (15:38), and a Roman centurion expresses admiration for Jesus (verse 39). Neither event alters the course of the story, and none of the participants even notices the occurrences. Yet the writer reports both events as of interest and importance. They warrant closer attention. Consider the centurion first.

The Jewish high court has condemned Jesus for accepting the titles "the Christ, the Son of the Blessed [God]." It is highly significant that at the moment of his death one of those present, a Roman soldier, confesses that Jesus is truly the Son of God. Yet, once again, there is ambiguity. The centurion's statement may also be translated, "Truly, this man was a son of God"—that is, he was a good man—perhaps meaning, as Luke interprets it, that he was innocent (Luke 23:47). Mark's commitment to telling his story at two levels leads one to see the ambiguity of the Greek as intentional. For the centurion, the statement expresses only a conviction that Jesus was not a criminal. For the reader, it is a Christian confession, the counterpart to the opening superscription of the Gospel, perhaps even a climax to the whole Gospel. At the most unlikely moment in the story, at Jesus' humiliating death, an unexpected and probably uncomprehending witness makes the ultimate confession: truly this is God's Son.

Once again, there is evidence that the narrative is carefully constructed. Earlier, two groups of people taunt Jesus as he hangs on the cross. The first group mentions the Temple: "Aha! You who would destroy the temple and build it in three days, save yourself, and come down from the cross!" (Mark 15:29). The second group is concerned with Jesus' identity: "He saved others; he cannot save himself. Let the Christ, the King of Israel, come down now from the cross, that we may see and believe" (verses 31-32).

The narrator makes certain that his readers, if not the characters in the story, know that two events, reflecting those two taunts, occur at the moment of Jesus' death—one dealing with the Temple and one with Jesus' identity. Further, both taunts are restatements, in slightly altered forms, of the two charges made at the trial before the Sanhedrin (14:55-65).

> And some stood up and bore false witness against him, saying, "We heard him say, 'I will destroy this temple that is made with hands, and in three days I will build another, not made with hands.'" (verses 57-58)

> Again the high priest asked him, "Are you the Christ, the Son of the Blessed?" And Jesus said, "I am." (verses 61-62)

Two charges at the trial, two taunts at the cross, two events at the moment of Jesus' death—in each case, one deals with the Temple, the other with Jesus as Messiah, Son of God. The relationship obviously is intended. The trial before the Jewish authorities introduces the two key issues; interpretation of the passion story must focus on these two charges. The second one is decisive: Jesus claims to be the Christ, the Son of God. At the trial Jesus openly acknowledges his identity for the first time, thus sealing his fate. For the reader, this full confession is one of the climaxes in the story. The taunt in 15:31-32 reminds the reader that although Jesus is on the cross, he is indeed the Messiah. Finally, at the moment of deepest despair, at Jesus' death, the centurion gives final testimony: "Truly this man is the Son of God." Although he dies, Jesus is nevertheless the Christ, the Son of God.

3. The Temple Veil. The first of the two charges is more difficult to understand. Witnesses testify (falsely) to something Jesus is alleged to have said about the Temple. Their testimony about a "temple made with hands" and "another temple not made with hands" is formulated with great precision, yet they disagree with one another about the facts (14:59). But how? Rather than supply information not found in Mark to explain this strange detail, one should examine how the charge functions within its own literary context.

The Temple is a focus of attention from the moment Jesus arrives in Jerusalem; it is the symbol of the Jewish religious establishment in Mark's Gospel. In fact, the confrontation between Jesus and the religious authorities in Jerusalem is in large measure a dispute about the Temple.

As his first act in the holy city, Jesus cleanses the Temple (11:15-17), a provocative deed that sets in motion the machinery that will eventually result in his death. Yet the description of this critical event is surprisingly terse. The reader is told simply that Jesus overturned the tables of merchants and money changers and that he would not allow anyone to use the Temple court as a shortcut. Jesus then explained his actions with two quotations from the Jewish Bible: "And he taught, and said to them, 'Is it not written, "My house shall be called a house of prayer for all the nations"? But you have made it a den of robbers'" (verse 17). The first quotation is from Isaiah 56:7, where the Hebrew or Greek word is usually translated *Gentiles* instead of "nations"; the second is from Jeremiah 7:11. The latter quotation, translated "den of robbers," does not mean "place of dishonest merchants," but rather, an asylum for a band of outlaws. According to Jeremiah, God's house has been transformed into such a hideout by God's own people:

> Will you steal, murder, commit adultery, swear falsely, burn incense to Baal, and go after other gods that you have not known, and then come and stand before me in this house, which is called by my name, and say, "We are delivered!"—only to go on doing all these abominations? Has this house, which is called by my name, become a den of robbers in your eyes? (Jer. 7:9-11)

Jeremiah's sermon ends with a prediction that God will destroy the Temple (7:13-14). Jesus' reference to Jeremiah, therefore, hints at what is to come: the Temple will be destroyed.

Furthermore, the cleansing of the Temple is framed by the story of cursing the fig tree (Mark 11:12-14, 20-25). As in other such instances, Mark means for the reader to interpret the two stories as having one meaning. The fig tree has borne no fruit and is cursed; those in charge of the Temple have turned the house of prayer into a den of robbers and will likewise be destroyed.

In yet another reference to the fate of the Temple, Jesus tells a parable about some wicked tenants who refuse to pay the owner of the vineyard his due at the time of the harvest and kill the owner's son (12:1-11). It is a thinly veiled allegory: Jesus is the owner's son who will be killed by his enemies. The parable concludes with a promise that the wicked tenants will be destroyed and that the "stone which the builders rejected has become the head of the corner" (Ps. 118:22). This is another prediction of the collapse of the Temple and of the heads of the cult. Again Jesus quotes scripture (Mark 12:10); again what is to come has been foretold.

Jesus' opponents—the chief priests, scribes and elders, the leaders of the Temple—"perceived that he had told the parable against them" (12:12). They attempt to trap him into incriminating himself. But a scribe ends up praising Jesus' answer to his question and adds his own significant comment about the Temple:

> And the scribe said to him "You are right, Teacher; you have truly said that he [God] is one, and there is no other but he; and to love him with all the heart and with all the understanding, and with all the strength, and to love one's neighbor as oneself, *is much more than all whole burnt offerings and sacrifices.*" And when Jesus saw that he answered wisely, he said to him, "You are not far from the kingdom of God." (12:32-34)

The polemic against the Temple comes to something of a climax in chapter 13, Jesus' farewell discourse to his disciples:

> And as he came out of the temple, one of his disciples said to him, "Look, Teacher, what wonderful stones and what wonderful buildings!" And Jesus said to him, "Do you see these great buildings? There will not be left here one stone upon another, that will not be thrown down." (13:1-2)

He now states explicitly what he had earlier hinted: the Temple will be destroyed. He has already given the reason: the Temple establishment is corrupt; the religious leaders have failed in their responsibilities and will be rejected.

Mark has made rather elaborate preparation for the court's charge about the destruction of the Temple. The precise formulation of the charge against Jesus, however, seems odd: "And some stood up and bore false witness against him, saying, 'We heard him say, "I will destroy this temple made with hands, and in three days I will build another, not made with hands""'" (14:57-58).

Like so much else in Mark, the charge is to be understood at two levels. At one level, as the last chapters in Mark indicate, the Temple officials view Jesus as a threat. The charge is that Jesus explicitly threatened to destroy the Temple personally. Even at the time of Jeremiah, such a threat was enough to warrant a death sentence. (See Jer. 26.) Furthermore, Jesus appears to claim the magical power to build a Temple in three days; such a claim would provide another basis in Jewish legal tradition for execution. The sense in which Jesus' opponents understand the charge is evident in the taunt in 15:29: Jesus has both threatened the Temple and made an absurd boast, another impossible assertion by one who cannot even help himself. At this level of meaning, the charge is part of what Mark tells us is "false testimony" at the trial—false perhaps because Jesus never made such a statement himself, perhaps because the reader is supposed to view the charge as part of the court's preconceived plot to have Jesus condemned.

At another level of meaning, however, the charge is true. Its precise wording has little impact on either the witnesses or the court, but for the reader the wording is indeed decisive. Only the reader understands what is meant by the other temple, "not made with hands" that Jesus will build "in three days." Jesus will build a new community of believers, the Church, as a result of his resurrection after three days.

A new Temple at the end of days was traditionally associated with the awaited Messiah-King.[1] The garbled charge by false witnesses, therefore, serves the reader both as a prediction of the birth of the church to replace the Temple and as another sign that Jesus is indeed the promised Messiah.

The charge represents the culmination of interest in the Temple throughout the latter half of Mark. It is as much a prophecy as Jesus' promise that his judges will see him enthroned at God's right hand and returning with the clouds of heaven. This latter prediction, part of Jesus' assertion that he is the Messiah and Son of God, is confirmed at his death by the confession of the Roman centurion. Similarly, the fate of the Temple and the promise of its replacement is symbolized by the tearing of the Temple veil. The doom of the Temple cult has been sealed. The stone that the builders have rejected will become the cornerstone of the new temple "not made with hands," while the builders will be cast aside.

II. Historical Reflections

Two problems noted earlier remain to be solved.[2] Why does messianic (royal) imagery suddenly become prominent when the story of Jesus gets to the passion narrative? And why do the narrators seem so interested in the role of the Jewish leaders in Jesus' death? Both questions are important to students of early Christianity and of the evangelists' literary methods.

All three Synoptic Gospels make clear from the outset that Jesus will eventually be hailed as Messiah-King. Mark begins with the messianic title (Mark 1:1). So does Matthew (Matt. 1:1, 16-18); he also reports that the magi worship Jesus as King of the Jews (2:1-11). In Luke, Mary is promised that her son will sit on "the throne of his father David" and "reign over the house of Jacob for ever" (Luke 1:32-33); an angel tells a group of shepherds about the birth of "a Savior, who is Christ the Lord" (2:11); and when an old man sees Jesus, he acknowledges that God has fulfilled his promise that "he should not see death before he had seen the Lord's Christ" (2:26).

Yet messianic imagery then disappears and is almost completely absent from the accounts of Jesus' ministry prior to his death. Apart from John, who reports that a crowd tried to make Jesus king by force (John 6:15), none of the gospel writers even suggests that Jesus' contemporaries suspected him to be the Messiah. Only Peter has an inkling that Jesus is indeed the long-awaited King, but even his perception is clouded.

After a ministry in which messianic titles are virtually absent, the image of Jesus as Messiah suddenly dominates the narrative of his last days. As already seen, Jesus is interrogated, mocked, and crucified as King of the Jews. Why, in all the Gospels, do the authors resume explicitly messianic imagery as they describe Jesus' trial and death?

A. The Messianic Tradition

The question is all the more intriguing when the Gospels' image of Jesus as the crucified Messiah is compared with traditional Jewish images of the expected Messiah immediately prior to and contemporaneous with the first Christian century. These traditions concerning the Messiah's role in establishing the messianic kingdom are diverse, but they seem to have shared a common stock of biblical passages and images. Even those groups with the most radically diverse messianic expectations—like the sectarians at Qumran who produced the Dead Sea Scrolls—drew on that traditional material. In all traditions he was to appear as a king; variations in his expected function probably reflect different views about kingship.

The following passages are descriptions of the Messiah that appear in literature roughly contemporary with the New Testament. The first is taken from the apocryphal Psalms of Solomon, believed to have been composed some time during the first century B.C.E.; the second is from the Dead Sea Scrolls. Both express the belief that the Messiah will reestablish the glorious reign of David.

1. Behold, O Lord, and raise up unto them their king, the son of David,
    At the time in which Thou seest, O God, that he may reign over Israel Thy servant.
    And gird him with strength, that he may shatter unrighteous rulers,
    and that he may purge Jerusalem from nations that trample [her] down to destruction.
    Wisely, righteously he shall thrust out sinners from inheritance,

He shall destroy the pride of the sinner as a potter's vessel;
With a rod of iron he shall break in pieces all their
    substance,
He shall destroy the godless nations with the word of his mouth;
At his rebuke nations shall flee before him,
And he shall reprove sinners for the thoughts of their heart.

. . . .

And he shall have the heathen nations to serve him under
    his yoke;
And he shall glorify the Lord in a place to be seen of all the
    earth;
And he shall purge Jerusalem, making it holy as of old;
So that nations shall come from the ends of the earth to see
    his glory. . .
And there shall be no unrighteousness in his days in their
    midst,
For all shall be holy, and their king the anointed of the Lord.
                                                (Ps. Sol. 17:23-38)[3]

2. May Adonai [rai]se [thee] to everlasting heights,
   and as a fortified tower upon a steep wall!
   And [thou shalt strike the peoples] by the might of thy [mouth;]
   thou shalt devastate the earth by thy sceptre,
   and by the breath of thy lips shalt thou slay the ungodly.
   [The Spirit of couns]el and eternal might [shall be upon thee],
   the Spirit of Knowledge and of the fear of God.
   And righteousness shall be the girdle [of thy loins],
   [and faith] the girdle of thy haunches.
   May He make thy horns of iron
   and thy shoes of bronze!
   May thou toss like a [young] bull [. . .]
   [and trample the peopl]es like the mud of the streets!
   For God has established thee as a sceptre over the rulers . . .
   [and all the peo]ples shall serve thee,
   and He shall exalt thee by His holy Name.
   And thou shalt be as a lion.[4]

Close reading of those two passages uncovers allusions to
several biblical texts that apparently formed the nucleus of
what were traditionally considered messianic prophecies. The
following were the most important:

A star shall come forth out of Jacob,
    and a scepter shall rise out of Israel;

it shall crush the forehead of Moab,
and break down all the sons of Sheth.
(Num. 24:17)

Judah is a lion's whelp;
from the prey, my son, you have gone up.
He stooped down, he crouched as a lion,
and as a lioness; who dares rouse him up?
The scepter shall not depart from Judah,
nor the ruler's staff from between his feet,
until he comes to whom it belongs,
and to him shall be the obedience of the peoples.
(Gen. 49:9-10)

There shall come forth a shoot from the stump of Jesse,
and a branch shall grow out of his roots.
And the Spirit of the LORD shall rest upon him,
the spirit of wisdom and understanding,
the spirit of counsel and might,
the spirit of knowledge and the fear of the LORD.
And his delight shall be in the fear of the LORD.
He shall not judge by what his eyes see,
or decide by what his ears hear;
but with righteousness he shall judge the poor,
and decide with equity for the meek of the earth;
and he shall smite the earth with the rod of his mouth,
and with the breath of his lips he shall slay the wicked.
(Isa. 11:1-4)

Why do the nations conspire,
and the peoples plot in vain?
The kings of the earth set themselves,
and the rulers take counsel together,
against the LORD and his anointed, saying,
"Let us burst their bonds asunder,
and cast their cords from us."
He who sits in the heavens laughs;
the LORD has them in derision.
Then he will speak to them in his wrath,
and terrify them in his fury, saying,
"I have set my king
on Zion, my holy hill."
I will tell of the decree of the LORD:
He said to me, "You are my son,
today I have begotten you.
Ask of me, and I will make the nations your heritage,
and the ends of the earth your possession.

You shall break them with a rod of iron,
   and dash them in pieces like a potter's vessel."
(Ps. 2:1-9)

In all these texts, the Messiah is a king. He will be fierce as a lion, he will "crush the forehead of Moab," (whomever Moab represents), and he will "slay the wicked" with the breath of his lips. He will rule not only over Israel but over all nations. Nowhere is there the slightest indication that death is part of the Messiah's career.

In Jewish tradition the only observable proof of Messiahship is success. Simon bar Kochbah, discussed in chapter 1, was originally hailed by many Jews as the Messiah, the star from Jacob promised in Numbers 24. His failure to defeat the Roman armies and inaugurate the messianic kingdom proved to his contemporaries that he was not the awaited Messiah and that his supporters had been mistaken. Seen in this context, Jesus' life, as described in the Gospels, was not messianic in the traditional sense, even though his teaching and healing may have convinced many that he was a prophetic figure.

Jesus makes no attempt to establish himself as king, though that alone does not disqualify him as the yet unrevealed Messiah. Some traditions held that the Messiah, when he came, would for a time be unrecognized; others taught that the Messiah had already been born and that he was presently living as a beggar at the gates of Rome.[5] All, however, believed that he would reveal himself at the proper time. Thus it is not altogether strange that the gospel writers should narrate the first stage of the career of Jesus the Messiah with minimal use of explicitly messianic imagery. What is strange is that the story should emphasize Jesus as the Messiah just when he has obviously failed the traditional test of Messiahship—at the moment of his arrest, trial, and death. Paradoxically, royal imagery is most prominent when Jesus is most powerless, least kinglike.

B. Jesus as Messiah

What could have convinced Jesus' followers that he was the Messiah? The usual answer to this question is that it was Jesus' resurrection from the dead. The New Testament does indeed teach that Jesus was raised from the dead and that for this reason his death did not mark the end of his movement. But resurrection was not part of the messianic tradition and would not by itself have convinced his contemporaries that he was the Messiah. Instead, he could have been accepted simply as the risen one, as the "living Jesus," or perhaps as a risen prophet. Why would his resurrection convince his followers that he was God's anointed one, the promised Messiah-King? It is still unclear why messianic imagery is so prominent in the accounts of Jesus' passion.

The inscription of the charge against Jesus may contain a clue. Jesus dies as King of the Jews; the title is the same in all the Gospels. Many students of early Christianity have held that believers added the title because of later theologizing. This is an unlikely explanation; neither Christians nor Jews would consider "King of the Jews" a messianic title. Furthermore, to a Jew, the epithet would have been "King of Israel" (Mark 15:32). There is little reason to doubt the authenticity of the gospel account: the charge against Jesus, as formulated by the Roman official, Pilate, is that he was a possible usurper and pretender to kingship.[6]

If Jesus was executed as a would-be king, then, for his followers, his resurrection by God was a vindication; he was the risen King (Messiah-King, for Jews). To them, it meant that Jesus' enemies had been wrong about him. If he died as King and if God vindicated him by raising him from the dead, then obviously it must be as King that Jesus was vindicated. This would explain why his contemporary and later followers viewed Jesus as the crucified and risen Messiah. The image of Jesus as Messiah sticks in Christian tradition despite the radically unconventional nature of his Messiahship because of the turn of events during his last days in Jerusalem and because of the centrality of Jesus' death and resurrection in Christian preaching. Here is one of the earliest confessional fragments in the New Testament:

> For I delivered to you as of first importance what I also received, that Christ died for our sins in accordance with the scriptures, that he was buried, that he was raised on the third day in

accordance with the scriptures, and that he appeared to Cephas, then to the twelve. (I Cor. 15:3-5)

Early Christians accepted the Jewish Bible as sacred scripture, and they were convinced that Jesus was the Messiah promised in that Bible. He fulfilled for them traditional messianic texts (Isa. 11; II Sam. 7:10-14; Ps. 2). In light of his unique ministry, however, they redefined Messiahship, omitting much of the traditional imagery because Jesus did not appear as a warrior-king. Most radical of all in the eyes of their fellow Jews, Christians insisted that the highest messianic action was Jesus' death: "Then he opened their minds to understand the scriptures, and said to them, 'Thus it is written, that the Christ should suffer and on the third day rise from the dead'" (Luke 24:46).

Christians assembled passages that were not traditionally viewed in Jewish circles as descriptions of the coming Messiah-King to prove the messianic nature of Jesus' death. To many Jews, such a belief seemed unreasonable. The apostle Paul, speaking about his attitude as a Jew toward Christians prior to his conversion, describes Jesus' death as a "scandal"; and after his conversion he insists that this scandal can be understood only by the faithful (I Cor. 1:21-24). Christian Jews were convinced that the crucified and risen Jesus was indeed the Messiah, and by the second century they had developed a full-blown Old Testament doctrine of the Messiah that looked very different from traditional Jewish messianic beliefs. Many biblical passages became messianic by their specific application to Jesus the Messiah. The Gospels seem to represent a rather late stage in this development, and part of their purpose is to redefine for their readers true Messiahship in light of Jesus' death.

The image of Jesus in the Gospels is a composite, reflecting a variety of biblical traditions about prophets, holy men, and divine beings. The Messiahship of Jesus lay at the very earliest stratum of Christian tradition and persisted in spite of the profound differences between Jesus and the more conventional image of the Messiah. Ironically, one of the more creative forces in the development of Christian tradition may have been Pontius Pilate. His order to crucify Jesus as the political King of the Jews may have guaranteed that all later generations of believers in the risen Jesus would call him "Christ"—that is, the religious Messiah-King. Had there been no inscription, had Jesus died as an ordinary insurrectionist, his followers might have chosen a more obvious designation for Jesus from their tradition—"prophet" for example. But since they believed God had vindicated their crucified King, they must have been convinced that the designation was appropriate in a way no one had dreamed. To use in their preaching the very title formulated by Jesus' opponents would have served as an appropriate testimony to the stunning reversal of values that Jesus' followers saw in his whole ministry.

This would also explain why the messianic imagery became so intimately associated with the story of Jesus' death. For his followers, his arrest, trial, death, and resurrection were the most significant and revealing events in his entire ministry. Here the point of his mission finally emerges clearly. Jesus is not confessed as Messiah until the proper moment; only in light of his death and resurrection, according to Christians, could one truly appreciate what it meant to call Jesus Messiah and Son of God.

Other historical questions, of course, remain unresolved. How did Pilate and the Jewish leaders hear that Jesus claimed to be king? Nowhere in the Gospels does Jesus ever publicly claim to be the Messiah. If it was a secret that he revealed to his followers, the evangelists are peculiarly ambiguous about Jesus' attitude toward such a title. In any case, the claim that Jesus was Messiah unquestionably surfaced among his followers at some point during the last stages of his ministry whether he made that claim or not. All the Gospels agree that when asked, Jesus did not deny that he was the Messiah. More than that today's reader does not know. It is difficult to believe, however, that he would have been crucified as king had he insisted at his trial that the title was wholly inappropriate. Surely his followers would not have made the confession of Jesus as Christ so fundamental had they known that Jesus himself steadfastly rejected the title. Here, however, one enters an area where historical certainty will always be unattainable, barring discovery of new sources.

C. Hostility Toward Jews

Another feature of the passion story requiring some comment is the hostility toward Jews in all the Gospels. The role of Jews in Jesus' arrest and ultimate fate is not a sufficient explanation for the tone of the narratives.

The Gospels differ significantly. In Mark and Luke, the hostility is directed toward the established leaders of the Jewish community—specifically, the scribes, the chief priests, and the elders. Matthew emphasizes the Pharisees, who were not as a group part of the Jerusalem establishment, as co-conspirators. His last chapters include a series of bitter denunciations of scribes and Pharisees, and when Pilate refuses to accept responsibility for Jesus' death, the people answer, "His blood be on us and on our children!" (Matt. 27:25). John says it is the Jews in general who demand Jesus' death, although the chief priests are the spokesmen in much of the dialogue with Pilate. The term "the Jews" serves John as a symbol for all who are God's enemies. The irony in John's passion story is almost savage. He reminds us that it is the Passover (when Jews remember Pharaoh and confess in the service that "we have no King but God") as the chief priests say to Pilate, "We have no king but Caesar" (John 19:15).

Today there is general agreement among scholars from a variety of religious perspectives that the responsibility for Jesus' death—that is, for the sentence itself—lies with Pilate. The authorities executed Jesus for political reasons, as a would-be king and as a threat to peace. This accords well with Josephus' descriptions of the typical Roman response to potentially seditious religious movements (and of Pilate's responses in particular). Even Matthew and John show clearly that Jesus is executed by the Romans and that the cross is a Roman instrument of execution.

There is also general agreement among students of early Christianity that those who handed Jesus over to the Romans were not the Pharisees or the common people but members of the Sanhedrin, the official governing body in Jerusalem. Jesus probably antagonized Pharisees and other pious Jews by teaching with untraditional methods, flaunting certain religious practices, and associating with irreligious Jews, but these matters would not have provided a sufficient basis for his death.

One of the major tasks of the Sanhedrin was to oversee the religious affairs of the capital city, Jerusalem. Passover was a time of potential unrest: the festival commemorated the liberation of Israel from oppression, and the city was hopelessly overcrowded with impassioned pilgrims. Chances of uprisings against the hated Romans were immeasurably greater. Many who followed Jesus undoubtedly did so because they were convinced he would eventually lead a revolutionary movement, regardless of his actual intentions. In the eyes of those responsible for the well-being of Jerusalem, therefore, Jesus certainly posed a threat to the peace.

Those who had most to lose from any revolt and who were held responsible for affairs within the Jewish community were members of the high court, the same group in charge of the Temple cult. According to Josephus, the chief priests opposed revolt against Rome to the very end (when the Zealots wrested control of the government from them) because they knew that revolution could only end in disaster. Obviously, a nonconformist, popular preacher with an unruly following would have greatly disturbed those responsible in the Jerusalem establishment. It is both unjust and historically naïve to say that the Sanhedrin delivered Jesus to the Romans simply out of envy. Precisely what role the Jewish high court was expected to play in the arrest, interrogation, and conviction of a revolutionary, and to what extent violations of Jewish law might have been considered significant in the eyes of the Romans—these are historical problems that may perhaps never be resolved.

In Roman law, indigenous courts in provinces might serve as grand juries.[7] If this pattern applied to Judea, the Sanhedrin might have been requested to prepare charges against Jesus—but not to try him themselves. Nothing in Jewish law, however, provides for any such legal proceedings. Furthermore, Judea was an exceptional province in so many respects that historians can only speculate how far legal patterns in other Roman provinces applied to Judea.

Whether the Jewish high court had the authority to try and to execute in capital religious cases is uncertain. According to John, the only reason the Jewish court does not execute Jesus on charges stemming from Jewish law is its lack of authority to do so (John 18:31). The Synoptics make no such comment. Even in Mark, where the Jewish court gives Jesus a full trial and condemns him as deserving death according to Jewish law, no attempt is made to have the Jewish sentence confirmed by Pilate; the court simply hands Jesus over to the procurator to be tried according to Roman law as "King of the Jews." And in Luke, there is no trial before the Jewish court, only a hearing. Is John correct, or did the Sanhedrin have the right to execute capital sentences? Scholars still debate the authority of the Jewish court and probably will never agree.

The Gospels tend to absolve Pilate of at least the moral responsibility, placing the blame for Jesus' death on Jews. The passion narratives can hardly have been designed to impress Romans: the portrait of a Roman official completely subject to the whims of a Jewish mob would not be flattering. Matthew and John make "the Jews," or "all the people," responsible; their persistence wears Pilate down, until he finally consents to have Jesus executed. In light of Josephus' record of Pilate as a ruthless tyrant, this portrait in the Gospels is highly unrealistic.[8] But why should they make Pilate the apologist and the Jews the villains? Why should the gospel writers be so obsessed with the role of the Jews or of the Jewish leaders in Jesus' death?

The reason is that the Jewish rejection of Jesus—both at the time of Jesus and in later Christian history—was more a religious than a historical problem. The fact that Jesus was executed by a Roman would be only a historical fact; the Romans were pagans, noted for hostility toward Jews, and could not be expected to recognize the Messiah, Son of God. Nevertheless, for the earliest Christians (Jews who believed that Jesus was the Jewish Messiah) the Jewish involvement in Jesus' death was a serious matter. It was scandalous enough that Jews would hand one of their own over to the hated Romans—but their own Messiah! How could the recognized leaders of the Jewish religious community do such a thing?

And why did the majority of the Jewish community still refuse to accept Jesus as the Messiah? Each evangelist offers answers. The leaders of the Jews were jealous; they were the wicked tenants who refused to pay the owner of the vineyard his due (Mark 12); they were the builders who rejected the stone (Matt. 21:42); they were the ones whose fathers always opposed the prophets (Acts 7); they were the Jews who could say something as totally un-Jewish as "We have no king but Caesar" (John 19:15).

Jewish opposition to Jesus came to a head as a problem for Christians some time near the end of the first century, when Christian Jews were excluded from the Jewish community. These people must have faced a terrible crisis of identity. They believed that they were the true people of God, that they were the children of Abraham, and that Jesus was the fulfillment of promises made to their own Jewish patriarchs and of prophecies made by their own Jewish prophets. They believed that the God who raised Jesus from the dead was the God of Abraham, Isaac, and Jacob. But they had to face the fact that other Jews, who did not share their convictions, now insisted that Christian Jews were outsiders, no longer even Jews, that they had no claim on the patriarchs and the prophets and were no longer members of the people of God.

Christian Jews reacted strongly. Beyond doubt the Jewish leaders in Jerusalem were involved in Jesus' death, but it is also clear that Christian tradition has exaggerated their role. The gospel writers consider themselves to be the true Jews at a time when the majority of the Jewish community regards them as not Jews at all. During this period of recrimination on both sides as to who were the true Jews and who were the apostates, Christian storytellers naturally focus on the Jewish role in Jesus' death, since the way a story is told reflects to a considerable extent the needs and questions of both the storyteller and his audience. The New Testament must plead guilty to the charge of anti-Semitism, but the sentiment arose as a struggle between two "Semitic brothers" regarding who was rightful heir to the promises, and the resulting bitterness in the Gospels reflects the feeling of the one brother who has been irreconcilably ousted by his family.

Summary

There were other martyr stories in the ancient world, but the story of Jesus' death in the Gospels is depicted as more than a triumph for a person or his ideals. It is seen as a fulfillment of scriptures, as God's victory through which a ransom has been paid. In death the martyr is revealed as Messiah, King, and God's Son. Jesus' last week in Jerusalem dominates the gospel stories. Whereas the writers had often been vague concerning details in the early part of his life, the accounts now become much more specific.

The Gospel of Mark has carefully prepared his reader for the denouement. The plotting against Jesus begins early; his career is closely tied to that of John the Baptist, who is beheaded. Although Jesus is popular with the multitudes, many are offended at what he says and does. Peter gets an inkling, but the subsequent behavior of the disciples underlines their inability to understand Jesus. The reader is not, however, prepared for the movement's radical collapse that begins with his arrest. Betrayed by one disciple, denied by another, forsaken by the rest, Jesus is mocked and misunderstood by Jewish and Roman authorities and even by the criminals with whom he is crucified.

The final chapters have been structured in Mark so that the story of Jesus' last days in Jerusalem can be understood at two levels. The reader is allowed to see him as he was commonly perceived—a would-be Messiah and false prophet arrested as a revolutionary. The irony continues as a real revolutionary is released and culminates with Jesus' being executed between two convicted revolutionaries. In his trials before the religious and political authorities there are two charges: he will destroy the Temple and rebuild another in three days, and he claims to be the Messiah-Christ. When he is crucified, the same two charges are hurled at him as taunts from the crowd.

But Mark also gives the reader a perspective that the participants in the drama could not have. Scriptural quotations point up a divine plan being fulfilled. When the cock crows twice one sees Jesus' prophecy to Peter being fulfilled at the moment he is proclaiming himself as Christ and prophesying his victorious return. At his death the Temple veil is torn and the Roman centurion confesses him as "Son of God," conforming to the dual pattern of the two trial charges and taunts.

Messianic motifs are introduced in the birth stories but dropped almost entirely in the rest of the story of Jesus—until he enters Jerusalem to die. And it is strange that messianic imagery is most stressed just when Jesus looks least like the traditional Messiah. In his death he certainly does not seem to be the long-awaited Messiah-King from the line of David who would return to judge the wicked and establish his worldwide rule of righteousness and peace.

Why did the early church stress Jesus as Messiah when he himself never referred to himself by that title? It is hard to know Jesus' thought, although if he had emphatically denied that title—in his trials or before his disciples—it is doubtful that the tradition would have persisted. It is suggested that the Romans, in putting the "King of the Jews" sign on the cross in his execution, may have contributed to this strong stress. The Romans had intended it ironically, but after the resurrection experience, the early church saw God's vindication of that title and proclaimed him as the risen Christ.

One also detects a new strident note of hostility againt the Jews in the passion stories, although Jesus was condemned and executed by the Romans as a political prisoner. The Pharisees might have disagreed with some of Jesus' interpretations of scripture and wondered at some of his friendships, but they would not have handed him over to the hated Romans for death. On the other hand, Judea was a volatile political entity, always susceptible to uprisings—especially in Jerusalem during the pilgrimage holidays. Both Jewish and Roman authorities would have been alert for anything unusual that could lead to riots and possibly insurrection. It is uncertain how much authority the Sanhedrin had in capital cases, but it is very possible that they would regard Jesus as a threat to the peace. The early Jewish Christians had to puzzle how the authorities in Jerusalem failed to recognize the Messiah when he appeared. The Gospels, however, were written in the latter part of the first century, as hostility between Jews and Christians began to mount and a major schism finally resulted. The blame and hostility heaped on the Jews, especially in Matthew and John, reflect the bitter feelings of a family feud, laying the blame against Jews rather than the real culprit, the Roman forces of occupation.

CHAPTER SEVEN

RESURRECTION STORIES
IN THE SYNOPTICS

Jesus' story does not end with his death. His disciples believed that God raised him from the dead, and their belief provided a new foundation for the movement, which had suffered almost total collapse with Jesus' crucifixion. The resurrection motivated the Christians to narrate Jesus' story; appropriately, therefore, it serves as a conclusion to all four Gospels, but in characteristically different ways. As in all literature, the conclusion of each Gospel demands close examination: here loose ends usually are tied up, the development of themes concluded, emphases highlighted, and problems in the narrative resolved.

Because of the centrality of Easter within the Christian community, the stories of Jesus' appearances to his disciples are familiar to many readers of the New Testament. As with the infancy narratives, such familiarity can be a barrier to full appreciation of the distinctiveness and artistry of the individual Gospels. For example, one should look at the Synoptic Gospels' accounts side by side, listing the variations in the three accounts, beginning with the women's visit to the tomb. (See Mark 16:1-8, Matt. 28:1-8, and Luke 24:1-12.)

1. *The women:* The list of names in the party is slightly different. According to Mark, the women are Mary Magdalene, Mary, the mother of James, and Salome (Mark 16:1). Matthew mentions only Mary Magdalene and "the other Mary" (Matt. 28:1). Luke identifies Mary Magdalene, Joanna, and Mary, the mother of James (Luke 24:10).

2. *Their purpose:* Mark and Luke say that the women are going to the tomb to anoint Jesus' body for a proper burial. Matthew says nothing about anointing; the women are going "to see the sepulchre" (Matt. 28:1).

3. *The stone:* According to Mark, the women have made preparations to anoint the body, but no provision for removing the stone in order to enter the tomb (Mark 16:3). Mark and Luke do not explain how the stone has been rolled away but note simply that the women found the entrance to the tomb open. Matthew says that the stone was removed by an earthquake that accompanied the descent of an angel from heaven (Matt. 28:2), revealing an already empty tomb.

4. *The angel:* In Mark, the women are greeted by "a young man . . . dressed in a white robe" (Mark 16:5); in Matthew, by an "angel of the Lord" whose "appearance was like lightning" and whose raiment was "white as snow" (Matt. 28:3); in Luke, by "two men . . . in dazzling apparel" (Luke 24:4).

5. *The message:* In Matthew 28:7 and Mark 16:7, the women are directed to deliver to the disciples a message, whose wording is almost identical. Both Gospels read "he is going before you to Galilee; there you will see him." Mark adds "as he told you"; Matthew inserts "lo, I have told you."

In Luke, the men give the women no message, but chide them for their perplexity at seeing the empty tomb: "Why do you seek the living among the dead?" (Luke 24:5). And instead of the statement "he is going before you to Galilee," Luke reads, "Remember how he told you, while he was still in Galilee" (verse 6). Nothing is said about a future meeting with Jesus in Galilee. In Luke, Galilee is the place where Jesus predicted his death and resurrection, not the place where the disciples are to meet the risen Lord.

6. *Their departure:* Mark reports that the women "fled" from the tomb, for "trembling and astonishment had come upon them" (Mark 16:8); in Matthew, they "departed quickly with fear *and* great joy" (Matt. 28:8)—a very different mood.

7. *Their report:* In Matthew and Luke, the women report to the disciples what they have seen. According to Mark, however, "they said nothing to anyone, for they were afraid" (Mark 16:8).

Some of these differences represent only varied word choice or simple embellishment. Others, however, are more significant. The mood created in Mark's account contrasts in a revealing way with that in Matthew and Luke. Luke's reporting the resurrection appearances as being in Jerusalem rather than in Galilee coincides, as will be seen later, with the writer's literary purpose. Even the smaller variations may help the reader appreciate the uniqueness of the individual Gospels. After the women's visit to the tomb, all agreement among the Synoptic Gospels about the Easter story ends.

Each of the resurrection stories should be considered within its own context.

I. Mark

The Gospel of Mark, according to the almost unanimous testimony of the oldest Greek manuscripts, ends with 16:8: "And they went out and fled from the tomb; for trembling and astonishment had come upon them; and they said nothing to any one, for they were afraid." The 350-year-old Authorized, or King James, Version of the New Testament contains another twelve verses. Many modern translations include such other endings in footnotes; their absence from the oldest manuscripts suggests that they were added later by scribes who were dissatisfied with what seems to be an incomplete conclusion at 16:8. The ending is indeed abrupt and completely unexpected—even more so in the original Greek than in English translations. Many scholars, insisting that no book could end with such a strange grammatical construction, have made a host of proposals about lost endings. Apart from the conclusions that seemingly were added in later manuscript traditions, however, there is no early evidence that Mark ever ended in any other way. (Significantly, Matthew and Luke agree with each other in recording the Easter story only up to the conclusion of the visit to the empty tomb. If both were using Mark as a source, and if this is where their common source ended, the lack of agreement from this point on makes sense.)

Why would a writer end his work on such a puzzling note? Why is Jesus going to Galilee? How did the disciples and the evangelist learn about the resurrection if the women "said nothing to any one"? Did the disciples meet Jesus in Galilee if the women did not deliver the message? Without the other Gospels, the reader would not know; Mark provides no answers. In fact, 16:8 is not really a conclusion: the story's loose ends are not tied up. Yet there are indications that this ending that is not really an ending is intentional; if so, then these concluding verses should be of primary importance for an understanding of the Gospel as a whole.

Throughout Mark's story, the narrator shows that he is familiar with resurrection traditions. Three times Jesus predicts that he will be raised "after three days" (Mark 8:31, 9:31, 10:34). He also instructs Peter, James, and John that they are to keep silent about the transfiguration experience "until the Son of man should have risen from the dead" (9:9). Again, he tells his disciples that he will go before them to Galilee "after I am raised up" (14:28). Obviously, the writer knows about the Resurrection and presumes that his readers also know. Nevertheless he chooses to end his story without reporting any actual appearances. From what perspective does this fulfill Mark's purpose?

Proposals about the purpose of Mark's Gospel will be offered in the next chapter, but a few anticipatory comments may be useful here. The ending, like the beginning, suggests that the Gospel is not a piece of missionary literature: it presumes some familiarity with the story of Jesus, and its purpose is to cast that story in a particular light—to offer a particular interpretation of it.

In one sense, the last verse represents the culmination of a theme encountered throughout Mark: the aura of mystery that enshrouds the whole of Jesus' ministry is sustained to the end of the Gospel. In another sense, however, the conclusion forces the reader beyond the events of the story itself. All along, the reader has known what the characters did not. The story was framed by the superscription at the outset; the reader must supply the end-frame. The mystery of Jesus the Messiah, Son of God, is resolved only outside of the story's boundaries. Rather than provide a neat resolution of all problems in the story, the conclusion forces on the reader the final challenge: what sort of good news concludes with "and they said nothing to any one, for they were afraid"?

II. Matthew

One might almost say that Matthew answers every question that Mark's story leaves open. The women do not flee the tomb in dumb terror; they run out "with fear and great joy" to tell the disciples what they have seen. They actually see the risen Jesus and take "hold of his feet"—both as a sign of worship and, in the context of the Gospel, as a proof that Jesus is not simply a spirit. They then report to the fearful disciples who, in turn, meet Jesus in Galilee (Matt. 28:16). There Jesus gives them final instructions, and the story concludes with his promise to remain with his followers "to the close of the age" (verse 20).

Notice that Matthew's Gospel ends on a mountain in Galilee. As with the Sermon on the Mount, the mountain is unnamed. Are unnamed mountains, not influencing the story's action, to be understood as symbols? The setting clearly enhances Jesus' exalted stature as one to whom "all authority in heaven and on earth has been given." More specifically, the Gospel's concluding concern is teaching. Jesus instructs his followers not simply to missionize the world, but to teach the new converts "all that I have commanded you" (28:20). The reader recalls that the basis of the disciples' teaching to others is what Jesus has taught them earlier—also from a mountain (5–7). Jesus as teacher and the teaching role of his followers are recurrent motifs in Matthew's Gospel, probably echoing Mosaic tradition. Like Moses, Jesus transmits God's message from a mountain. And like Moses, Jesus gives a last testament on a mountain. The audience would not miss the symbolism.

The story of the Roman guards at the tomb who witness the resurrection (27:62-66; 28:4, 11-15) is unique to Matthew. At the instigation of the chief priests and the Pharisees, Pilate places a guard at the tomb to prevent any tampering by Jesus' followers. These guards see the angel descend from heaven, and although they become as "dead men," they recover and report what happened—not to their Roman commander but to the Jewish leaders. Subsequently these leaders bribe the guards to spread malicious rumors about the disciples' having stolen the body from the tomb—rumors that, Matthew observes, have been "spread among the Jews to this day" (28:15).

The episode supports Matthew's preoccupations, one of which is an unusual hostility toward Jews, particularly the Pharisees. Only Matthew reports any alliance between the chief priests and Pharisees (27:62). His mention of derogatory rumors spread among Jews to his own day presumes that his readers know about the hostility toward Jesus and his followers from within the Jewish community. The story of the guards' report and the bribe, whatever its historical accuracy, is a response to those rumors. The insistence on having guards at the tomb provides ironic substantiation of the truth of the resurrection. At the same time, the story reveals the unscrupulous nature of the Jewish authorities who will stop at nothing to discredit the Christian message. The story, as shall be examined in greater detail, tells one a good deal about the situation of Matthew and his audience.

In one respect, the ending of Matthew, like Mark, is unfinished. The drama closes with Jesus still on earth, although, as the reader knows, he eventually takes his place at God's right hand (26:64). As in Mark, Matthew's seemingly inconclusive ending is appropriate to his Gospel. The life of Jesus is the first part of the continuing story of his followers, who are to preach, baptize, and teach "all that I have commanded you." Although Jesus does not explain how he will be present with his followers, he does promise to be with them "to the close of the age." The audience might recall one of the names given to Jesus earlier in Matthew: "Emmanuel (which means, God with us)" (1:23). The continuing story will conclude only with the final scene in the great drama, when the Son of man comes to "gather his elect from the four winds" (24:30-31). Until that day comes, followers of Jesus must preach, baptize, and teach. They do so in the knowledge that the risen Jesus is present and that some day he will return to bring the story to its fitting climax. Matthew concludes with that assurance.

III. Luke

Luke's resurrection stories are a transition to part two of his work, the book of Acts. Although separated in the present New Testament canon, the two parts apparently were conceived as a unified work and should be read as a unit. Thus only Luke brings Jesus' story to a formal conclusion and relates it to the early church. Jesus ascends into heaven (Acts 1:6-11); the band of disciples is renewed (verses 12-26); and with the coming of the Spirit, the new era of missionary activity begins (2). Luke tells the story of Jesus as part of a history that extends into Christian times.

Although transitional, Luke's account of Jesus' appearances after his death does close the first part of his work and thus warrants examination within that context. Luke's verson is by far the longest, and it paints a distinctive picture of the events. As in Matthew, the women return to the disciples with their message, but in Luke, no one believes them, for "these words seemed to them an idle tale" (Luke 24:11). The disciples do not travel to Galilee, but remain in Jerusalem where they themselves see the risen Lord (verses 36-43). The audience clearly understands that this is a bodily resurrection. Jesus invites his disciples to touch him, and he eats food in their presence, demonstrating that he is not a spirit. Evidently, Luke considers the question of body versus spirit important.

Luke's most notable contribution to the stories is Jesus' appearance to the travelers on the road to Emmaus. Found only in Luke, it is also unique in its intimacy and fullness of detail. A stranger joins the two men as they are talking about Jesus' death and their disappointment because they "hoped that he was the one to redeem Israel" (24:21). The mysterious stranger to whom they have given this news turns out to be none other than Jesus himself, and after the two men recognize him, he vanishes as suddenly as he appeared. The recognition scene is climactic: "When he was at table with them, he took the bread and blessed, and broke it, and gave it to them. And their eyes were opened and they recognized him" (verses 30-31).

Readers may link this episode to other passages in Luke. Most important of these is the breaking of bread at Jesus' last meal with his followers: "And he took bread, and when he had given thanks he broke it and gave it to them" (22:19). The wording is so similar that Luke must intend for his readers to connect the events at Emmaus and in the upper room.

Luke shows special interest in the fellowship Jesus enjoys with his followers at meals. References to the "breaking of bread" in Acts 2:46 and 20:7 also suggest a sacred meal shared by believers. The symbolic element in the Emmaus resurrection story impresses the two travelers; when they report to the circle of disciples in Jerusalem, they tell "how he was known to them in the breaking of the bread" (24:35). Luke's inclusion of the episode is, therefore, thematic.

Jesus' conversation with the travelers is also significant. He gives them a Bible lesson:

> And he said to them, "O foolish men, and slow of heart to believe all that the prophets have spoken! Was it not necessary that the Christ should suffer these things and enter into his glory?" And beginning with Moses and all the prophets, he interpreted to them in all the scriptures the things concerning himself. (24:25-27)

Matthew uses the same method of instruction. His Gospel begins with several references to biblical passages that he says have been fulfilled by Jesus' birth. Although Luke's account cites no specific passages from Moses and the prophets at this point, the importance in Luke of scriptural fulfillment is obvious. Jesus' suffering and death are completely in accordance with scripture; that is, with God's will. In his last meeting with his disciples, Jesus gives them the same lesson he gave the travelers:

> Then he said to them "These are my words which I spoke to you, while I was still with you, that everything written about me in the law of Moses, and the prophets and the psalms must be fulfilled." Then he opened their minds to understand the scriptures, and said to them, "Thus it is written, that the Christ should suffer and on the third day rise from the dead, and that repentance and forgiveness of sins should be preached in his name to all nations, beginning from Jerusalem." (24:44-47)

These two statements by Jesus about the fulfillment of scriptures reaffirm the theme introduced in the opening sections of the Gospel: the events of the story fulfill promises made to Abraham. Jesus continues the story of Israel. His last lecture ends where his ministry began in Nazareth (4:16-21), with emphasis on fulfillment of scriptures. Furthermore, the story that began in the Temple with Zechariah, the priest, ends in the Temple with Jesus' followers worshiping God as good Jews. Luke does not imply that a new religious movement has been born. Rather, the history of Israel has moved through an important new stage.

Still, Jesus' last speech is a transition as well as a conclusion. It is a programmatic description of what will follow. The book of Acts traces the progress of those who preach repentance and forgiveness of sins to all nations, from holy Jerusalem (Acts 1–7) to imperial Rome (28). Acts records the second half of the fulfillment of scripture; the story of the early church, like that of Jesus, is continuous with the story of Israel. Luke's concern to demonstrate this continuity, based on proper interpretation of scripture, abounds in Acts. His reports of the great speeches of Peter, Stephen, and Paul (2, 3, 7, and 13) include specific scriptural proofs. This concern is an important key to the interpretation of the two-volume work as a whole.

Summary

All four Gospels end with an account of Jesus' resurrection, yet each Gospel tells it with slight differences in accordance with the themes being developed. This chapter compares the three Synoptic Gospels and suggests some reasons for their variant accounts.

The resurrection theme has been woven into the story, mentioned by Jesus five times before he dies. Yet Mark's ending—describing the women fleeing from the empty tomb in astonishment and fear, telling no one—is extremely abrupt and leaves many questions unanswered. How did the others find out? Why are there no post-resurrection appearances, as in the other Gospels? The abrupt ending culminates the theme of mystery that has enshrouded the whole of Jesus' ministry in this Gospel. Mark has forced the resolution of the story and its meaning onto the reader at a level outside the story's boundaries.

Matthew ties together everything that Mark had left unresolved. The women flee in joy, meet the risen Jesus on the way, and tell the disciples, who go to Galilee as they have been commanded. There they encounter Jesus on a mountain: as in the life of Moses, Jesus gives his major teaching (the Sermon on the Mount) and his farewell address from a mountain. Matthew pursues another theme when he includes a story of Pilate's placing guards at the tomb. From the evangelist's perspective, the story serves to substantiate the claim that Jesus has been raised, while it mocks the attempts of Jewish leaders to discredit that claim.

Yet, as in Mark, Matthew's ending is also intentionally unfinished. The disciples are commanded to go out and win converts, secure in Jesus' promise to be with them to the end of the age. Thus the story's ultimate conclusion will be on that last day, which is anticipated but not described in Matthew's Gospel.

In Luke, the women tell of the empty tomb, but the tale is not believed until Jesus appears to them while the disciples are still in Jerusalem. Jesus also appears to two travelers on the road to Emmaus. He explains how his suffering and death have all been in accordance with scripture, showing Luke's concern to develop the continuity between the story of Israel and the story of Jesus.

An equally strong concern for Luke is to point up the continuity between the story (era) of Jesus and the story (era) of the church. The travelers recognize the stranger when he "took the bread and blessed, and broke it, and gave it to them"—the language making a bridge between Jesus' last supper and the communion meal of the early church. Thus the ending of the Gospel concludes only the first part of Luke's story; it also serves as a transition into the Acts of the Apostles, where the story of Jesus (and of Israel) is continued as the story of the church bringing its message from Jerusalem to Rome.

CHAPTER EIGHT

THE GOSPEL OF MARK

The Gospel of Mark has been something of an embarrassment to the church. If the majority of critical scholars are correct, two thorough revisions of Mark—by Matthew and Luke—appeared not more than a decade later and very nearly displaced the original. The church fathers rarely quote Mark; the historic lectionary cycles (series of texts read at public worship) virtually ignore him.

One reason for the Gospel's lack of popularity was its ostensibly coarse and "unliterary" quality. The earliest extant reference to Mark in the early church comes from about the first quarter of the second century:

> Mark, who had been Peter's interpreter, wrote down carefully, but not in order, all that he remembered of the Lord's sayings and doings. For he had not heard the Lord or been one of His followers, but later, as I said, one of Peter's. Peter used to adapt his teaching to the occasion, without making a systematic arrangement of the Lord's sayings, so that Mark was quite justified in writing down some things just as he remembered them. For he had one purpose only—to leave out nothing that he had heard, and to make no misstatement about it.[1]

Papias, a bishop in Asia Minor, here reflects a widespread concern about the ultimate source of Mark's Gospel. The precise outline of the New Testament canon was not settled until the time of Irenaeus, Bishop of Lyons (about 185 C.E.), and disputes about individual books continued within the Roman Catholic Church until the Council of Trent in 1548. The classic defense for accepting the four canonical Gospels as the only authorized stories of Jesus was that they derived from apostles who traveled with Jesus and were selected by him for such special purposes. Mark's Gospel presented a problem, since it bore the name of one who was not a member of the apostolic circle. According to Papias and all later tradition, Mark's Gospel has its authority from Peter: Mark was his interpreter.

Papias singled out the real problem, however, in his first sentence: Mark did not write things "in order." At first glance, the comment may seem unreasonable, since both Matthew and Luke follow the same chronological order as Mark. But the Greek term for order as used here probably refers to literary symmetry and style: Mark's work does not look like literature. Papias attempts to excuse this apparent failing by arguing that Mark never intended to write a polished piece of literature. He was simply Peter's traveling secretary, concerned only with accurately recording everything Peter said, and Peter evidently never delivered any structured narrative of the life of Jesus.[2]

The main reason the church ignored Mark in favor of the other Gospels was that Mark had so many enigmatic aspects. It does not look like a Gospel: nothing about Jesus' background, little of his teaching, a highly unflattering portrait of the disciples, and—most strange—no account of Jesus' appearance to them after his resurrection. The baffling ending, even more abrupt in the Greek syntax, led more than one scribe to add an appropriate conclusion, as the manuscript evidence indicates.[3] It is ironic that the writer who seems to have invented the literary form and labeled it "the Gospel of Jesus Christ" was ignored by later generations of Christians because his work looked so little like a Gospel.

It is relevant, therefore, to inquire, What is a Gospel? To what sort of literature would his early readers have compared Mark? What were its literary antecedents? To what should it or can it be compared? There are no satisfactory answers to these questions. People have always read Mark in light of the Gospels of Matthew, Luke, and John. In the last decade and a half, however, scholars have become increasingly convinced that when they study Mark by itself and do not measure it by later standards of what a Gospel should be, it reveals signs of artistry and of a unique literary achievement.

Mark's literary "genius" must not be exaggerated, however. As mentioned in an earlier chapter, his Gospel lends itself to piecemeal study because he makes little effort to integrate individual events into the flow of the narrative. Form critics see in this episodic style a suggestion that Mark limited himself to following the contours of the individual story-units from oral tradition, though he may have preserved some stories as parts of cycles. The finished book is "literature" only in a special sense. As Eric Auerbach has pointed out, Mark makes no attempt to respect aesthetic conventions.[4] The Gospel is, nevertheless, carefully written; its form and content support each other. Its genius can be appreciated only when it is understood on its own terms.

I. Narrative Method of Understanding: Two Levels of Meaning

As noted, Mark's narrative does not flow evenly. The first chapters are particularly episodic. Transitions, where they are inserted, are highly artificial and unimaginative: "immediately" or "and immediately" occur six times in the first chapter alone. Such crudities may indicate the unrevised form of the material prior to its incorporation into the literary work. Yet it cannot simply be assumed that the Gospel has no structure, that stories about his hero have been randomly juxtaposed by an editor who has no real awareness of what he is doing. Is there a perspective that will justify or make sense of Mark's stylistic peculiarities? Auerbach suggests that they signal an interest in the narrative at another level of reality.[5]

Unlike most writers of the time, Mark presents few details of setting, characters, or events. Seemingly essential information is often lacking, so that some passages appear incomprehensible. Beneath the surface, however, even the most puzzling details and omissions do seem to have a function. In Auerbach's opinion, Mark includes only what is essential to his purpose, and since his overall purpose controls his material, the work must be studied as a unity. To interpret the Gospel, one must try to develop some view of Mark's own conception of his work and his principles of selection.

A. Healing the Blind

It has already been noted that Mark's account of Jesus' trial and death must be read at two levels. On the surface, the characters in the drama play out their roles as they understand them; beneath is the level at which only the reader understands the real meaning of the events. Dramatic irony runs through Mark's passion story.

The same device characterizes Mark's strangely isolated accounts of the restoration of sight to blind men. Most of the miracle stories in Mark cluster in blocks in chapters 5–8. He includes only two reports of Jesus' healing of blind men, both of them outside those clusters. Like the other miracles, these healings give evidence of Jesus' power. Their most important function in the narrative, however, is figurative. Both occur at points in the story when the "blindness" of those around Jesus is most pronounced.

The first of the two stories, one in which a blind man is healed in two stages (Mark 8:22-26), occurs immediately after Jesus has reproached his disciples for failing to understand the two feeding miracles ("Having eyes do you not see, and having ears do you not hear?" [verse 18]) and just prior to Peter's confession (verses 29-33). Peter's confession that Jesus is the Christ indicates that he has "seen" something, although his inability to accept Jesus' suffering implies that he has not seen everything. Peter also needs two stages before his eyes will be completely opened. Mark's juxtaposition can hardly be accidental.

Similarly, just before the healing of blind Bartimaeus, Jesus' disciples argue once again about status, proving their continued lack of insight. After healing Bartimaeus, Jesus enters Jerusalem, to be rejected by the Jewish leaders, executed by the Romans, and mocked as "Christ, the King of Israel" and "King of the Jews." Yet blind Bartimaeus recognizes Jesus as the true "Son of David" (10:48). Those with eyes are blind, while the blind see. Although Mark has made little effort to integrate these two healings aesthetically into the surface flow of the story, they have important illustrative functions at the second level.

B. The Demons' Confessions

Mark's method of narrating both these healings and the passion story indicates his preoccupation with this second deeper level of meaning—to the exclusion of other considerations. Some things he mentions do not make sense. For example, Mark reports that whenever demons beheld Jesus, "they fell down before him and cried out, 'You are the Son of God'" (3:11). The Gerasene demoniac cries out "with a loud voice" that Jesus is "Son of the Most High God" (5:7). There is no hint that Jesus was alone when this happened; yet when Jesus asks his disciples whom people believe him to be, no one suggests that he is the Son of God. How could the disciples have failed to hear the cries of the demons or to understand what they said? Here again, some commentators view the confessions of the demoniacs as unassimilated tradition that the evangelist has unthinkingly incorporated into his work.

From a different perspective, however, Mark seems to be in control of his method. Unlike characters in the story, the reader has known from the beginning of the Gospel that Jesus is Christ and Son of God; he knows that God called Jesus his "Son" (1:11). The confessions of supernatural beings are evidently intended to corroborate the narrator's claims about Jesus' identity.

A better artist might have written the story so that it made sense on both levels of the narrative, with its transitions smooth and its details fitting more neatly into larger wholes. Mark's interest lies elsewhere, and it is no service to him to try to fill in narrative lapses (for example, adding that the disciples were busy with something else while the demoniacs were making their confessions). There is no evidence that Mark has even tried to sketch a consistent picture—at least at one level of the story. Study of the trial, of the healings of the blind men, and of the confessions of the demons reinforces the opinion that the unity of the work lies at the deeper level of the story, the level that reads the "gospel of Jesus Christ, the Son of God." Mark makes sense only when one is constantly aware of the distance the writer has imposed between the reader and the characters and events of the story.

II. Structure: Galilee/Jerusalem

Geography structures Mark's Gospel quite simply. Jesus' preaching and healing ministry takes place in Galilee (chaps.

1–10); his final confrontation with the Jewish and Roman leaders occurs in Jerusalem (chaps. 11–15). The story ends with a promise to return to Galilee after his resurrection (16:7). This geographical division is most general, however; one cannot trace Jesus' movements in detail on a map because too much is left out. Yet the movement from Galilee to Jerusalem seems to be a significant pattern in Mark's Gospel. The Gospel of John demonstrates that Mark's is not the only pattern possible. In John, Jesus visits Jerusalem frequently; furthermore, Jesus travels to Galilee only when he encounters hostility in Judea (John 7:1-9). Why has Mark structured his story with only one visit to Jerusalem? In Luke, Jesus appears in Jerusalem to his disciples after the resurrection. Why, according to Mark, does Jesus tell his disciples to meet him in Galilee (Mark 14:28; 16:7)? For Mark, Galilee and Jerusalem may serve as symbols as well as geographical locations.

The variety of explanations scholars offer for Mark's interest in Galilee indicates uncertainty as to its significance, but that of Jerusalem is easier to appreciate.[6] Jerusalem symbolizes the climactic events toward which the Gospel's story relentlessly moves. It is the religious capital of Israel, the place where the Temple is located. It is also the seat of the religious and political authorities, who will, in the name of tradition and political stability, have Jesus arrested and executed. Jerusalem is important not simply as a location but as the place where Jesus will die.

The Jerusalem phase of Jesus' career dominates Mark's Gospel. Although it comprises only one week out of Jesus' total ministry, Mark devotes more than one-third of his Gospel to that week, almost one-sixth to the last day. Early in the Gospel, one hears rumblings from the storm gathering in Jerusalem. Even while Jesus is still in the north, the "scribes who came down from Jerusalem" (3:22) characterize him as a demoniac, and in chapter 6, the Pharisees and "some of the scribes, who had come from Jerusalem" verbally attack Jesus again. In 8:31, Jesus announces to his disciples that he is going to Jerusalem to die, a prediction repeated twice in subsequent chapters (9:31; 10:33). Tying the story together, at least in a general way, is the inexorable movement toward Jerusalem, the place of death.

III. Theme: The Hidden Messiah

A. Revelation to the Reader

The main unifying theme of Mark's Gospel might be called the unveiling of the hidden Messiah. Ever since Wilhelm Wrede's work at the turn of the century, scholars have referred to "the messianic secret motif" in Mark.[7] Jesus' identity is a mystery to the participants in the story, and although the opening says that Jesus is the "Christ, the Son of God," even for the reader there is still an enigma. What does it mean to be Messiah and Son of God? This, too, is a messianic secret. The narrator gives no definitions, tells no birth stories, presents no genealogy. As the story unfolds, the reader can readily see that Jesus is not Messiah in any traditional sense. Without background information, Jesus' Messiahship is puzzling. The reader must assume that the story will explain in just what sense Jesus is Messiah and Son of God, and why the book should be viewed as "gospel"—that is, as "good news."

The reader gets no help from character development or from intrusion into the consciousness of Jesus. The narrator never reports what led Jesus to submit to baptism by John, to preach, or suddenly to "set his face toward Jerusalem." Nevertheless, as the story progresses, the reader does learn what it means to call Jesus Messiah and Son of God. This process of revelation is the thread that ties Mark's story together for the reader.

But only for the reader. Even Jesus' disciples never achieve full enlightenment. The characters react to each new bit of revelation with either misunderstanding or heightened hostility. Study of the trial and passion narratives showed that the most important revelations about Jesus come at moments when misunderstanding is at its peak, when the participants in the drama are utterly incapable of enlightenment. Even the empty tomb only terrifies the group of women into withholding the good news of the resurrection. The reader's interest here, however, lies not in the obstacles of Jesus' unveiling of his identity to the characters in the story but in Mark's exposing of the meaning of Jesus' Messiahship to the reader. An examination of five aspects of this latter revelation is necessary: (1) the trial and crucifixion, (2) Peter's confession, (3) Jesus as Son of Man, (4) the confessions of demoniacs, and (5) discipleship.

1. Trial and Crucifixion. Mark's opening sentence calls Jesus "Christ" (Greek for Messiah, or anointed one) and "Son of God," and his later use of these terms is significant. The former is notably absent from much of the story. Together with related royal titles and imagery, it appears almost exclusively in the account of Jesus' trial and execution. Although the second term, "Son of God," occurs more frequently in Mark, the trial and crucifixion narratives seem to give it a special importance too. The full confession with which the Gospel begins, using both terms, recurs only once in the story, in the question from the high priest at the trial: "Again the high priest asked him, 'Are you the Christ, the Son of the Blessed?' And Jesus said, 'I am'" (14:61-62).

For the first and only time in the Gospel, Jesus openly acknowledges his identity, and his titles are those of 1:1. From there on, the two terms—Christ (and its implied synonym, the anointed King of the Jews) and Son of God—appear frequently in accusations, mockings, and condemnations. (The Jewish equivalents are "King of Israel" and "Son of the Blessed.") At the moment of his death, another climactic moment in the story, a centurion unknowingly testifies that the King of the Jews is the "Son of God." This recurrent use of the two titles, and their synonyms, suggests that the decisive revelation occurs—paradoxically—at Jesus' trial and crucifixion. As seen earlier, Jesus is revealed as Messiah and Son of God through events that, on the surface, appear least messianic in the traditional sense and least characteristic of what one might expect of the Son of God.

2. Peter's Confession. Although the decisive stage of the revelation of Jesus begins with his trial and death, earlier turning points in the story are critical in the process of the unveiling. Peter's confession (8:30) is the first occasion on which Jesus is called Messiah. Prior to this, Mark provides a great deal of information about Jesus. Jesus is a worker of wonders with power over demons and disease, a teacher, a person with the authority to forgive sins (2:5), and one whom "even wind and sea obey" (4:41). Mark reports to the reader that God himself calls Jesus "Son" at his baptism, and the demons recognize him as "the Holy One of God," "Son of God," and "Son of the Most High God"—regardless of what people present heard or understood.

Peter's confession represents both a summary of what has preceded and the transition to a new phase of the story. Jesus' ministry in Galilee has ended; he now begins his fateful trip to Jerusalem. The story pauses for an evaluation, echoing an earlier question of the astounded disciples: "Who then can this be?"

> And Jesus went on with his disciples, to the village of Caesarea Philippi; and on the way he asked his disciples, "Who do men say that I am?" And they told him, "John the Baptist; and others say, Elijah; and others one of the prophets." And he asked them, "But who do you say that I am?" Peter answered him, "You are the Christ." And he charged them to tell no one about him. (8:27-30)

Those who have witnessed Jesus' healings, exorcisms, miraculous feedings of five and four thousand people, and teaching "with authority" consider him a prophet (or perhaps *the* prophet) because his Galilean ministry has been in the prophetic tradition, as noted. Those who interpret the signs and wonders as the work of the awaited prophet have understood something—but they do not yet know the real secret of his identity. Peter's confession is presented as a contrast: "But who do you say I am?" Until now, evidently, no one thought of Jesus as the Messiah; Peter's perception is something new. Jesus' strange response, "And he charged them to tell no one about him," leaves some question in the reader's mind about the appropriateness of the confession. Its timeliness rather than its truth, however, seems at issue. The contrast between Peter and "others" as well as the importance the title "Christ" assumes later in the story suggest that Peter is correct; Jesus is more than a prophet. His order to keep this information silent probably should be viewed as similar to the commands directed to the demons, especially in 3:11-12.

Peter's confession of Jesus as Messiah is not the only signal that the revelation both of his identity (to the disciples) and of the meaning of that identity (to Mark's readers) has moved to another important stage. On this occasion, Jesus for the first time explicitly predicts his death. Mark's transitions are abrupt, but his placement of the first prediction of the passion immediately after the confession of Jesus as Christ is a careful choice. Jesus' prediction of his impending death conflicts with Peter's image of Jesus as Messiah:

> And he began to teach them that the Son of man must suffer many things, and be rejected by the elders and the chief priests and the scribes, and be killed, and after three days rise again. And he said this plainly. And Peter took him, and began to rebuke him. But turning and seeing his disciples, he rebuked Peter, and said, "Get behind me, Satan! For you are not on the side of God, but of men." (8:31-33)

Peter's confession is another example of the ambiguity that runs through the story: he understands, yet he does not understand. He has seen something the crowds have not, but something more remains to be revealed.

Some scholars have suggested that Jesus' rebuke here definitely implies his total rejection of the messianic concept, because his coming suffering conflicts with that concept as Jews of his day knew it. The suggestion is based on the profound differences between later Christian conceptions of Messiah and traditional Jewish views. The Jewish Messiah was expected to be a king and deliverer; he was not expected to fail, much less to die at the hands of foreigners.

The form and content of Peter's confession and the importance of the messianic titles at the beginning and end of the story do not support such an interpretation. Jesus is the Messiah; the reader has known that from the beginning of the Gospel. Peter has come to believe that Jesus is the Christ—but he does not yet perceive what that means. The tension between Peter's confession and Jesus' prediction of his death appropriately reflects the contrast between traditional Jewish messianic conceptions and the Christian confession of Jesus as Messiah. At this point in the Gospel, the writer seems to be leading the reader to arrive at a new definition of Messiahship, a process that continues until the end of the story. Jesus is Christ, but he is the Christ who dies on a cross as a ransom for many.

Peter's confession thus divides the Gospel into two parts. In the first, devoted to Jesus' teaching and healing ministry, the predominant imagery is prophetic. As teacher and healer and worker of signs and wonders, he is accepted by contemporaries as a prophet. Huge crowds follow him; his activities elicit amazement and awe.

Following Peter's confession, Mark portrays Jesus primarily as the one who must die—but also, as seen in the study of the trial and passion stories, as the crucified Messiah. For Mark, the suffering and death are the key to the reader's understanding of Jesus. Yet the prediction of these crucial events initiates the period of greatest misunderstanding, culminating in the flight of Jesus' disciples, Peter's denial, and Jesus' condemnation and death. The revelation in this second stage of the story does not supplant what has been learned about Jesus in the first eight chapters, but it does suggest that the real secret of Jesus' identity does not lie simply in his teaching or his miracles.

3. The Son of Man. In Mark's Gospel, others refer to Jesus as the Messiah and Son of God. But he calls himself the Son of man. Scholars have puzzled over this strange title without reaching a consensus.[8] Jesus uses the expression without qualification throughout the early passages (2:10, 28; 8:31, 38; 9:9, 31; 10:31, 45).

In chapters 13 and 14, Jesus becomes more specific, identifying himself repeatedly as the Son of man described in Daniel.

> I saw in the night visions, and behold, with the clouds of heaven there came one like a son of man, and he came to the Ancient of Days and was presented before him. And to him was given dominion and glory and kingdom, that all peoples, nations, and languages should serve him. (Dan. 7:13-14)

In Mark 13:24-27, Jesus promises his followers that he will return as Son of man "in clouds with great power and glory," to gather the "elect" who have remained faithful from the ends of the earth. At his trial before the Sanhedrin Jesus tells his judges: "And you will see the Son of man seated at the right hand of Power, and coming with the clouds of heaven" (Mark 14:62). In these two passages, the expression "Son of man" seems to be a title that refers to a definite figure. Yet that meaning of the title is not apparent elsewhere in Mark—or in the other Gospels.

This title is used only by Jesus to speak of himself; the only exceptions in the New Testament are in Acts 7:56; Hebrews 2:6; Revelation 1:13, 14:14. Nowhere else does anyone confess Jesus as Son of man. Little is lost by accepting the term as merely an enigmatic self-designation (except in the two instances in chaps. 13 and 14). What is important is not that Jesus called himself Son of man, but what he says about himself as Son of man. The occurrence of the expression in Daniel is certainly important for the New Testament writers, but it is not at all clear that the scriptural connotation is present whenever the title is used.

Some scholars have proposed that the revelations of Jesus as Daniel's coming Son of man are the primary ones in Mark's Gospel and that the title itself has a special meaning, having little to do with the portrait of Jesus as Messiah. On the contrary, however, these two Son of man passages—Mark 13:26 and 14:62—function precisely within the messianic theme. In both of these references to Daniel, two promises about the Son of man point the reader to the vindication of Jesus as Messiah. The first assures his followers that those who remain faithful and refuse to follow false Christs and prophets (13:21-22) will be vindicated in the eyes of all the world. The second vows that those chief priests, scribes, and elders who believe the claims about Jesus as "the Christ, the Son of the Blessed" to be blasphemous, "will see." When Jesus is enthroned at God's right hand at his resurrection, and when he returns from heaven, they too will know that he is the Messiah, the Son of God.

4. The Son of God. Mark's Gospel begins, as the reader recalls, with two titles: "Christ" (Messiah, anointed King) and "Son of God." Both are prominent toward the end of the Gospel, but the former title is not used until Peter's confession, as a step in the progressive unveiling of Jesus—to the disciples (who he is) and to the reader (what it means to call him Jesus Christ, the Son of God). The use of the title "Son of God," however, is more complicated, for it is applied to Jesus in passages of considerable significance in the early portion of the Gospel.

1:11: At his baptism, Jesus is called "Son" by God himself: "Thou art my beloved Son; with thee I am well pleased."

3:11: Summarizing Jesus' ministry at the sea, the narrator comments: "And whenever the unclean spirits beheld him, they fell down before him and cried out, 'You are the Son of God.'" But strangely, Jesus commands them "not to make him known." He presumably does not wish to be recognized as the Son of God.

5:7: The Gerasene demoniac cries out that Jesus is the "Son of the Most High God."

9:7: On the mount of transfiguration, God once again calls Jesus "Son."

In a sense, these revelations of Jesus as the Son of God seem gratuitous. None of the episodes has much impact on the story. The voice at Jesus' baptism is intended for him alone (God addresses him in the second person). At his transfiguration, the disciples appear too dumbfounded to understand what has just happened. And no one seems to hear (or, at least, pay any attention to) the demoniacs. Prior to the question of the high priest in 14:61, only supernatural beings use the words "Son of God." Only God himself and the demons know that Jesus is God's Son. To the characters in the story, Jesus' true identity is unknown and, according to Mark, that is what Jesus intends.

Obviously, if the confessions of the demoniacs and the baptism and transfiguration have virtually no impact on the characters in the story, Mark must include them for the sake of the reader. They provide momentary flashes of light, glimpses into the mystery of Jesus' identity, reinforcing what the reader has been told at the beginning of the story. These four flashes of insight are necessary reminders to the reader in a story which, at least for the characters, provides so little real illumination: contrary to appearances, Jesus is really God's Son.

5. Discipleship. Understanding what it means to call Jesus "Christ" and "Son of God" has existential implications for his followers, for Christians. This is clearest in chapters 8–10. Jesus' first prediction of his own suffering in 8:31 introduces a discussion of discipleship that comes to a climax in 10:45: "For the Son of man also came not to be served but to serve, and to give his life as a ransom for many."

A person who truly understands Jesus' messianic role and copies his example will "take up his cross and follow" (8:34). One who would be first must be last and servant of all (9:35). Again, whoever desires to be great among Jesus' followers must be the slave of all (10:42-44). The revelation of the pattern of real discipleship is simply the other side of the revelation of true Messiahship. And, according to Mark, the disciples miss the point in both cases. The disciples' role in the Gospel as a whole is varied and complex, but, in chapters 8–10, they serve almost exclusively as examples of poor discipleship. Each of Jesus' predictions of suffering is followed by an inappropriate response from his followers. In 8:32, Peter "rebukes" Jesus for suggesting that he must die; suffering has no part in Peter's conception of either Messiahship or discipleship. As Jesus is predicting his death for the second time in 9:31, his disciples are discussing which of them is the greatest (9:34). Jesus' last announcement of his imminent death is followed by a request from the two sons of Zebedee for special status in the messianic kingdom. Each of these unsuitable reactions provides an occasion for a discourse on true discipleship.

Mark's portrait of the disciples is congruent with the basic motifs in his Gospel: the revelation of the hidden and the ironic contrast between appearance and reality. The disciples exemplify those who confuse appearance and reality, less perverse than the scribes and chief priests who condemn Jesus to death, but equally fatal for living a meaningful life. Ambitious self-seeking is an equally false response to the Christ who, as Mark says, has come to "give his life as a ransom for many" (10:45). The ironic mode pervades the book, from theme to the role of characters.

B. Mystery for the Characters

The progressive revelation of what sort of Messiah Jesus is seems intended only for the reader. For those in the story, the mystery surrounding Jesus becomes more and more impenetrable. Those who witness Jesus' miracles and listen to his teachings "see, but do not perceive, hear but do not understand." Their increasing confusion is a basic motif in the Gospel and acts as a counterpoint to the revelation that occurs for the reader. Following is an examination of the motif as Mark develops it, first with the crowds and Jewish religious figures, then with the insiders, the disciples.

1. Outsiders. In explaining the parable of the sower, Jesus makes a division. There are those—presumably his followers—to whom the secret of the kingdom of God has been given, and there are others "outside" (4:11). From the beginning of Jesus' ministry, outsiders challenge his ministry.

2:1-12: In the course of healing a paralytic, Jesus declares that the man's sins are forgiven; Jesus then tells his audience that he will heal the paralytic, so "that you may know that the Son of man has authority on earth to forgive sins." Some witnesses are amazed, but the scribes view Jesus' claim of authority to forgive sins as blasphemous—the same charge by which Jesus is condemned at the trial before the Sanhedrin.

3:1-6: Jesus cures a man with a withered hand on the sabbath, a violation of tradition that occasions a plot against Jesus by the Pharisees and the Herodians.

3:20-27: Jesus has demonstrated his power to cast out demons, who recognize him as Son of God (3:11). The "scribes who came down from Jerusalem," however, attribute his power over demons to his own demonic possession (verse 22). In the same incident, his relatives believe that he is "beside himself" (verse 21) and try to take him home; in that crowd, according to Mark, are his brothers and mother (verses 31-32).

6:1-6: After a successful ministry elsewhere, Jesus

returns to his "own country" where his former
neighbors take offense at the now-famous carpenter. Even Jesus "marveled because of their
unbelief."

This unbelief, challenges, and hostility, as we have seen, are
most pronounced at the conclusion of the Gospel and most
pronounced among the religious and political leaders of the
people. Those to whom others turn for enlightenment are
themselves the least enlightened. Members of the Sanhedrin
consider Jesus' claim blasphemous, and on that basis, they
condemn him to death. The Romans interpret the claims to
royalty as seditious, and on that basis, they execute Jesus with
two other revolutionaries as "King of the Jews." Even Jesus'
final cry of dereliction is misinterpreted. His death is the
culmination of the misunderstanding and hostility of outsiders
that he encountered throughout his ministry.

2. The Disciples. On the one hand, Mark makes a clear
distinction between Jesus' disciples and others. Jesus chooses
a small group to be "fishers of men" (1:17); he appoints
twelve "to be with him, and to be sent out to preach and have
authority to cast out demons" (3:14). His disciples accompany
him throughout his ministry. They are insiders to whom the
secret of the kingdom of God has been given (4:11), including
private explanations of all the parables (verse 34). On three
occasions, Jesus explicitly tells them that he will die (8:31;
9:31; 10:33); five times he predicts that he will be raised from
the dead (8:31; 9:9, 31; 10:34; 14:28). There is evidence that
the disciples are enlightened: sent out on a mission to preach,
heal, and cast out demons (6:7-13), they apparently enjoy
some measure of success. As the spokesman, Peter recognizes, as others have not, that Jesus is more than a prophet, he
is the Messiah (8:27-30). The disciples are among those who
have "left everything and followed" (10:28).

On the other hand, Mark repeatedly shows that even the
disciples, like the outsiders, never really understand. Twice
Jesus calms the elements and twice he feeds the multitudes; all
four miracles baffle his disciples:

4:35-40: Immediately after the parables (all of which have
been explained to the disciples), the disciples and
Jesus are caught in a storm crossing the Sea of

Galilee. Jesus calms the storm, then asks his disciples: "'Why are you afraid? Have you no faith?' And they were filled with awe, and said to one another, 'Who then is this, that even wind and sea obey him?'" Those to whom the secret of the kingdom of God has been given do not know who Jesus is.

6:45-52: After the feeding of the five thousand, the disciples put out to sea without Jesus. When they see him walking on the water, they are terrified. Jesus tries to calm them and gets into the boat with them, at which time the wind ceases. The narrator continues: "And they were utterly astounded, for they did not understand about the loaves, but their hearts were hardened."

8:14-21: After the feeding of the four thousand, Jesus makes a comment about the "leaven of the Pharisees and the leaven of Herod," which his disciples completely misunderstand. Jesus says to them, "Why do you discuss the fact that you have no bread? Are your hearts hardened? *Having eyes do you not see, and having ears do you not hear?* And do you not remember?" Jesus uses the same words to describe his followers (taken from Isa. 6:9-10) that he used for the "outsiders," those to whom the secret of the kingdom had not been given (4:11-12). Astonishingly, Jesus' followers are equally unenlightened at this point.

As noted previously, each of Jesus' predictions of his impending suffering and death is immediately followed by some indication that his followers misunderstand his words.

8:31—First prediction

8:32. Peter rebukes Jesus for suggesting that Jesus, the Messiah, will suffer and die.

9:31—Second prediction

9:32-37. It is revealed that while Jesus was talking about his impending death, his disciples were discussing which of them is the greatest.

10:33-34—Third prediction

10:35-37. The two sons of Zebedee request that they be

given places of honor in Jesus' kingdom, which makes the rest of Jesus' disciples indignant.

Despite Jesus' repeated and detailed predictions, his followers are completely unprepared for what is to come; and under the pressure of events, the circle collapses. Judas betrays him; after the arrest, all but Peter flee; and finally, Peter, who swore he would never fall away (14:29), denies him three times. Even the women who learn about the resurrection run away in terror, unprepared for what they find at the tomb. None of the characters in the story ever resolves the Christ-mystery.

Jesus' followers differ greatly from the hostile chief priests and scribes, who reject Jesus in favor of their own tradition. The disciples have been prepared to continue his ministry of preaching, healing, and casting out demons. They lack only the final insight, the decisive illumination. Although they do not achieve it in Mark's Gospel, he clearly implies that it will come.

> And he said to them, "Is a lamp brought in to be put under a bushel, or under a bed, and not on a stand? For there is nothing hid, except to be made manifest; nor is anything secret, except to come to light." (4:21-22)

The present is a time of uncertainty and secrecy, but this will not always be so. The parables in Mark contrast a time of small, unpromising beginnings with the coming time of harvest, which is also the time of openness. Jesus emphasizes and clarifies the contrast: "And as they were coming down the mountain, he charged them to tell no one what they had seen, *until the Son of man should have risen from the dead*" (9:9).

In a sense the failure of the disciples to understand Jesus shows an almost incomprehensible stupidity and provides a contrast to proper discipleship. In another sense, however, their failure is not so much their fault as it is due to the inherent nature of the Christ-mystery. The kingdom of God and Jesus' messianic office are matters outside normal human understanding. Mark presents them as a challenging mystery or secret beyond the grasp of all but the demons. The disciples can not know who Jesus is during his ministry because it is not yet the time of openness. This is as Jesus and, indeed, God himself intend. Even the misunderstanding is part of the plan. The Son of man "goes as it is written of him" (14:21). The secret is not to be kept forever; it will be disclosed—after the Resurrection. The time of unveiling is also the time of mission; that is, the time of the church.

Mark clearly assumed that by the time he wrote his Gospel the secret had been revealed to the reader as well as to the disciples. From the outset, his readers know that Jesus is the Messiah, Son of God; that he was raised after three days; that he is presently seated at God's right hand; and that he will soon return to gather his elect. If this is the case, why do the characters never solve the mystery of Jesus' identity and mission within the story? If the Gospel is intended to enlighten the reader about Jesus' Messiahship and about proper discipleship, why does the writer take such pains to underline again and again the absolute inability of Jesus' contemporaries to understand him? Or to put the question in literary terms, how is one to reconcile the two strands—the mystery that eludes the characters and the revelation that the reader already knows about? What is revealed to the reader is a "mystery"—but in a different sense.

C. Mysterious Revelation

At the surface level, within the world of the characters, Mark's story is a tragedy: a potentially great man's aspirations outrun his abilities. Jesus defies tradition and institutional powers, even implies that his power is from God himself. Ultimately he is unable to communicate with anyone, even his followers; his movement collapses, and he is crushed by the tradition and institutions he opposed.

Beneath that level, in the world of Mark and his reader, the hero, Jesus Christ, the Son of God, is vindicated. Contrary to all appearances, Jesus is the true Messiah, and all that happens to him is according to God's plan. Even the hostility and ridicule are part of his plan, to provide further confirmation that Jesus is the Messiah-King who was foretold. Mark's method of narration, telling the story at two levels, makes possible the literary expression of the fundamental Christian paradox: Jesus is most messianic when he looks least like the traditional Messiah; his greatest spiritual triumph occurs at the moment of greatest ostensible weakness.

Mark does not falsify Jesus' historical career in telling the story as he does. Jesus' contemporaries did not hail him as Messiah. The leaders of the Jewish community rejected him, and the Romans executed him as a political criminal. The tension in Mark between the two motifs—the revelation and the lack of understanding—reflects the tension between Jesus and tradition. For the characters in the story, particularly the representatives from the Jewish religious establishment, reality is defined by tradition, by institutions, and by common sense. Measured by these standards, the claim that Jesus is the Messiah and that his ministry represents the inauguration of God's kingdom appears absurd. Yet that is precisely the claim the Gospel makes. Jesus' resurrection has exploded the old standards of reality and appearance, truth and absurdity. Those to whom this is revealed and who understand the secret can no longer measure reality and truth by convention, by institutional standards, or even by common sense.

Although the gospel account ends without the resolution of this final mystery, the whole narrative presupposes that Jesus' followers did eventually see the risen Lord and understand the meaning of his life and death. Mark emphasizes the mystery of the Gospel of Jesus Christ, the Son of God. Jesus is the awaited Messiah—but an unconventional King who has come to give his life as a ransom for many. The story discloses this mysterious paradox, but only to those who have the eyes to see beneath the surface, those for whom the Resurrection has provided insight. To be a true disciple of the crucified Messiah, the reader must be prepared to accept a new definition of Messiahship, based on a new standard of reality and truth. To succeed where the disciples failed, the reader must be prepared to abandon the security of tradition and institutions, even of common sense, to find security where there appears to be none. The gospel of Jesus Christ is not for everyone, says Mark. It is only for those to whom this mystery has been revealed.

Yet even the elect need reminders. Like the disciples, the readers may be unprepared for the difficult times ahead and found wanting in the hour of crisis. Even the Easter story in Mark serves as a warning. The frightened women at the tomb provide a final, graphic reminder of the need for constant watchfulness and of the ever-present possibility of failure. For Mark, Jesus' resurrection does not inaugurate the time of harvest and openness and safety anticipated in the parables. Public vindication of Christians and the return of the Son of man are still to come (13:24-27). The present is a time of danger and temptation. Jesus' words to his followers prior to his death appropriately summarize one of Mark's major concerns: "And what I say to you I say to all: Watch" (verse 37).

IV. Authorship, Date, and Purpose

Critical study of the New Testament cannot resolve conclusively the problems of authorship and date of the Gospel of Mark. The Gospel does not mention its writer's name or refer explicitly to sources. Papias is the source of the tradition that the writer was John Mark, who in turn received his information from Peter. One suspects that Papias' comments about authorship were the result of some detective work, in which today's reader may also indulge.[9] Assume that the work now known as the Gospel According to Mark carries that designation early in the second century. Mark is hardly a distinctive name; without further information it would not point to a specific person. But there is a person named Mark elsewhere in the New Testament:

> Acts 12:12, 25: "When he [Peter] realized this, he went to the house of Mary, the mother of John whose other name was Mark, where many were gathered together and were praying. . . .And Barnabas and Saul returned from Jerusalem when they had fulfilled their mission, bringing with them John whose other name was Mark."
>
> Colossians 4:10: "Aristarchus my fellow prisoner greets you, and Mark the cousin of Barnabas."
>
> I Peter 5:12-13: "By Silvanus, a faithful brother as I regard him, I have written briefly to you, exhorting and declaring that this is the true grace of God; stand fast in it. She who is at Babylon, who is likewise chosen, sends you greetings; and so does my son Mark."

This is not a great deal of information about Mark, but it is perhaps sufficient to explain the origin of the tradition. The key passage is the last one. There is no way of knowing whether this reference is to the same Mark who traveled with Paul and Barnabas. In the absence of other information, the indication that someone named Mark was associated with Peter would have provided for early Christians the necessary link between Mark and Peter, one of Jesus' group, thus conferring apostolic authority on the Gospel.

The majority of scholars today question the tradition. They base their arguments on the character of the Gospel itself. Although the Greek is far from polished, it is not the product of a resident of Jerusalem, whose mother tongue presumably was Aramaic. More important, the formal characteristics of the stories in Mark suggest that his source was not the reminiscenses of an eyewitness but oral tradition. His writing bears the unmistakable stamp of popular forms of story-telling. This does not imply that Mark had no access to eyewitnesses or that his information is inaccurate. It does make the tradition about Mark as the secretary of Peter questionable. Some scholars still believe the writer was an associate of Peter, however, and they argue that the work betrays a Petrine element. The only certainty is that without further information about the early Christian movement scholarship can not decide the issue definitely.

Evidence for dating the work is even more ambiguous. Recently, scholars tend to date the composition around 70 C.E. because of the particular interest in the destruction of the Temple toward the end of the Gospel. In this view, the narrative is intended to interpret this catastrophic event for troubled people.

If authorship and date are uncertain, one can speak with a bit more assurance about Mark's audience and purpose. Particularly in the thirteenth chapter, the reader senses that a crisis is imminent. The destruction of the Temple ("let the reader understand . . . the desolating sacrilege," 13:14) will signal not the end of the age but the beginning of a time of testing:

> And when you hear of wars and rumors of wars, do not be alarmed; this must take place, but the end is not yet. For nation

> will rise against nation, and kingdom against kingdom; there
> will be earthquakes in various places, there will be famines; this
> is but the beginning of the birth-pangs. (13:7-8)

Christians can expect opposition from Jews (13:9-11) and
dissension within families (verse 12); they can expect false
Messiahs and false prophets who will attempt to "lead astray,
if possible, the elect" (verses 21-22). The whole chapter
presumes an impending difficult period, followed by the
return of Jesus (verses 24-27). Its tone is summarized in the
injunction to believers that they remain firm and alert:

> Watch therefore—for you do not know when the master of the
> house will come, in the evening, or at midnight, or at cockcrow,
> or in the morning—lest he come suddenly and find you asleep.
> And what I say to you I say to all: Watch. (13:35-37)

The Gospel gives other hints about its audiences and
purpose. Mark insists that proper understanding of Jesus has,
as its correlate, proper discipleship. The true follower of Jesus
will take up his cross and follow, and even—like Jesus—give
his life in service to others. The three chapters (8–10) that
discuss discipleship constantly contrast proper and improper
behavior. Those who dispute about which one is the greatest
(9:34-35) or who seek status or authority to lord it over others
(10:35-45) have failed to grasp the meaning of following the
crucified Messiah as true disciples.

This concern with discipleship may be one of Mark's
motives for composing the Gospel. It is not a biography or a
history. Nor does it appear to be missionary literature; a work
that omits any account of Jesus' resurrection appearance can
not have been designed to convince nonbelievers. The Gospel
makes sense if viewed as written for the benefit of believers
who are familiar with the story of Jesus and confess him as
Christ and Son of God. It seems intended as a reminder or
corrective for believers rather than as new information for
potential converts.

The good news that Christians preached to others was that
the crucified Messiah had been raised from the dead, that he
had been enthroned as Lord at God's right hand, and that he
would return to judge the world. In Mark, the emphasis is

reversed. His story of the Messiah and Son of God is of a person whose most revealing act was his death—humiliated, forsaken by his friends, and ridiculed by all—a person who cries, "My God, my God, why have you forsaken me?" Christians at Mark's time, facing times of crisis, may have before them an image of Jesus as hero—a successful miracle-worker and preacher, now triumphantly enthroned in heaven. They may expect victory too soon, by his return and intervention or through their own efforts. Discipleship may have become a matter of success, with Christians competing with one another for power. Have followers of Jesus, in other words, begun to make the measure of truth the same traditional and institutional standards by which Jesus was judged and executed? Such suggestions intrigue the historian of early Christianity.

The literary critic is also looking for the writer's audience and purpose, to furnish a perspective from which Mark's Gospel has literary unity and coherence. Despite some obvious shortcomings of technique, the Gospel deserves to be studied as literature. If the literary form is unconventional, perhaps its unusual subject matter and theme demand an original method of narration. As Auerbach suggests, Mark deserves admiration, not because his work exhibits artistry by traditional standards, but because his Gospel represents a remarkably successful attempt at something new. The old wineskins are no longer sufficient for the new wine.

Summary

The narrator of Mark's Gospel addresses an audience that knows more than the characters in the story, and he tells his story at two levels. Events on the surface are disordered and sometimes baffling, presented with little literary artistry. Beneath that surface, however, the reader may discover a harmonizing perspective and ingenious planning.

In an earlier chapter, this dualism was noted in Mark's account of the trial and death of Jesus. Similarly, the two healings of blind men, which seem to be strangely placed in the story, take on new significance for the reader when they are considered in their contexts. Both healings are preceded by confrontations between Jesus and people who have eyes but cannot "see." Similarly, Mark's structuring the story as a movement from Galilee to Jerusalem may seem fairly crude on the surface. But the careful reader sees that Jerusalem symbolizes the culmination and goal of Jesus' ministry; the story prepares one to see him as the Messiah who must suffer and die.

The theme that gives perspective to Mark's Gospel and controls his selection and ordering of details is the revelation of the mystery of the hidden Messiah. At one level, the mystery for the participants in the story is "Who is Jesus?" At another level, Mark assumes that the reader knows that Jesus is the Christ/Messiah and God's Son; here the mystery is "What does it mean to be Messiah?"

Several episodes reveal answers to the reader's question: As already discussed Jesus is finally and fully revealed to the reader as Messiah and God's Son at the trial and death; this suffering and martyrdom is what it means to be Messiah. Before this, the reader gets the clue from what follows Peter's confession that Jesus is the Messiah—he turns toward the judgment in Jerusalem.

Jesus hints at his identity when, on two occasions, he accompanies his customary self-designation as the Son of man with allusions to Daniel's prophecy. At the baptism and the transfiguration, God calls Jesus his "Son"; so do the demons that Jesus exorcises. Yet Mark clearly indicates that these supernatural revelations are for the benefit of the readers, not for the characters in the story. Furthermore, Mark presents many instances of wrong actions by the disciples; these can only be cautionary examples for the reader.

As for the mystery of Jesus' identity that the characters confront, the Jewish and Roman leaders and the crowds—the outsiders—challenge and finally persecute Jesus; they never catch a glimpse of who Jesus is. The insiders, the disciples, are exposed to the secret of the Kingdom; Jesus explains his parables to them; they preach and heal successfully; their leader, Peter, even says Jesus is the Messiah. Yet they refuse to accept a Messiah who suffers and is put to death, and they think that discipleship is measured by success and power. They never really get to know who Jesus is or fully grasp Jesus' definition of discipleship. The story even stops short of their discovery of the resurrection.

The method of narration on two contradictory levels—mystery for the characters and revelation for the reader—has literary integrity. What is revealed to the reader about the nature of Messiahship and discipleship is a paradox, a mystery: the Messiah triumphs by being defeated; the disciple is first to the extent that she or he is last.

Most critical scholars challenge the tradition that the writer of Mark's Gospel was the John Mark mentioned in Acts and the Epistles, and they date it around 70 C.E., but there is no certainty about the authorship and date. The internal evidence reviewed gives more assurance, however, about Mark's audience and purpose. He writes for believing Christians who know of the resurrection; they are at a period when they need a lesson in the meaning of Messiahship and in the requirements of discipleship.

CHAPTER NINE

LUKE-ACTS

I. Some Problems about Luke's Purpose

Unlike the other Gospels, Luke is only the first part of a two-volume series. Despite their separation in the present New Testament canon, the book belongs with the Acts of the Apostles. Both are dedicated to someone named Theophilus (Luke 1:3; Acts 1:1), and, in the introduction to Acts, the writer refers to his Gospel as "the first book." Each book has a recognizable beginning and ending, so each might justifiably be studied as a separate unit. The total scope of the author's conception—and the place of each book in that conception—can be understood, however, only by studying the Gospel and Acts as part of a single work—referred to as Luke-Acts.

A. The Preface

Uniquely among the evangelists, the author introduces his work (presumably both volumes) with a formal preface—the first four verses of Luke—reflecting the conventions of contemporary historiographers. (One scholarly suggestion, not widely accepted, is that dedicating a work to someone of wealth and position was in antiquity a request for publication, the patron assuming responsibility for the copying and dissemination.)[1] Luke-Acts does seem to be modeled on different literary genre than the other Gospels. The writer appears to have some literary pretension. Like to the Epistle to the Hebrews, the four-verse introduction is one of the finest examples of Greek composition in the New Testament.

The preface is most revealing. Momentarily stepping from the shadows of anonymity typical of the evangelists, Luke tells something about his audience and his conception of his task. He addresses one Theophilus; the passage allows us to say with certainty only that Theophilus is no stranger to the story that follows. He has already "been informed" (Luke 1:4). Therefore, we may assume that Luke does not conceive of his two-part history of Jesus and the Christian movement as missionary literature. Nor does he suggest that he is the first to write a story of Jesus: many others have "undertaken to compile a narrative." Whether the "many" is simply a rhetorical convention or actually refers to several written works familiar to the writer is uncertain, but at least Luke acknowledges that his work is second-generation literature. Unlike the "many others," the writer is no eyewitness to the events; he is, therefore, dependent for his information on traditions "delivered to us by eyewitnesses and ministers of the word."

The preface is not quite clear about why the evangelist has written the two-part history. The answer may lie partially elsewhere, but a proper understanding of this introduction is of considerable importance in determining the writer's purpose. The Greek can be translated variously, and renderings in major recent English versions of the New Testament differ in ways that suggest at least two quite dissimilar views of the purpose and, ultimately, the meaning of Luke-Acts.

> Inasmuch as many have undertaken to compile a narrative of the things which have been accomplished among us, just as they were delivered to us by those who from the beginning were eyewitnesses and ministers of the word, it seemed good to me also, having followed all things closely for some time past, to write an orderly account for you, most excellent Theophilus, *that you may know the truth concerning the things of which you have been informed.* (1:1-4 RSV)

> Many writers have undertaken to draw up an account of the events that have happened among us, following the traditions handed down to us by the original eyewitnesses and servants of the Gospel. And so I in my turn, your Excellency, as one who has gone over the whole course of these events in detail, have decided to write a connected narrative for you, *so as to give you authentic knowledge about the matters of which you have been informed.* (NEB)

> Seeing that many others have undertaken to draw up accounts of the events that have taken place among us, exactly as they were handed down to us by those who from the outset were eyewitnesses and ministers of the word, I in my turn, after carefully going over the whole story from the beginning, have decided to write an ordered account for you, Theophilus, *so that your Excellency may learn how well founded the teaching is that you have received.* (JB)

Why has the author prepared his own version of the story for Theophilus? According to the Revised Standard Version, it was so "that you may know the truth." This presumes that Theophilus and other potential readers do not know the truth, that they may be ignorant or misinformed at some points. Luke conceives of his work as a corrective. This view is even more pronounced in the New English Bible: the writer wishes to provide "authentic knowledge." The implication is that other information is inauthentic, inaccurate, or untrue.

The Jerusalem Bible translation is strikingly different: the writer's purpose is to demonstrate how "well founded" the teaching is. His work is not necessarily a corrective but rather a persuasive reinforcement. Possibly Theophilus will be more likely to believe the story on the basis of Luke's account. If the translation in the Jerusalem Bible is correct—and it is closer to the literal meaning of the Greek—the preface says nothing about accuracy or authenticity. It suggests that Luke's purpose is to reinforce beliefs, to inspire confidence in a way others have not. His history has a purpose beyond the preservation of an accurate record, according to the Jerusalem Bible version.

The rendering of the preface will have a significant impact on the way the reader understands the work. These introductory verses may help explain why the two books were written, and they may contain clues to the thematic unity of the work. Conversely, the translator must base any decision about how to render verse 4 on a reading of Luke-Acts as a whole. Readers need to be aware of the alternatives. Which translation is most appropriate to the work? Does the writer seem preoccupied with accuracy and correcting faulty versions of the story? Or does he seem concerned with persuading the reader that the story is "well founded"? If the latter, how does the evangelist go about achieving his purpose, and how does his goal explain the form of his work? Does one's view of the preface help to explain why the books begin and end where they do and as they do?

One additional term, in the first verse of Luke, deserves mention. The Greek verb translated "accomplished" (RSV), "happened" (NEB), and "taken place" (JB), is an uncommon word that means literally "fill completely," or "fulfill." Since it is not the usual verb for "occur" or "happen," one may ask whether there is some special significance in its use here. The writer evidently wishes to convey the image of events that fill up or fill out some established measure. His story is a "fulfilling," his language implying at the outset that the events that follow occupy an important place in some larger story. He is about to narrate "the things that have been fulfilled in our midst." As shall be seen, this rendering of the Greek, which the Revised Standard Version most closely approximates, is an appropriate introduction to Luke's work.

B. Beginnings and Endings

Biblical interpreters, like literary critics, generally find the beginnings and endings of narratives particularly illuminating. If the preface to Luke's work suggests a distinctive view of his literary task compared with the other gospel writers, the beginning of the actual narrative is no less unusual and thought provoking. Unlike the other evangelists, Luke begins the story of Jesus in Jerusalem, at the Temple. The first characters he introduces are John the Baptist's prospective parents, a priest and his wife, also from a priestly family. He explicitly characterizes both man and wife as pious Jews. In what sense do these characters represent the beginning of Jesus' story? Does the opening of the narrative provide any clues to the major themes of Luke's history or to his purpose?

The ending of Luke's Gospel raises similar questions. His work does not conclude with the termination of Jesus' ministry; he continues on, with the story of Jesus' followers and the spread of the gospel and the church. How is this second half of Luke's history linked to the first? What, if anything, does the mission of the church have to do with

Jerusalem and with the pious and priestly parents of John the Baptist? What does Acts as a whole have to do with the preface to Luke's Gospel and with Theophilus? Any proposal about the purpose of Luke-Acts must deal with such questions.

The conclusion to the book of Acts raises still more intriguing questions. It represents the completion of a story that began at Luke 1:5, and it should also be related in some sense to the author's opening statement in Luke 1:1-4. The story of Jesus did not end with his return to heaven. It continued among his followers, who were commissioned to preach "repentance and forgiveness of sins . . . to all nations, beginning from Jerusalem" (24:47). Jesus promised his disciples that they would "receive power when the Holy Spirit has come upon you; and you shall be my witnesses in Jerusalem and in all Judea and Samaria and to the end of the earth" (Acts 1:8). The reader has been led to anticipate that the book of Acts would recount the spread of the Christian movement from Jerusalem to the end of the earth.

At least at the beginning of Acts, these expectations are met. The account begins with the mission of Jesus' followers in Jerusalem then moves to Samaria (chap. 8). They convert the first non-Jews, opening a new missionary field (chap. 10). Quite appropriately, the last stage in the spread of Christianity "to the end of the earth" begins with the appearance of the apostle Paul, the great missionary to the Gentiles, and the last half of the book of Acts concerns his career. It seems only fitting that Acts should end with the great missionary in Rome, where, according to tradition, he was martyred under the Emperor Nero. The good news has at last reached the end of the earth—or, to use another image more appropriate to the political situation at the time, the center of the earth.

Yet the actual ending is not the fulfilling conclusion the reader has expected. When Paul arrives in Rome, he meets not with Christians but with the Jewish community. Acts describes a last appeal to the Jews in the capital city. The result of this effort to convince his countrymen of Jesus' Messiahship is typical of what occurs throughout Paul's ministry as described in Acts: some Jews believe; some do not

(28:24). Paul then makes one final pronouncement that includes a lengthy quotation from Isaiah:

The Holy Spirit was right in saying to your fathers through Isaiah the prophet:

> "Go to this people, and say,
> You shall indeed hear but never understand,
> and you shall indeed see but never perceive.
> For this people's heart has grown dull,
> and their ears are heavy of hearing,
> and their eyes they have closed;
> lest they should perceive with their eyes,
> and hear with their ears,
> and understand with their heart,
> and turn for me to heal them."

Let it be known to you then that this salvation of God has been sent to the Gentiles; they will listen. (28:25-29)

Acts closes with a brief, anticlimactic comment about Paul's continuing to preach in Rome. The ending raises questions. What happened to Paul? Was he martyred? Did Paul ever visit the Christians in Rome (those to whom Paul sent his Epistle to the Romans)? Did he get to make his trip to Spain (Rom. 15:28)? Who continued the ministry to the Gentiles?

A number of other loose ends also remain untied. Why did Luke end his history of the noted apostle to the Gentiles with a formal termination of Paul's mission to the Jews, with his extended quotation from Isaiah? How can this episode be the conclusion of the story that begins in Jerusalem with the parents of John the Baptist? What does it have to do with Theophilus and the purpose of Luke-Acts? These questions are particularly important for an understanding of the work, yet they traditionally have not been raised.

Interpreters customarily have viewed Luke as the most un-Jewish of the Gospels and Luke-Acts as the story of the coming of a Savior and the message of forgiveness to all people and all nations. Still, the Gospel begins among pious Jews in Jerusalem and ends with an address to Jews in Rome. If one interprets these two books properly, then one should be able to explain why the story begins and ends where it does, what major themes unify the work, and how all this relates to the author's purpose as stated in Luke 1:1-4. With this task of interpretation in mind, our study begins with the Gospel of Luke.

II. Two Themes in the Story of Jesus

The infancy narratives and the resurrection cycle have been studied in previous sections of this book. Here, analysis of the Gospel will be restricted to two of its major themes, both of which tie it to Acts.

A. Jesus and the Outcasts

In Luke, the birth of Jesus in large measure foreshadows his career. From the beginning, Jesus' place is with outsiders, those ignored or despised by the religious establishment. The ones who take note of Jesus' birth are simple shepherds, not magi. Jesus is born in an animal's stall because the inn has no more room. All the Gospels portray Jesus as a friend of tax-collectors and sinners, eliciting criticism from religious Jews, but this interest in the outcasts and in the poor is more pronounced in Luke's Gospel. It is one of the major themes of his story, beginning with Mary's Magnificat:

> He has shown strength with his arm,
> he has scattered the proud in the imagination
>   of their hearts,
> he has put down the mighty from their thrones,
> and exalted those of low degree;
> he has filled the hungry with good things,
> and the rich he has sent empty away. (Luke 1:51-53)

Those about whom God is most concerned, throughout Luke, are the helpless and the despised. Those whose lives are held up as examples of piety are people who share that concern. According to all the Synoptic Gospels, John the Baptist preached a baptism of repentance. Matthew and Luke include a short account of his message, but only Luke provides concrete advice for the crowds who come to John: "And the multitudes asked him, 'What then shall we do?' And he answered them, 'He who has two coats, let him share with him who has none; and he who has food, let him do likewise'" (3:10-11).

In his inaugural address at Nazareth, Jesus describes his ministry in the following words:

> The Spirit of the Lord is upon me,
> because he has anointed me to preach good news to
>   the poor.
> He has sent me to proclaim release to the captives
> and recovering of sight to the blind,
> to set at liberty those who are oppressed,
> to proclaim the acceptable year of the Lord. (4:18-19)

→ Ships (r Audin)

Again and again, the story returns to the plight of the poor, the problem of wealth, and the need for generosity. Only Luke reports Jesus' famous parable of the Good Samaritan about a man who proved himself a neighbor by showing compassion (10:29-37). Jesus was responding to a question about inheriting eternal life: real piety means living as a neighbor to others, giving aid to those who need help. The Samaritan, despised by religious Jews, is the example of piety; the ostensibly religious priest and the Levite, who both refuse to help the injured man, are irreligious in a more important sense. Luke portrays all his major characters as almsgivers: Peter and John (Acts 3:1-10); the whole Christian community (2:44-45; 4:32); Cornelius, the first Gentile to be converted (10:1-2); and Paul (24:17). When a notorious tax collector named Zacchaeus is converted, he tells Jesus: "Behold, Lord, the half of my goods I give to the poor" (Luke 19:8).

-no one to Icarus

There is no attempt to spiritualize the poor. The Gospel records the famous speech about the lilies of the field, found also in the Sermon on the Mount in Matthew, but with the following addition in Luke:

> Fear not, little flock, for it is your Father's good pleasure to give you the kingdom. Sell your possessions, and give alms; provide yourselves with purses that do not grow old, with a treasure in the heavens that does not fail. (12:32-34)

The advice illustrated by the lilies of the field, not to be anxious about such things as food and clothing, is not merely a call to be spiritual; it is an invitation to be generous.

Corresponding to this invitation is a warning about riches. Only Luke includes the parable of the rich farmer who, when faced with a bumper crop, elects not to give anything away but to build larger barns. He discovers, to his dismay, that his earthly wealth is useless and that he has no treasure in the heavens (12:13-21). Jesus condemns the Pharisees in Luke's account because they are "lovers of money" (16:14). A few verses later there is the story of the rich man and Lazarus, also unique to Luke (verses 19-31). The rich man ends in Hades, in eternal torment, while Lazarus, a destitute beggar, takes his place in Abraham's bosom. The only virtue of Lazarus is that he is poor; the fatal sin of the rich man is his lack of generosity.

The most striking example of this thematic interest in the poor and the centrality of compassion in Luke's Gospel is the so-called Sermon on the Plain (6:12-49), Luke's version of Jesus' great Sermon on the Mount in Matthew. This sermon is not as extensive as the one in Matthew, but there are similarities in both structure and content. Luke also begins with Beatitudes and ends with the parable of the house built on sand. Several of the sayings in Luke are also found in Matthew's version. There are some important differences, however, typified by the opening blessings and corresponding woes:

Blessed are you poor, for yours is the kingdom of God.	But woe to you that are rich, for you have received your consolation.
Blessed are you that hunger now, for you shall be satisfied. (6:20-21)	Woe to you that are full now, for you shall hunger. (6:24-25)

In Luke, Jesus says that the kingdom of God is primarily for the poor and hungry and abused—not, as in Matthew, for the poor *in spirit* or for those who hunger and thirst *after righteousness.*

And those who understand God's concern for the poor will respond appropriately:

For if you love those who love you, what reward have you? Do not even the tax collectors do the	If you love those who love you, what credit is that to you? For even sinners love those who love

same? And if you salute only your brethren, what more are you doing than others? Do not even the Gentiles do the same? You, therefore, must be perfect, as your heavenly Father is perfect. (Matt. 5:46-48)

them. And if you do good to those who do good to you, what credit is that to you? For even sinners do the same. And if you lend to those from whom you hope to receive, what credit is that to you? Even sinners lend to sinners, to receive as much again. But love your enemies, and do good, and lend, expecting nothing in return; and your reward will be great, and you will be the sons of the Most High; for he is kind to the ungrateful and the selfish. *Be merciful, even as your Father is merciful.* (Luke 6:32-36)

In both versions of the injunctions Jesus focuses on behavior that is truly praiseworthy. The distinctive emphasis in Luke, however, is on selfless love of enemies and on the appropriateness of mercy. In Luke, Jesus speaks not simply of saluting brothers but of doing good and of lending money. In Luke, God is not simply and remotely perfect; he is essentially a God of mercy.

Jesus' ministry as reported in Luke is principally to the poor and the outcast. Consequently, the mark of a true disciple is compassion, the willingness to help the needy. Precisely this feature of Jesus' ministry, however, scandalizes respectable Jews: "Now the tax collectors and sinners were all drawing near to hear him. And the Pharisees and the scribes murmured, saying, 'This man receives sinners and eats with them'" (Luke 15:1-2).

In response to such criticisms, Jesus tells the parable of the prodigal son, which might better be termed the parable of the loving father. The father's fundamental characteristic is his willingness to show mercy: he rejoices at the return of his renegade son, who has wasted his inheritance. The response of the older brother is equally important. This faithful son cannot share his father's joy: his brother is unworthy of his father's love, and he alone has earned that love through his faithfulness. The parable, however, suggests that the older brother has missed the whole point of belonging to a family. A true brother, and a true son of his father, would be able to share his father's joy. He cannot—because he does not understand what is essential: love means mercy. He does not know what it means to live the life his father has invited him to emulate.

Jesus is separated from the religious leaders by his willingness to associate with the outcasts, his readiness to show mercy. In this sense, according to Luke, he is a true Son of his Father. God is essentially a God of mercy. He is like the woman who sets aside all her work to find the one coin that has been misplaced or like the shepherd who leaves the flock to seek out the one sheep that has strayed (15:4-9). His goal is to bring all those who stray back into the flock: "Just so, I tell you, there will be more joy in heaven over one sinner who repents than over ninety-nine righteous persons who need no repentance" (verse 7).

Luke's history is one in which the poor and the lost have a prominent place. One might even say it is their history. Fittingly, Jesus commissions his followers to preach the message of "repentance and forgiveness of sins" (24:47). Jesus' followers in Acts accordingly pool their resources to provide for the needy (Acts 2:45; 4:34-35). The contrast with the establishment is never forgotten: according to Luke, "uneducated, common men" confound the religious leaders of the people (4:13). This is the conflict of values foreshadowed in the Magnificat.

B. Jesus as Savior for Israel: The Jewish Emphasis

To an extent unparalleled even in the Gospel of Matthew, Luke's Gospel portrays Jesus as Israel's savior, the Jewish Messiah. His story opens with a priest in the Temple in Jerusalem and concludes in the Temple with Jesus' disciples "blessing God" (Luke 24:52). All the earliest characters are pious Jews, zealous for the Law of Moses. Zechariah and Elizabeth are "righteous before God, walking in all the commandments and ordinances of the Lord blameless" (1:6). Luke alone notes that the parents of John the Baptist and of Jesus have their sons circumcised on the eighth day, precisely as the Law of Moses commands. On four separate occasions,

Luke emphasizes how scrupulous Jesus' parents were in observing all that the Law commanded (2:21, 22-24, 39, 41). Simeon and Anna, two minor characters who appear in the episode in the Temple, are both pious Jews of Jerusalem, looking for the "consolation of Israel" or the "redemption of Jerusalem."

In language familiar from Jewish tradition, Luke describes the work of John the Baptist and of Jesus as ministries to Israel. With John, he alludes to the book of Malachi, which prophesies Elijah's return (Mal. 4:5-6). As a new Elijah, John will "turn many of the sons of Israel to the Lord their God" (Luke 1:16).

In the case of Jesus, the angel Gabriel says that Jesus will be the Davidic Messiah and as king will rule over the house of Jacob (1:32-33). Jesus' role is described in advance as "a horn of salvation for us [Israel] in the house of his servant David" (verse 69). God will do "as he spoke by the mouth of his holy prophets from of old" (verse 70). God intends "to perform the mercy promised to our fathers, and to remember his holy covenant, the oath which he swore to our father Abraham" (verses 72-73). Luke refers to these familiar Jewish traditions in describing a ministry almost exclusively aimed at Jews, fulfilling promises made by God to Jewish partriarchs and by Jewish prophets to more recent generations.

This theme pervades Luke's Gospel. Jesus does not travel to Tyre and Sidon—that is, non-Jewish territory—as he does in Mark and Matthew. He does not preach in the Greek cities of the Decapolis. Those rare occasions of communication with non-Jewish people are especially noted as exceptions.

An example is the story of the healing of a Roman centurion's slave. It appears in Matthew as well, making a comparison possible. According to Matthew, the Roman comes to Jesus with a request for help, which Jesus grants (Matt. 8:5-10). In Luke's version, Jesus has no direct contact with the centurion:

> Now a centurion had a slave who was dear to him, who was sick and at the point of death. When he heard of Jesus, he sent to him elders of the Jews, asking him to come and heal the slave. And when they came to Jesus, they besought him earnestly, saying,

> "He is worthy to have you do this for him, for he loves our nation, and he built us our synagogue." (Luke 7:2-5)

The request from a non-Jew is clearly something exceptional, and the elders' description obviously is not of a typical Gentile—yet even so, the centurion still needs Jews to approach Jesus for him.

Other comments throughout the Gospel hint that Jesus' mission is particularly to Jews. Jesus heals a woman on the sabbath; a dispute arises over his action. Responding to the criticism, Jesus says to his adversaries:

> You hypocrites! Does not each of you on the sabbath untie his ox or his ass from the manger, and lead it away to water it? And ought not this woman, *a daughter of Abraham* whom Satan bound for eighteen years, be loosed from this bond on the sabbath day? (13:15-17)

When Zacchaeus, the notorious Jewish tax collector, decides to reform his life, Jesus says: "Today salvation has come to this house, *since he also is a son of Abraham.* For the Son of man came to seek and to save the lost" (19:9-10). Jesus came to save the lost and the outcasts, but in Luke, that means only the lost within Israel. Gentiles are not considered strays; from the Jewish perspective, they were never within the fold.

Luke does record some indications that Gentiles will eventually share in what Jesus has begun. Simeon describes God's sending Jesus not only for "glory to thy people Israel" but also as "a light for revelation to the Gentiles" (2:32). In talking of his relation to his own people, Jesus makes an enigmatic reference to Elijah and Elisha, both of whom performed miracles for foreigners (4:24-27). The time for admission of Gentiles has not yet come, however; this is a time of preaching and healing directed to Jews. In Luke, Jesus' ministry is described with imagery familiar from Jewish tradition, even when foreshadowing the mission to non-Jews. Simeon's reference about light to the Gentiles uses language from Isaiah (Isa. 42:6, 49:6), and Jesus' provocative remarks to his neighbors in Nazareth about miracles for foreigners cite the examples of two of Israel's greatest prophets.

The resurrection stories in Luke provide the transition

between the Gospel and Acts. Luke says that Jesus spends some time with his disciples, prior to his formal return to the Father, preparing them for what is to come. Jesus' last instructions in the Gospel predict the events in Acts:

> Thus it is written, that the Christ should suffer and on the third day rise from the dead, and that repentance and forgiveness of sins should be preached in his name to all nations, beginning from Jerusalem. You are witnesses of these things. And behold, I send the promise of my Father upon you; but stay in the city, until you are clothed with power from on high. (Luke 24:46-49)

Once again emphasis is on the sense in which Jesus' whole ministry is to be viewed as the fulfillment of scripture and of Israel's history. All has been "written." The fulfillment of scripture is not concluded with Jesus' ministry; the message of forgiveness that will reach even "the nations" is part of the same scriptural plan. The story of Jesus and that of the early church are continuous, not only with each other, but also with a history that extends back to Abraham. Both the ministry of Jesus and the mission of the church fulfill promises God made directly to the Jewish patriarchs and to their descendants through the Jewish prophets.

After taking leave of Jesus, the disciples return to the Temple in Jerusalem. This is not the birth of a new religion; rather, the prophecies about the Jewish Messiah have now been fulfilled. God has kept his promises and oaths. Jerusalem, the religious capital of Israel and site of the Temple, is where Jesus' story began and, according to Luke, where he appeared after he was raised from the dead. It is also the place where the new stage of the story begins at Pentecost.

To understand more fully the predominant emphases in Luke's Gospel and their relationship both to the form of Luke-Acts and to the purpose of the work expressed in the preface, our study will now turn to Acts.

III. The Restoration
of Israel and the Mission to Gentiles

The beginning of part two of Luke-Acts formally concludes the ministry of Jesus.[2] After giving his followers final instructions, he ascends to heaven (Acts 1:9). His departure ends the period of Jesus' ministry; the coming of the Holy Spirit, the "power from on high" promised by Jesus, begins the era of mission. In another important shift, the message of repentance and forgiveness is now to be extended beyond the confines of the Jewish community, to all mankind. Jesus' last instructions to his disciples before ascending predict both the mission and its course: "But you shall receive power when the Holy Spirit has come upon you; and you shall be my witnesses in Jerusalem and in all Judea and Samaria and to the end of the earth" (verse 8).

Chapters 1–7 of Acts recount the mission in Jerusalem; chapter 8, the mission in Judea and Samaria; and chapters 9–28, the mission "to the end of the earth." At the beginning of Acts the characters are familiar from the Gospel—chief among them being Peter. As the story progresses, new characters are introduced, especially Stephen, who becomes the movement's first martyr, and Paul, a Pharisee who is converted from a fierce opponent to Christianity's greatest missionary. Luke devotes almost half the book to Paul.

The writer's preface to his Gospel both states and illustrates his intention to write history in the prevailing literary manner: "an orderly account." But not until Acts does he display his abilities as a classical historian. The most significant literary feature of Acts not found in the Gospel of Luke is its many extended speeches. In antiquity, such speeches were characteristic and illuminating features of historiography; readers expected a good historian to be a master of speech composition. So it is with Acts. Through these orations, Luke develops basic themes, interprets crucial events, and advances the story. Here the fulfillment theme noted in the Gospel is most pronounced. These speeches interpret events as the fulfillment of Israel's traditional hopes, spelling out in considerable detail what was stated in general terms in the Gospel.

A. Peter's Sermon at Pentecost

The first of these speeches in Acts is Peter's sermon at Pentecost.[3] During this Jewish pilgrimage festival, which celebrated the end of the barley harvest, the Holy Spirit is poured out on the small group of Jesus' followers gathered in an upper room in Jerusalem. They are able to speak in other tongues, and people from all over the world can hear about the "mighty works of God" in their own languages (2:1-12). The event marks the formal inauguration of the apostolic mission—a new stage in a continuing history, not the beginning of a new history.

Peter's speech interpreting the Pentecost experience is carefully constructed, its arguments intricate. As an excellent literary composition, it warrants careful study, but space permits only a few observations. First, the speech is addressed to Jews. Those who gather to hear him out of curiosity are "Jews, devout men from every nation under heaven" (2:5). Peter speaks to "men of Judea" (verse 14), "men of Israel" (verse 22).

In this oration to Jews, Peter explains, by reference to the book of Joel, that the speaking in foreign languages that some have interpreted as drunkenness is a sign that the spirit of prophecy has been poured out:

> But this is what was spoken by the prophet Joel:
> "And in the last days it shall be, God declares,
> that I will pour out my Spirit upon all flesh,
> and your sons and your daughters shall prophesy,
> and your young men shall see visions,
> and your old men shall dream dreams." (2:16-17)

According to Peter's interpretation of Joel, a prophecy about the "last days" has been fulfilled. A decisive new stage in Israel's history, foreseen in scripture, has now arrived.

This new era brings a special call to repentance and an offer of forgiveness, as the conclusion of Peter's quotation from Joel suggests: "And it shall be that whoever calls on the name of the Lord shall be saved" (2:21). According to Peter, the Lord referred to in Joel's words is none other than the crucified and risen Jesus. It is not self-evident, however, that Jesus may even be called Lord, since the title in Jewish tradition is reserved for God himself. So beginning with 2:22, the speech offers detailed proof from scripture that Jesus is Lord, concluding in 2:36: "Let all the house of Israel therefore know assuredly that God has made him both Lord and Christ, this Jesus whom you crucified."

The scriptural interpretation in the speech is intricate, following principles of interpretation accepted among the rabbis. Passages from Psalms 16, 132, and 110 are quoted to demonstrate that Jesus' resurrection identifies him as the Christ and that because he has been elevated to the right hand of God he must be the second Lord referred to in Psalm 110:1. Having demonstrated that Jesus is Lord, Peter can then urge his audience to accept the offer of forgiveness promised in Joel by being "baptized every one of you in the name of [the Lord] Jesus Christ" (2:38).

The pouring out of the Spirit at Pentecost is thus linked both to the ministry of Jesus and to the history of Israel. The conversion of three thousand Jews begins a new era in the history of God's people, an era foretold in scripture. There is no suggestion that the converts have broken with Jewish tradition: they attend the Temple daily (2:46).

B. Peter's Second Speech: "The Prophet Like Moses"

Peter's speech in chapter 3 is equally significant. It is set in the Temple, where Peter and John have healed, in Jesus' name, a man lame from birth; like the first speech, it addresses "men of Israel." Peter explains that the healing is due not to his own powers but to the "name" of Jesus—whom they had delivered to Pilate for execution but whom God has raised from the dead (3:12-16). Once again Peter tells an audience of Jews that God has fulfilled what he "foretold by the mouth of all the prophets," that Jesus' death and resurrection mark the beginning of a time of crisis, and that this provides a special opportunity for repentance and forgiveness (verses 17-19). Quoting Moses this time, Peter describes the crisis more precisely:

Moses said, "The Lord God will raise up for you a prophet from your brethren as he raised me up. You shall listen to him in whatever he tells you. And it shall be that every soul that does not listen to that prophet shall be destroyed from the people." And all the prophets who have spoken, from Samuel and those who came afterwards, also proclaimed these days. You are sons of the prophets and of the covenant which God gave to your fathers, saying to Abraham, "And in your posterity shall all the families of the earth be blessed." God having raised up his servant, sent him to you first, to bless you in turning every one of you from your wickedness. (3:22-26)

Peter's reference to the coming of a prophet like Moses comes from Deuteronomy 18.[4] He interprets the passage as a prophecy pointing to his own day: Jesus is the prophet like Moses. The significance of this fulfillment of scripture is not simply what it reveals about Jesus but what his coming really means for Peter's audience. Deuteronomy says that the coming of the prophet like Moses will signal a time of crisis within the people of God. Membership within the Jewish community will depend on the response of each person to the prophet and his teaching. Those who refuse to heed the words of the prophet like Moses (Jesus) will be rooted out from the people, forfeiting their right to call themselves Jews. According to Peter (and Luke-Acts as a whole), only those who believe in Jesus can properly consider themselves Jews. This is indeed an extreme position. The apostolic mission is not the birth of a new religious sect. It is a reform movement within the Jewish community of such consequence that it represents the decisive purge foretold in scripture, the formation of a holy remnant.

The reader can now appreciate more fully how the strands that have been isolated—the consistent portrayal of the main characters as pious Jews, the tying of Jesus' story to Jerusalem, the many references to fulfillment of patriarchal promises and of later prophecies in scripture—are drawn together into the fabric of the narrative. For Luke, the story of Jesus has religious significance for Jews, looking both to the past and to the future. Jesus' life and ministry are part of a whole that began with Abraham and includes the story of the religious community that will carry the message about the crucified and risen Messiah to the end of the earth. In this sense Luke tells Jesus' story not as a biographer but as a historian, interested in relating that life and teaching to a larger context. In detail, he traces lines from the time of Jesus to the time of the church; more broadly, he carefully integrates the combined story of Jesus and the Christian movement into the history of Israel.

The reader must appreciate the distinctiveness of this characteristic of Luke-Acts. Mark tells the story of Jesus as a mysterious revelation; Matthew, as the authorized interpretation of the Law of Moses; John, as the decisive testimony of the one who has come from the Father. Only Luke tells Jesus' tale as an episode in a story that has an earlier as well as a later stage. He relates the entire Christian story, not to the history of the world or of the Roman Empire, but to that of Israel. Luke describes every event in the life of both Jesus and the early church as a fulfillment, a consummation.[5] They represent neither more nor less than the latest and decisive stage in the story of Israel. Jesus' coming signals a critical winnowing out among Jews. The God who raised Jesus from the dead is the God of Abraham, Isaac, and Jacob; he is also the God of the remnant that continues on.

The writer of Luke-Acts, in other words, is updating the history of Israel. Ample precedent for such an enterprise occurs in Jewish tradition, even within the sacred Scriptures themselves. The writer of I and II Chronicles, for example, undertook just such a task of retelling the story of God's people, taking into account new events and new perspectives. Even the style of Luke-Acts is reminiscent of the historical writings in the Greek Old Testament; one may legitimately suggest that Luke conceived of himself as a biblical historian. Considered as an addition to the corpus of Jewish historical writings, both the form of Luke-Acts and its overwhelming interest in relating the new events to Israel's past make sense.

Yet some features of this history remain unexplained. One is the ending of Acts. Why does the account close on the verge of the Gentile mission, when that mission seems to be implied from the opening of Acts? Why is nothing said about the death of Paul? A second is the relationship between the two-part history and Theophilus, or, more properly, its audience. Why was the work written? What was it intended to accomplish? A further investigation of major themes in Luke-Acts may furnish a perspective that will throw light on these two issues.

C. A Divided Israel

A significant feature of Luke's history is that many Jews reject the claims made by Jesus and his followers. These opponents include the most influential members of the Jewish community, the leaders of the people. Opposition to Jesus culminates in his arrest, trial, and death, but it also continues into the story of the early church. Peter and John are arrested; Stephen is stoned; Paul is persecuted wherever he goes and is finally arrested in Jerusalem, barely escaping death at the hands of a Jewish mob. Although Romans are involved in the death of Jesus and in the arrest of Paul, Luke's story clearly focuses on the role of the Jews. In the case of both Jesus and Paul, Roman officials testify that these persons have committed no crime against Roman law (Luke 23:1-25; Acts 23:26-30; 25:13-27; 26:30-32).

Some scholars suggest that Luke includes these declarations of innocence to convince Roman officials that Christianity is not a seditious movement, even though certain of its prominent figures have been arrested for political crimes. Yet Luke-Acts would have been ill-conceived as an apologetic work directed primarily to Roman officials. Roman officials in the two books are less than noble characters. Pilate, the representative of Roman law, permits himself to be swayed by a Jewish mob; Felix, procurator of Judea, leaves Paul in prison both because he has not received a bribe from him and out of deference to the Jews (Acts 24:26-27). Romans have not been able to make sense out of the dispute between Paul and the Jews (23:28-29; 25:18-20, 25-27), and there is little reason to believe that Roman officials to whom Luke-Acts might have been addressed would have understood any better.

Like Mark, Luke seems much more interested in Jewish than Roman opposition to Jesus and his followers. He makes no attempt to disguise opposition within the Jewish community; in fact, Acts is largely an attempt to account for that opposition and to interpret the division within the Jewish community.

As already noted, Peter's speeches demonstrate that what he preaches is according to Scripture and that those who believe in Jesus are true Jews, in fact *the* true Jews. Peter's opponents, and the opponents of the movement in general, take precisely the opposite view. *They* are the Jews. They insist that Jesus' followers are false Jews, who pervert the truth and forsake tradition. Almost every major character in Luke-Acts is accused by the leaders of the Jewish community of being a heretical Jew who has broken the sacred Law of Moses. Consider the following three instances.

In Acts 4–5, the rulers of the Jews, notably the Sadducees, call Peter and John perverters of the truth. The real issue of dispute is not Jesus himself but the resurrection: "And as they were speaking to the people, the priests and the captain of the temple and the Sadducees came upon them, annoyed because they were teaching the people and proclaiming in Jesus the resurrection from the dead" (4:1-2). The opposition is understandable since Sadducees did not believe in resurrection.

In Acts 6, Stephen, a Greek-speaking Jew, is brought by the "elders and the scribes" to the Sanhedrin on a charge of blasphemy. They allege that he spoke "blasphemous words against Moses and God" (6:11). As in Matthew's and Mark's description of Jesus' trial, false witnesses testify against the accused: "This man never ceases to speak words against this holy place and the law; for we have heard him say that this Jesus of Nazareth will destroy this place, and will change the customs which Moses delivered to us" (verses 13-15).

In Acts 21, elders in the Jerusalem congregation summarize the Jewish opposition Paul has encountered throughout his ministry in Acts:

> You see, brother, how many thousands there are among the Jews of those who have believed; they are all zealous for the law, and they have been told about you that you teach all the Jews who are among the Gentiles to forsake Moses, telling them not to circumcise their children or observe the customs. (21:20-21)

In sum, the story of Jesus and of the Christian movement is one of controversy, and Luke-Acts does not tell it from a neutral point of view. This dispute about who are the real Jews lies behind Luke's entire narrative. It seeks to convince the reader that the events described constitute "fulfillment." All the main characters are pious Jews, zealous for the Law—from Zechariah and Elizabeth to Paul. Jesus tells his followers that his death and resurrection, as well as their mission, fulfill scripture. In Acts, Peter amplifies the argument with references to Joel and the Psalms, and Paul ends with a quotation from Isaiah.

The ministry of the apostles begins with the formation of a holy "remnant" within the Jewish community in Jerusalem. According to Peter, those who refuse to accept the prophet like Moses exclude themselves from the Jewish community (chap. 3). This separation of true from false Jews continues throughout the rest of Acts, even into the ministry of Paul, known in tradition as the great apostle to the Gentiles. The story concludes with the divided response of one last group of Jews in Rome, the imperial capital. The writer apparently means to demonstrate, in the face of opposing views, that this group and its history represent Israel and the continuation of its history. Thus the followers of Jesus meet the charge of heresy from the leaders of the Jewish establishment: those who refuse to believe in Jesus are the real heretics.

D. Stephen's Defense: The Temple Made with Hands

Luke uses the medium of historical narrative to interpret for his readers a disputed matter in which they have something important invested. At issue is the right of a religious group to claim the past as its own, in this case the past history of Israel as recorded in scripture. For any religious movement to remain alive, it must reinterpret the past, applying the past to new questions and new events and even accounting for opposition. For Luke and his contemporaries, the importance of Jewish tradition was fundamental. As historian and partisan, Luke must show not only that the movement he chronicles can legitimately lay claim to tradition but also that tradition explains the opposition it encounters from fellow Jews. This perspective of the two-volume work is nowhere clearer than in Stephen's speech, which takes up nearly all of chapter 7.

This lengthy oration marks the culmination of opposition to

the followers of Jesus in Jerusalem. (It also marks an important turning point in the narrative: with chap. 8, the mission extends to Samaria, moving inexorably to Rome in chap. 28.) Stephen, identified simply as a Hellenistic Jew of unusual piety and wisdom, is involved in a dispute with other Hellensitic Jews (6:9), as a result of which he is brought before the Sanhedrin on charges that recall those lodged against Jesus: "This man never ceases to speak words against this holy place and the law; for we have heard him say that this Jesus of Nazareth will destroy this place, and will change the customs which Moses delivered to us" (verses 13-14).

Stephen's defense against the charges of heresy and blasphemy begins with a review of Israel's history. Let us examine which events and people from that long history he selects, how he interprets them, and what functions they serve in his defense. The survey includes:

Abraham (the story begins with God's promise to him)
Isaac (only mentioned)
Jacob (simply identified as the father of the patriarchs)
Joseph (his rise to power in Egypt is recounted)
Slavery in Egypt
Moses
Exodus
Erection of the golden calf
Receiving the Law on Sinai
Building the tent of witness in the wilderness
Joshua (briefly)
David (very briefly)
Solomon

The most important figures in Stephen's condensed history of Israel are Abraham and Moses. The time of Abraham, the sojourn in Egypt, and the wilderness era get his greatest attention. After Moses, the period of the settlement and the Davidic era are mentioned briefly. The great David and Solomon merit notice only in relation to God's "habitation"—the tent of witness in the wilderness and the Temple Solomon eventually builds. The survey ends with the building of that Temple.

Stephen returns to the present and concludes with a scathing denunciation of his judges:

You stiff-necked people, uncircumcised in heart and ears, you always resist the Holy Spirit. As your fathers did, so do you. Which of the prophets did not your fathers persecute? And they killed those who announced beforehand the coming of the Righteous One, whom you have now betrayed and murdered, you who received the law as delivered by angels and did not keep it. (7:51-53)

One of the lessons derived from this review of Israel's history is that divisions have split God's people since the time of Moses. Much of the information about Moses included in the speech relates to these divisions. After saving the lives of two Hebrews, Moses attempts to settle a quarrel between them; but they "thrust him aside" with the rebuke, "Who made you a ruler and a judge over us?" (7:27). Moses leads his people out of bondage and ascends Mount Sinai to receive the Law from God; at that same moment, the people are building a golden calf, a sign that they have "refused to obey him, but thrust him aside" (verse 39). Stephen emphasizes that Moses, God's spokesman, is repeatedly rejected by those he is attempting to serve. The significance is clear: "This is the Moses who said to the Israelites, 'God will raise up for you a prophet from your brethren as he raised me up'" (verse 37).

Moses is important not simply because of his climactic role in Israel's history, but because Jesus is identified as the promised prophet like Moses. The pattern in the time of Moses still persists in Israel at the time of Jesus and his followers: there are those who "always resist the Holy Spirit," persecute God's spokesmen, and do not honor the Law. Jesus and his followers are on the side of Moses and the Law, while those presumed to be religious leaders are "stiff-necked people, uncircumcised in heart and ears." They, not Stephen, are guilty of apostasy and no longer deserve to call themselves Israelites.

Appropriately, Stephen's historical survey ends with Solomon's Temple, ostensibly fulfilling God's promise to Abraham that his posterity would "come out and worship me in this place" (7:7). Yet Solomon's Temple was "made with hands," and Stephen recalls the value of such works: false Israelites built the golden calf and offered a sacrifice to the idol and "rejoiced in the works of their hands" (verse 41). The analogy is clear: the Temple has become an idol, its cult idolatry. Stephen is on trial for statements allegedly made against the Temple. His judges are primarily Temple officials, committed to defend a thing "made by hands." Apparently they forget the biblical text according to which God does not dwell in temples made with hands, so Stephen reminds them:

> Yet the Most High does not dwell in houses made with hands; as the prophet says,
> "Heaven is my throne,
> and earth my footstool.
> What house will you build for me, says the Lord,
> or what is the place of my rest?
> Did not my hand make all these things?"
> (Acts 7:48-50; quoting Isa. 66:1-2)

Stephen clearly implies that those who have made the Temple the ultimate symbol of their religion have failed to understand both that religion and their own history.

Stephen does not specify which Temple practices, if any, he objects to; his speech contains no sustained polemic against sacrificial cults. After all, followers worship in the Temple. Rather, he seems to make the point that the Temple does not represent the final stage in the spiritual history of Israel, as some seem to believe. When "the time of the promise drew near" (7:17), God raised up a deliverer in the person of Moses and led his people out of bondage. According to Stephen, God has now fulfilled another promise to his people, for a prophet like Moses. Witnesses are to go from Jerusalem to the end of the earth: God has intervened again, and history must move on, as it always has. Just as there were those whose hearts remained in Egypt, who worshiped the "works of their hands" and refused to accept Moses as God's spokesman, so now there are those for whom God's promises remain bound to Jerusalem, who worship the actual building "made with hands" and refuse to accept the prophet like Moses. Stephen's judges will be judged; like their fathers, they will be removed "beyond Babylon."

Because space permits only a brief examination of the major blocks of material that comprise the last two-thirds of Acts, this study will concentrate on their relation to basic themes in the narrative.

E. "To the End of the Earth"

Luke has prepared the reader for the story to go beyond Jerusalem, and with chapter 8 the new movement reaches Samaria. With chapter 9, Luke concentrates on Paul, devoting more than half the book of Acts to the career of this influential and controversial missionary. A zealous Jewish opponent of the Christian movement who was dramatically converted to it, he was more responsible than any other figure for the spread of its message to the end of the earth. The later church knew him as the preeminent apostle to the Gentiles; as such, his importance to Luke's history seems self-evident.

Quite contrary to what might be expected, however, the first missionary to non-Jews is not Paul but Peter.[6] After recounting Paul's extraordinary conversion, his dramatic escape from Damascus, and his activities in Jerusalem, Luke suddenly interrupts Paul's story with a detailed account of Peter's activities, including his visit to a Roman centurion named Cornelius (9:32–11:18).

1. Peter and Cornelius. Luke portrays Peter as anything but a willing missionary to Gentiles. It takes three visions and a communication from a heavenly messenger to persuade him to visit Cornelius (a Gentile more pious than most Jews, 10:2). As he is preaching to Cornelius, he and his Jewish friends are stunned to see the Holy Spirit poured out on uncircumcised men precisely as it was on the Jerusalem circle at Pentecost. Despite Jesus' instruction about carrying the message of forgiveness to all nations (Luke 24:47) and the prophecy Peter quoted from Joel according to which the Spirit would be poured out on "all flesh" (Acts 2:17), Jesus' followers seem ill-prepared for this radical departure from tradition. For them, Peter's very presence in a Gentile home violates Mosaic Law and seems to imply that Peter is guilty of heretical behavior (11:1-3).

The episode formally introduces the problem of Gentile status within the community of believers. Before the mission to non-Jews begins on a large scale, admission must be justified—from a Jewish perspective. The issue centers on Peter in chapters 10 and 11; it is not settled until chapter 15, when Paul's case arises.

After visiting Cornelius, Peter returns to Jerusalem, where he meets the "circumcision party": "So when Peter went up to Jerusalem, the circumcision party criticized him, saying, 'Why did you go to uncircumcised men and eat with them?'" (11:2-3). Peter explains Cornelius' conversion: the visit was not Peter's idea; visions, heavenly messages, and finally God's pouring out of the Holy Spirit compelled him to accept Gentiles within the community *as Gentiles.*

The question is not whether to accept Gentiles into the family of believers, but on what terms. The circumcision party comprises those who insist—as would all good Jews—that converts who wish to become members of the people of God must be circumcised. The Cornelius story demonstrates that this is not necessary among those who believe in Jesus. Peter's experience indicates that Gentiles are to enter the group as Gentiles, and Jews will be permitted to enjoy social intercourse with them. This is the case, however, not because Christianity is a new religion, but because the God who gave the Law of Moses has now made a special dispensation. God has "cleansed" Gentiles, making it possible for them to join Jews who believe in Jesus—without undergoing circumcision. They do not have to be children of Israel (by circumcision) in order to be followers of Jesus; by being followers of Jesus, they become children of Israel. This is the implication of Peter's experience with Cornelius.

The issue is still not settled, however; the same dispute arises within the church in Antioch between Paul and Barnabas on one side and some men "from Judea" on the other. The Jerusalem church calls a formal meeting to settle the matter once and for all (chap. 15). Paul, whose reputation among Jews is highly questionable, only testifies; he does not participate in making the decision. Peter recounts the story of Cornelius once again; and James, the apparent authority in the council, confirms Peter's position by citing a passage from scripture (15:13-21). The group's decision to accept Gentiles into the church without requiring circumcision is supported by visions and signs from heaven and is sealed by a passage from the Bible. The "fallen tent of David" is now raised up; that is, a holy remnant of faithful Jews has now been formed, so that now the "rest of men may seek the Lord.'" Those who actually make the decision, Peter and James, are men whose faithfulness to the Mosaic Law is unquestioned. Thus, the narrator calls attention to the fact that even this somewhat radical decision about Gentiles is orthodox by Jewish standards.

2. Paul and the Jews. Paul's story, interrupted by the episode of Peter and Cornelius, resumes in Antioch (11:25 and, after another interruption, 13:1). At this point, the mission begun among Jews in Jerusalem is moving beyond the borders of Israel and is taking a special interest in Gentiles. According to Luke's report in Acts (Paul's version in his letters differs), Paul's missionary work with Barnabas in Antioch forces a decision on the status of non-Jews in the church. Since Christian tradition has crystalized Paul's description of himself as the apostle to the Gentiles (Gal. 1 and 2), one might reasonably expect Paul's work from Antioch on to be his mission to non-Jews.

His ministry in Antioch begins, however, with Jews, not Gentiles (Acts 13). Paul delivers his first oration to an audience gathered at a synagogue in the city. It concludes with a clear indication that a new era in the church's mission is at hand:

> It was necessary that the word of God should be spoken first to you. Since you thrust it from you, and judge yourselves unworthy of eternal life, behold, we turn to the Gentiles. For so the Lord has commanded us, saying, "I have set you to be a light for the Gentiles, that you may bring salvation to the uttermost parts of the earth." (13:46-47)

After such a rejection and his declaration of intention to turn to Gentiles, it is a bit surprising to learn that Paul continues to preach to Jews after leaving Antioch: "Now at Iconium they entered together into the Jewish synagogue, and so spoke that a great company believed, both of Jews and of Greeks ['God-fearers']" (14:1).

After the conference in Jerusalem, the pattern continues. One learns that Paul customarily visited synagogues not simply to find interested Gentiles ("God-fearers," a special category of Gentiles who participated in synagogue worship, but were not full proselytes to Judaism) but also to preach to

Jews, despite his formal pronouncement in Antioch. He seeks out Jews in Thessalonica, Beroea, Athens, and Corinth.

In 17:1, when Paul comes to Thessalonica, he goes into the "synagogue of the Jews," where he remains for three weeks arguing with them. He is forced to leave when the Jews become jealous and make trouble.

In 17:10, immediately upon arriving in Beroea, Paul proceeds to the synagogue, where he finds that "these Jews were more noble than those in Thessalonica, for they received the word with all eagerness" (verse 11). He is again forced to leave, however, when Jews from Thessalonica arrive and stir up trouble.

In 17:16-17, even in Athens, that most Greek city, Paul begins by arguing with Jews in a local synagogue.

In 18:4, in Corinth, Paul "argued in the synagogue every sabbath, and persuaded Jews and Greeks." When Silas and Timothy arrive, they find Paul "occupied with preaching, testifying to the Jews that the Christ was Jesus" (verse 5).

When Paul encounters hostility from these Corinthian Jews, he reiterates his intention to preach to Gentiles: "And when they opposed and reviled him, he shook out his garments and said to them, 'Your blood be upon your heads! I am innocent. From now on I will go to the Gentiles'" (18:6).

Nevertheless, as soon as Paul leaves Corinth and arrives in Ephesus, he goes to the synagogue, where he "argued with the Jews" (18:19). He even promises to return to them if he has an opportunity (verses 20-21). Furthermore, upon returning to Corinth, Paul once more goes to the synagogue, where he argues for three whole months (19:8)—peculiar behavior for the man who says in his letters that he was called primarily to preach to Gentiles.

Luke concludes his book with a last attempt by the great missionary to convert a group of people, but once again they are Jews, the leaders of the Jewish community in Rome, the imperial capital. Luke tells us virtually nothing about Paul's visits with Christians, to whom, as is known from other sources, he had already written (the Letter to the Romans). Rome may be an appropriate setting for the climax of the story, but there is no climax; the reader does not learn Paul's fate, whether he is condemned by Romans or released to continue his ministry. It stretches prophecy to view the imperial capital as the "end of the earth" or as one of the "uttermost parts of the earth" (13:47). How can this be the conclusion to the mission promised by Jesus (Luke 24:47; Acts 1:8)? How can it be the conclusion to Acts?

The result of Paul's final confrontation with a Jewish community follows the pattern typical of his ministry. There is a division among the people: some believe; some do not. Paul responds with an extended quotation from the prophet Isaiah about the unbelief the prophet was to expect from God's own people, and he follows with one final repetition of his pronouncement: "Let it be known to you then that this salvation of God has been sent to the Gentiles; they will listen" (28:28).

The end of Acts does not conclude the Christian effort. It is only on the verge of the Gentile mission; the uttermost parts of the earth have yet to be visited. What is formally concluded is the mission to Israel, in Judea and beyond. Paul has given these people of God, scattered all over the world, an opportunity to hear about God's new act of salvation through Jesus. Many Jews have accepted the message and joined the community of believers, not only in Jerusalem but throughout the Roman empire and in the capital itself. The righteous remnant has now been formed, the fallen tent of David raised up. The missionaries now turn their backs on those Jews who have refused the message; they have, from the perspective of the narrator, denied their own heritage. From now on, the messengers will go to Gentiles: the future of the church lies with them; "they will listen."

F. An Apology for Paul

Although Luke devotes more space in Acts to Paul than to anyone else, his portrait of Paul does not differ strikingly from that of Peter or of Stephen. All the major figures in Acts are extraordinary wonder-workers, and Paul is no exception (13:4-12; 14:4-8; 16:16-18; 18:11-20). Like Peter and Stephen, he is a superb orator (esp. 13:26-41; 17:22-31). The outstanding feature of Luke's sketch of Paul, however, is his Jewishness. Paul was a Jew not only in the past; he remains a

Pharisee throughout Acts, faithful in keeping the Law of Moses and believing everything written in the Law and the prophets.

The writer's interest in Paul's Jewishness emerges even in places where it might not be expected: his Roman trial is over a purely Jewish matter. Luke devotes half of his account of Paul's career to the apostle's imprisonment and trial at the hands of the Romans. Yet in the course of this trial—in progress for six chapters—no Roman official lodges a single charge against Paul, and Acts concludes before the emperor gives a final verdict. Roman officials call attention to the dispute between Paul and his Jewish opponents, disputes about matters of Jewish law bewildering to Romans (23:29; 25:18-19, 25; 26:30-31). The narrator seems little interested in the confrontation between Paul and the Roman authorities.

The extended trial narrative (chaps. 21–28) provides Paul with the occasion for several apologetic speeches in which he defends his fidelity to Jewish tradition. The allegations to which Paul replies are summarized by the elders of the Jerusalem church in their initial conference with Paul as he returns to Jerusalem just prior to his arrest:

> You see, brother, how many thousands there are among the Jews of those who have believed; they are all zealous for the law, and they have been told about you that you teach all the Jews who are among the Gentiles to forsake Moses, telling them not to circumcise their children or observe the customs. (21:20-21)

In 22:3-21, Paul insists that he has been raised as a Jew and educated by a leading rabbi and that he is "zealous for God as you all are this day." Paul recounts his conversion to explain why, as a good Jew, he is preaching about Jesus. He notes that Ananias, a devout Jew, told him that the "God of our fathers" had chosen him for the special service; further, Paul received his commission in the Jerusalem Temple.

In 23:6, Paul says he is a Pharisee, on trial simply because he believes in resurrection. Thus his opponents are revealed as Sadducees—the same group responsible for the arrest of Jesus and his followers in Jerusalem.

In 24:10-21, Paul affirms that he worships "the God of our

fathers, believing everything laid down by the law or written by the prophets." His opponents charge him with defiling the Temple. On the contrary, he protests, he was arrested while "purified in the temple," having come to Jerusalem "to bring my nation alms and offerings." Again he argues that the real issue at his trial is belief in resurrection.

In 26:4-23, Paul reviews his career to King Agrippa. He epitomizes his position in verses 5-7:

> According to the strictest party of our religion I have lived as a Pharisee. And now I stand here on trial for hope in the promise made by God to our fathers, to which our twelve tribes hope to attain, as they earnestly worship night and day. And for this hope I am accused by Jews.

In Luke's account, Paul—successful but controversial missionary—is admirably suited for his predominant role as gatherer of the scattered people of God in the Diaspora. The amount of space Luke devotes to Paul's defense and the intensity of the apologetic speeches suggest that the issue of Paul's Jewishness was important to Luke and to his audience. Was Paul a Jewish apostate who had turned from the religion of his birth to teach against the Mosaic Law and Jewish tradition? Certainly not, says Luke. He depicts Paul as a Pharisee whose problems arise principally because of his Pharisaic belief in resurrection. In Acts, the confrontation between Paul and the Jews who do not believe in any resurrection, let alone in the resurrection of Jesus, mirrors the conflict between Pharisees and Sadducees that divided the Jewish community until Pharisaic scholars assumed control of the religious courts after 70 C.E. and pronounced the Sadducees heretics. The Paul of Acts is principally a Pharisaic Jew who believes in Jesus.[8]

This portrait has implications for Jews who hounded Paul throughout his ministry and finally succeeded in having him arrested in Jerusalem. They have thereby demonstrated their solidarity with those who caused Jesus' death, persecuted Peter and the apostles, and stoned Stephen. Furthermore, they are like the Israelites of old who rejected Moses and all the prophets (7:51-52). Like their predecessors, they have rejected God's spokesmen and separated themselves from

God. The history of God's people will continue within the community of true Jews; the success of those who believe in Jesus is certain. The persecutors of Jesus' followers, those who continue to view Paul as a heretic, have excluded themselves from that history and, therefore, from the world to come.

IV. Purpose

Literary models of historiography furnish the pattern for Luke-Acts: as historian, however, Luke does not present his two-stage history as a disinterested observer. He seeks to persuade the reader to adopt the writer's perspective from the outset: the story is not only well known, it is also "well founded"; it is firmly anchored within the tradition of Israel. One of Luke's main purposes is to provide legitimacy to a religious movement.

In antiquity, one way of legitimizing a new movement was to demonstrate that the beliefs of the group were ancient, traditional, historical. Similarly, for the writer of Luke-Acts, Christianity is not a new religion, its ideas not mere novelties. Its history began with the first Jew, with Abraham; in fact, it can be traced back to the first man, to Adam (Luke 3:23-38). More specifically, the story of Jesus and the early church belongs to the story of Israel. These recent events fulfill God's promises made to Jewish patriarchs and through Jewish prophets; the birth of this religious movement is the beginning of the latest and decisive stage in the history of the one people of God. What started with Zechariah and Elizabeth will conclude only at the uttermost parts of the earth.

Most likely, Luke wants his two-part history to convince readers of this truth despite strong objections from other Jews—probably the recognized leaders of the Jewish community. He needs to explain a seeming paradox: the history of God's people, Israel, will continue to involve more and more Gentiles, while the gulf separating these "true" Jews from the rest of the Jewish community will continue to widen. Those Jews who have believed in Jesus are the legitimate heirs of the patriarchs, the true defenders of the Mosaic Law and the Jewish way of life. If the two-part work was not written specifically for Jewish-Christians, they certainly must have represented an important element in his constituency.

V. Author, Date, and Setting

The Gospel of Luke and Acts are traditionally ascribed to a traveling companion of Paul named Luke. The writer never gives his own name; in the prologue he reveals only that he did not witness the events he records in the Gospel, but knows of earlier written accounts that need support or correction. The origin of the traditional Lucan identification is lost, although several clues in the New Testament might have led to such an inference:

1. In certain portions of Acts, the narrator shifts from "they" to "we"—the first time at 16:10. One plausible explanation for the use of the first person plural is that the writer/narrator at one time traveled with Paul.
2. Letters attributed to Paul contain several references to someone named Luke:

Ephaphras, my fellow prisoner in Christ Jesus, sends greetings to you, and so do Mark, Aristarchus, Demas, and Luke, my fellow workers. (Philem. 23-24)

Luke the beloved physician and Demas greet you. (Col. 4:14)

For Demas, in love with this present world, has deserted me and gone to Thessalonica; Crescens has gone to Galatia, Titus to Dalmatia. Luke alone is with me. (II Tim. 4:10-11)

3. The tradition that Luke was a Gentile as well as a physician may stem from Colossians. Paul sends greetings from several co-workers—including Luke the beloved physician; but Luke's name is not included in the list of those with Paul who are "men of the circumcision" (Col. 4:11).

Some scholars find the evidence for the traditional identification insufficient. The traditional arguments about a "physician's perspective" are unconvincing.[9] Luke omits the passage in Mark which criticizes physicians for their inability to heal the woman with a hemorrhage and for their high fees, but so does Matthew (Matt. 9:20; Luke 8:43). The use of technical medical language does not mark the writer as a physician. As one scholar points out, Josephus, the Jewish historian, also uses such phrases.[10] Writers often take pains to use appropriate terminology in their work. Consider, for example, the description of Paul's shipwreck in Acts 27, where Luke uses many specialized nautical terms. The writer may be a sailor as well as a physician; on the other hand, he may be merely discharging his literary responsibility to use a convincing vocabulary in both contexts.

A more important matter is the writer's relationship to Paul, whose career occupies more than half of Acts. Paul's own letters provide few specifics about his travels, but he does confirm some facts reported by Luke, who seems to be well informed.[11] Most reconstructions of Paul's travels rely almost totally on Acts. If, as many believe, the "we" passages identify the writer as a traveling companion of Paul, such detailed information and the occasional confirmations would make sense.

Unfortunately, there are major discrepancies between the Paul of Acts and the Paul of the Epistles. The greatest differences occur where Luke is fitting the story of Paul into his major theme in Luke-Acts, the restoration of Israel. For example, the Paul of Acts is preeminently a thoroughly orthodox Jew, who sees in Christianity no basic discontinuity with the past. This hardly fits the image of Paul that emerges from his letters. Paul speaks about his conversion as a radical break with Judaism and counts his achievements while a zealous Pharisee as garbage (Phil. 3:4-11). He insists on the absolute freedom of Gentiles from the Mosaic Law (Gal. 3:23-29, 5:2-6). He can even make the radical statement, "Christ is the end of the law [of Moses]" (Rom. 10:4).

This may, as some scholars suggest, simply represent a difference in emphasis between Paul's letters and Acts. There are other scholars, however (among whom I would include myself), who believe that the real Paul would have scandalized the writer of Luke-Acts. The problem of comparing the Paul of Acts and the Paul of the Epistles is more thoroughly discussed elsewhere.[12] Here it is necessary to note only that the comparison raises problems for the traditional view of the relationship between Paul and his biographer. Could the person who traveled with Paul have described the self-styled apostle to the Gentiles as such a zealous defender of the Jewish way of life? Opinion is divided.

Dating the two-part work is even more problematic. Some scholars explain the rather abrupt ending of Acts by dating it prior to the outcome of Paul's trial and martyrdom. That seems unlikely: the narrator leaves little doubt that Paul will eventually be martyred. One is on firmer ground if the ending of Acts is viewed as the writer's intended conclusion to his story rather than as a sign of a lack of further information and a token of literary ineptitude.

A clue to the dating of Luke-Acts lies in whether it reflects knowledge of the destruction of Jerusalem, which ocurred in 70 C.E. One can reasonably expect that an event of such crucial important would leave some trace in a work like Luke-Acts. Yet the one bit of evidence that does appear is ambiguous. Luke's version of Jesus' instructions to his disciples about the future differs from Mark's. In Mark, Jesus predicts the destruction of the Temple (Mark 13:2), seemingly as part of a series of worldwide catastrophes that will culminate in the end of the age. In Luke, Jesus predicts that Jerusalem will be destroyed, and the event is separated from the catastrophes that follow. The "great distress" and "wrath" apply to the inhabitants of Jerusalem alone (Luke 21:20-24). The form of this prediction may suggest that the writer knows that it already has been fulfilled and that history has not come to an end. The differences between the two Gospels may reflect Luke's modifications of Mark's prediction in light of subsequent events. It is at least possible, though by no means certain.

There is another possibility for dating the composition of Luke-Acts. As has been suggested repeatedly, this version of Christian history seems to have been conceived as an apologetic for a movement whose legitimacy was in question. The dispute apparently focuses on identity: Who are the real Jews? In this book's introductory historical survey, it was noted that at some point toward the end of the first Christian century, a formal separation took place between Jews who believed in Jesus and Jews who did not. Christian Jews were banned from the synagogue. For such believers, there would have been an intense identity crisis. The leaders of the Jewish community told them that they were no longer Jews. If that were true, they could not properly call Jesus the Jewish Messiah, could not appeal to the Jewish Bible as their Bible, could not accept the Jewish God as their God. It would not have occurred to such Jewish Christians that they were members of a different religion, a "new Israel." From their perspective, there could be only one Israel; the only question that could arise was, Who were the true Jews?

There seem to be good reasons to date Luke-Acts soon after this identity crisis began to penetrate the Christian community, when it became apparent that there would be no reconciliation with the established Jewish community. The suggestion is hypothetical, but it does provide a plausible relationship among major themes, literary devices, purpose, and the period in which Luke-Acts was composed. Such a hypothesis takes the reader beyond the piece of literature itself, but it is offered as a solution to problems raised by literary analysis. It may indicate the importance of literary analysis even for the student of early Christian history.

Summary

The Gospel of Luke and the book of Acts are two parts of a sequential account of Jesus and the early church. Among the themes that unite the two books, the principal one is the continuity of the Christian movement with the history of Israel: Christians are the only legitimate Jews; their opponents renounced their Jewish heritage when they refused to acknowledge Jesus as the fulfillment of Israel's scripture and tradition.

This theme seems to lie beneath the opening and closing of each part of the two-volume work. The Gospel begins and ends with pious Jews in Jerusalem and in the Temple. Acts begins and ends with missions to Jews, at first in Jerusalem and finally in Rome.

It also underlies two subsidiary themes in the Gospel. Luke emphasizes Jesus' interest in the outsiders—the sinners and the poor—whom the established leaders scorn, in violation of the spirit of Jewish tradition. Luke also focuses on the leader's rejection of Jesus as the Jewish Messiah, the promised prophet like Moses, just as they have always rejected God's spokesmen.

In Acts, Luke portrays Peter, Stephen, and Paul as echoing these themes. Peter's sermons give detailed scriptural support to the new movement's claims to historical legitimacy. Stephen's speech points up the long-standing division between believers and nonbelievers within Israel and depicts his opponents as resisting the fulfillment of God's promises. His oration accuses the establishment Jews of worshiping the Temple building itself rather than God, whose true temple is not built with hands.

As for Paul, Luke's picture of him conflicts with the traditional view of Paul, which is mainly derived from his self-portrait in his letters. Paul says his Christianity is a radical break with Jews and with Pharisaic Judaism; he was called to be the apostle to the Gentiles. As Luke tells the story, however, Paul's speeches throughout his extended trial defend him against the charge of heresy and insist on his orthodoxy.

In Luke's account, it was Peter who first accepted a non-Jew into the movement without the convert's first becoming a Jew, and it was Peter and James who were mainly responsible for the Jerusalem council's final approval of such a practice, whereas Paul merely reported to the council on his activities. More important, Luke reports that Paul went to synagogues and tried to convert Jews nearly everywhere he went. Even at the end, he is talking to Jews in Rome, meeting the usual divided reaction, and repeating his old threat to the dissidents that he will go to the Gentiles instead.

As suggested above, one of the main purposes of Luke-Acts seems to be to convince readers that Jewish Christians are the legitimate heirs of Israel's tradition. Just who wrote the books, and when, are by no means settled. Christian tradition says that Luke was a traveling companion of Paul, but the internal evidence is inconclusive, and the discrepancies between Luke's presentation of Paul's mission and Paul's own report in his Epistles cast doubt on that theory. Dating the books is even more uncertain, but one hypothesis helps explain Luke's major themes and apparent purpose: the work reflects a serious cleavage that took place near the end of the first Christian century between establishment Jews and Christians, when each group was insisting that its members were the true Jews and that the others were apostates.

CHAPTER TEN

THE GOSPEL ACCORDING TO MATTHEW

I. Point of View and Purpose

A. Matthew and Mark

Of the Four Gospels, Mark and Matthew seem to be the most clearly related. Virtually all the stories and sayings recorded in Mark also appear in Matthew, usually in the same order and frequently with identical wording. One can find similarities among all the Gospels, but nowhere is careful columnar comparison as necessary, and as illuminating, as with Matthew and Mark. A slightly different nuance—the use of a variant term or a minor shift in setting—will often reveal a distinctive point of view. Therefore, this study of Matthew will begin with a series of comparisons with Mark.

1. Mystery in Mark. Matthew and Mark begin their stories quite differently. Mark plunges the reader directly into the baptism of Jesus with only a superscription ("the Gospel of Jesus Christ, the Son of God") and a paragraph about John's preaching as preparation. Matthew provides a proper genealogical introduction: Jesus Christ is the "son David, the son of Abraham." At the outset, Matthew establishes his hero's credentials: as a descendant of Abraham, he is an Israelite; as a son of David he is qualified for his title of Christ. Before launching into his career, Matthew gives Jesus' background—his ancestry, the nature of his birth, signs of his identity as King of the Jews—and even some foreshadowing of the trouble the young King will encounter.

Matthew begins paralleling Mark with his account of John the Baptist's ministry and Jesus' baptism (Matt. 3:1-17). Matthew's version of the baptism fills in some of the puzzling gaps in the story. Anyone reading Mark's account of Jesus' baptism must wonder why Jesus—the Christ and Son of

God—would submit to baptism by John the Baptist, who administers a "baptism of repentance for the forgiveness of sins" (Mark 1:4). Did the Son of God require forgiveness? Was the Messiah a follower of John? Matthew anticipates such questions. He does not call John's action a "baptism of repentance for the forgiveness of sins," and John is as surprised as anyone at Jesus' request for baptism:

> Then Jesus came from Galilee to the Jordan to John, to be baptized by him. John would have prevented him, saying, "I need to be baptized by you, and do you come to me?" But Jesus answered him, "Let it be so for now; for thus it is fitting for us to fulfil all righteousness." (Matt. 3:13-15)

John's question is not really answered, but Matthew's report at least acknowledges for the reader that Jesus is doing something extraordinary: John asks the reader's question. Note also that John recognizes Jesus as someone special, a detail absent from Mark.

A bit later, the slight difference in the wording of the voice from heaven ("This is my beloved Son" instead of "You are my beloved Son") is significant. Matthew portrays the baptism scene as an epiphany rather than as a transaction between God and Jesus. The writer does not tell that others heard the voice, but one should not be surprised to discover that they did. Matthew is not so careful to conceal Jesus' glory as Mark is.

Consider also the different attitudes that Jesus expresses toward his teaching as reported by Mark and by Matthew. The first detailed presentation of Jesus' teaching in Mark occurs in the fourth chapter, which is composed of a small group of parables for the crowds. In this context, Jesus says to his disciples:

> To you has been given the secret of the kingdom of God, but for those outside everything is in parables; *so that* they may indeed see but not perceive, and may indeed hear but not understand; lest they should turn again, and be forgiven. (Mark 4:11-12)

In Mark, Jesus' teaching is filled with secrets and mysteries; apparently, he does not intend that everyone should understand his message. Interpreting something as obvious as the parable of the sower is possible only for those who have eyes to see and ears to hear. Even the disciples, to whom everything has been explained, who know the secret of the kingdom of God, seem unable to penetrate the mystery of that parable. Similarly, when Jesus rebukes the wind and sea at the end of the chapter, his disciples can only respond with amazement: "Who then is this, that even wind and sea obey him?" (verse 41).

Matthew, on the other hand, introduces Jesus' teachings not with enigmatic parables but with the pointed, unambiguous injunctions of the Sermon on the Mount. In Matthew, the parables themselves serve a different function. Several of those in Mark 4 also appear in Matthew 13. Again, Jesus comments about his use of parables in response to a question by his followers. His reply is almost identical to that found in Mark, with a significant exception:

> To you it has been given to know the secrets of the kingdom of heaven, but to them it has not been given. . . . This is why I speak to them in parables, *because* seeing they do not see, and hearing they do not hear, nor do they understand. (Matt. 13:11-13)

In Matthew's account, Jesus says he uses the parable not because it obscures but because it clarifies and is a way of reaching those who are imperceptive—because people are so blind. The narrator adds his own (and quite typical) embellishment to the explanation:

> All this Jesus said to the crowds in parables; indeed he said nothing to them without a parable. This was to fulfil what was spoken by the prophet: "I will open my mouth in parables, I will utter what has been hidden since the foundation of the world." (13:34-35)

The chapter concludes with a clear indication that the disciples have been enlightened. When Jesus asks his followers whether they have understood, they say yes (13:51). Unlike Mark, Matthew does not end the group of parables with the story of Jesus' calming the sea and the disciples' bewilderment. Nothing in the chapter suggests that Jesus has failed to communicate with his disciples.

Matthew fills in gaps left in Mark. Jesus' disciples are not so obtuse as in Mark, and Jesus does not seek to conceal his message. One final comparison—the two versions of the story of Jesus' walking on the water (Mark 6:45-52; Matt. 14:22-23)—has revealing conclusions:

And he got into the boat with them and the wind ceased. And they were utterly astounded, for they did not understand about the loaves, but their hearts were hardened. (Mark 6:51-52)	And when they [Jesus and Peter] got into the boat, the wind ceased. And those in the boat worshiped him, saying, "Truly, you are the Son of God." (Matt. 14:32-33)

In Mark, the apostles do not understand; in Matthew, they do.

In Mark, the ultimate collapse of Jesus' disciples at the moment of arrest can hardly come as a surprise. Again and again the narrator points up their almost supernatural inability to understand Jesus and his mission, an emphasis that seems to fit the writer's conception of the Christian message as being profoundly mysterious. In Matthew, however, the disciples genuinely have eyes to see; their failure to remain steadfast seems to be a failure of will. The sense of the mysterious and the paradoxical that pervades Mark's Gospel is virtually absent from Matthew's.

2. Didacticism in Matthew. Matthew emphasizes other facets of the story than Mark does. At a similar point in Jesus' ministry, they both summarize Jesus' activity.

That evening they brought to him many who were possessed with demons; and he cast out the spirits with a word, and healed all who were sick. This was to fulfil what was spoken by the prophet Isaiah, "He took our infirmities and bore our diseases." (Matt. 8:16-17)	And he healed many who were sick with various diseases, and cast out many demons; and he would not permit the demons to speak, because they knew him. (Mark 1:34)

In Mark, Jesus is concerned, as usual, that the demons not reveal his identity as God's Son. Matthew's interest is quite different. His climactic quotation from Isaiah 53:4 emphasizes that the exorcisms and healings demonstrate Jesus' ministry as occurring according to scriptures. To understand these events fully, one must see them in their proper context: Jesus' ministry is a fulfillment of prophecy.

The same interest dominates the narrative of Jesus' birth, as observed in chapter 3 of this book. Except for brief pauses to examine the reactions of Joseph and King Herod to the announcement of Jesus' birth, the narrator records events in rapid succession with little descriptive detail. Each incident concludes with a quotation from scripture: "This was done in order to fulfill what was written." Matthew does not develop characters or exploit dramatic possibilities. He is careful, however, to impress on the reader the nature of his story: it is "scriptural." In the birth narrative, Matthew seems to be more interested in justifying the events than in describing them: the reader must above all appreciate the religious significance of the story, understood in light of the scriptures of Israel.

The authors of the Gospels—or editors, as they are frequently called—were not completely free to write as they chose. The tradition about Jesus that they had received limited their creative freedom. Within these limits there is, nevertheless, considerable room for individual expression. Matthew's distinctive emphasis seems to be edification, often to the exclusion of the picturesque details of Jesus' ministry that Mark seems to relish. Consider the following passages from two stories narrated by both Matthew and Mark. The first is from Jesus' encounters with demoniacs.

Matt. 8:28-32	Mark 5:1-13
28 And when he came to the other side, to the country of the Gadarenes, two demoniacs met him, coming out of the tombs, so fierce that no one could pass that way.	1 They came to the other side of the sea, to the country of the Gerasenes. 2 And when he had come out of the boat, there met him out of the tombs a man with an unclean spirit, 3 who lived among the tombs; and no one could bind him any more, even with a chain; 4 for he had often been bound with fetters and chains, but the chains he wrenched apart, and the fetters he broke in pieces; and no one had the strength to subdue him.

29 And behold, they cried out, "What have you to do with us, O Son of God? Have you come here to torment us before the time?"

5 Night and day among the tombs and on the mountains he was always crying out, and bruising himself with stones. 6 And when he saw Jesus from afar, he ran and worshiped him; 7 and crying out with a loud voice, he said, "What have you to do with me, Jesus, Son of the Most High God? I adjure you by God, do not torment me." 8 For he had said to him, "Come out of the man, you unclean spirit!" 9 And Jesus asked him, "What is your name?" He replied, "My name is Legion; for we are many." 10 And he begged him eagerly not to send them out of the country.

30 Now a herd of many swine was feeding at some distance from them. 31 And the demons begged him, "If you cast us out, send us away into the herd of swine." 32 And he said to them, "Go." So they came out and went into the swine; and behold, the whole herd rushed down the steep bank into the sea, and perished in the waters.

11 Now a great herd of swine was feeding there on the hillside; 12 and they begged him, "Send us to the swine, let us enter them." 13 So he gave them leave. And the unclean spirits came out, and entered the swine; and the herd, numbering about two thousand, rushed down the steep bank into the sea, and were drowned in the sea.

The second is the episode of the woman with a hemmorhage.

Matt. 9:20-22

20 And behold, a woman who had suffered from a hemorrhage for twelve years

came up behind him and touched the fringe of his garment; 21 for she said to herself, "If I only touch his garment, I shall be made well."

Mark 5:25-34

25 And there was a woman who had had a flow of blood for twelve years, 26 and who had suffered much under many physicians, and had spent all that she had, and was no better but rather grew worse. 27 She had heard the reports about Jesus, and came up behind him in the crowd and touched his garment. 28 For she said, "If I touch even his garments, I shall be made well." 29 And immediately the

hemorrhage ceased; and she felt in her body that she was healed of her disease. 30 And Jesus, perceiving in himself that power had gone forth from him, immediately turned about in the crowd, and said, "Who touched my garments?" 31 And his disciples said to him, "You see the crowd pressing around you, and yet you say, 'Who touched me?'" 32 And he looked around to see who had done it. 33 But the woman, knowing what had been done to her, came in fear and trembling and fell down before him, and told him the whole truth.

22 Jesus turned, and seeing her he said, "Take heart, daughter; your faith has made you well." And instantly the woman was made well.

34 And he said to her, "Daughter, your faith has made you well; go in peace, and be healed of your disease."

Matthew's version of the exorcism omits the extended description of the man's condition. Furthermore, Jesus simply commands the demons, and they depart, whereas Mark reports an extended dialogue between the exorcist and the demons. In the healing of the woman with a hemorrhage, Matthew proceeds directly to the climax: "Take heart, daughter; your faith has made you well." He is obviously less interested in the extraordinary aspects of the healing or in the dramatic confrontation with a demoniac than he is in making a point about the efficacy of faith. In both cases, the lesson is central. As a rule, although Matthew's accounts are less picturesque than those of Mark or even Luke, he is quite clear about a story's meaning and moral. Perhaps this feature of Matthew's Gospel made it the favorite of the church fathers.

B. Structure: The Mosaic Analogy

One of the more important indications of the Gospel's focus is its structure. Overall, Matthew divides into three parts: a brief introduction (the infancy narratives) and a lengthy central portion (the ministry), and a conclusion (death and resurrection). Within each part there are subdivisions. For example, even in his report of Jesus' ancestry, Matthew purposely separates the list of progenitors into three neat groups of fourteen names.

The story of Jesus' ministry easily subdivides into five blocks, each built around a major discourse, the first of which—the Sermon on the Mount—has already been studied in some detail. Each block concludes with the formula: "And when Jesus finished these sayings—" Some teachings do fall outside these five blocks, but the fivefold division covers most of Jesus' sayings. Particular attention will be paid to the five groups of teachings.

I. Infancy narratives (chaps. 1–2)
II. The ministry of Jesus
   A. Narrative: The preaching of John, Jesus' baptism and temptation, beginning of Jesus' ministry, 3:1–4:25
     Concluding formula: "And he went about all Galilee, teaching in their synagogues and preaching the gospel of the kingdom and healing every disease and every infirmity among the people" (4:23-25).
     Teaching: The Sermon on the Mount, 5–7
     Concluding formula: "And when Jesus finished these sayings . . ." (7:28).
   B. Narrative: Jesus' mighty works, 8–9
     Concluding formula: "And Jesus went about all the cities and villages, teaching in their synagogues and preaching the gospel of the kingdom, and healing every disease and every infirmity" (9:35-38).
     Teaching: Discourse on mission, 10
     Concluding formula: "And when Jesus had finished instructing his twelve disciples . . ." (11:1).
   C. Narrative: Response to Jesus' mighty works and the opening of hostilities, 11:2–12:50
     (No concluding formula)
     Teaching: The parables of the Kingdom, 13
     Concluding formula: "And when Jesus had finished these parables . . ." (13:53).

    D. Narrative: Insiders and outsiders: signs of faith and increased hostility, 13:54–17:27
(No concluding formula)
Teaching: Rules for the common life, 18
Concluding formula: "Now when Jesus had finished these sayings . . ." (19:1).

    E. Narrative (and debate): Open conflict between Jesus and the religious establishment, 19:2–23:27
(No concluding formula)
Teaching: Instructions about the close of the age, 24–25:46
Concluding formula: "When Jesus finished all these sayings . . ." (26:1).

III. Death and resurrection, final commission of disciples (26–28)

One feature of the structure stands out: the body of the Gospel (chaps. 3–25) appears to be intentionally divided into the five parts mentioned above. Some subsidiary parts of the outline, of course, may be artificially imposed, the result of overly ingenious interpretation. The separations into narrative and discourse in the first two subdivisions are clearly delineated; in the remaining three, however, the narrative portions have no formal conclusions. Also, the last narrative section (19:2–23:39) contains numerous sayings, including a chapter-long attack on the Pharisees (chap. 23). Nevertheless, one can surely identify five major units of teaching, each concluded with a formula.

In each of the teaching sections, Jesus seems to focus on a separate issue. (A) He provides some indications about the life-style appropriate for his followers, (B) he sends out his disciples to preach and to heal after giving instructions about their mission, (C) in his parables, he discusses the nature of the kingdom of God, (D) he offers guidelines for communal life, and (E) he instructs his disciples about what is to come, including several parables that serve as warnings to the faithful.

At the very end of the Gospel, Matthew again emphasizes Jesus' teachings:

> And Jesus came and said to them, "All authority in heaven and on earth has been given to me. Go therefore and make disciples of all nations, baptizing them in the name of the Father and of the Son and of the Holy Spirit, *teaching them to observe all that I have commanded you*; and lo, I am with you always, to the close of the age." (28:18-20)

Of course, Matthew sees Jesus as the Messiah, the Son of God, who is born of a virgin, crucified, and raised from the dead, and who will return with the clouds to gather his elect. For Matthew, however, Jesus is more specially a great teacher, not only founding a new movement but also providing for his followers an authoritative interpretation of the will of God. As discussed earlier, Matthew does not portray Jesus as a revealer of cosmic secrets—in contrast, for example, to the Gospel of Thomas, a book that also emphasizes Jesus' teachings (see above, chap. 4). Jesus' teachings in Matthew have a more practical orientation.

For Matthew, it is the authority of Jesus' interpretation of God's will that is important. On what basis does Jesus claim to teach the will of God? Matthew's Gospel contains hints of a seemingly revolutionary attitude or an extraordinary claim to authority: "You have heard it said to men of old. . . . But I say to you."[1] But Matthew undercuts any tendency to interpret Jesus' teachings as subversive by first placing them in their proper context:

> Think not that I have come to abolish the law and the prophets; I have come not to abolish them but to fulfil them. For truly, I say to you, till heaven and earth pass away, not an iota, not a dot, will pass from the law until all is accomplished. (5:17-18)

Matthew sees Jesus not as a revolutionary or even as an innovator but as a spokesman for tradition and as an expositor of the Law of Moses. In Matthew, Jesus insists that his teaching falls within a thoroughly Jewish framework, which has led many to believe that the Gospel of Matthew is the most Jewish of the four.

Viewed from this perspective, the fivefold structure of the ministry in the Gospel becomes even more interesting. The obvious and obtrusive division of the entire account, as shown in the outline, raises the question of the significance of the division. One suggestion is that the writer, whose interest in Jewish scripture is pervasive, has patterned his work after another that is divided into five parts: the Torah, or first five books of the Bible, also known as the Five Books of Moses. He introduces his Gospel as the genesis of Jesus Christ (a more accurate translation than "genealogy"), perhaps corresponding to the "Genesis of the World" (the title of the first book in the Greek Septuagint). Parallels between Jesus and Moses seem clear in the infancy narratives (only Matthew tells of the baby's escape from Herod's slaughter) and, notably, in the giving of the "Law" from the mountain. The structure of Matthew may be simply one more indication that the author sees Jesus as a new Moses and his teaching as a new Law.

Scholars have raised several objections against this interpretation of the structure of Matthew.[2] The most serious is that the five-book analogy would relegate the infancy narratives and the death/resurrection sequence to the status of preface and epilogue. Yet the proposal continues to intrigue interpreters of Matthew. The use of the term "genesis" in the opening verse is too striking to be coincidental. The symbolic setting of Jesus' sermon (chapters 5–7) on an unidentified "mountain" reminiscent of Sinai seems to reinforce the parallel of Jesus and Moses. Only Matthew divides Jesus' ministry into five parts, arbitrarily imposing a structure even where it is not quite suitable.

Matthew does seem to have in mind a pattern for his Gospel. Luke's literary models were historical writings; the only literary model for Matthew's Gospel seems to be the books of the Law, or Torah (Genesis–Deuteronomy). In both Matthew and the Torah, teaching is primary. Like Moses, Jesus is not simply a great leader or miracle-worker but also an expositor of God's will. For Matthew, Jesus is more than a great hero or prophet like Moses: he is the Messiah, God's own Son, the Son of man to whom all authority has been given. Nevertheless, Matthew chooses to emphasize Jesus' activity as teacher, and the distinct features of his Gospel are reminiscent of patterns and themes, even of the structure, of the Torah.

C. Some Themes

1. "Not like the scribes": Jesus as Rabbi. If Matthew sees Jesus as the new Moses, he at least does not characterize Jesus' teachings as a new Law. He has come "not to abolish . . . but to fulfil" (5:17); he will merely interpret the Law and the prophets. Note, however, that scribes, Pharisees, and Sadducees also appear in the Gospel as interpreters of the Law. Since the Sadducees, who also oppose Jesus, do not believe in a developing, oral law beyond Scripture, Jesus' main quarrel is with scribes and Pharisees, whose interpretive traditions he considers incorrect. (In addition, Matthew may have been writing at a time when the Pharisees had replaced the Sadducees as Jewish leaders. But more of that later.) The major point of conflict in Matthew centers on the proper interpretation of the Law and of tradition.

Matthew clarifies Jesus' position by contrasting Jesus with the scribes. His listeners observe that "he taught them as one who had authority, and not as their scribes" (7:29). Jesus demands that his followers display a righteousness greater than that of the scribes and Pharisees if they hope for admittance to the kingdom of heaven (5:20). Scribes and Pharisees appear as actors for the first time in Matthew in chapter 9, and as in all the Gospels, their role is negative. Their first response to Jesus is an accusation that he is blaspheming in presuming to offer forgiveness of sins beyond the teacher's prerogative and power, according to tradition (9:3). Pharisees then object when Jesus violates their understanding of tradition and sits down to eat with sinners and tax collectors. "And when the Pharisees saw this, they said to his disciples, 'Why does your teacher eat with tax collectors and sinners?'" (verse 11).

In Matthew, as in Mark and Luke, Jesus responds with a pronouncement about his mission to the sick and to those in need of forgiveness. Matthew's account subtly emphasizes the relationship between Jesus' practice and his teaching. The Pharisees, who take the Law seriously, imply by their question that this teacher either has misunderstood the Law or is deliberately violating its precepts by associating with irreligious people. Jesus' reply reinforces his proclaimed purpose of his mission with a quotation from Hosea 6:6. "Go and learn what this means, 'I desire mercy, and not sacrifice'" (9:13).

Appealing to biblical authority was a familiar rabbinic method of argumentation. Jesus here is a rabbi—a teacher, interpreting the Law and advancing tradition by applying a scriptural passage to a contemporary situation. He defends his association with "untouchables" by quoting Hosea. He, not his opponents, is acting in accordance with Scripture. In Matthew's version of the conflict, the point is not that Jesus himself authorized associating with sinners and tax collectors, but that he justified his practice by appeal to Jewish Scripture.

In chapter 15, Matthew further specifies the issues that separate Jesus from the Pharisees and scribes. After miraculously feeding five thousand people (14:13-21), Jesus returns with his disciples, only to be attacked by his opponents:

> Then Pharisees and scribes came to Jesus from Jerusalem and said, "Why do your disciples transgress the traditions of the elders? For they do not wash their hands when they eat." He answered them, "And why do you transgress the commandment of God for the sake of your tradition?" (15:1-3)

Jesus then lists examples of traditions that violate the Torah. He contrasts his opponents' false tradition (the basis for their criticism of him and his followers) with the Law. The issue here is not whether one should follow the Law rather than interpretations; Jesus boldly interprets the ancient commands himself in the Sermon on the Mount. The question is rather who interprets the Law properly; that is, who speaks for God? The Pharisees were certain that their interpretations were valid expositions and extensions of the Law. In sweeping terms, however, Jesus condemns them for their failure to understand the real thrust of God's commands. His opponents are concerned with externals—with hand washing—while they overlook things that truly defile: evil thoughts (15:19-20). In their concern for details, they miss the essentials. And once again, Jesus introduces Scripture into the debate: "You hypocrites! Well did Isaiah prophesy of you, when he said: 'This people honors me with their lips, but their heart is far from me; in vain do they worship me, teaching as doctrines the precepts of men'" (verses 7-8).

The dispute between Jesus and the Pharisees reaches a climax in his scathing attack on the scribes and Pharisees (chap. 23). Luke also records these harsh words, but less prominently; Matthew includes them in Jesus' final confrontation with the religious leaders of the people. He denounces the heads of the Pharisaic movement within Israel as pietistic hypocrites: these would-be followers of the Law have become so obsessed with minutiae that their tradition has finally succeeded in obscuring the will of God. Jesus condemns them for not practicing the Law zealously and for misleading others, in addition to missing the real point of Torah. The attack concludes with as bitter a statement as any in the pages of the New Testament:

> Woe to you, scribes and Pharisees, hypocrites! for you build the tombs of the prophets and adorn the monuments of the righteous, saying, "If we had lived in the days of our fathers, we would not have taken part with them in shedding the blood of the prophets." Thus you witness against yourselves, that you are sons of those who murdered the prophets. Fill up, then, the measure of your fathers. You serpents, you brood of vipers, how are you to escape being sentenced to hell? Therefore I send you prophets and wise men and scribes, some of whom you will kill and crucify, and some of whom you will scourge in your synagogues and persecute from town to town, that upon you may come all the righteous blood shed on earth, from the blood of innocent Abel to the blood of Zechariah the son of Barachiah, whom you murdered between the sanctuary and the altar. Truly, I say to you, all this will come upon this generation. (23:29-36)

Matthew's Gospel is not simply Jewish; it is also anti-Jewish. Jesus' opponents are a segment of his own people. In this climactic speech, Jesus places the conflict within the perspective of Israel's experience. Jesus aligns himself and his disciples with the ancient prophets. By opposing Jesus, the scribes and Pharisees demonstrate that they are true sons of those who traditionally persecuted the prophets. God will vent his accumulated wrath on them in a special way.

Matthew reports that "all the people" answered Pilate,

saying, "His blood be on us and on our children" (27:25). Their fate, according to the writer, has been sealed: Jerusalem will be destroyed. The vineyard will be taken from them and given to another nation (21:43). For Matthew, the destruction of Jerusalem will provide a striking if brutal vindication of Jesus and his followers. It is they, not the scribes and Pharisees, who have properly understood the Law and deserve the name "people of God." The end of the chapter will consider the importance of the claim and the vehemence with which it is argued in Matthew.

2. *"Unless your righteousness exceeds that of the scribes and Pharisees": Models of Pious Behavior.* Matthew uses the same device in the narrative portions of Jesus' ministry as he does in the sections devoted to his teachings. As already seen, to clarify what is distinctive about Jesus' teaching, Matthew presents Jesus' interpretation of the Law in response to attacks from scribes and Pharisees, the guardians of traditional interpretation. Similarly, he provides models of real piety, on the part of true people of God—in contrast to the behavior of scribes and Pharisees, who serve as foils. From their very first appearance in the Gospel, the scribes and Pharisees cannot accept Jesus and what he stands for because of their view of tradition, their understanding of what it means to be a Jew. Others, however, do accept Jesus.

Apart from the disciples and Jesus' parents, other such characters begin to appear in chapter 8, after the Sermon on the Mount. The first one to express faith in Jesus and appeal to him for help is a leper, considered ritually "unclean" by usual standards of Jewish law. His faith is rewarded when Jesus cleanses him from the leprosy. The second is a Roman centurion, who asks Jesus to heal his slave. When Jesus agrees to come with him, the soldier replies:

> Lord, I am not worthy to have you come under my roof; but only say the word, and my servant will be healed. For I am a man under authority, with soldiers under me; and I say to one, "Go," and he goes, and to another, "Come," and he comes, and to my slave, "Do this," and he does it. (8:8-9)

The centurion understands power; he is confident that Jesus has the authority to command and the power to have his commands fulfilled. According to Matthew's account, the centurion understands Jesus in a way many Jews do not:

> Truly, I say to you, not even in Israel have I found such faith. I tell you, many will come from east and west and sit at table with Abraham, Isaac, and Jacob in the kingdom of heaven, while the sons of the kingdom will be thrown into the outer darkness; there men will weep and gnash their teeth. (8:10-12)

Matthew introduces Jesus as the Jewish Messiah and his teachings as expositions of the Mosaic Law. His examples of true piety are an unclean leper, contact with whom was defiling to religious Jews, and a non-Jew who is an agent of the oppressors of God's people. Matthew's conception of proper Jewishness strikingly reverses the values and expectations of the scribes and Pharisees. They feel that they are the righteous ones and criticize Jesus for associating with untouchables (9:10-13). On the contrary, Jesus says that those who consider themselves to be good Jews and "sons of the kingdom" will find themselves without a place at the great table (22:1-10). The theme echoes John the Baptist's earlier warning:

> Do not presume to say to yourselves, "We have Abraham as our father"; for I tell you, God is able from these stones to raise up children to Abraham. Even now the axe is laid to the root of the trees; every tree therefore that does not bear good fruit is cut down and thrown into the fire. (3:9-10)

Matthew uses the device of contrast again in the group of stories in chapters 14–16, all built around food imagery: feeding the five thousand (14:13-21), what defiles a person (15:1-20), the Canaanite woman (15:21-28), feeding the four thousand (15:32-39), discourse on leaven (16:5-12).

The feeding of the five thousand elicits from scribes and Pharisees only criticism of Jesus based on his followers' failure to wash properly before eating (15:1-20). The ensuing discussion of defilement is followed by a story of Jesus' encounter with a Canaanite woman. (Mark refers to her as Syrophoenician.) The narrator gives no reason for Jesus' withdrawal to the vicinity of Tyre and Sidon; the only point of the story is the contrasting Gentile and Pharisaic responses to

Jesus. The woman, identified only as a non-Jew, comes to Jesus for help. He meets her pleas first by silence, then by the statement that he was sent only to Jews (15:22-24). Matthew makes no attempt to play down the priority of Israel as God's people and the object of his concern. The woman persists:

> But she came and knelt before him, saying, "Lord, help me." And he answered, "It is not fair to take the children's bread and throw it to the dogs." She said, "Yes, Lord, yet even the dogs eat the crumbs that fall from their master's table." Then Jesus answered her, "O woman, great is your faith! Be it done for you as you desire." (15:25-28)

Jesus defends the priority of Israel, even concurs in the widespread Jewish view of Gentiles as "dogs." The woman is willing to accept that priority and the epithet, if only Jesus will condescend to help her. The contrast with the Pharisees is striking. Ignoring the fact that Jesus has miraculously fed the multitudes with actual bread, the self-important Pharisees and scribes are concerned only with washing properly; the Gentile woman is willing to sacrifice her self-respect for mere crumbs, and Jesus feeds her spiritual bread.

Elsewhere, Jesus pictures the kingdom of heaven as a banquet (8:11; 22:1-10; 25:1-13). When offered real food, those alleged to be religious Jews cannot see beyond superficial ritual. They will discover too late that their place at the great banquet has been taken by others, who recognize which teacher speaks for God and what true righteousness means.

3. "Teaching them to observe all that I have commanded you": Rules of Behavior. Like the other evangelists, Matthew defends the claims and teachings of the Christian movement against attack. Thus, the contrast between Jesus, the teacher, and other teachers within the Jewish community is an essential element of Matthew's Gospel. The Gospel has another didactic element, however, that has little to do with defining Jesus' position by contrast or defending the movement against attack. Many of Jesus' teachings are guidelines for the everyday life of his followers. They handed his sayings on from generation to generation for this reason, and Matthew is no exception. In fact, this interest in the relevance of Jesus' teachings for the life of believers is more pronounced in Matthew than in any of the other Gospels.

Consider Matthew's treatment of parables compared with Luke's. Luke tells the parable of the lost sheep (Luke 15:3-7) as Jesus' response to criticism of his association with sinners and tax collectors (verses 1-2). "Just so, I tell you, there will be more joy in heaven over one sinner who repents than over ninety-nine righteous persons who need no repentance" (verse 7).

In Matthew, the same parable is part of Jesus' instruction to his followers. It illustrates the lengths to which members of the community should go in seeking out errant brothers and sisters who stray from the flock of those who believe in Jesus. Matthew's parable ends very differently: "So it is not the will of my Father who is in heaven that one of these little ones should perish" (Matt. 18:14). The parable is an exhortation to persevere in preserving the community rather than an explanation of why Jesus associated with outcasts.

Another parable that establishes rules of behavior is the wedding feast (Matt. 22:1-14; see Luke 14:15-24), which warns that many of the supposed chosen of God will not enter God's kingdom. Though confident that they know what to expect from God, they will discover to their dismay that they failed to recognize God's messenger and to take his invitation to the feast seriously. To their surprise and consternation, the hall will be filled not with the chosen but with outcasts.

In Matthew, the parable does not end at the filling of the hall, as it does in Luke. Those who fill the hall are "both bad and good" (Matt. 22:10), a circumstance that leads to another stage in the story. The host discovers a man without a wedding garment:

> And he said to him, "Friend, how did you get in here without a wedding garment?" And he was speechless. Then the king said to the attendants, "Bind him hand and foot, and cast him into the outer darkness; there men will weep and gnash their teeth." For many are called, but few are chosen. (22:12-14)

Now the parable presents difficulties. It seems unfair that someone unexpectedly invited to attend a wedding should be faulted for not having a wedding garment. What does the wedding garment symbolize in the parable? Joachim Jeremias, a well-known student of Jesus' parables, found in the Talmud a strong parallel to Jesus' parable:

> R. Eliezer said: "Repent one day before your death." His disciples asked him, "Does then one know on what day he will die?" "Then all the more reason that he repent today," he replied, "lest he die tomorrow, and thus his whole life is spent in repentance." And Solomon too said in his wisdom, "Let thy garments be always white; and let not thy head lack ointment." R. Johanan b. Zakkai said: "This may be compared to a king who summoned his servants to a banquet without appointing a time. The wise ones adorned themselves and sat at the door of the palace, ['for,'] said they, 'is anything lacking in a royal palace?' The fools went about their work, saying, 'can there be a banquet without preparations?' Suddenly the king desired the [presence of] his servants: the wise entered adorned, while the fools entered soiled. The king rejoiced at the wise but was angry with the fools. 'Those who adorned themselves for the banquet,' ordered he, 'let them sit, eat and drink. But those who did not adorn themselves for the banquet, let them stand and watch.'"[3]

The point of the rabbinic story is that one must always be prepared for God's coming—at death—at peace with God and man. The image of the white robe, similar to the parable's wedding garments, is a symbol for a pure heart, with which to appear before God. Whether the wedding garment in Jesus' parable literally meant simply a clean robe, the symbolism suggested by the rabbinic story would fit well into the context of the last chapters in Matthew's Gospel. For Luke, the parable teaches that some who expect to get into the kingdom of God won't be there; Matthew goes further and tells his followers how to behave so that they may remain among the chosen.

Together with the parable of the householder whose return is delayed (24:45-51) and the parable of the wise and foolish maidens (25:1-13), the story of the man who had not prepared clothing appropriate to the wedding feast would serve as a warning for followers of Jesus who had become neglectful about righteous behavior. These three parables reveal an interest in the post-Easter Christian movement. They serve as a warning, not to Jesus' enemies, but to his followers—in

Matthew's times as well as in Jesus'. In the first, the hall is filled with "both bad and good." Some who believe that they are secure, now that they have joined the movement, will discover that even belonging to the new movement will not guarantee their status before God. In the second, if those entrusted with the affairs of the household do not exercise their responsibility faithfully, they too will be cast into the outer darkness (24:45-51). In the third, even some believers will be unprepared when the Son of man comes. They too must be watchful; like Jesus' own followers, Matthew's readers might be unprepared for what is to come: "Watch therefore, for you do not know on what day your Lord is coming. . . . Therefore you also must be ready; for the Son of man is coming at an hour you do not expect" (verses 42-44).

Matthew portrays Jesus as the authorized interpreter of the Torah who provides guidelines so that his followers can live in accordance with God's will. Teaching is one of the important tasks of Jesus' followers. In his parting words to his disciples, Jesus orders them not simply to preach the gospel and baptize converts but to teach these converts "to observe all that I have commanded you" (Matt. 28:20). Instruction is an essential task; they must carry it out before the close of the age. The order to teach what he has commanded precedes Jesus' promise of his continued presence with his followers until the close of the age. The angel told Joseph that Jesus was to be called "Emmanuel"; that is, "God [is] with us" (1:23). To his followers, his presence represents God's presence in the world. Jesus promises them that "where two or three are gathered in my name, there I am in the midst of them" (18:20.)[4] In light of the concluding verses of the Gospel, one may suggest that for Matthew, it is in remembering and obeying Jesus' commandments and instructions that his followers perceive his presence in their midst.

II. Background

A. Author, Date, and Context

Tradition provides little information about the background of the Gospel of Matthew. The first reference to the book in

Christian literature is an enigmatic two-line comment by Papias, Bishop of Hierapolis in Asia Minor, which the historian Eusebius includes with the comment on Mark noted in chapter 8. Scholars dispute whether the comment by Papias is even a reference to the Gospel of Matthew as it is now known. The text from Eusebius reads:

> Mark who had been Peter's interpreter, wrote down carefully but not in order, all that he remembered of the Lord's *sayings and doings.* For he had not heard the Lord or been one of His followers, but later, as I said, one of Peter's. Peter used to adapt his teaching to the occasion, without making a systematic arrangement of the Lord's *sayings,* so that Mark was quite justified in writing down some things just as he remembered them. For he had one purpose only—to leave out nothing that he had heard, and to make no misstatement about it. Such is Papias's account of Mark.[5]

Of Matthew he has only this to say: "Matthew compiled the sayings in the Aramaic language, and everyone translated them as well as he could."

If this translation is correct, and it is the most common, the reference can hardly be to the present Gospel of Matthew, which was most certainly composed in Greek and includes stories about Jesus in addition to his sayings. Many have therefore concluded that Papias must be referring to a now-lost collection of Jesus' sayings in Aramaic that might have been a basis for the hypothesized Greek collection of Jesus' sayings known as "Q".[6]

A German scholar named Kürzinger has proposed an alternate translation of the two lines on Matthew that eliminates these difficulties and provides an interesting literary evaluation of Matthew:

> Matthew compiled the sayings [and doings—as in the elliptical use of "sayings" in line 7 of the comment on Mark] in Hebrew style—and each one [i.e., Matthew and Mark] interpreted them [Jesus' sayings and deeds] as best he could.[7]

According to this reading, Papias is describing the literary character of Matthew as he has with Mark. Papias says that Mark does not write "in order," meaning not in proper form, while Matthew writes "in a Jewish manner." The manner might well be that of the Jewish Bible or perhaps rabbinic models. Like Mark, Matthew does not follow proper literary conventions; but at least his book has a model. Kürzinger's proposal is attractive because it requires no hypothetical Hebrew collection of sayings and accords well with the apologetic tone of Papias' comments about Mark, as noted in chapter 8. Whatever the case, the earliest extant comment on Matthew tells little about the writer of the Gospel and nothing about the circumstances of its composition.

According to tradition, the writer was one of Jesus' original disciples. The evangelist never identifies himself, but some have found clues to his identity in the list of disciples. In Matthew 9:9, the tax collector whom Jesus invites to follow him is named Matthew, while in Mark and Luke he is Levi. In the lists of disciples (Matt. 10:3; Mark 3:18; Luke 6:15), when all three call him Matthew, only in the Gospel of Matthew is he identified—once again—by his occupation. Many students of the Gospel nevertheless consider the traditional attribution unlikely: if the writer used the Gospel of Mark and a collection of Jesus' sayings as his main sources, he probably was not an eyewitness (see chap. 2). Those who find the arguments about the sources of Matthew unconvincing will obviously have less difficulty accepting apostolic authorship.

Dating the work is also uncertain. Once again, much depends upon an interpreter's evaluation of the arguments about sources. If Matthew is based on the Gospel of Mark, a date after 70 C.E. is almost certain. One piece of evidence that many interpreters consider significant is in Matthew's version of the parable of the marriage feast. It mentions the destruction of the murderers and the burning of their city by the king's troops (22:7). Some scholars (with whom I agree) believe this to be a reference to the destruction of Jerusalem that is read back into the parable of Jesus; others do not. Students of the Gospel must evaluate the various supporting arguments in order to determine for themselves how relevant such details are for dating the work.

The context of Matthew's composition is clearer. The Gospel presupposes the existence of a community of believers, a "church," which is engaged not simply in spreading the Word but also in the day-to-day business of communal life. The book provides practical help for those who must serve as leaders. In fact, some have even proposed that Matthew composed his Gospel as a handbook for church leaders.[8] The proposal surely overstates the case: the Gospel belongs to a different genre than the "Manual of Discipline" discovered among the Dead Sea scrolls at Qumran, for example. Matthew has other purposes, as already discussed; but he is continually concerned with relating Jesus' story to the practical matters of Christian living.

The institution whose existence the Gospel presupposes is under attack. Jesus warns his followers that they can expect hostility—from Jews as well as from Gentiles (10:16-23; 23:34-35)—and emphasizes the opposition of Jewish leaders throughout. In telling the Easter story, the narrator refers to rumors circulating among Jews, rumors with which his readers presumably are familiar (28:11-15). Matthew singles out as Jesus' typical opponents the scribes and Pharisees. In his version, Pharisees were involved even in the plot against Jesus in Jerusalem and in the intrigue prior to his resurrection (21:45; 27:62). Jesus launches his most vituperative attacks at the scribes and Pharisees.

The reason for the heightened hostility toward the Pharisees in Matthew, as compared with Mark, may be that the Gospel was composed when Pharisaic scholars, not Sadducean priests, headed the Jewish community—the situation after the destruction of the temple in 70 C.E.[9] The scribes and Pharisees dispute the claims of Jesus' followers that he is the Messiah and that his disciples are true Jews, claiming that they distort the Law and violate traditional Judaism. The dispute between Jesus and his opponents is especially intense in Matthew. The bitterness and hostility toward scribes and Pharisees may well reflect a collapse in the relations between community leaders and those Jews who believed Jesus to be the Messiah. Representatives of the official establishment may have even persecuted Christian Jews.

In many respects the problems with which the writer of Matthew's Gospel wrestles seem similar to those in Luke-

Acts. Like Luke-Acts, the Gospel of Matthew seeks to make sense out of the traumatic experiences of his group. The crisis in both cases appears to be a rupture within the Jewish community. Each writer claims the heritage and Scripture of Israel for his own group in the face of opposition. The greater vehemence of the controversy in the Gospel of Matthew suggests that for his community, the conflict with established Judaism was more intense.

Each writer deals with the group's identity crisis in a distinctive way. Luke-Acts interprets events by relating them to the history of Israel—that is, by writing history; Matthew casts the division within the Jewish community in the form of a debate over proper interpretation of the Law. Matthew portrays Jesus as the authoritative interpreter of the Law. Those who practice righteousness as Jesus describes it are faithful to the Law and the true tradition; they will enter the kingdom of heaven—unlike the scribes and Pharisees.

B. Interpretation of Scripture in Matthew

Among the frequent references to Scripture in Matthew, eleven are introduced by a formula: "This was done in order to fulfil what was spoken by the prophet." Their content also marks these quotations as distinctive. In several cases the quotations deviate from the Septuagint, suggesting modification of the text, knowledge of the Hebrew original, or use of a different Greek translation of the Old Testament—but not poor rabbinic technique.[10]

Matthew's use of some of the quotations reveals what may seem to be a rather unconventional approach to interpreting Scripture. For example, Matthew calls Jesus' return from Egypt with his parents the fulfillment of a biblical prophecy. "This was to fulfil what the Lord had spoken by the prophet, 'Out of Egypt have I called my son'" (2:15). The words are from the book of Hosea:

> When Israel was a child, I loved him,
> and out of Egypt I called my son.
> The more I called them,
> the more they went from me. (Hos. 11:1-2)

Matthew is not merely relating events to obvious parallels. In Hosea, the metaphor is clear and traditional; the nation Israel is personified as God's son. The calling out of Egypt is a reference to the Exodus. If so, how can Matthew argue that Jesus' return from Egypt fulfills this prophecy? Matthew, like his Jewish contemporaries, read the biblical text quite differently from the way most modern scholars read texts.

This approach to a text has been explored in our first chapter. An interpreter may read the text as a prediction, despite the intention of the original writer. Furthermore, the interpreter assumes that each text has several meanings in addition to the literal one. Matthew is interested in the hidden meaning, according to which the prophetic text points to the coming of the Messiah. His method of approaching the biblical text is common among Jewish interpreters, particularly noticeable in the Dead Sea Scroll writers, as well as among Christians.

What distinguishes Matthew from other Jewish writing of the time is the acceptance of Jesus as the Messiah, and what distinguishes Matthew from other Gospels is the ingenuity and sophistication of his interpretation. Many of these formula quotations seem to show careful work with the biblical text, the sort one might expect within a scholarly community. One interpreter has in fact suggested that this Gospel is the product of a "school."[11] Although debatable, the proposal does suggest that the Gospel of Matthew emerges from a context with striking affinities to rabbinic communities. The writer might well be viewed as a "scribe trained for the kingdom of heaven," in the words of the author himself (Matt. 13:52).

Summary

Matthew is mainly interested in establishing Jesus' authority as a teacher whose interpretations of the Mosaic Law correct the tradition upheld by scribes and Pharisees. More specifically, Matthew emphasizes that Jesus' teachings define true righteous behavior for his followers, both of his own time and of Matthew's time.

The distinctiveness of Matthew's Gospel stands out when

compared with Mark's. Mark centers on the unique mystery of Jesus' mission. Matthew demystifies Mark's Gospel; he takes pains to have his readers understand the meaning of events in Jesus' life and of his teachings, showing that both are grounded in Scripture.

Matthew's overwhelming preoccupation with Jesus' teachings is reflected in the structure of the Gospel. It has relatively short accounts of the infancy and of the trial, death, and resurrection. The far larger main body of the book is clearly divided into five sections. Each centers on a major didactic theme, and each contains both narrative and teachings. (Some scholars see this fivefold division as an echo of the Pentateuch, reinforcing other parallels in Matthew between Jesus and Moses.) In addition, the Gospel ends with Jesus telling his disciples that one of their main duties is to teach others what he has taught them to do and to be.

Jesus' quarrel with the scribes and Pharisees is most intense in Matthew's Gospel. Both sides are especially vicious here. Jesus, and Matthew as narrator, insist that their Jewish opponents misunderstand the Law and violate its true meaning—especially by not accepting Jesus as the true interpreter of the Law and as the Messiah. Jesus exhorts his followers to behave with true righteousness and not follow the teachings and examples of the Pharisees. To this end, he presents to his disciples specific rules of behavior and examples of righteousness.

According to tradition, this Gospel is the work of the apostle Matthew, but most critical scholars feel that the evidence indicates otherwise. Matthew's Gospel seems to be based on Mark's and on a hypothesized collection of Jesus' sayings preserved by tradition, so that the writer of Matthew probably was not an eyewitness. Its emphasis on the proper behavior for a community of believers presupposes the existence of some sort of institutionalized church. It seems to allude to the destruction of Jerusalem, which took place in 70 C.E. Its rage against the scribes and Pharisees suggests that they had by then replaced the Sadducees as the established leaders of the Jewish community and were possibly even persecuting Christians.

Still, Matthew, like Luke, insists that it is the followers of

Jesus, not his opponents, who are the true Jews. Matthew differs from Luke in his method of arguing. Luke sets Jesus within the continuity of the history of Israel, past and future. Matthew argues in the traditional rabbinic manner, reinterpreting Scripture to account for the contemporary situation.

CHAPTER ELEVEN

THE GOSPEL OF JOHN

> In the beginning was the Word, and the Word was with God, and the Word was God.

With these words, John introduces his readers to a world of symbols distinctly different from that of the Synoptic Gospels. Several peculiarities of both content and form reinforce the distinctiveness of the Fourth Gospel:

1. The Johannine Jesus does not speak in concise, aphoristic statements or in parables taken from rural life in Palestine. Instead, he delivers extended, often complex and abstract discourses.

2. Jesus preaches not about the imminent coming of the kingdom of God but about himself and his role as emissary of his Father.

3. The miracle stories in John are fewer and unique to this Gospel, with the exception of feeding the five thousand and walking on water (John 6:1-21).

4. The narrative mentions three Passovers, suggesting to some commentators that Jesus' ministry, as portrayed by John, lasts at least two years.

5. Jesus works primarily in Judea, in the south, and is frequently in Jerusalem. His ministry in Galilee, so important for the other evangelists, is an exception occasioned by his rejection in Judea. Judea, not Galilee, is Jesus' country in which, as a prophet, he has no honor (4:44).

6. John's account of Jesus' last meal with his followers does not include the famous words instituting the Eucharist.

7. The dating of the crucifixion is singular.[1]

John's form is no less distinctive. The language is often highly symbolic, and the relatively limited vocabulary masks an often complex and bewildering style that makes frequent use of double entendre, misunderstanding, and irony. For those unfamiliar with the original Greek, a commentary is more useful with John than with any other Gospel.

Another prominent feature of John is startlingly illogical actions or words:

11:5-6: Jesus' close friends, Mary and Martha, send word that their brother is at the point of death. "Now Jesus loved Martha and her sister and Lazarus. So when he heard that he was ill, he stayed two days longer in the place where he was."

7:7-9: Jesus' brothers, who are planning to go up to Jerusalem for the feast of Tabernacles, ask Jesus whether he plans to come. "Go to the feast yourselves; I am not going up to this feast, for my time has not yet fully come." So saying, he remained in Galilee. But after his brothers had gone up to the feast, then he also went up.

5:31: "If I bear witness to myself, my testimony is not true."

8:14: "Even if I do bear witness to myself, my testimony is true."

8:15-16: "I judge no one. Yet even if I do judge . . ."

These examples indicate something of the elusiveness of the narrative. John seems to delight in strikingly unexpected statements, giving the impression that he is purposely confusing or paradoxical and that his story has a mysterious dimension just beyond reach.

Some students of John's Gospel argue that several of these confusions are due to careless editing. Indeed, much evidence indicates that the work is in fact the end product of a rather complex process of editing.[2] Parenthetical editorial comments explain names (1:38, 41), interpret symbols (2:21; 12:33), and correct mistaken impressions or errors (4:2; 6:6; 7:22). Yet the paradoxes and the unexpected turns in the narrative are so frequent and so pronounced that they cannot be accidental or signs of poor craftsmanship. They represent simply one more indication of a singular literary style characteristic of the Fourth Gospel.

I. Structure

Outlining the Gospel of John presents problems. In all three of the Synoptic Gospels, the major divisions in the material are clearly marked: Peter's confession and Jesus' first prediction of his passion are a watershed, and Jesus' ministry has clearly Galilean and Jerusalem phases. This geographical division in particular makes the direction of the narrative and its dramatic development obvious. In John, one cannot recognize the familiar blocks of material. The first eleven chapters generally seem to have carefully selected narratives from Jesus' life integrated with major discourses. There is no obvious logical movement, however, and certainly no clear overall geographical progression: Jesus is frequently in Jerusalem, and his movements between Jerusalem and Galilee in chapters 5–7 are difficult to follow.

The chronology and the dramatic development are equally baffling. One of the first incidents recorded in the Fourth Gospel is Jesus' provocative cleansing of the Temple (2:13-22), which occurs at the end of his ministry in the other Gospels. John reminds the reader (verse 17) that this act initiates a process that will end in Jesus' death, as it does in the other Gospels. He reports the Jerusalem authorities' plotting to destroy Jesus in chapter 5 (verse 18), much earlier than in the Synoptics, and several attempts on Jesus' life are made before his last visit to Jerusalem (5:16-18; 7:32, 44; 8:20, 59; 10:39). The story does not build up gradually to its tremendous climax. On the contrary, in John, the reader can only marvel that Jesus is able to survive as long as he does.

A. "My Hour"

Fortunately, John does provide some clues to a structure. Jesus talks of "my hour," and so does the narrator. For some time, Jesus is mysteriously immune to arrest and harm from his enemies. The reason, according to the narrator, is that his hour has not yet arrived:

> So they sought to arrest him; but no one laid hands on him, because his hour had not yet come. (7:30)

> These words he spoke in the treasury, as he taught in the temple; but no one arrested him, because his hour had not yet come. (8:20)

This turning point toward which the story moves is the hour of Jesus' death, which, in the Gospel of John, paradoxically is also his glorification.

> And Jesus answered them, "The hour has come for the Son of man to be glorified. Truly, truly, I say to you, unless a grain of wheat falls into the earth and dies, it remains alone; but if it does, it bears much fruit. . . . Now is my soul troubled. And what shall I say? 'Father, save me from this hour?' No, for this purpose I have come to this hour." (12:23-27)

> Now before the feast of the Passover, when Jesus knew that his hour had come to depart out of this world to the Father . . . (13:1)

The expression not only provides clues to a major division in the story but it also reveals the perspective from which the story is narrated. Nothing in Jesus' life occurs by chance: all has been ordained or "has been written." Precisely how Jesus manages to elude his would-be executioners is unimportant; more decisive is the fact that his death occurs according to the will of God, at the moment—the hour—chosen for the purpose. John's task is to narrate what "really" happens, what the story "really" means.

B. Coming and Going Back

A related structural feature is a pair of images connected with Jesus' ministry. A major theme, to be examined below in some detail, is the coming of Jesus into the world: as the Word of God, the emissary from the Father, Jesus has come. He must also go back to the Father:

> Jesus then said, "I shall be with you a little longer, and then I go to him who sent me; you will seek me and you will not find me; where I am going you cannot come." (7:33-34)

> And again he said to them, "I go away, and you will seek me and die in your sin; where I am going, you cannot come. . . . You are from below, I am from above; you are of this world, I am not of this world." (8:21-23)

> "I came from the Father and have come into the world; again, I am leaving the world and going to the Father." (16:28)

John tells of Jesus' coming into the world in the first eleven chapters. They record his public ministry, mighty acts or signs, and teaching. With chapter 13, the focus shifts to his going from the world and his return to his Father. Most of the rest of the book deals with the preparation of his followers for that departure. Chapter 12 marks the transition from the first to the second phase of his ministry, summarizing what has happened and anticipating what is to come.

II. Thematic Analysis

A. Prologue

> In the beginning was the Word, and the Word was with God, and the Word was God. He was in the beginning with God; all things were made through him, and without him was not anything made that was made. In him was life, and the life was the light of men. The light shines in the darkness, and the darkness has not overcome it.
>
> There was a man sent from God, whose name was John. He came for testimony, to bear witness to the light, that all might believe through him. He was not the light, but came to bear witness to the light.
>
> The true light that enlightens every man was coming into the world. He was in the world, and the world was made through him, yet the world knew him not. He came to his own home, and his own people received him not. But to all who received him, who believed in his name, he gave power to become children of God; who were born, not of blood nor of the will of the flesh nor of the will of man, but of God.
>
> And the Word became flesh and dwelt among us, full of grace and truth; we have beheld his glory, glory as of the only Son from the Father. (John bore witness to him, and cried, "This was he of whom I said, 'He who comes after me ranks before me, for he was before me.'") And from his fulness have we all received, grace upon grace. For the law was given through Moses; grace and truth came through Jesus Christ. No one has ever seen God; the only Son, who is in the bosom of the Father, he has made him known. (1:1-18)

The Fourth Gospel prefaces the story of Jesus with these poetic verses. They give neither the narrator's sources nor a list of Jesus' ancestors; instead, John presents a picturesque sketch of the career of the Word of God. This mysterious "Word," which plays a decisive role in creation and is "the true light that enlightens every man," is Jesus of Nazareth, confessed by his followers as Messiah.

It is a peculiar prologue, difficult even to classify formally. It seems to be a hymn, similar to others in the New Testament (e.g., Phil. 2:5-11), to so-called wisdom hymns (e.g., Wisdom of Sirach 24:1-22), or to the non-Christian hymn to Zeus by Cleanthes.[3] The hymn has no obvious match, but it does exhibit certain stylistic features found in Semitic poetry, like staircase parallelism:

> In the beginning was the Word,
>> and the Word was with God,
>>> and God was the Word.
> In him was life,
>> and the life was the light of men.
>> The light shines in the darkness,
>>> and the darkness has not overcome it.

The prologue is different from the rest of the Gospel. Its poetic form does not appear again. Jesus is described as the Word only in these verses. "Grace," used four times in the first eighteen verses, does not recur in John. John uses the "tenting" metaphor for Jesus' incarnation only here ("the Word became flesh and dwelt [lit., tented] among us," 1:14). Indeed, the differences in the prologue have led several scholars to believe that the hymn was composed separately and only later added as an introduction.[4]

In any event, the prologue is a most appropriate introduction to the Gospel. Most of the major motifs in John appear in it: light/darkness, son/father, enlighten, life. John mentions the light/darkness opposition of 1:5 in 3:19-21 and develops it in chapters 8 and 9. The "only son" (1:14) occurs in one of the most familiar verses in the New Testament, John 3:16, and father/son language pervades the Gospel. Jesus frequently speaks of himself as the revealer (verse 18), notably in 5:19-22 and 6:46. The term "life" appears nearly forty times, and in 20:31, John summarizes the purpose of the Gospel with these words: "These are written that you may believe that Jesus is the Christ, the Son of God, and that believing you may have life in his name." The prologue also introduces one of the most basic themes of the story, Jesus' coming into the world and his rejection by "his own people" (verse 11). Thus, the prologue contains most of the important clues for interpreting the work and deserves a more detailed examination:

1. Creation and Revelation. John begins "in the beginning": the story of the itinerant preacher from Galilee extends back before the foundation of the world.

> In the beginning God made the heavens and the earth. (Gen. 1:1)

> In the beginning was the Word, and the Word was with God, and the Word was God. He was in the beginning with God; all things were made through him. (John 1:1-3)

The similarities between Genesis and the Gospel continue. God's first act is the creation of light in the pervading darkness: in John, the creative Word is also the source of light:

> And God said, "Let there be light"; and there was light. And God saw that the light was good; and God separated the light from the darkness. (Gen. 1:3-4)

> In him was life, and the life was the light of men. The light shines in the darkness, and the darkness has not overcome it. (John 1:4-5)

Even the image of the Word by which the world was created echoes Genesis 1. God creates by speaking: God said, "Let there be . . ." (Gen. 1:3, 6, 9, etc.). As the psalmist expresses it: "By the word of the LORD the heavens were made, and all their host by the breath of his mouth" (Ps. 33:6).

In his expression "Word of God," John borrowed the Greek term for "word" used in the Septuagint, *logos.* This borrowing takes on added significance when we consider that Jews had been speculating about the power of God's Word to create. Before the Christian movement, Jewish tradition had hypostasized the creative Word of God—given to his word a substantial reality.[5] John here identifies this Word with an historical person, Jesus of Nazareth, the Word who "became flesh" (1:14). God's creative word, the agency that fashioned the universe, has become embodied, incarnate. The horizons of Jesus' ministry as described in the Fourth Gospel are cosmic.

The imagery from the creation story of Genesis becomes a superb vehicle for John's purposes. Through his word, God created physical light. John gives this act a further meaning: "The true light that enlightens every man was coming into the world" (1:9).

Darkness is as appropriate a description of the human situation as it is of the cosmic order. Without God's Word, human life is darkness, chaos. John sees a parallel between creation and revelation. He links the enlightenment, or revelation that Jesus' coming brings, with God's first act of creation, the bringing of light into darkness. One can find this same attempt to correlate creation and revelation in Jewish tradition. The word through which God creates is identified with Wisdom (Prov. 8:22-31; Wisd. of Sol. 9:1-2) or with Torah: the principles God has given, which are to govern life, are the blueprint for creation itself.[6]

For the writer of John's Gospel, as for the narrator in Genesis, darkness is not a neutral image. In Genesis, the primeval state is a potentially threatening chaos; so also in John, human spiritual darkness is hostile to enlightenment:

The light shines in the darkness, and the darkness has not overcome it. (John 1:5)

The true light that enlightens every man was coming into the world. He was in the world, and the world was made through him, yet the world knew him not. He came to his own home, and his own people received him not. (1:9-11)

The prologue forecasts that the light that is to enlighten every person will not meet universal enthusiasm. In fact, it will bring about a division. Some will receive him: "But to all who received him, who believed in his name, he gave power to become children of God; who were born, not of blood nor of the will of the flesh nor of the will of man, but of God" (1:12-13).

But others will not receive him. Ironically, it is his own, those who should most naturally be expected to recognize him and to accept him, who will not. The statement is puzzling. How can anyone not recognize and accept the Word of God, to whom each person owes his or her very existence? Who are "his own" who will not receive him, and who are the others who do? The prologue does not say; instead, it becomes more confusing: "For the law was given through Moses; grace and truth came through Jesus Christ" (1:17).

Is there a contrast between "law" on the one hand and "grace and truth" on the other? Between Moses and Jesus Christ? Did not the God who created the world through his Word, who sent his Son into the world to "enlighten every man," also give the Torah and enlightenment to Moses? The conclusion of the prologue is even more mystifying, not to say mystical: "No one has seen God; the only Son, who is in the bosom of the Father, he has made him known" (1:18).

Why does the introduction to the Gospel end on this note? The mention in the previous verse of Moses, who spoke with God face to face, may be a clue that for some people only Moses is God's authorized revealer, perhaps to the exclusion of Jesus.

Even without further clues, the reader can sense in the prologue a dominant feature of the ensuing story. Jesus will encounter opposition from the very beginning of his career; some will not understand that he is from God. In John's Gospel this is a paradox. On the one hand, Jesus enlightens everyone, openly reveals who he is; on the other hand, most of his own people live in an impenetrable darkness through which they cannot see. The dispute between those who believe Jesus and those who do not will focus on their understanding of Moses and Torah and tradition. That much is learned from the prologue. The prologue further suggests that this conflict will not be simply an episode in the history of Israel. It is nothing less than the cosmic struggle between light and darkness that has existed since the world began.

2. John the Baptist: The Witness. In several places, John interrupts the poetic movement of the prologue with prose comments, the first time at verse 6: "There was a man sent from God, whose name was John. He came for testimony, to bear witness to the light, that all might believe through him. He was not the light, but came to bear witness to the light" (1:6-8).

At first glance, this intrusion seems superfluous: despite the seeming reversal of roles in his baptism of Jesus, John the Baptist is of secondary importance, only preparatory to the story of Jesus. Nevertheless, the evangelist evidently felt that his readers needed this reminder—both for negative and positive reasons. The narrator explicitly denies an extraordinary list of offices to John the Baptist in the first verses: he is not the light (1:8); he is not the Christ, not Elijah, not the prophet (1:20-21, also 3:27-29). The Baptist himself says that Jesus ranks before him (1:15), and in answer to a concerned question from one of his followers, he states that "he must increase, but I must decrease" (3:30). The forceful way the writer plays down his role indicates that for some people John the Baptist was more than simply Jesus' forerunner.

More important for interpreting the Gospel as a whole is the positive role attributed to the Baptist. He is a witness: "He came for *testimony,* to *bear witness* to the light. . . . He was not the light, but came to *bear witness* to the light" (1:7-8); "John *bore witness* to him" (verse 15); "And this is the *testimony* of John" (verse 19).

The use of the verb "to bear witness" and the related noun "testimony" becomes particularly significant when one notes that this terminology is remarkably rare elsewhere in the New Testament. The verb occurs only twice in the other Gospels combined, while it appears thirty-two times in John. The noun appears three times in Mark and once in Luke, compared with thirteen times in John. Though used by John in a variety of contexts, both are legal terms, whose connotations John may fully intend in these opening verses. John the Baptist may be a witness whose task is to give testimony for someone on trial. Both the Baptist and the evangelist may be arguing a case. Further study of the Gospel as a whole may support this view.

B. The Story

Each evangelist unifies his Gospel by different means. In Mark, the mystery of the suffering Christ ties together the episodes in the story. In Luke-Acts, one might say that the basic unifying theme in the two-volume composition is the establishment of a restored Israel, a holy remnant, understood within the perspective of the whole history of Israel. For

Matthew, the main issue is Jesus as the true teacher/interpreter of the Mosaic Law. In John, on the other hand, the unifying elements in the story seem to be certain basic and pervasive motifs. Following is an examination of two of the more important ones: Jesus as the Coming One and Jesus' entire ministry as a trial, culminating in the episode with Pilate.

1. The Coming One. From the prologue on, John stresses Jesus' advent into the world of humanity. Jesus is "the true light that enlightens every man" (1:5); that is one purpose of his coming: "I have come as light into the world, that whoever believes in me may not remain in darkness" (12:46).

This reason for Jesus' coming is illustrated in the episode of his healing of the man born blind (chap. 9). Jesus can bring such enlightenment only because he has come "from God" (3:2) or "from above" (verse 4): "No one has ever seen God; the only Son who is in the bosom of the Father, he has made him known" (1:18). "But he who sent me is true, and I declare to the world what I have heard from him" (8:26).

Another purpose for the advent appears even more pervasively in the Fourth Gospel—that Jesus has come to offer the possibility of life:

"I came that they may have life, and have it abundantly." (10:10)

In him was life. (1:4)

For God so loved the world that he gave his only Son, that whoever believes in him should not perish, but have eternal life. (3:16)

These are written that you may believe that Jesus is the Christ, the Son of God, and that believing you may have life in his name. (20:31)

This purpose is also illustrated by an episode in the story—the raising of Lazarus (chap. 11).

As the Coming One, Jesus fulfills expectations; his advent has been anticipated.

The woman said to him, "I know that Messiah is coming (he who is called Christ); when he comes, he will show us all things." Jesus said to her, "I who speak to you am he." (4:25-26)

When the people saw the sign which he had done, they said, "This is indeed the prophet who is to come into the world!" (6:14)

She said to him, "Yes, Lord; I believe that you are the Christ, the Son of God, he who is coming into the world." (11:27)

What has he come to reveal that will enlighten and give life? John uses many images, but offers few details. Almost the sole content of Jesus' revelation is that he is the one who has come. Jesus is called revealer, Christ, prophet, Son of God, good shepherd, the living water, bread from heaven, resurrection and life. John does not elaborate further, preferring only to emphasize the arrival of the emissary from above, the fulfillment of hopes.

The advent provides the drama in the story; it provokes a crisis, forcing people to make a decision for or against Jesus. They dispute about where Jesus has come from:

Some of the people of Jerusalem therefore said, "Is this not the man whom they seek to kill? And here he is, speaking openly, and they say nothing to him! Can it be that the authorities really know that this is the Christ? Yet we know where this man comes from; and when the Christ appears, no one will know where he comes from." (7:25-27)

And they reviled him, saying, "You are his disciple, but we are disciples of Moses. We know that God has spoken to Moses, but as for this man, we do not know where he comes from." (9:28-29)

When Pilate heard these words, he was more afraid; he entered the praetorium again and said to Jesus, "Where are you from?" (19:8-9)

The prologue introduces the conflict between light and darkness. Jesus comes because there is darkness, and his advent causes confrontation between the two forces. In making a decision about Jesus, the characters in the story reveal something about themselves: whether they are of the light or of the darkness, whether they will inherit life or death. Jesus has come to bring light and life, but his advent has its negative aspect as well, because he has come for judgment. "And this is the judgment, that the light has come into the world, and men loved darkness rather than light, because their deeds were evil. For every one who does evil hates the light, and does not come to the light, lest his deeds should be exposed" (3:19-20).

2. The Trial Motif: Its Two Levels. The conflict between Jesus and his opponents climaxes in the legal trial before Pilate (18:28–19:16), but forensic imagery is introduced much earlier in the Fourth Gospel. The first of many witnesses to offer testimony is John the Baptist: "There was a man sent from God, whose name was John. He came for testimony, to bear witness to the light" (1:6-7).

The list of witnesses is impressive:

a. Jesus has come to bear witness:

> He who comes from heaven is above all. He bears witness to what he has seen and heard. (3:32)

> "[The world] hates me because I testify of it that its works are evil." (7:7)

> "Even if I do bear witness to myself, my testimony is true." (8:14)

> "For this I was born, and for this I have come into the world, to bear witness to the truth." (18:37)

b. God is a witness:

> "I bear witness to myself, and the Father who sent me bears witness to me." (8:18)

c. Miracles are signs that provide testimony:

> "For the works which the Father has granted me to accomplish, these very works which I am doing, bear me witness that the Father has sent me." (5:36)

> "The works that I do in my Father's name, they bear witness to me." (10:25)

d. The Spirit, called the Counselor, will give testimony:

> "But when the Counselor comes, whom I shall send to you from the Father . . . he will bear witness to me." (15:26)

e. Followers of Jesus are appointed to be witnesses:

"You also are witnesses, because you have been with me from the beginning." (15:27)

f. The narrator is a witness:

He who saw it has borne witness—his testimony is true, and he knows that he tells the truth—that you also may believe. (19:35)

The consistent use of courtroom language indicates that John has fundamentally cast the story in the form of a trial. Jesus is being judged. Is he the prophet coming into the world (6:14) who works true signs (20:30-31) and speaks God's words? Or is he a false prophet whose signs and teaching are perversions intended to lead people astray (7; 18:19-23)? If Jesus is a false prophet, then according to the Torah, he deserves to die:

If a prophet arises among you, or a dreamer of dreams, and gives you a sign or a wonder, and the sign or wonder which he tells you comes to pass, and if he says, "Let us go after other gods," which you have not known, "and let us serve them," you shall not listen to the words of that prophet. . . . But that prophet or that dreamer of dreams shall be put to death. (Deut. 13:1-5)

John never quotes the passage above, but it seems to provide the traditional backdrop for one aspect of the controversy. Jesus' teaching is the issue at his hearing before the Jewish court (John 18:19-23).

The authenticity of his teaching as a prophet is one of the many controversial aspects of Jesus' ministry. Is he the true Messiah or only a would-be King of the Jews? Is he from God, or are his incredible claims blasphemous (5:17-18; 8:39-59; 19:7)? The prologue, the miracle narratives, Jesus' teaching, even the literary patterns in the story emphasize the controversial nature of Jesus.

Jesus' signs are one form of testimony in his trial. Jesus says he has come to bring life. The stories of the woman at the well (4:7-42) and the raising of Lazarus (11:1-44) support his claim, and each story suggests a different nuance of the life Jesus has come to make possible. He also says he has come to bring light to those in darkness (8:12). As evidence, the narrator offers the story of the healing of the man born blind. These remarkable signs provide testimony that Jesus' claims are true and that he is indeed from God: "If this man were not from God, he could do nothing" (9:33). The signs testify—for those who have the eyes to see—that Jesus is the prophet coming into the world (6:14), the Christ (7:31), and the Son of God (11:27; 20:31).

In addition to signs, Jesus presents as evidence the testimony of Scripture and tradition. The "lifting up" of the brazen serpent in the wilderness points to his death and exaltation (3:14-15), which will bring life to those who fix their gaze on him. It is of Jesus that the enigmatic biblical text about "bread from heaven" spoke (6:31). The narrator also calls Scripture as a witness: Jesus' ministry, John says, fulfills the statement about the unbelief of God's people in Isaiah (12:38-40), and Jesus is the true paschal lamb (19:36).

Even Jesus' enemies ironically become unknowing witnesses to the truth. The comment of the Pharisees at the interrogation of the blind man ("but as for this man, we do not know where he comes from," 9:29) becomes testimony to Jesus as the Messiah because it corroborates an earlier statement made by the crowd: "Yet we know where this man comes from; and when the Christ appears, no one will know where he comes from" (7:27). The high priest offers the sage political advice that Jesus should be stopped before bringing the Romans down on Israel; he puts it in prophetic terms: Jesus should "die for the people" (11:50). Pilate's inscription, "King of the Jews," is a climactic piece of ironic testimony.

On one level, Jesus is on trial throughout the Fourth Gospel. The characters in the story, notably the leaders of the Jewish people, must judge him. They have to weigh the testimony and decide what to do with him. For the reader, however, the trial has a deeper level. The reader sees no ambiguity about Jesus: The Father has sent Jesus, the Christ and Son of God, as the only revelation of his will. Jesus is to bear witness to the truth, to give enlightenment and life. Truth is not simply a matter of intellectual curiosity; life itself hinges on knowledge of that truth. Those who judge correctly and accept Jesus' testimony, who believe that he is from God and has the words of life, receive life and become children of God (6:67-68). Those who do not believe are condemned:

> For God so loved the world that he gave his only Son, that whoever believes in him should not perish but have eternal life. For God sent the Son into the world, not to condemn the world, but that the world might be saved through him. He who believes in him is not condemned; he who does not believe is condemned already, because he has not believed in the name of the only Son of God. And this is the judgment, that the light has come into the world, and men loved the darkness rather than light, because their deeds were evil. (3:16-19)

As discussed, although Jesus has come to bring life, his coming also involves judgment—by the people and upon them. Those who see Jesus' signs and hear his words face a crisis; they must decide who he is and whether to believe him. Everything depends on that decision; it is a matter of life and death. This personal crisis represents, John implies, an anticipation of the final judgment. How people judge Jesus determines how they themselves will be judged.

In this sense, it is not really Jesus who is on trial, but those who presume to be his judges, those to whom he has been sent. Jesus' signs and teachings have a different meaning at this deeper level: they unmask the characters in the story and provide testimony for God's verdict. Those who attempt to use Moses and tradition against Jesus will find, to their dismay, that Moses has become not their advocate in the heavenly court, but their accuser (5:45). The climax of this level of the story comes when the religious leaders of the people, like the Pharisees in the story of the healing of the man born blind, must commit themselves. They condemn Jesus to temporal death—and in so doing sign their own eternal death warrants.

This double meaning of the trial is reflected in the literary patterns and even in the narrative style of the Gospel. The discourse on bread from heaven unfolds with progressive misunderstanding on the part of the crowd precisely as the discourse offers greater insight into the nature of Jesus' ministry (6:25-65). The most profound statement (from the perspective of the believer) about the body and blood of Jesus causes the deepest lack of insight and even hostility from the crowd. Similarly with the climactic sign: Jesus' most spectacular miracle, the raising of Lazarus, becomes the catalyst that finally crystalizes the plot against Jesus' life (11:17-53).

Like Mark, John tells the story at more than one level. The perspective of the characters is narrower than that of the readers. John tells his readers at the outset who Jesus is, that he has enemies, that his own will reject him. The ensuing story gives the readers the details: what Jesus' role is, who his enemies are, why his own do not receive him, and what their rejection means. Jesus' signs and discourses, which provide this information about Jesus for readers, confront the characters in the story with the necessity of making a decision about Jesus. Their rejection of Jesus serves as a counterpoint to the revelation for the reader.

3. The Trial before Pilate. The trial (18:28–19:16) is the culmination of the development of the "witness" and "testimony" imagery in the Fourth Gospel. Again like Mark, John emphasizes the language of the charges in order to instruct the reader about Jesus. Jesus is interrogated, mocked, and executed as "King of the Jews" (18:33-37; 19:2-5, 14-15, 19-22). John is even more explicit than Mark, leaving no doubt that Jesus really is the Messiah-King. Jesus is also tried as "Son of God," as he is in the other Gospels (19:17). Both titles form one of the basic Christian confessions and are related to the stated purpose of John's Gospel (20:30-31).

The testimony offered to Pilate against Jesus is at the same time testimony for the reader that all the claims made by, and for, Jesus are true. Once more, Jesus' enemies unwittingly provide this testimony in their accusations, as they do in Mark. Here, however, John is more interested in the witnesses themselves, in the would-be judges of Jesus—Pilate and the Jewish leaders. He permits the reader to see into the real trial—that of the leaders and the people.

a. Pilate. On the one hand, Pilate is depicted as an apologist for Jesus. Although his persistent attempts to have Jesus released are ultimately unsuccessful, he at least makes the attempt. The rather bewildering movement in and out of the praetorium throughout the trial serves to heighten the suspense, but it also makes Pilate a more favorable person than the Jewish leaders.

On the other hand, Pilate is not really of the light; he is not even a neutral figure. Jesus has come to bear witness to the truth, but Pilate mocks him with "What is truth?" (18:38) and does not wait for an answer. He does not know and does not want to know. Like most of the characters in the story, he is in the dark about where Jesus is from (19:9).

Pilate does his best to avoid having to make a decision about Jesus. He suggests that the Jews judge Jesus according to their own law (18:31); he tries to release Jesus in his customary Passover gesture of goodwill (verse 39). He has Jesus scourged, hoping thus to satisfy the mob (19:1-4). He insists that he can find no crime that Jesus has committed. Nevertheless, when forced to choose between the King of the Jews and the favor of Caesar, he decides against Jesus. Pilate, therefore, is no less culpable than the Jewish leaders, according to John. He too belongs to the darkness.

b. The Jewish Leaders and the Jews. Like the other evangelists, John focuses principally on the role of his own people at Jesus' trial. Here the words of the prologue become clear. From the perspective of the narrator, the trial completely unmasks Jesus' "own" people. Insisting upon Jesus' death, they steadfastly resist every attempt of Pilate to have Jesus released. Their comments become more and more revealing.

First they choose Barabbas for clemency in place of Jesus. The incident, reported only briefly, concludes with one of the parenthetical remarks that are often significant: "Now Barabbas was a robber" (18:40).

As noted in the chapter on Mark, the term that is used here, *lestes,* can mean either "robber" or "revolutionary." In this case, the proper translation is "robber" because of other associations the term has for John. In Jesus' discourse on the good shepherd, he draws a contrast between himself as the true shepherd and others whom he characterizes as "thieves and robbers" (10:1, 8). Here also the term is *lestes.*

Jesus also says that the sheep who belong to his fold will

recognize his voice (10:3-5). This image is echoed just before the Barabbas episode, in Jesus' response to Pilate's question about his identity: "Every one who is of the truth hears my voice" (18:37). In their choice of the robber Barabbas, the Jews have demonstrated that they have not heard Jesus' voice; they do not follow the true shepherd, but belong to the thieves and robbers.

The most stunning revelation occurs at the most dramatic point in the confrontation between Pilate and the Jews. Pilate has made his final plea to have Jesus released, once again to no avail. He then brings Jesus out and either sits himself or places Jesus on the judgment seat—where the judge is supposed to sit!

Most commentators have preferred the translation of 19:13 found in the Revised Standard Version: "He brought Jesus out and sat down on the judgment seat." The Greek verb is *kathizo,* which is transitive, meaning "to set, place." It may be translated as the intransitive "sit," in the sense of "sit oneself down." In this case, the latter seems sensible to most translators, since it would be incomprehensible for Pilate to place Jesus on the judgment seat. Yet it may not be necessary to translate the transitive Greek verb in this way; there is, after all, a separate word in Greek for the intransitive "sit." John may have purposely sketched what, at least on the surface, seems an absurd picture: the final verdict at Jesus' trial is about to be pronounced while Jesus himself is sitting at the judge's bench.[7] The irony would be wholly appropriate, for Jesus has come to sit in judgment.

John introduces the last response of the Jewish leaders, which decides Jesus' fate, with unusual solemnity and an uncustomary concern for precise detail:

> Now it was the day of Preparation for the Passover; it was about the sixth hour. He [Pilate] said to the Jews, "Behold your King!" They cried out, "Away with him, away with him, crucify him!" Pilate said to them, "Shall I crucify your King?" The chief priests answered, "We have no king but Caesar." (19:14-15)

The real force of this last statement would be apparent only for those hearers (and readers) who knew something about the Jewish celebration of Passover, the observation of which actually begins with ritual preparations on the preceding day.[8]

The following lines conclude an ancient hymn that is part of the liturgy:

> From everlasting to everlasting thou art God;
> Beside thee we have no king, redeemer, or savior,
> No liberator, deliverer, provider,
> None who takes pity in every time of distress and trouble.
> We have no king but thee.[9]

Unfortunately, it cannot be determined precisely when this hymn, the *Nishmat,* became part of the Passover celebration. The first reference to it occurs in the Babylonian Talmud in a statement attributed to a Palestinian scholar who lived from the end of the second into the third century of the Common Era.[10] It is not known for certain, therefore, that this hymn was part of the Passover celebration at the time the Fourth Gospel was written.

In any event, the themes of the hymn were certainly familiar and especially appropriate to the Passover. To be a member of God's people meant to acknowledge, regardless of consequences, that God is the only King, certainly above pagan rulers. It was the confession of God's sole lordship that occasioned the rise of the resistance movements against Rome when Judea became a Roman province, since for some Jews submission to Roman rule meant acknowledging Caesar as lord instead of God. At the opening of the great festival of Passover, when Jews acknowledged their complete dependence on and hope for God's deliverance, John reports that the leaders of the Jewish nation were confessing their sole allegiance to Caesar. By their response to Pilate, the leaders of the Jewish people have rejected their God and their tradition and have consequently forfeited the right to be called the people of God. They, not Jesus, are judged and condemned.

4. Humanity Divided. John's Gospel represents a distinctive point of view. He does not portray Jesus' ministry as a new stage in the history of Israel, as does Luke. Rather, Jesus' ministry represents a challenge or charge to which everyone must respond as at a trial. In their response lies the Judge's verdict, their destiny. Everything in John's Gospel focuses on

Jesus and the two possible responses to him. This division among humanity resulting from Jesus' coming is nothing new. It is part of the continuing struggle between light and darkness, from the dawn of creation to the end of time. The historical response to Jesus among the people of Israel—in Jesus' time or in John's—is simply a manifestation of an eternal confrontation between God and his world. The heavenly court will make a decision in the case of every person, basing it on his or her response to Jesus. There is light and life or darkness and death. Those who believe have life already; those who do not are already condemned.

This highly dualistic conception of the universe and of humanity has led many students of John to compare the Gospel with other dualistic religious literature. For John, reality seems inherently an opposition between light and darkness, with little room left for anything in between. This opposition, however, has no mythological dimensions, common in later Gnostic literature. The Gospel does not tie the division in the universe and within the human race to a dualistic cosmogony or to a Manichean polarity. John makes remarkably little use even of that aspect of dualism, common in the other Gospels, which depicts Jesus in conflict with demonic powers. The Father who sends his Son into the world has no apparent rival in the heavenly realm. The emissary from the Father is the Word by which the cosmos was created.

Nevertheless, the Gospel assumes a crucial division among humankind. Some belong to the light; others, to the darkness. For some God is their father; for others, the devil (8:42-47). Reality is a struggle between these two sides. According to John, Jesus' ministry does not introduce a new struggle into history or even inaugurate a new epoch in the struggle. It simply brings to the surface the divisions that have always been present but until now were unrecognized.

The struggle focuses on Jesus' ministry to his own people. From John's perspective, "the Jews" stand for those who consider themselves the people of God, but are actually God's enemies, forfeiting the right to that designation. They should be God's people; having Moses and the prophets, the Jews above all should recognize the truth. Moses and the whole of tradition have provided one consistent witness to Jesus

(5:39-47). The Jews who oppose Jesus believe that in Scripture and tradition they can find eternal life. Yet in their rejection of Jesus, they reveal their misunderstanding of, and opposition to, God and Jewish Scripture and tradition.

John's Gospel is an artistic accomplishment. By the use of misunderstanding, irony, and double entendre, the narrator enlightens the reader about Jesus and at the same time exposes the blindness of those who saw Jesus' signs and heard his teachings. John's literary genius lies in his telling a simple story with remarkable subtlety and power.

III. Author, Context, and Purpose

A. Authorship

Ostensibly, the Fourth Gospel appears to offer fewer problems about its authorship and date than the other Gospels, largely because of its suggestion that the information comes from an eyewitness: "He who saw it has borne witness—his testimony is true, and he knows that he tells the truth—that you also may believe" (19:35). The Gospel addresses readers directly in this parenthetical comment to guarantee the reliability of the story.

But who speaks—the original author of the Gospel or a later editor? Who is the eyewitness—our narrator or someone else to whom the narrator refers as "he"? Most commentators believe that the eyewitness must be the mysterious "beloved disciple" (lit. "the disciple whom Jesus loved"), who first appeared with that title in John 13:23 and, only in John's account, was present at the foot of the cross (19:26-27). The suggestion that this eyewitness is the beloved disciple, and that the same person has written at least part of what is in the Gospel, receives further support from the last chapter: "This is the disciple who is bearing witness to these things, and who has written these things; and we know that his testimony is true" (21:24). The antecedent of "this" is clear: he is "the disciple whom Jesus loved, who had lain close to his breast at the supper" (verse 20).

Yet this whole last chapter poses a number of problems. It seems anticlimactic from the rest of the Gospel. It also goes out of its way to settle the question of whether Jesus had implied that the "beloved disciple" would not die until Jesus returned:

> Peter turned and saw following them the disciple whom Jesus loved, who had lain close to his breast at the supper and had said, "Lord, who is it that is going to betray you?" When Peter saw him, he said to Jesus, "Lord, what about this man?" Jesus said to him, "If it is my will that he remain until I come, what is that to you? Follow me!" The saying spread abroad among the brethren that this disciple was not to die; yet Jesus did not say to him that he was not to die, but, "If it is my will that he remain until I come, what is that to you?" (21:20-23)

The most obvious occasion for such an explanation of what Jesus really said would be that the beloved disciple, the putative author of the Gospel, had died and Jesus had not yet returned. In any case, the Gospel contains claims that the information included at least stems from an eyewitness.

Which disciple is it? The Gospel itself does not say. The tradition that it was John derives from Irenaeus, the great Bishop of Lyons, who wrote during the latter part of the second Christian century.[11] Irenaeus said that his information came from Polycarp, Bishop of Smyrna, who was martyred in 155 C.E., but there the trail ends. For those interested in a careful evaluation of the evidence provided by Irenaeus, Raymond Brown has discussed the matter thoroughly and clearly in his commentary.[12]

Tradition holds that the apostle John was not only the beloved disciple and the eyewitness but also the author of the book present today. There is evidence, however, that the work has undergone revisions. Father Brown, who is a careful scholar, sees at least five separate stages in its composition. Complicating the matter further, many scholars argue that behind the finished literary product stand more than one source, the most important of which is a "signs source," a collection of the distinctive miracle stories included in this Gospel. Traditionalists might reply that a writer's use of sources does not rule out the writer's being an eyewitness; furthermore, evidence of various stages in the editing of the work does not prove that work was not written and edited by one individual. Nevertheless, all of these details raise questions about the traditional view that the eyewitness and the person who wrote the finished product are the same person.

According to Irenaeus, the Gospel was composed in Ephesus. While that is conceivable, the reliability or unreliability of the tradition cannot be proven. External and internal evidence is scant. Dating the work depends to some extent upon evaluation of the authorship question. But even if one rejects the traditional ascription of the Gospel of John, the son of Zebedee, a date later than 100 C.E. is unlikely. A papyrus fragment of a copy of the Gospel, discovered in Egypt in 1935 (p^{52}), has been reliably dated shortly after the beginning of the second century.[13] Some scholars have argued that the distinctive character of the Gospel is evidence that it was composed later than the three Synoptic Gospels, but such arguments are tenuous. Criteria for distinguishing between what is late and what is simply distinctive are unreliable.

B. Context

Scholars are in a better position to venture some opinions about the situation in which the Gospel was written. One important clue is the term "the Jews." Although John occasionally does make distinctions among the various groups within the Jewish community, he more often lumps them together as "the Jews." More significantly, the term is clearly pejorative; it stands for those who are enemies of Jesus. Not all Jews are hostile to Jesus: the narrator does refer to Jews who believe in Jesus (8:31), but this instance is followed by a scene in which even these Jews are scandalized by Jesus. The overwhelming number of references to the Jews is negative. Those who demand Jesus' death are, alternately, the Jews and the chief priests. The Jews have decided to exclude from the synagogue anyone who confesses Jesus to be the Christ (9:22). The pejorative term "Jews" sometimes appears to mean anyone hostile to Jesus, even a Gentile. Pilate's question at Jesus' trial, "Am I a Jew?" (18:13) is for the reader—and for John—more than the taunt it seems on the surface. His inability to recognize truth and his question about where Jesus is from place him on the side of those who demand Jesus' death. Even Pilate is a "Jew" in the sense in which John uses the term.

One may well ask why John should choose this expression to characterize the people opposed to Jesus and, by implication, the world in its opposition to God. He says virtually nothing about opposition from non-Jews to Jesus or to his followers, as do the other Gospels. Jesus simply warns his followers that they will be put out of synagogues and killed (16:1-4); this is the opposition they can expect from "the world" (15:18-27). Yet the Gospel also consistently claims Moses and Jewish tradition as witnesses for Jesus (5:39-47; 8:56-58; 12:37-42). Jesus and his followers have not rejected Judaism. John does not use special terminology for those who believe in Jesus; they are never called Christians. In one passage, Jesus refers to Nathaniel, who later becomes a disciple, as an "Israelite" (1:47), a less pejorative term to John than "Jew." Like Luke and Matthew, John questions the right of the Jews to consider themselves children of Abraham and members of the people of God because they have rejected God's emissary. Those who have recognized and accepted Jesus as God's emissary are the only true children of Abraham; they alone are Israelites.

"The Jews," like the phrase "their synagogues" in Matthew, expresses a deep division within the Jewish community between those who believe in Jesus and those who do not. John describes the break:

> His parents said this because they feared the Jews, for the Jews had already agreed that if any one should confess him to be the Christ, he was to be put out of the synagogue. (9:22)

> "I have said all this to you to keep you from falling away. They will put you out of the synagogues; indeed, the hour is coming when whoever kills you will think he is offering service to God." (16:1-2)

In *History and Theology in the Fourth Gospel*, J. Louis Martyn attempts to reconstruct the situation in the Jewish and Christian communities portrayed in the Fourth Gospel.[14] His study reads like a detective novel, and the reconstruction of the puzzle from scattered pieces is fascinating. Although absolute clarity or universal agreement will probably never be achieved, Professor Martyn makes a good case for the theory that the Gospel of John was written for a community of Jewish believers in Jesus, a group who had been recently excluded from the synagogue as part of the broader purge within the Jewish community, discussed briefly in this book's opening chapter.

The evangelist, in this view, must deal with a problem to which Matthew and Luke also address themselves: Who are the true people of God? Because of this recent action of the official Jewish community, the question is vital. The intensity of the debate and the bitterness of the polemic against "the Jews" indicate that John and his readers feel keenly about the problem they face. Their anti-Jewish sentiment should be understood as the hatred between estranged members of a family who are fighting for the right of inheritance and identity.

C. Purpose

John's interpretation of the situation is distinctive. Those who believe in Jesus do not form a new Israel; Jesus' ministry does not inaugurate a new epoch in the history of God's people, as in Luke. There is not even a debate about who interprets the Law properly, as Matthew emphasizes. The Gospel does not debate issues of proper interpretation of tradition and rights of inheritance. The sole criterion by which such questions are settled is one's attitude toward Jesus. Those who believe that he is God's emissary and has the "words of eternal life" demonstrate that they are "of the light," that they are God's own people. Those who reject the Christian message belong to "the world" and to the darkness; they have no part in the people of God. The division between those of the darkness and those of the light has been present since creation and will continue until the close of the age. Jesus' followers must offer testimony, as Jesus did, so that the division may be brought to light and Jesus' "flock" may be gathered; the decisions reached in the case argued during Jesus' ministry are now to be extended to the ends of the earth.[15]

The Gospel of John, like the Synoptic Gospels, is minority

literature. John seeks to interpret for his audience a bewildering world in which reality does not conform to expectations. God's own people have rejected his Son and continue to reject and persecute those who confess Jesus as Messiah. Those who ally themselves with the Word of God receive not blessings but curses. Their confession of faith brings not life but death. The story suggests that those who are "from above" can always expect hostility from those who are "of the world"; they will be hated by those who belong to the darkness just as Jesus was.

Nevertheless, John's Gospel reassures its readers that their faithful testimony is accomplishing God's will. The present moment anticipates the final judgment, and the fate of God's enemies is already sealed. Those who believe have already passed from death to life. Whatever that means with respect to external circumstances, it at least suggests that for those who belong to the new community of believers, some quality of existence transcends the normal range of human experience, over which the world has no power.

In composing his Gospel, the evangelist sought to interpret this "eternal life" for his readers. Aside from judging the success of his endeavor as a witness, which many find powerful, the reader must recognize the literary achievement of John's subtle and fascinating work.

Summary

John's Gospel differs from the other three in style, content, and emphasis. His language is symbolic, abstract, and complicated. The Gospel's facts are often unique, and at times they seem to conflict with those of the Synoptics. Jesus' discourses center on his role as an emissary from his Father, rather than on the coming of the kingdom of God.

In the Gospel of John, the advent of Jesus precipitates a crisis within the Jewish community that is an example of cosmic and human divisions. The conflict between those who accept Jesus and those who reject him represents the opposition between the forces of light and darkness in the universe and among humanity, between eternal life and damnation for human beings.

The prologue concentrates all these distinctive characteristics and motifs into eighteen verses. It is an almost mystical hymn to Jesus' incarnation and his role as God's creative Word: just as God's Word created light and life "in the beginning," so Jesus, God's Son, will bring light and eternal life to humanity. It also introduces elements of the conflict: a witness for Jesus, opponents who reject Jesus, and cosmic and human darkness.

In dramatizing this crisis, John presents the life and mission of Jesus as a trial and judgment—on two levels. On the first level, "witnesses" give testimony for and against Jesus. Pilate, the community leaders, and his own people—the Jews—condemn him. On the second level, it is those who judge him that are on trial. In rejecting Jesus, they unwittingly testify for him and convict themselves.

This double perspective on the trial reflects the universal dualism. The human judges are in darkness, and their verdict is physical death. God, whose Word is light, has already anticipated the final judgment and sentenced them to eternal death.

All four Gospels preach that Jesus is the Messiah, but each has its own major unifying theme. In Mark, it is the mystery of the suffering Christ. In Luke-Acts, it is the place of Jesus and the church in the continuing history of Israel. In Matthew, it is the issue of the true interpretation of Scripture. In John, it is the people's response to Jesus, the decision they make when forced to judge him.

Like Mark, John writes at two levels; but here Jesus does not hide his identity. He marshals witnesses to testify that he is God's Son; his miracles are signs—pieces of evidence. Like Luke and Matthew, John especially scorns those Jews who reject Jesus: they are being untrue to God's (and their own) Scriptures and tradition. But the Fourth Gospel argues against them less from the authority of history or Scripture than from his one criterion—the people's acceptance or rejection of Jesus as God's Son and his message as the word of God.

Tradition says that the Fourth Gospel is the work of the apostle John, the son of Zebedee, the "beloved disciple." Many critical scholars concede the possibility of the Gospel's own claim that the facts come from an eyewitness, but suggest that the original account was put into final form much later by someone else.

The book seems to respond to a situation in which the Jewish leaders have already cast the Christians out of the community. By that decisive action, they reveal that they are on the side of darkness. Their "trial" of Jesus—and by him—has found them wanting. They have forfeited eternal life and the right to call themselves the heirs of Moses and the people of God. John, and presumably his Christian readers, vehemently condemn "the Jews" and insist on their own exclusive right to the family inheritance—of that tradition and that identity.

CHAPTER TWELVE

❧

PAULINE LETTERS

Letters had always been indispensible in diplomacy, but by the first century C.E. they were a familiar feature of public life in the Roman Empire. Written communication had become increasingly important in administering the empire as it grew in size and complexity. Anyone wishing to enter public life needed skill in writing letters, and many of the rhetorical handbooks preserved from the period include instructions about their proper form and style.[1]

This proliferation of letter writing extended beyond official circles. Thousands of letters from the period survive, both in published form and by accident, in official archives or unearthed by archaeologists in city dumps.[2] The subjects range widely: brief orders by merchants, private letters, elaborate essays composed in letter form by great philosophers and statesmen of the day.[3] Scholars have long recognized that letters in the New Testament are closer in form to nonliterary than to literary letters; that is, they resemble private correspondence more than letter essays.

One characteristic of the common Greek letter is its lack of detail, partially because the private messengers, unlike modern mail carriers, could provide an oral commentary and supply missing information. A more striking characteristic is the extremely stereotyped form of Greek letters, followed for centuries. The usual pattern, essentially unchanged from the fourth century B.C.E. to the fourth century C.E., included three parts, the first of which is quite formalized:

Introduction: sender, recipient, greetings (and wish for health)

Body

Conclusion: greetings, wishes, final greetings (and date)

Even the most personal letters were restrained, closely adhering to convention. Here are two examples:

Serapion to his brothers Ptolemaeus and Apollonius, greeting. If you are well, it would be excellent. I myself am well. I have made a contract with the daughter of Hesperus and intend to marry her in the month of Mesore. Please send me half of chous of oil. I have written to let you know. Goodbye. Year 28, Epeiph 21.
Come for the wedding day, Apollonius.[4]

Serapias to her children Ptolemaeus and Apolinaria and Ptolemaeus heartiest greeting. Above all I pray that you may be in health, which is for me the most necessary of all things. I make my obeisance to the lord Serapis, praying that I may receive word that you are in health, even as I pray for your general welfare. I rejoiced when I received letters that you are well and recovered. Salute Ammonous with his children and wife and those who love you. Cyrilla salutes you, and Hermias the daughter of Hermias, Hermanoubis the nurse, Athenais the teacher (?), Cyrilla, Casia . . . Empis, in fact all who are here. Please therefore write me what you are about, for you know that, if I receive your letters, I am glad on account of your well-being. I pray that you may prosper.[5]

Similarities in form between such personal letters and New Testament epistles are obvious. Most of Paul's letters, for example, begin with his name, the names of the people addressed, a greeting, and an assurance that Paul prays daily for them and is concerned about them. Paul's modifications of the normal salutation and concluding greeting do not obscure the formal parallels. The letters in the New Testament were not as carefully polished as were the literary efforts of philosophers and statesmen that were intended for publication; they were real, personal letters, addressed in most cases to specific individuals or groups.

Yet, New Testament epistles also differ markedly from personal letters found among the papyri. First of all, they are far longer than most letters, more personal, and less stereotyped. Further, most were written by men who regarded themselves as more than just private individuals, so that some of the letters exhibit characteristics of official correspondence. Although the New Testament letters are, in the main, private correspondence, no one category of ancient letters will cover all of their features.

Study of ancient epistolography helps to clarify some conventions of letter writers in the Greco-Roman world. It also serves to highlight the distinctive features of the New Testament letters and the particular genius of their authors, who came to play such dominant roles in the life of the early Christian movement.

I. The Letters of Paul

A. The Apostle

More is known about Paul than about any other early Christian. The book of Acts provides some information about this famous missionary and his travels, and his letters reveal a good deal about his character and his career as spiritual father of his congregations.[6] About his life prior to his conversion, for example, he gives little information. He was apparently born in Tarsus, a commercial city near the northeastern corner of the Mediterranean. Paul reports that he was a Pharisee (Phil. 3:5); but a Diaspora Jew, born and raised outside Palestine, would also have been familiar with intellectual currents in the Greco-Roman world. His letters indicate that he was a thoroughly Hellenized Jew. The only other definite piece of information Paul provides about his life prior to his conversion is that out of loyalty to his Jewish tradition he won a reputation as a fierce opponent of Christianity (I Cor. 15:9; Gal. 1:23; Phil. 3:6).

The record shows that Paul was a man of extremes. The extraordinary zeal for his beliefs that led him to persecute Christians made him their equally energetic advocate after an experience that changed his life. Paul attributes his conversion to an appearance before him by the risen Christ—an experience granted only to a select group beginning with Peter and the Twelve—in which he was called to become a missionary to Gentiles (I Cor. 15:3-10; Gal. 1:15-16). According to his letters, the exclusionist Jew became a missionary to non-Jews. The defender of the restrictive Mosaic Law argued the case of complete freedom from it for Gentile Christians within the church. On this issue more than on any other Paul staked his career. His position probably caused the unrest in Jerusalem that resulted in his arrest, described in Acts. Acts concludes with Paul under arrest in Rome, where, according to tradition, he was martyred.

B. The Letters

No single person has had as great an impact on the shape of the New Testament as Paul. As many as fourteen of the twenty-seven New Testament books have been attributed to him. Little doubt remains for critical scholars that at least one of those—the Epistle to the Hebrews—actually was not his; Hebrews is the only one of the so-called Pauline letters that does not mention his name. Of those writings that do, some others still may not be his. Although disagreements continue, there is a consensus among scholars about the core of the unquestioned Pauline corpus. It includes the following seven:

Romans
I and II Corinthians
Galatians
Philippians
I Thessalonians
Philemon

Three more, if not composed by Paul, were probably written by an associate:

II Thessalonians
Colossians
Ephesians

The authorship of the so-called Pastoral Epistles—First and Second Timothy and Titus—is more controversial. Many scholars, including some conservatives, doubt that these are Paul's, dating them as late as 100-125 C.E., long after Paul's death.[7]

Paul's letters played an essential role in his ministry. As a missionary, he was primarily an evangelist, traveling from city to city and establishing churches. He was also a pastor, sustaining his churches, helping them through difficult times, and providing guidance. When unable to visit them personally, he exercised his pastoral functions both through epistles and through personal envoys like Timothy and Titus. Paul's letters were personal and dealt with specific situations, but they were also official communications. The writer considered himself an authority within the Christian movement, appointed by God himself:

Paul, a servant of Jesus Christ, called to be an apostle . . . (Rom. 1:1)

Paul, called by the will of God to be an apostle of Christ Jesus . . . (I Cor. 1:1)

Paul, an apostle of Christ Jesus by the will of God . . . (II Cor. 1:1)

Paul an apostle—not from men nor through man, but through Jesus Christ and God the Father, who raised him from the dead . . . (Gal. 1:1)

Paul, more than anyone else, seems to have fashioned from existing models a new letter form suited to the needs of pastoral care and church administration. His letters are far less stylized than others known from the period. They are lively, often exhibiting characteristics of street preaching. And they serve a remarkable variety of functions: The letters answer questions (I Cor.), warn against false teaching or combat false teachers (II Cor. and Gal.), encourage I Thess.), correct false impressions (II Thess.), or defend a position (Rom.). Their length, liveliness, and variety of function all set Paul's letters off from both the highly stylized personal letters and the typical official correspondence in the Greco-Roman world.

C. Structure

A recognizable structure is fairly consistent throughout Paul's epistles:

Opening
    Sender
    Recipient
    Salutation
Thanksgiving
Body
"I appeal to you"
Closing
    Benediction
    Concluding greeting

Consider three of these recurring elements.

Opening. It has already been noted that in Greek letters of the period, the sender customarily mentions his name (and title, if appropriate), the name of the recipient, and a one-word salutation. Paul frequently expands this convention, adding information about himself or the group to which he writes. As his letters vary in function, frequently the specific opening sets a tone for the letter and provides important clues for interpreting what follows, as will be observed.

Thanksgiving. In this portion of the letter, Paul reveals his attitude toward the recipients and, on occasion, the circumstances under which he is writing (Rom. 1:8-15; I Cor. 1:4-9). Almost two-thirds of First Thessalonians appears to be a thanksgiving, indicating that relations between Paul and his congregation in Thessalonica are excellent and that Paul sees no imminent threat to their survival. On the contrary, the thanksgiving is conspicuously absent from Galatians and Second Corinthians. Study of Galatians will show why Paul has shifted from his usual "I thank my God always for you" to "I am astonished" (Gal. 1:6).

"I appeal to you." Knowledge of ancient epistolography helps to explain this feature, found in all the undisputed Pauline epistles (Rom. 12:1, 15:30, 16:17; I Cor. 1:10, 4:16, 16:15; II Cor. 2:8, 6:1, 10:1; Phil. 4:2; I. Thess. 4:1, 5:14; Philem. 9, 10).[8] The phrase "I appeal to you" usually introduces a request, often related to the purpose of the letter. Philemon provides the clearest example:

> Accordingly, though I am bold enough in Christ to command you to do what is required, yet for love's sake I prefer to appeal to you—I, Paul, an ambassador and now a prisoner also for Christ Jesus—I appeal to you for my child, Onesimus, whose father I have become in my imprisonment. (Philem. 8-10)

This distinction between "commanding" and "appealing" occurs most frequently in diplomatic correspondence when an official making a request wishes to convey to the recipients of the letter his sense of their autonomy or equality. The writer is confident that the recipient will respond to the request appropriately. Paul's use of the expression sheds some light on the relationship he sought to cultivate between himself and his churches. The only letter in which Paul does not appeal to a church is Galatians, where he "begs" the congregation (Gal. 4:12). Study of Galatians should explain this departure from Paul's normal usage as well.

Understanding of such structural elements in Paul's letters guides these studies.[9] Two Pauline letters, Galatians and First Corinthians, will be considered. They lend themselves to literary analysis, and they reveal different, even contending, aspects of Paul's thought. In Galatians, Paul is a polemicist, combating a fundamental perversion of the Christian message; here he appears as an advocate of Christian freedom from the past. In First Corinthians, he writes as a pastor, helping his congregation cope with life as believers; he has to deal with a freedom that has left community life in shambles. This tension between liberation and bondage, between new and old, is a basic aspect of Paul's understanding of Christianity. To resolve that tension is to misunderstand him.

II. Galatians

Paul's letter to the churches of Galatia has a desperate tone; he considers the congregations to be verging on apostasy. The letter is also passionately defensive, touching on issues central to Paul's role as a missionary to non-Jews and to his own religious experience. And it reveals the more revolutionary side of Paul's gospel, particularly contrasted with his first letter to the Corinthians.

A. Structure

1. Opening.

Paul an apostle—not from men nor through man, but through Jesus Christ and God the Father, who raised him from the dead—and all the brethren who are with me,
    To the churches of Galatia:
    Grace to you and peace from God the Father and our Lord Jesus Christ, who gave himself for our sins to deliver us from the present evil age, according to the will of our God and Father, to whom be the glory for ever and ever. Amen. (Gal. 1:1-5)

Paul firmly states his authority, a stance that he emphasizes in the first chapters and carries through the letter. One of Paul's purposes in writing is to reestablish his authority, which is under attack.

Paul also expands his customary salutation, adding "who gave himself for our sins to deliver us from the present evil age." According to Paul, the age to come is actually a present reality for those who believe in Christ. For them, the "present evil age" is the old world, from which they have already been delivered. Thus, Paul can say, a bit later, that distinctions recognized in the old world no longer apply within the community of the faithful: "For as many of you as were baptized into Christ have put on Christ. There is neither Jew nor Greek, there is neither slave nor free, there is neither male nor female; for you are all one in Christ Jesus" (3:27-28). Paul can even refer to the new life in faith in terms of a re-creation: "For neither circumcision counts for anything, nor uncircumcision, but a new creation" (6:15).

Throughout the letter Paul uses terms like "new" and "free." The break with the past that occurs when one becomes a Christian is a basic theme of the letter.

2. Thanksgiving. There is no thanksgiving in this letter. Where one normally would expect at least a polite expression of thanks for the churches and what they have meant to him, Paul launches an attack:

> I am astonished that you are so quickly deserting him who called you in the grace of Christ and turning to a different gospel—not that there is another gospel, but there are some who trouble you and want to pervert the gospel of Christ. But even if we, or an angel from heaven, should preach to you a gospel contrary to that which we preached to you, let him be accursed. (1:6-8) .

Relations between Paul and his congregations in Galatia, strained almost to the breaking point, give him nothing to be thankful for. Instead of offering thanks, Paul hurls anathemas at the "troublers," as he calls them, who are about to lead the Galatians away from Christ (1:8-9).

3. "I appeal to you." Another customary expression is absent, here replaced by a more emotional term: "Brethren, I beseech you, become as I am" (4:12). Paul no longer trusts the Galatians to make the appropriate response to a polite, simple appeal. He finds it necessary to beg his congregations to make the proper decision. The issue is clear-cut: the Galatians must choose between Paul and the newcomers whose preaching he condemns. They must heed his warning and support him and his position. To understand the choice Paul puts before his churches, the reader needs to know something about his opponents and their gospel.

B. Opponents

Who were the troublers Paul accuses of trying to "pervert the gospel of Christ," and what was their message that Paul found so offensive? Unfortunately, only Paul's letters exist as a source of information. Paul may not have been fully informed about his adversaries, and he may be distorting their position. Any sketch of the controversy is necessarily hypothetical.

In any case, the core of the dispute seems to be the issue of the observance of the Jewish Law, including circumcision, from which Paul says Christians should be liberated:

> O foolish Galatians! Who has bewitched you, before whose eyes Jesus Christ was publicly portrayed as crucified? Let me ask you only this: Did you receive the Spirit by works of the law, or by hearing with faith? (3:1-2)

> Now I, Paul, say to you that if you receive circumcision, Christ will be of no advantage to you. (5:2)

> It is those who want to make a good showing in the flesh that would compel you to be circumcised. (6:12)

Paul also attacks the preaching of his opponents on the observance of certain holy days—presumably Jewish. Yet these days are not simply festivals stipulated in Scripture. Paul talks of holy days related to "elemental spirits," and although the Greek term is ambiguous, here it probably means stars or planets. Paul seems to be arguing against an astrological reckoning of lucky and unlucky days—typical of popular piety throughout the Greco-Roman world—that has evidently been combined with the calendar of Jewish holy days:

> Formerly, when you did not know God, you were in bondage to
> beings that by nature are no gods; but now that you have come
> to know God, or rather to be known by God, how can you turn
> back again to the weak and beggarly elemental spirits, whose
> slaves you want to be once more? You observe days, and
> months, and seasons, and years! I am afraid I have labored over
> you in vain. (4:8-11)

As to the identity of Paul's opponents, one of the more
plausible portraits suggested by scholars is the following.[10]
They appear to have been Jewish Christians who, upon
arriving in Galatia, began to encourage Gentile Christians to
undergo circumcision and to adopt Torah as a way of life.
These new missionaries felt that Gentiles should become
bona fide members of the people of God. Obedience to the
Torah's commandments would likewise insure morality. For
Jewish Christians, Christianity was true Judaism, not a novel
religious movement. They undoubtedly found Paul's message
of total freedom from Torah both puzzling and dangerous.
Conversely, their position appears to be the major target of
Paul's polemic.

If this reconstruction is accurate, Paul's opponents did not
threaten Christianity either as sophisticated rabbinic thinkers
or as purveyors of deep religious mysteries. They were
Hellenized Jewish Christians who criticized Paul for neglect-
ing circumcision—the symbol of the covenant with God—in
his preaching to the Gentile believers in Galatia. They also
felt that Paul's radical exclusion of Torah would lead to
immorality; his moral exhortation at the end of his letter is
probably a defense against this charge (5:13–6:10). His
opponents questioned such teaching and such a teacher, and
their message was making sense to the Galatians.

C. Paul's Reply

1. Apology: Independence and Consistency. After his
startling introduction, Paul defends himself and his office at
length. He focuses on two issues: his independence from
Jerusalem and his consistency.

a. "Not from men nor through man" (1:1). Paul establishes
that his office as apostle was not conferred upon him by the

recognized leaders of the church in Jerusalem. He needed no authorization from them, nor did he ever seek their approval of his call. He went up to Jerusalem only twice: once, three years after his conversion and his call to be an apostle, at which time he met with Peter and James (verses 18-20); the second time, fourteen years later, when God directed him to settle with the Jerusalem leaders the sensitive issue of Gentile status within the church. Paul's legitimacy as an apostle does not depend upon the Jerusalem leaders.

b. *"Am I now seeking the favor of men?"* (1:10). Paul's opponents have evidently accused him of preaching different things in different places, adapting his message to his audiences in an unprincipled, two-faced way, to please people.

> Even if we, or an angel from heaven, should preach to you a gospel contrary to that which we preached to you, let him be accursed. (1:8)

> Am I now seeking the favor of men, or of God? Or am I trying to please men? If I were still pleasing men, I should not be a servant of Christ. (1:10)

The charge centers on his teaching about the Law. In defense of his integrity, Paul cites the unfavorable reaction of some Jewish Christians. He has consistently advocated freedom from the Law for Gentiles. (His principled consistency may also counter the opposite charge of unpopularity, an argument used against Paul in Corinth.)

Paul's recital of his long relationship with James, Peter, and John—"reputed to be pillars" (2:9)—substantiates the steadfastness of his view that the Law does not apply to Gentiles. He forced their approval of his position by bringing with him to Jerusalem Titus (an uncircumcised Gentile Christian) for the conference on Gentile status in the church, a singularly provocative and undiplomatic act (2:1-3). Later, Paul boldly tried to embarrass Peter publicly in Antioch when Peter appeared to back away from complete table fellowship with Gentiles—in Paul's eyes, an essential test of faithfulness to the gospel (verses 11-15). Such actions are not those of one whose primary goal is unprincipled seeking after popularity with the multitudes or acceptance by reputed leaders.

2. Freedom from the Law. The Galatians may have been bewildered by the vehemence of Paul's attack. To them, the new position advocated by the recently arrived missionaries could supplement rather than replace Paul's message. Paul argues, however, that reliance on the Jewish Law is not simply an unnecessary addition but is totally unacceptable:

> Now I, Paul, say to you that if you receive circumcision, Christ will be of no advantage to you. I testify again to every man who receives circumcision that he is bound to keep the whole law. You are severed from Christ, you who would be justified by the law; you have fallen away from grace. (5:2-4)

Interpreters have traditionally seen in Paul's attack an opposition between works and grace. What Paul opposes, they argue, is the desire to expect salvation as earned compensation rather than to receive it as a gift. But the real issue goes even further. The opposition Paul sees is between works of the Mosaic Law and faith in Christ—not only works versus faith, but also Torah versus Christ. The question is whether the Law of Moses has any continuing validity for Gentile Christians or in Christian life at all. Paul vehemently insists that the Torah's validity lies only in its testimony to the sole efficacy of faith in Jesus Christ. In rabbinic fashion, he offers sophisticated arguments from the Jewish Scriptures, including the Torah, to substantiate his position. Precisely where Paul argues most like a rabbi in form, however, he is least like a rabbi in substance. He uses Torah to prove that Torah is no longer valid—both for Gentile Christians and for Jewish Christians as well. He never presents a detailed argument for nonobservance of Torah by Jewish Christians except by implication. He insists that essential features of Torah piety have been abrogated. For example, Jewish Christians are not to observe the distinction between Jews and non-Jews. Paul also argues that as a Christian, Peter is obligated to disobey Jewish dietary laws.

As suggested, the issue lies at the heart of both Paul's theology and his personal experience. As a former Pharisee, Paul understands the meaning of strict adherence to the Torah.

He says that his opponents in Galatia do not understand the consequences of living by the Law. Anyone committed to observing Torah must keep the whole Law, not just part of it (5:3-4); if not, they are considered cursed (Gal. 3:10, quoting Deut. 27:26). Elsewhere Paul argues that in fact no one keeps the whole Law (Rom. 1:18–3:20). All are thus under a curse, and the only deliverance is from Christ who "redeemed us from the curse of the law" (Gal. 3:13).

Paul's opposition to observance of Torah is even more deeply rooted than this theological argument. His profound awareness of the power of sin and an almost demonic misuse of the Law stems from his own experience as a Jew. Faithfulness to the Torah drove Paul to persecute Christians; it was a mark of his religious zeal as a Jew (Phil. 3:4-6). According to the Torah, Jesus died accursed by God, since he died by "hanging on a tree" (Gal. 3:13, quoting Deut. 21:23). To hail a crucified man as God's Messiah was for Paul the devout Pharisee nothing short of blasphemy. As a Jew, Paul saw that the message of a crucified Messiah could not be reconciled with his faithfulness to Torah.

When he was converted, Paul did not change his mind about the irreconcilability of the Christian gospel with Jewish piety. He simply changed sides, arguing as a Christian that faith in Christ must mean the complete abrogation of Torah as a way of life, not merely freedom from its rituals. When God raised Jesus from the dead, God did not change his mind about the Torah and tradition; he simply revealed that they had been custodial orders that had served their functions and were no longer needed (Gal. 3:23-25).

Paul's position is complex but logical. He saw more clearly than other early Christians a radically new consequence of the gospel of the crucified Christ. Thus in his eyes, submission to the Torah by Galatian Christians meant a denial of Christ, apostasy.

3. The New Morality. Appended to the body of the letter is a series of moral exhortations. Paul does not fear that his opponents encourage license; on the contrary, he is answering their charge that freedom from Torah will inevitably lead to moral anarchy. Paul maintains that freedom is the hallmark of the life of faith, but freedom must be exercised within the context of love. In a statement much like that of Jesus and of the famous Rabbi Hillel, Paul cites a passage from Leviticus as a summary of the Torah: "For the whole law is fulfilled in one word, 'You shall love your neighbor as yourself'" (Gal. 5:14, quoting Lev. 19:18).[11]

Paul's inference from that rule, however, is radically different than that of Jesus or Hillel. If love fulfills the Law, then the commands of the Torah are superfluous for one who has love.

The brief injunctions at the end of Galatians provide an insufficient basis on which to reconstruct Paul's approach to ethics. Whatever his precise views, Paul never appeals to a particular code as an authoritative statement of morality. Yet he can assume that the works of the flesh and works of the spirit are obvious to the Galatians (5:19-24). Paul relies heavily on the direct guidance of the Spirit (verses 16-18, 25). It seems clear from his letter to the Romans that many felt his theology took insufficient account of morality (Rom. 6), and his letter to the church at Corinth points up some of the practical difficulties of living by the Spirit.

Paul's epistle to the Galatians is expressed in extremes, composed in the heat of what Paul saw as a life-and-death battle. Invectives against his opponents are extravagant (Gal. 1:8; 5:12). His emphasis on the radically new situation of the believer in Jesus and on their freedom from tradition is to some extent qualified in Corinthians. Nevertheless, these positions, further spelled out in Romans, are based on the foundations of Paul's religion. For good reasons students of Paul consider this letter one of his most important.

III. First Corinthians

Paul's first letter to the church at Corinth contrasts with Galatians. Here, Paul faces no competition from outsiders. With one exception, the issues are practical and do not involve the struggles that engage Paul in Galatians. He responds to questions raised in a letter from his congregation.

> Now concerning the matters about which you wrote . . . (I Cor. 7:1)
> Now concerning food offered to idols . . . (8:1)

> Now concerning spiritual gifts . . . (12:1)
> Now concerning the contribution for the saints . . . (16:1)

Some scholars have tried to find in the problems confronting the Corinthian church some consistency that might suggest a full-blown religious position, like Gnosticism, that Paul must combat.[12] It seems more likely that the difficulties facing the church derive largely from tendencies inherent in Paul's preaching. The Corinthians seem to have understood in one sense the note of liberation sounded in Paul's gospel, which we have heard in Galatians. In oversimplified terms, Paul's letter to the Corinthians represents his struggle to understand with his congregation how his gospel of liberation can be translated into stabilized, united practice in a community that must live in a world not yet fully liberated.

The purpose and focus of the second half of First Corinthians are relatively clear. In chapters 7–16, Paul deals one by one with problems facing the church, making an outline relatively simple. The function of the first six chapters presents a more difficult problem. Why does Paul begin by discussing gossip he has learned from "Chloe's people" (1:11), rather than with the letter he has received? One must look at the opening verses in relation to other structural elements of the letter.

A. Structure

1. Opening.

> Paul, called by the will of God to be an apostle of Christ Jesus, and our brother Sosthenes,
> To the church of God which is at Corinth, to those sanctified in Christ Jesus, called to be saints together with all those who in every place call on the name of our Lord Jesus Christ, both their Lord and ours. (1:1-2)

As in Galatians, Paul's opening statement of his authority suggests that it is under attack. Again, one of the purposes of the letter is to reestablish his authority as the spiritual father of the congregation (4:14-21).

The second verse amplifies the usual meaning of the

recipient as well. His mention of all the others who call on the name of the Lord Jesus may stress the unity of the Christian family—an appropriate emphasis for a church that the reader soon learns is divided into factions (1:10-12). It may even be a barb aimed at some who consider themselves the only true Christians. This theme of unity will recur throughout the letter.

2. *Thanksgiving.*

I give thanks to God always for you because of the grace of God which was given you in Christ Jesus, that in every way you were enriched in him with all speech and all knowledge—even as the testimony to Christ was confirmed among you—so that you are not lacking in any spiritual gift, as you wait for the revealing of our Lord Jesus Christ; who will sustain you to the end, guiltless in the day of our Lord Jesus Christ. (1:4-8)

The presence of a thanksgiving means that the relationship between Paul and his congregation is not in serious jeopardy. In the context of the first six chapters, however, Paul's effusive praise of the Corinthian Christians is more than a little ironic. The reader learns that these Christians, who have been given "all knowledge," are embroiled in controversies that have resulted in brother hauling brother into pagan courts for judgment (6:1-8). The Corinthians have been boasting of immoral acts that are abhorrent even to pagans (5:1-2). Finally, the "speech" and the "spiritual gifts" lavished on the Corinthians have become occasions for schisms within the church (12–14). The congregation, though richly blessed, is in turmoil.

3. "I appeal to you." Departing from his custom, Paul makes a request before beginning the body of the letter: "I appeal to you, brethren, by the name of our Lord Jesus Christ, that all of you agree and that there be no dissensions among you, but that you be united in the same mind and the same judgment" (1:10).

His request is not based on their letter, but on other information: "For it has been reported to me by Chloe's people [perhaps slaves] that there is quarreling among you, my brethren. What I mean is that each one of you says, 'I

belong to Paul,' or 'I belong to Apollos,' or 'I belong to
Cephas,' or 'I belong to Christ'" (1:11-12).

Paul's problem is difficult. His church has asked his opinion
about several matters in a letter. But he learns from Chloe's
people that the church is split into factions and that Paul
himself is a major focus of the disruption. The majority of the
congregation must still "belong to Paul." After all, the letter
from the church was sent to him. Yet for many, allegiance lies
elsewhere.

The situation in Corinth is by no means clear, but the
factions within the congregation are not necessarily highly
organized, on the evidence of Paul's letter.[13] Apparently, the
decision to ask the advice of an outsider about problems
within the church has crystalized some of that opposition to
Paul. Most believe they should seek Paul's advice, since he
founded the church; others challenge his authority. Paul's
defensive statements in the opening chapters suggest that the
following criticisms had been leveled:

a. Paul baptized few and was thus not really the spiritual
   father of the congregation. (See 1:14-17.)
b. Paul had left the church and had not returned, implying
   a lack of real concern for the Corinthians. (See 4:18.)
c. Paul was not an eloquent speaker, and his preaching
   seemed mundane compared with that of others. (See
   1:17–2:5 and 3:1-2.)

Paul's detractors may have suggested writing to Apollos, a
figure associated with the Corinthian church in Acts 18:24-28.
Others may have suggested Peter (Cephas), since Paul
himself spoke of Peter as a recognized leader in the church
(I Cor. 15:5; Gal. 1:18). Those belonging to the otherwise
unexplained Christ party ("I belong to Christ") may have
voted against sending a letter to anyone outside the
congregation, insisting that they had been given "all
knowledge" as Christians and were capable of solving their
own problems.[14]

Whatever the precise nature of the controversies, Paul finds
it necessary to begin his letter with an appeal for unity. He
must convince the Corinthians to accept his authority,
eliminating that cause of factionalism, if he is to gain a hearing

for his answers to their questions. Both of Paul's appeals, in 1:10 and 4:16, deal with the preliminary but essential issue of conflict about his role within the church.

B. Chapters 1–6: "One father in Christ"

1. Paul's Lack of Eloquence. Paul opens his appeal for unity with a statement about his call: "For Christ did not send me to baptize but to preach the gospel, and not with eloquent wisdom, lest the cross of Christ be emptied of its power" (I Cor. 1:17).

His comments sound defensive. Evidently, he has been criticized for not having baptized many and for being a second-rate orator. Paul quickly disposes of the baptism issue (1:14-15), but takes the criticism of his unsophisticated manner of preaching seriously. In the Greco-Roman world, skill in rhetoric was essential for molding public opinion. Great orators were among the most highly regarded members of society. In a congregation that professed to have all wisdom and knowledge and speech, some may have found Paul a poor spokesman for the Christian community.

Rather than apologize for his lack of rhetorical skill, Paul makes a virtue of his lack of eloquence; it is a clear sign that he is a true messenger of the gospel. The form of his message, he argues, is appropriate to the message itself. Clever expression clothes the wisdom of this world, not God's true wisdom. With verse 18 Paul introduces his message, the "word of the cross," with a series of contrasting parallels.

> For since, in the wisdom of God, the world did not know God through wisdom, it pleased God through the folly of what we preach to save those who believe. . . . For the foolishness of God is wiser than men, and the weakness of God is stronger than men. (1:21, 25)

These abstractions become more specific through an appeal to the experience of the Corinthians:

> For consider your call, brethren; not many of you were wise according to worldly standards, not many were powerful, not many were of noble birth; but God chose what is foolish in the

world to shame the wise, God chose what is weak in the world to shame the strong. (1:26-27)

Conventional wisdom would have considered the motley crowd in Corinth unlikely to be God's people. But they are. Their success, which Paul does not dispute, should be viewed as a sign of God's shaming the worldly wise by exalting the weak and despised. The congregation itself embodies the inversion of worldly values that Paul's gospel implies. The passage is, of course, full of irony. While illustrating his theme of wisdom and folly, of strength and weakness, Paul also reminds the Corinthians of their origin. If God's grace alone has enriched them, and if their common life manifests God's power, they have no basis for boasting.

Returning to the original issue, Paul says that they have little reason to criticize him for not measuring up to worldly ideals of eloquent wisdom. If the Christian gospel is an affront to worldly wisdom, it is only appropriate that the same is true of Paul's preaching. He masterfully turns what must have been criticisms into arguments for himself: "When I came to you, brethren, I did not come proclaiming to you the testimony of God in lofty words or wisdom. . . . that your faith might not rest in the wisdom of men but in the power of God" (2:1-5). His lack of rhetorical polish and his unimposing appearance are testimonies to that overturning of worldly values that the Gospel proclaims and that the Corinthians themselves experienced.

2. Wisdom and Folly. In verse 6, Paul's argument enters a new stage, a discussion of wisdom. He preaches a secret wisdom, revealed only in Jesus Christ and understandable only to the spiritual, those whose eyes are open to the truth. Again Paul illustrates his abstraction with an appeal to the Corinthians' experience, but with a surprise twist: the Corinthians, who believe themselves to be spiritual, are actually worldly (3:1). They are still novices, babes in the faith. Initially, Paul could expect them to understand only the most elementary precepts of the faith, and they have not yet matured. The evidence of their continued immaturity is the presence of factions.

> I fed you with milk, not solid food; for you were not ready for it; and even yet you are not ready, for you are still of the flesh. For while there is jealousy and strife among you, are you not of the flesh, and behaving like ordinary men? For when one says, "I belong to Paul," and another, "I belong to Apollos," are you not merely men? (3:2-4)

There can be no competition among God's servants. Each has a role to play in the construction of the church. What is essential is laying the foundation and completing the edifice. Those who argue about which worker is the most important endanger the temple itself, and to such people Paul issues a solemn warning: "If anyone destroys God's temple, God will destroy him" (3:17). The wholeness and unity of the church are paramount.

In 3:18-23, Paul recapitulates the initial discussion (1:12-17) and summarizes his argument: those who boast of men, who form parties around various figures, are the fools; they consider themselves wise, but will be caught by God in their own craftiness. Corinthians may have used the terms "wise" and "foolish" to differentiate between church members and outsiders. Paul uses them against dissident elements within the church; they are still like outsiders, not yet having penetrated the exterior of the gospel they profess.

3. The Corinthians' Need of Paul. Paul is not merely a true preacher of God's word; as founder of the congregation, he is its only proper spiritual adviser: "For though you have countless guides in Christ, you do not have many fathers. For I became your father in Christ Jesus through the gospel. I urge you [I appeal to you], then, be imitators of me." (4:15-16).

Some of the Corinthians have disputed Paul's claims to authority. Though human, they have presumed to judge Paul "before the time" of enlightenment, before all the evidence is in (4:3-5). Their arrogance, according to Paul, arises from their exalted conception of themselves. They boast (verse 7); they are "puffed up" (verse 6). Making use of the contrasts between the strong and the weak, rich and poor, wise and foolish, employed earlier, Paul sarcastically reproaches the Corinthians for their audacity:

> Already you are filled! Already you have become rich! Without us you have become kings! And would that you did reign, so that

we might share the rule with you! For I think that God has exhibited us apostles as last of all, like men sentenced to death; because we have become a spectacle to the world, to angels and to men. We are fools for Christ's sake, but you are wise in Christ. We are weak, but you are strong. You are held in honor, but we in disrepute. (4:8-10)

Largely through Paul's efforts, the once poor Corinthians have been spiritually enriched since becoming Christians. They have witnessed dramatic changes in their lives and see themselves as new people, in touch with new sources of power. To some, Paul now appears second-rate, weak, and unsophisticated. He is unpopular because his worldly career does not mirror the same radical transformation they have come to expect in their leader. Some probably suggest that they have outgrown their need for Paul.

Their attitude toward him shows Paul that they are immature as Christians. They still judge by the standards of this world, standards of the flesh. Only the worldly would see a liability in Paul's trials and his lack of polish. For those with understanding, his whole career exemplifies the radically new standards of personal status and wisdom revealed in the crucified Christ. To the worldly, Paul appears to be "the refuse of the world, the offscouring of all things" (4:13). Just so, the word of the cross is "folly" to those who are not being saved (1:18).

Problems in the Corinthian church and opposition to Paul are largely due to their extravagant expectations, derived at least in part from Paul's own message. The people accepted Paul's message of liberation, experienced the transforming power of the gospel, and consequently came to expect complete spiritual liberation and worldly transformation. As initiates into the mysteries of the gospel, enriched with "all spiritual gifts," they are ready to pass judgment on all whose lives do not show the appropriate signs of newness. They are, to use a term commonly employed by biblical scholars, "enthusiasts"—people religiously possessed; today's word might be "fanatics."

Paul directs his attack against this distorted anticipation of external success. He points to himself as an embodiment of the gospel he preaches—not only his successes and talents, but also his failures and incompetences. The gospel is not simply a blessing of success and a source of power. It is itself an assault on worldly standards. The Corinthians' criticism of Paul's worldly inadequacies is a sign of their failure to understand the gospel—and an indication of how desperately they need the advice of their "father" in Christ. The first four chapters of the letter are Paul's attempt to point this out, so that the Corinthians will be prepared to accept as authoritative his answers to their questions.

Chapters 5 and 6 provide a transition to the second half of the letter, in which Paul responds to the questions specifically raised by the church. The matters discussed, probably stemming from information provided by Chloe's people, further support Paul's contention that his congregation needs help and should welcome his advice.

C. Chapters 12–14: Gifts of the Spirit

Beginning with chapter 7, Paul treats successive issues presumably raised in the letter he received:

Marriage—7
Food offered to idols—8–10
Behavior of women—11:2-16
Practice of the Lord's Supper—11:17-34
Gifts of the Spirit—12–14
Resurrection—15
Contribution for the saints—16:1-5

As an example of Paul's responses, this study will examine his discussion of gifts of the Spirit, a portion of the letter that includes Paul's famous hymn to love.

1. Chapter 12: The Body Metaphor. Paul's discourse on spiritual gifts, or *charismata,* begins with 12:1 and extends through chapter 14. Paul does not say what he has been asked or why spiritual gifts are a problem.

More perplexing is his shift in chapter 14, where he suddenly narrows his discussion to only two gifts, speaking in tongues and prophecy. Paul includes these two phenomena, examined in detail below, in his two lists of gifts of the Spirit in chapter 12, but he does not single them out for special attention:

> To one is given through the Spirit the utterance of wisdom, and
> to another the utterance of knowledge according to the same
> Spirit, to another faith by the same Spirit, to another gifts of
> healing by the one Spirit, to another the working of miracles, to
> another prophecy, to another the ability to distinguish between
> spirits, to another various kinds of tongues, to another the
> interpretation of tongues. (12:8-10)

> And God has appointed in the church first apostles, second
> prophets, third teachers, then workers of miracles, then
> healers, helpers, administrators, speakers in various kinds of
> tongues. (12:28)

Speaking in tongues appears in both lists—in the second,
deliberately ranked last in order of importance. As will be
seen, this visible, spectacular form of ecstatic speech is the
subject of controversy within the Corinthian church and is
Paul's focal point.

After mentioning some basic distinctions between God's
Spirit and demonic spirits, Paul stresses the common source of
the charismata: "Now there are varieties of gifts [charismata],
but the same Spirit" (12:4). This emphasis on unity—"one
Spirit" and "same Spirit"—recurs in almost every sentence.
Shifting to another image in verse 12, Paul again highlights
unity in diversity:

> For just as the body is one and has many members, and all the
> members of the body, though many, are one body, so it is with
> Christ. For by one Spirit we were all baptized into one
> body—Jews or Greeks, slaves or free—and all were made to
> drink of one Spirit. (12:12-13)

The problem of spiritual gifts has obviously resulted in
more factions within the church: evidently, some "parts of the
body" claim more importance than others. Though he may
strain the metaphor, Paul uses it to argue that each spiritual
gift is equally indispensable and interdependent, just as the
various organs of the body are necessary to the whole:

> On the contrary, the parts of the body which seem to be weaker
> are indispensable, and those parts of the body which we think
> less honorable we invest with the greater honor, and our
> unpresentable parts are treated with greater modesty, which
> our more presentable parts do not require. But God has so

composed the body, giving greater honor to the inferior part, that there may be no discord in the body, but that the members may have the same care for one another. (12:22-25)

From Paul's comments in chapter 14, it seems that many Corinthians considered speaking in tongues and prophesying the most prestigious manifestations of the Spirit of God. The members with these abilities regard themselves as an elite group, causing a dispute within the church.

There is often confusion about the meaning of "speaking in tongues" and "prophecy" in First Corinthians. They are two distinct forms of inspired speech. Speaking in tongues is mentioned in the book of Acts; apart from Acts 2 (where it seems to mean speaking in foreign languages) the phrase refers to ecstatic speech. The same is true in First Corinthians. Tongues refers to inspired speech that is unintelligible to others and requires interpretation. Prophecy is a form of inspired speech that is intelligible ("he who prophesies speaks to men for their upbuilding and encouragement and consolation," I Cor. 14:3). Prophecy in this sense seems to mean "forthtelling" rather than "foretelling."

Inspired speech did not originate with early Christians. Scripture records both the incoherent, ecstatic prophecy of Saul (I Sam. 19:24) and the coherent prediction of the seer Elisha speaking under the influence of the "power of the LORD" (II Kings 3:15-19). Yet its appearance within Christian circles seems to have been unusual enough to attract attention. Extraordinary speech, both intelligible and unintelligible, was a phenomenon the Corinthian Christians interpreted as a clear-cut sign of God's presence in their midst.

Paul was faced with a paradox. He himself believed that inspired speech was evidence of the presence of the Holy Spirit. He boasts to the Corinthians that he speaks in tongues "more than you all" (I Cor. 14:18). Yet the Holy Spirit would never be disruptive, and in Corinth, the activity of the Spirit that works for the unity of the church is resulting in the division of the congregation. Paul's task is to restore unity without denying the validity of tongues as a true gift of the Spirit.

His first move is to place these two gifts within a broader

context. The Holy Spirit inspires not simply particular kinds of speaking but also other activities that are equally important to the well-being of the church (healing, helping, miracle-working, etc.). Those who brag about their gift of tongues must recognize that it is one among several and cannot sustain the whole congregation by itself. Like parts of a body, they must acknowledge their dependence upon other members and their gifts.

Paul's argument has a second thrust; this book must now turn attention to the famous chapter on love.

2. Chapter 13: The Hymn to Love. Scarcely a chapter in the New Testament is more familiar than I Corinthians 13. Scholars have customarily studied the hymn as a self-contained whole, apart from its context in the letter. This procedure has some justification, since the passage is unique within the letter. The style is more universal, less obviously related to particular issues within the life of the congregation. Although the chapter is not in verse, it has a certain hymnic quality that sets it off from the rest of the letter.

Chapter 13 also has a recognizable literary form. It is an encomium, a hymn offered in praise of a virtue—in this case, love. The genre was well known among ancient authors. One can recognize certain affinities with other encomia, two examples of which are included here for purposes of comparison.

I Corinthians 13

Verse   *Line*

1   If I speak in the tongues of men and of angels,
      but have not love,
        I am a noisy gong or a clanging cymbal.

2   And if I have prophetic powers,
      and understand all mysteries and all knowledge,   5
      and if I have all faith, so as to remove mountains,
      but have not love,
        I am nothing.

3   If I give away all I have,
      and if I deliver my body to be burned,   10
      but have not love,
        I gain nothing.

4   Love is patient and kind;
      love is not jealous or boastful;

5   it is not arrogant or rude.   15
     Love does not insist on its own way;
         it is not irritable or resentful,
6   it does not rejoice at wrong,
         but rejoices in the right.
7   Love bears all things,   20
         believes all things,
         hopes all things,
         endures all things.

8   Love never ends;
         as for prophecies,   25
             they will pass away;
         as for tongues,
             they will cease;
         as for knowledge,
             it will pass away.   30
9   For our knowledge is imperfect
         and our prophecy is imperfect;
10   but when the perfect comes,
         the imperfect will pass away.
11   When I was a child,   35
         I spoke like a child,
         I thought like a child,
         I reasoned like a child;
     when I became a man,
         I gave up childish ways.   40
12   For now we see in a mirror dimly,
         but then face to face.
     Now I know in part;
         then I shall understand fully,
         even as I have been fully understood.   45
13   So faith, hope, love abide,
         these three;
     but the greatest of these is love.

A hymn to love from Plato's *Symposium*

Thus I conceive, Phaedrus, that Love was originally of surpassing beauty and goodness, and is latterly the cause of similar excellence in others. And now I am moved to summon the aid of verse, and tell how it is he who makes—

Peace among men, and a windless waveless main;
Repose for winds, and slumber in our pain.

He it is who casts alienation out, draws intimacy in; he brings us together in all such friendly gatherings as the present; at feasts and dances and oblations he makes himself our leader; politeness contriving, moroseness outdriving; kind giver of amity, giving no enmity; gracious, benign; a marvel to the wise, a delight to the gods; coveted of such as share him not, treasured of such as good share have got; father of luxury, tenderness, elegance, graces and longing and yearning; careful of the good, careless of the bad; in toil and fear, in drink and discourse, our trustiest helmsman, boatswain, champion, deliverer; ornament of all gods and men; leader fairest and best, whom every one should follow, joining tunefully in the burthen of his song, wherewith he enchants the thought of every god and man.[15]

I Esdras 4:33-41 (In praise of truth)

And he began to speak about truth: "Gentlemen, are not women strong? The earth is vast, and heaven is high, and the sun is swift in its course, for it makes the circuit of the heavens and returns to its place in one day. Is he not great who does these things? But truth is great, and stronger than all things. The whole earth calls upon truth, and heaven blesses her. All God's works quake and tremble, and with him there is nothing unrighteous. Wine is unrighteous, the king is unrighteous, women are unrighteous, all the sons of men are unrighteous . . . and all such things. There is no truth in them and in their unrighteousness they will perish. But truth endures and is strong for ever, and lives and prevails for ever and ever. With her there is no partiality or preference, but she does what is righteous instead of anything that is unrighteous or wicked. All men approve her deeds, and there is nothing unrighteous in her judgment. To her belongs the strength and the kingship and the power and the majesty of all the ages. Blessed be the God of truth!"

Paul's hymn to love is composed in three strophes: verses 1-3, 4-7, and 8-13.

a. Strophe 1. The dominant feature in the three verses is the pattern "If I ____ but have not love, I am [or, I gain] ____." Love is the essential element without which other virtues or achievements have no value. In the first sentence, tongues, a physical manifestation, is likened to a gong, also physical. In the second, prophecy, understanding, knowledge, and faith—abstract qualities—are appropriately coupled with an abstraction, personal identity ("I am nothing"). In the third, generosity and martyrdom, evidence of a living faith, are evaluated in terms of achievement ("I gain nothing").

In the second and third sentences, the virtues selected tend toward a climax. The second sentence ends with faith that can remove mountains (probably an allusion to the familiar saying of Jesus recorded in Matt. 17:20). The ending of the third climaxes both the individual sentence and the series with the supreme test of religious devotion, martyrdom. Even this most extravagant testimony to one's convictions gains nothing without selfless love (*agape*).

b. Strophe 2. In the second stanza the hymn personifies love and describes it in terms of what it does and does not. Contrast is basic to the structure of the strophe. Verses 4 and 5 state the first contrast, positives (line 13) followed by a series of negatives.[16] Verse 6 is a self-contained contrast, this time beginning with the negative and ending with a positive. The two series of contrasts are carefully balanced, forming a chiasm: positive, negative—negative, positive.

The description of love in this strophe is reminiscent of the hymn from Plato's *Symposium.* Some may feel that Plato is the superior stylist, making full use of rhyme, balance, and grammatical variety. But Paul's hymn, also quite complex, may be equally worthy of admiration. The final accumulation of predicates in verse 7, strung together without conjunctions, produces a particularly impressive effect. This translation balances "bears" with "endures" and "believes" with "hopes"—another chiasm.

c. Strophe 3. The third unit picks up three virtues introduced in the first strophe and develops the contrast between them and more lasting virtues, notably love. Three virtues introduced at the beginning, at verse 8 (prophecy, tongues, and knowledge), are balanced by three virtues at the end: faith, hope, and love (verse 13). The contrasts in the strophe point up the transient, impermanent character of tongues, prophecy, and knowledge. The child metaphor (verse 11) and the mirror metaphor (verse 12) stress that the present strains toward a future, the partial toward completion. Tongues, prophecy, and knowledge—so noteworthy and seemingly important in the present—will no longer be necessary in the time to come, when childish things are put away, when the partial will be replaced by the complete, and when we see face to face. Love alone endures.

The short hymn to love is an excellent and carefully wrought composition. During this brief encomium the particular, sometimes mundane problems of the Corinthian church fade from view. There is nothing parochial—or even necessarily Christian—about this vision of love; it does not even mention the name of Jesus Christ. Yet it is part of Paul's letter to the Corinthians, and readers have not fully comprehended the chapter or the entire letter until they understand its contribution to that letter.

Whether the chapter was composed independently of the letter (as most scholars believe), the hymn to love is appropriate to this epistle to the Corinthians. Chapter 13 says that the gift of tongues and prophecy about which the Corinthians have been arguing are valueless without love—which they obviously lack. So are wisdom and knowledge, to which Paul often refers sarcastically. Love is not jealous or boastful—yet the congregation is split up into factions over boasting and jealousy. Love does not "puff up," yet on four occasions Paul has spoken about members of the congregation who are puffed up (4:6, 18, 19; 5:2). He has also commented that knowledge, which the Corinthians believe they possess, can also puff up (8:1-3). The major problems in Corinth stem from a woeful lack of love.

The hymn to love is also important in the immediate context of the consideration of spiritual gifts. Love is not a spiritual gift that displaces those mentioned in chapter 12. When Paul returns to the specific problem of the Corinthians in chapter 14, he discusses tongues and prophecy—not love. But love is now assumed to be the precondition for proper and effective use of all spiritual gifts, even the most spectacular.

3. Chapter 14: Speaking in Tongues. The Corinthians have asked which gifts are the most important. As a practical standard for evaluating spiritual gifts, Paul suggests the basic principle of love—selfless concern for one's neighbor: to what extent do such gifts edify and build up the community? By this criterion, Paul finds tongues less essential to the church than other gifts, including prophecy. The gift of tongues benefits only individuals because others cannot understand the incoherent speech. Prophecy that upbuilds, encourages, consoles, and judges benefits everyone. In fact, its chief purpose is to build up the community—and that is the primary work of the Spirit.

Paul does not so much take sides in the dispute about spiritual gifts, however, as view it from another perspective. Those who would boast of their own glittering manifestations of the Spirit must recognize first of all that some deceptively unspectacular gifts are equally necessary to the proper functioning of the community. Then they must exercise their gifts for the well-being of brothers and sisters. Gifts that benefit others are the more desirable and valuable ones. For Paul, one of the greatest of miracles has been the birth of a new community, the church. First Corinthians is largely an exploration of the conditions for, and the circumstances of, life within that new community. Christian freedom means a binding commitment—to a church founded on selfless love.

Summary

Paul's letters give us a many-sided picture of the man, his message, and his relationships with the congregations of which he was the spiritual father. In all three respects, his diversity is often perplexing, though part of a fundamental integrity. One cannot explain away the perplexity either by saying that Paul was erratic or by trying to resolve the basic tensions among his potentially conflicting ideas. To compound the problem, Paul makes some extreme statements, depending on the situation of the people he is addressing. Paul affirms now one polarity and now another, attempting to hold the paradoxes in creative tension.

For example, Paul is basically committed to Christian liberation. Yet he demands that this not be misconstrued as being freed from responsibility to the community. Two of his more carefully written letters, Galatians and First Corinthians, illustrate contrasting emphases in Paul's thought.

In Galatians, Paul stresses Christian freedom from the past. Baptism alone inducts one into the community of God's people. Circumcision, Torah, and tradition are unnecessary, even a hindrance. In First Corinthians, Paul insists that the people of Corinth are not mature enough in their Christianity to handle freedom and so have formed destructive factions. They must submit their individuality to the good of the community, through love for one another.

Paul's epistles follow the form of ancient Greek letters in many respects. One can gain insight into his mind by examining the way he treats some conventional literary elements: (a) the opening salutation and identification of sender and recipient; (b) the thanksgiving, usually for the worthiness of the recipient; and (c) the request that the sender makes.

Paul sees the situation in Galatia as desperate. He feels that his gospel is being subverted by new Jewish Christian missionaries who are telling the Gentile Christians that they must be circumcised or they are not within God's covenant and that they must obey Mosaic Law or they will be immoral. Paul's preaching, they claim, leads away from God and into immorality. For Paul, this position replaces grace with ritualistic observance as the source of salvation. And as a former Pharisee, he is convinced that Torah Judaism and missionary Christianity are incompatible. He must defend himself as apostle to the Gentiles and must attack the Jewish Christians.

Therefore, in his epistle to the Galatians, Paul's opening identifies him as having received his apostleship directly from Jesus Christ and not from men—the Jewish Christian leaders in Jerusalem—and he emphasizes the grace of God in his salutation. He is so agitated that he omits the customary thanksgiving and launches into an attack. And rather than use the confident, formal request, he "beseeches" the Galatians to accept his values.

The situation in Corinth is different. The majority of the community has asked Paul's advice about certain congregational problems, but he has found that the community is divided. One dispute is over Paul's authority, because he has not baptized many converts in their church and because he has not been spectacularly successful as a preacher in general. Another controversy centers on the claims of certain members of the community to be more important by reason of their various superior spiritual gifts, or charismata: ecstatic speech, prophecy, faith, healing, miracles, and so forth. Paul argues in the first instance that his lack of eloquence is a sign that he shares the values of the crucified Christ: outward success is a false indicator of truth. Second, they are wrong to boast of their gifts, because they have neglected the only truly essential gift, selfless love (*agape*).

In this epistle, Paul's opening is unusual in calling attention to the unity of all Christians—an appropriate note for the contentious Corinthians. His thanksgiving ironically exaggerates their spiritual gifts, of which they are so blindly boastful. His appeal focuses on reports of their dissension. Thus, an analysis of literary elements of Paul's letters helps clarify their main themes.

The Epistle to the Corinthians especially repays closer literary examination. The first half (chaps. 1–6) deals with the people's inability to judge Paul's authority correctly because they confuse worldly wisdom and success with God's wisdom and truth. The second half (chaps. 7–16) answers the specific congregational question they have asked him to settle, and again Paul points to their reversal of values.

Pivotal in that second half is Paul's discussion of spiritual gifts (chaps. 12–14). Central to that discussion is his famous and ingeniously crafted "hymn to love" (chap. 13). Here the theme is similar to that of the first part of the letter: the people have missed the real substance of Christianity. Selfless love is the basic gift, and their contentiousness about him and about their own gifts shows that this is the one gift they lack. The gift of tongues or of prophecy should not make people important in the community. Love would make them submerge their competition and serve the whole, in cooperation—just as various members of a human body are equally necessary to the complete organism.

CHAPTER THIRTEEN

THE REVELATION TO JOHN

The last book in the New Testament bears little formal resemblance to other New Testament writings. It is neither a Gospel nor a historical narrative like Acts; and although its first three chapters consist of letters to seven churches, the book of Revelation, or Apocalypse, cannot be classed as an epistle. Scholars generally call it an apocalypse, a generic term based on the Greek word meaning to uncover or reveal. The narrator uses the word to characterize the work itself. "The revelation [apocalypsis] of Jesus Christ, which God gave him to show his servants what must soon take place; and he made it known by sending his angel to his servant John" (Rev. 1:1).

The work intends to uncover secrets concerning the immediate future ("what must soon take place"), hitherto concealed. The medium of this revelation is a seer, who introduces himself simply as John.

> I John, your brother, who share with you in Jesus the tribulation and the kingdom and the patient endurance, was on the island called Patmos on account of the word of God and the testimony of Jesus. I was in the Spirit on the Lord's day, and I heard behind me a loud voice like a trumpet saying, "Write what you see in a book and send it to the seven churches, to Ephesus and to Smyrna and to Pergamum and to Thyatira and to Sardis and to Philadelphia and to Laodicea." (1:9-11)

This introduction is part of John's three-chapter prefatory address to his readers in the seven Asian churches, for whom the visions, which begin in chapter 4, are intended. The number seven symbolized fullness, suggesting that John speaks to Asian Christianity as a whole, though he seems to be familiar with actual situations in each of the seven churches.[1]

In the visions that follow the seven letters, Christ himself reveals through John what must soon take place. The visions themselves are extraordinary—sometimes powerful and stirring, often bewildering. One difficulty in interpreting them may be the inadequacy of language to communicate an ineffable visionary experience. Yet John believes that the imagery will reveal its own message. He records what he has seen and expects his readers to know what is coming. Another difficulty for today's readers is not being a part of the religious and cultural milieu within which John wrote. John's work may have an artistry and an originality that transcend cultural or temporal boundaries, but there is still a considerable gap between the literary world of the writer's audience and today's. Knowledge of the literary traditions and historical context out of which Revelation arose will render some of the imagery less obscure and enhance an understanding of, and appreciation for, the finished literary product.

I. Visionary Literature

A. Prophetic Literature

Visionary literature antedates the Revelation of John by centuries. Seers claimed to speak on behalf of the gods, under the guidance of a divine spirit, in many cultures since the beginning of the second millennium B.C.E. Written accounts still exist of visions and oracles in the Greco-Roman world outside Jewish and Christian circles.

The most important literary parallels to Revelation, however, occur within the Jewish tradition. Similarities between John and the prophets of ancient Israel are obvious. Though he stops short of calling himself a prophet, John does refer to his work as "prophecy" (1:3, 22:7, 10, 18, 19), and an angel includes him among the fellowship of the prophets (22:9). John's experience of God and his conception of his role are also reminiscent of the great prophetic figures. Like Isaiah and Ezekiel, he reports a vision and a call. In a vision of the very court of God he, like Isaiah and Ezekiel, receives a commission as God's spokesman.

The detailed similarities between John's first vision in

chapter 4 and those of Isaiah and Ezekiel are striking, extending to identical images and even wording:

At once I was in the Spirit, and lo, a throne stood in heaven, with one seated on the throne. And he who sat there appeared like jasper and carnelian. (Rev. 4:2-3)

And above the firmament over their heads there was the likeness of a throne, in appearance like sapphire; and seated above the likeness of a throne was a likeness as it were of a human form. (Ezek. 1:26)

And round the throne was a rainbow that looked like an emerald. (Rev. 4:3)

Like the appearance of the bow that is in the cloud on the day of rain, so was the appearance of the brightness round about. (Ezek. 1:28)

And round the throne, on each side of the throne, are four living creatures, full of eyes in front and behind: the first living creature like a lion, the second living creature like an ox, the third living creature with the face of a man, and the fourth living creature like a flying eagle. (Rev. 4:6b-7)

And from the midst of it came the likeness of four living creatures. . . . As for the likeness of their faces, each had the face of a man in front; the four had the face of a lion on the right side, the four had the face of an ox on the left side, and the four had the face of an eagle at the back. (Ezek. 1:5-10)

And the four living creatures, each of them with six wings, are full of eyes all round and within, and day and night they never cease to sing, "Holy, holy, holy, is the Lord God Almighty, who was and is and is to come!" (Rev. 4:8)

Above him stood the seraphim; each had six wings. . . . And one called to another and said: "Holy, holy, holy is the LORD of hosts; the whole earth is full of his glory." (Isa. 6:2-3)

The writer of Revelation and his readers obviously shared a world of images with the prophets of ancient Israel. Curiously, however, although Revelation looks almost like a mosaic of excerpts from prophetic writings, John never directly quotes a single passage with an attributive phrase, "as it is written" or the like. The Jewish Bible appears to function differently for John than for other New Testament writers. It provides the images out of which he constructs his visions, but authority is invested in the visions and not in Scripture. John does not reinterpret the old message; for him biblical texts serve a quite distinct and original message. Very much in the manner of the prophets in ancient Israel—and unlike other New Testament writers—John draws freely on his tradition and adapts it to transmit what God has revealed to him. Yet as shall be seen, Revelation cannot be described as prophetic literature in the classic sense.

B. Apocalyptic Literature

The biblical work most closely related to Revelation is the second half of Daniel. The two books share numerous images, as footnotes in Bibles point out, but their similarities extend beyond, to structure and overall conception. Both are part of a visionary tradition that stems from the ancient prophetic movement in Israel. Yet they belong to a distinct literary genre that transformed the prophetic writing into a new mode of expression, called apocalyptic. Daniel 7–12 and Revelation are two apocalyptic writings that came to be included in scriptural canons; others appear in noncanonical literature.[2]

Most Old Testament introductions have included some account of the rise of apocalyptic literature, and there are important new studies.[3] The following characteristics of the genre are particularly relevant to this study of Revelation:

1. Symbolic Language and Monstrous Beasts. Visions and figurative language occur elsewhere in the Bible, but nowhere as profusely as in Daniel and Revelation. Some of the images are so bizarre as to defy the mind's eye:

> After this I saw in the night visions, and behold, a fourth beast, terrible and dreadful and exceedingly strong; and it had great iron teeth; it devoured and broke in pieces, and stamped the residue with its feet. It was different from all the beasts that were before it; and it had ten horns. I considered the horns, and behold, there came up among them another horn, a little one, before which three of the first horns were plucked up by the roots; and behold, in this horn were eyes like the eyes of a man, and a mouth speaking great things. (Dan. 7:7-8)

> And I saw a beast rising out of the sea, with ten horns and seven heads, and ten diadems upon its horns and a blasphemous name upon its heads. And the beast that I saw was like a leopard, its feet were like a bear's, and its mouth was like a lion's mouth. And to it the dragon gave his power and his throne and great authority. One of its heads seemed to have a mortal wound, but

its mortal wound was healed, and the whole earth followed the
beast with wonder. (Rev. 13:1-3)

However outlandish, their interpretation is fairly certain.
The bewildered Daniel hears that the vision of the beast
depicts the succession of empires (Dan. 7:15-28).In Revelation the beast clearly symbolizes the Roman Empire.
Evidently, monstrous beasts were appropriate symbols for
reigning world powers. Some of the bizarre images probably
derive from ancient Near Eastern mythology. Beasts rising
from the sea (Rev. 13:1) and from the land (verse 11) may be
Leviathan and Behemoth, encountered in other Jewish
apocalyptic writings and in the psalms.

Other symbols appear to be rather artificial creations,
referring to some contemporary person or event. The
blasphemous name on the heads of the beast (13:1) may refer
to inscriptions on imperial coinage, calling the emperors
gods.[4] For example, Domitian, probably on the Roman
throne when Revelation was written, wished to be addressed
as lord and god. The whore seated on a beast with seven heads
(17:1-6) represents the city of Rome; the angel tells the seer
that the seven heads stand for seven hills (verse 9),
eliminating any doubt about the meaning of the vision. The
mysterious number of the beast, 666, which requires wisdom
to understand (13:18), in all probability refers to Nero.[5]

One explanation for John's use of elaborate symbolism is
that his work is part of a tradition. Many of his images had
long been assimilated into Jewish tradition from earlier
cultures and had become an established feature of the new
literary genre. Another reason is that the writer probably
shares the ancient conception of the interrelationship of the
heavenly and the earthly realms. The struggles between
Christians and their enemies are a reflection of a cosmic battle
between God and his forces on one side, and the beast, the
personification of evil, and its forces on the other. It seems
unlikely that the symbolism was employed as a code language
for insiders. The image of a harlot seated on seven hills, for
example, could scarcely have symbolized anything but Rome
to a contemporary of John, whether Christian or non-

Christian. Historians will continue to debate the derivation of the symbols and the reasons for this distinctive use in apocalyptic writings. It is necessary to observe simply that Revelation is an example of a literary tradition that brought about a dramatic rebirth of ancient images.

2. Pessimism about the Present Age and Hope for the End of Time. Both Daniel and Revelation were written at a time of crisis: Daniel presumably during the terrible persecutions under Antiochus Epiphanes (175-164 B.C.E.); John, most likely in the reign of Domitian (81-96 C.E.), when open conflict with the emperor seemed certain. In both works, the seer has little hope that the fortunes of the elect will improve in this age. From the rulers of this world the elect can expect only persecution. Revelation portrays the Roman government as an agent of the dragon, the personification of evil (chaps. 12–13). For the present, God allows the forces of evil to rule on earth: "Also it was allowed to make war on the saints and to conquer them. And authority was given it over every tribe and people and tongue and nation" (13:7).

The apocalyptist paints history in black and white. The only important distinction between people is their allegiance. One is a worshiper of either the beast or God. People's names are either written in the "book of life of the Lamb that was slain" (13:8) or excluded as unworthy.

The visions sketch no program of reform or plan of human resistance against the powers of evil. Rather, through the visions of what is to come—what *must* come (1:1)—readers are assured that however desperate things appear, history is in God's hands. The triumph of his justice and the vindication of his elect are inevitable. For the present, the unequal battle against evil and against its personification in the Roman emperors, is all-consuming. The elect have no hope either of accommodation or of victory. Their only comfort is the knowledge that the days of the forces of evil are numbered. The ultimate triumph, for which this struggle is only an unhappy prelude, has been assured. The angel calls the faithful to hold fast and to live in anticipation of the final vindication soon to come (22:6-13).

3. Authorship. With the demise of the prophetic movement

in postexilic Israel, seers who felt the call could no longer speak for God in their own names. Apocalyptic writings are therefore pseudonymous, attributed to important figures from Israel's past like Enoch, Ezra, Baruch, or Daniel. For example, Daniel's apocalypse claims throughout to have been the experience of Daniel during the Babylonian exile (sixth century B.C.E.). An apparition tells him to write what he has seen and to seal it, until a time when God will reveal the existence of the scroll to those for whom it is intended (Dan. 12:9).

The Revelation of John, however, breaks with apocalyptic tradition. John writes under his own name for his own time. The angel explicitly instructs him to reveal his prophecy: "And he said to me, 'Do not seal up the words of the prophecy of this book, for the time is near'" (Rev. 22:10).

This Christian apocalypse addresses people who believe that God has again poured out the prophetic spirit, as Acts 2 plainly states. New beliefs have led to a significant departure in the apocalyptic literature.

II. Revelation as Literature: The Two Kingdoms

Reconstruction of the historical context of Revelation is useful for interpretation. For literary analysis and full appreciation of the writer's creative genius, however, it is only a prelude. The book of Revelation has never lacked its admirers, though most readers have been more attracted by its potential disclosures of the secrets of time and history than by its artistic qualities. Yet the book has proved as baffling to literary critics as to would-be prophets. A casual survey of the many outlines of the work's structure offered by commentators shows how it resists literary analysis.[6] There may even be no structure within the central portion of the book.

The closer one examines the work, however, the more the signs of artistry emerge. Interpreters have called attention to numerous such indicators.[7] Following is an examination of just one aspect of Revelation that shows deliberate literary craftsmanship: the careful and detailed juxtaposition of the kingdom of God and the kingdom of evil (chaps. 17–22).

A. The Beast vs. Christ

The first contrast begins with parallels between the opposing characters who will enact the drama of the end. Enter the beast in chapter 17 (who appeared in an earlier scene), a terrifying creature that "was and is not and is to come" (17:8). It is the "eighth" that "belongs to the seven" (verse 11). The "seven" were undoubtedly Caesars, and the eighth that was and is to come probably refers to a new Nero, the dreaded ruler whose return from the dead came to be a feature of popular mythology. More significantly, the words that describe the beast ironically echo earlier words, which described God: "'I am the Alpha and the Omega,' says the Lord God, who is and who was and who is to come, the Almighty" (1:8). The beast is a usurper, full of blasphemous names that proclaim its divinity (17:3). It claims dominion that belongs to God and his Lamb, which also serves as a contrasting parallel to the beast.

In an earlier scene, the beast miraculously recovers from a mortal wound: "One of the heads seemed to have a mortal wound, but its mortal wound was healed, and the whole earth followed the beast with wonder" (13:3). Christ, on the other hand, is the one who "died, and behold I am alive for evermore" (1:18); he is the Lamb that was slain (5:6; 8–9). The beast, like Christ, returns—but with a different destiny. The beast is to "go to perdition" (17:18, 11), whereas the Lamb will defeat the beast and be hailed as "Lord of lords and King of kings" (17:14; 19:11-21).

The parallel expands to include the opposing "trinities" who face each other in battle. On one side stand God, Christ, and Christ's prophet, John; on the other, the Satanic dragon, his agent the beast, and the false prophet. John's vision of the great heavenly drama climaxes with the defeat of the evil triumvirate:

> And the beast was captured, and with it the false prophet who in its presence had worked the signs by which he had deceived those who had received the mark of the beast and those who worshiped its image. . . . Then I saw an angel coming down from heaven. . . . And he seized the dragon, that ancient serpent, who is the Devil and Satan, and bound him for a

thousand years. . . . And the devil who had deceived them was thrown into the lake of fire and sulfur where the beast and the false prophet were, and they will be tormented day and night for ever and ever. (19:20–20:10)

B. Babylon vs. Jerusalem

The visions also include detailed portraits of two opposing cities, Babylon (Rome) and Jerusalem, both personified as women. Babylon is a whore, seated on the beast and decked in finery; she is the epitome of power and arrogance. "A queen I sit," she boasts, "I am no widow, mourning I shall never see" (18:7). At the same time, she radiates corruption and decadence: "The woman was arrayed in purple and scarlet, and bedecked with gold and jewels and pearls, holding in her hand a golden cup full of abominations and the impurities of her fornication" (17:4). And she willingly participates in the carnage of the beast, "drunk with the blood . . . of the martyrs of Jesus" (verse 6). Finally, the reader is given a vivid description of her eventual fall. Appropriately, the bestial lover of the faithless woman turns on her and destroys her: "And the ten horns that you saw, they and the beast will hate the harlot; they will make her desolate and naked, and devour her flesh and burn her up with fire" (verse 16).

Jerusalem, by contrast, will become the bride of the Lamb. She is modest, prepared for her husband, clothed in simple but fine linen:

"Hallelujah! For the Lord our God the Almighty reigns.
Let us rejoice and exult and give him the glory,
for the marriage of the Lamb has come,
and his Bride has made herself ready;
it was granted her to be clothed with fine linen, bright and pure"—
for the fine linen is the righteous deeds of the saints. (19:6-8)

The songs of rejoicing in chapter 19 contrast vividly with the dirges in chapter 18. The bounty and splendor of the new Jerusalem offset the deprivation and destruction of Babylon.

And the kings of the earth, who committed fornication
and were wanton with her, will weep and wail over her. . . .

And the merchants of the earth weep and mourn for her. . . .
And they threw dust on their heads, as they wept and mourned.
(18:9-11, 19)

God himself will be with them; he will wipe away every tear from
their eyes, and death shall be no more, neither shall there be
mourning nor crying nor pain any more, for the former things have
passed away. (21:3-4)

Babylon's fire and famine give way to Jerusalem's refreshment and abundance:

Behold, I make all things new. . . . To the thirsty I will give from the
fountain of the water of life without payment. (21:5-6)

On either side of the river, the tree of life with its twelve kinds of
fruit, yielding its fruit each month; and the leaves of the tree were for
the healing of the nations. (22:2)

Babylon's ruins and desolation are succeeded by the fantastic
splendor of the new Jerusalem: "The wall was built of jasper,
while the city was pure gold, clear as glass. The foundations of
the wall of the city were adorned with every jewel; the first
was jasper, the second sapphire, the third agate" (21:18-19).

The concluding vision of the new Jerusalem clearly aims at
instilling hope in a generation that had little reason to hope.
Passionately and movingly, it points to the ultimate triumph
of justice. The vision is no less impressive as a work of art. Its
elements are not particularly original, many of them deriving
from prophetic books, particularly Ezekiel. And yet the final
portrait is something distinctive. The old images are reborn.
The book of Revelation itself provides the words that capture
the spirit of the work: "Behold, I make all things new."

Summary

The Revelation to John is unique among New Testament
books: it is not gospel, history, or epistle. It is, however, well
within the tradition of ancient Near Eastern visionary
literature in general and of apocalyptic literature in
particular. Even more specifically, the book draws freely on
Ezekiel's visions for its imagery and shares both the imagery
and the apocalyptic features of the latter half of Daniel.

Jewish and Christian apocalyptic literature grows out of prophetic writing. Some of its earmarks are: a heavy use of symbolic language and images of monstrous beasts; pessimism about the reign of evil in the present age, coupled with an expectation of vindication for the elect at the end of time; and attribution of the authorship of the work to a prophetic figure of the past.

The book of Revelation fits all these criteria except the last. The writer identifies himself as a contemporary. He does not feel that prophecy ended forever after the Exile, nor does he consider himself an interpreter of tradition. He is a prophet like those of old, directly inspired in accordance with the example in Acts 2.

At first reading, the book is bewildering; but its fantastic imagery can be fairly well deciphered. There is less consensus among scholars about its literary aspects—especially its structure after the initial three chapters containing letters to the seven Asian churches. Literary analysis is enlightening, however; the book does show attention to craftsmanship.

For example, the last six chapters center on a series of contrasting and quite detailed parallels between the kingdom of God and the kingdom of evil. God, Christ, and the seer John confront the dragon Satan, the beast, and the false prophet. Babylon the whore is contrasted with the new Jerusalem, bride of Christ the Lamb. Explicitly depicted destruction and suffering await Babylon and its inhabitants, while vivid splendor and refreshment attend the new Jerusalem.

These parallels reinforce the message: evil now rules, but readers must resist steadfastly; their struggle mirrors the cosmic conflict at the end of the age; God will triumph over Satan and his evil hordes and will usher in a new age and a new Jerusalem; the elect, who now suffer and struggle, will be the heirs in the coming age in which Christ will rule.

NOTES

Chapter 1

1. The expression "Jewish Bible" is more appropriate than "Hebrew Bible." Most early Christians, like Jews living outside Palestine, spoke Greek and read the Bible in Greek translation. The term "Bible" may be a bit anachronistic for the early part of the first century C.E., since the formal outlines of the present Jewish canon were not drawn up until the last decade of the first century. Nevertheless, the decisions of the rabbinic community were principally confirmations of earlier practice rather than innovations.

2. For a discussion of the purge, see J. Louis Martyn, *History and Theology in the Fourth Gospel* (New York: Harper, 1968), pp. 23-40.

3. Josephus, *Jewish Wars,* II, 117-18.

4. *Ibid.,* pp. 258-60.

5. Fortresses still standing after the fall of Jerusalem were Herodium, Machäerus, and Masada. Masada, the last to be captured, fell to Flavius Silva and his legions in 73 C.E. The story of the seige of this extraordinary fortress is narrated in Josephus, *Wars,* VII, 252-406. Rather than surrender to the Romans, the Jewish defenders committed mass suicide. The whole story, including pictures of the fortress, has been retold in the superb work by Yigael Yadin, *Masada: Herod's Fortress and the Zealot's Last Stand,* trans. M. Pearlman (New York: Random House, 1966).

6. In *Roman History,* Cassius Dio states: "Very few of them in fact survived. Fifty of their most important outposts and nine hundred and eighty-five of their most famous villages were razed to the ground. Five hundred and eighty thousand men were slain in the various raids and battles. . . . . Thus nearly the whole of Judea was made desolate." *Dio's Roman History,* Loeb Classical Library (London, 1925), VIII, 449-51.

7. For studies of Hellenistic Judaism, see E. R. Goodenough, *Jewish Symbols in the Greco-Roman Period* (New York: Pantheon Books, 1953–68). An important work recently published is Martin Hengel, *Judaism and Hellenism,* trans. by John Bowden (Philadelphia: Fortress Press, 1974). See also Morton Smith, "Palestinian Judaism in the First Century," *Israel: Its Role in Civilization,* ed. Moshe Davis (New York: Harper, 1956), pp. 67-81.

8. The legend is recounted in the "Letter of Aristeas," which can be found in translation in R. H. Charles, *Apocrypha and Pseudepigrapha of the Old Testament* (Oxford: Clarendon Press, 1913).

9. Reference to the sects is made in Josephus, *Antiquities,* XVIII, 2-25, and *Wars,* II, 119-66. See also Hengel, *Judaism;* Smith, "Palestinian Judaism"; and Jacob Neusner, *From Politics to Piety: The Emergence of Pharisaic Judaism* (Englewood Cliffs, N. J.: Prentice-Hall, 1973).

10. This view of the Pharisees, still hotly debated, is represented by Neusner, *Politics to Piety.*

11. The dating of Marks' Gospel is still a matter of dispute. See my discussion of the matter in chap. 8.

12. Millar Burrows, *The Dead Sea Scrolls* (New York: Viking Press, 1955); John Trever, *The Untold Story of Qumran* (Old Tappan, N.J.: Fleming H. Revell, 1965).

13. See Charles, *Aprocrypha and Pseudepigrapha.*

14. See especially Hengel, *Judaism,* and Smith, "Palestinian Judaism."

Chapter 2

1. See Eusebius, *The History of the Church,* trans. G. A. Williamson (Baltimore: Penguin Books, 1965), pp. 309-13.

2. Augustine's principal concern is to defend the Gospels against critical assaults by opponents of the Christian movement. His solution to the complex pattern of interrelationships among the first three Gospels is that Mark was an epitomizer of Matthew.

3. Augustine, "The Harmony of the Gospels," book I, chap. 2.

4. One of the most important discussions of such assimilations and harmonizations can be found in B. H. Streeter, *The Four Gospels,* rev. ed. (London: Macmillan & Co., 1964), chap. 6.

5. Streeter, *ibid.,* chap. 9, was willing to attribute almost all minor agreements between Matthew and Luke against Mark to textual corruptions. Other scholars are not convinced that his explanations account for all the evidence that might be used to discount the priority of Mark. See especially William Farmer, *The Synoptic Problem* (New York: Macmillan, 1964).

6. *The Gospel According to Thomas,* trans. A. Guillaumont *et al.* (New York: Harper, 1959).

7. Emma J. and Ludwig Edelstein, *Aesclepius: A Collection and Interpretation of the Testimonies* (Baltimore: Johns Hopkins Press, 1945), pp. 231-32.

8. Philostratus, *The Life of Apollonius of Tyana,* Loeb Classical Library (London, 1912).

9. The German term translated as "form criticism" is *Formgeschichte.* The most famous proponents of the method in the study of the New Testament are Rudolf Bultmann and Martin Dibelius.

10. Martin Dibelius, the famous form critic, characterized the gospel writers as "collectors, vehicles of tradition, editors." See *From Tradition to Gospel,* trans. B. L. Woolf (New York: Scribner's, 1935), p. 3.

11. Examples are the contributors to *Literary Interpretations of Biblical Narratives,* ed. Kenneth R. R. Gros Louis *et al.* (Nashville: Abingdon, 1974).

12. Eric Auerbach, *Mimesis: The Representation of Reality in Western Literature,* trans. W. Trask (Princeton: Princeton University Press, 1946).

13. Evidence indicates that the Gospel of Mark originally ended with 16:8.

14. Auerbach, *Mimesis,* pp. 40-49.

Chapter 3

1. The titles used in English translations of the Old Testament are taken from the Greek translation: Genesis, Exodus, etc.

2. Early Christian and Jewish interpretation of Scripture is now the subject of a vast literature. David Daube provides an excellent introduction to the field in *The New Testament and Rabbinic Judaism* (New York: Arno Press, 1973).

3. One suggestion is that the name "Nazareth" is related by Matthew to the

term *netzer* in Isa. 11:1, a term that means "branch" and that, in Jewish tradition, was taken to be a reference to the coming Messiah.

Chapter 4

1. Among the many studies of Jesus' parables, one that has been of particular importance is Joachim Jeremias, *The Parables of Jesus,* trans. S. H. Hooke (New York: Scribner's, 1963).

2. An important study of such parables is Nils A. Dahl, "Parables of Growth," *Jesus in the Memory of the Early Church* (Minneapolis: Augsburg, 1976), pp. 141-66.

3. Jeremias, *Parables of Jesus,* devotes a lengthy portion of his study to an examination of the various influences he sees at work in the oral transmission that have resulted in alterations of the original parable. They include embellishment, influence of the Old Testament and of folk-story themes, change of audience, etc.

4. A particularly important study was done by W. D. Davis, *The Setting of the Sermon on the Mount* (Cambridge: Cambridge University Press, 1964). The substance of the book has appeared in more popular form in *The Sermon on the Mount* (Cambridge, 1966).

5. The last position was popularized by Albert Schweitzer in his extraordinary work, *The Quest of the Historical Jesus,* trans. by W. Montgomery (New York: Macmillan, 1964). The book, first published in 1906, has had an enormous impact on subsequent scholarship and is still a classic.

6. See for example W. F. Albright and C. S. Mann, *Matthew,* The Anchor Bible (Garden City, N. Y.: Doubleday, 1971), p. 45.

7. For examples of the antithetical form in rabbinic literature, see Daube, *New Testament and Rabbinic Judaism,* pp. 55-62.

8. The various lists of principles of interpretation are listed in H. Strack, *Introduction to the Talmud and Midrash* (New York: Harper, 1931), pp. 93-98.

9. See esp. 300-304 and 316-18 below.

10. *Gospel According to Thomas,* p. 3.

11. Raymond Brown, *The Gospel According to John,* The Anchor Bible (Garden City, N. Y.: Doubleday, 1966), pp. 265-66.

12. The quotation in John corresponds to no single scriptural text. It is reminiscent of Exod. 16:4, 16:15; Ps. 78:24; Wisd. 16:20.

13. This is the typical designation for Jesus' enemies in John's Gospel.

14. Wayne A. Meeks, *The Prophet-King* (Leiden: E. J. Brill, 1967), pp. 295-301.

Chapter 5

1. The cursing of the fig tree also provides a demonstration of the power of prayer that is picked up in Mark 11:22-24.

2. Babylonian Talmud, *Taanith* 24b, from H. Kee, *The Origins of Christianity* (Englewood Cliffs, N. J.: Prentice-Hall, 1973), p. 227.

3. Babylonian Talmud, *Shabbath* 119a, *The Talmud,* trans. H. Freedman (London, 1948), vol. 2, part 2.

4. Babylonian Talmud, *Berakoth* 33a, *The Talmud,* trans. M. Simon (London, 1948), vol. 1, part 1.

5. Edelstein, *Aesclepius,* pp. 231-32.
6. *Ibid.,* p. 235.
7. Philostratus, *Life of Apollonius,* IV, 45.
8. See, for example, Paul Achtemeier, "The Origin and Function of the Pre-Markan Miracle Catanae," *Journal of Biblical Literature,* 91 (1972), 198-221; and R. T. Fortna, *The Gospel of Signs* (Cambridge: Cambridge University Press, 1970), a study of possible sources of the Gospel of John.
9. This assertion, though vigorously denied in the past, has been proved correct by the scrolls from Qumran.
10. Martyn, *History and Theology in the Fourth Gospel,* believes this is what the narrator intends to convey by the use of "we." Professor Martyn sees here evidence of a two-level narrative in which there is a consistent interrelationship between the story of Jesus and the situation of John's audience.

Chapter 6

1. This issue has been hotly disputed for some time. The arguments are reviewed in my book *Messiah and Temple,* Society of Biblical Literature Dissertation Series, 31 (Missoula, Mont.: Society of Biblical Literature, 1976).
2. Many studies of the trial and death of Jesus have appeared in the last decades. Among the most important are: J. Blinzler, *The Trial of Jesus,* trans. I. and F. McHugh (Westminster, Md.: Newman Press, 1959); H. Cohn, *The Trial and Death of Jesus* (New York: Harper, 1967); Nils A. Dahl, "The Crucified Messiah," *The Crucified Messiah and Other Essays* (Minneapolis: Augsburg, 1974), pp. 10-36; P. Winter, *On the Trial of Jesus* (Berlin: Gruyter, 1961).
3. See Charles, *Apocrypha and Pseudepigrapha,* vol. 2.
4. See A. Dupont-Sommer, *The Essene Writings from Qumran,* trans. G. Vermes (New York: Meridian Books, 1967).
5. For the tradition that the Messiah has been born and is a leper at the gates of Rome, see Babylonian Talmud *Sandedrin* 98 a and b. For the tradition that the Messiah was born on the day the Temple was destroyed, see Talmud Yerushalmi *Berakoth* 2, 5a.
6. This is argued persuasively in Dahl, "Crucified Messiah."
7. A. N. Sherwin-White, *Roman Society and Roman Law in the New Testament* (Oxford: Clarendon Press, 1963).
8. Accounts of Pilate's career are found in Josephus *Antiquities* XVIII, 55-89, and *Wars* II, 169-77.

Chapter 8

1. Eusebius, *History of the Church,* p. 152.
2. This interpretation of Papias' comments has been proposed in an article that is unfortunately untranslated: J. Kürzinger, "Das Papiaszeugnis und die Erstgestalt des Matthäusevangeliums," *Biblische Zeitschrift,* 1960, pp. 19-38.
3. The ending of Mark's Gospel occurs in four distinct forms in manuscripts: (a) 16:1-20; (b) 16:1-20, with an additional verse inserted between vv. 14 and 15; (c) 16:1-8 plus the "shorter ending"; and (d) 16:1-8. In

all of the major Greek manuscripts of the greatest antiquity, the Gospel ends with 16:8. The other endings seem to represent attempts to conclude the Gospel in a more "appropriate" way. Most recent translations of the New Testament indicate in some way that the "longer" and "shorter" endings are not found in the oldest manuscripts. These ancient manuscripts were not available to the translators of the King James Version, prepared in 1611, which explains why in old Bibles the Gospel of Mark ends only with 16:20.

4. Auerbach, *Mimesis,* pp. 47-48.

5. *Ibid.,* chap. 2.

6. Scholars who have observed more than geographical interest in reference to Galilee and Jerusalem included Willi Marxsen, *Mark the Evangelist,* trans. Donald Juel *et al.* (Nashville: Abingdon, 1969), chap. 1; and R. H. Lightfoot, *Locality and Doctrine in the Gospels* (New York: Harper, 1938).

7. W. Wrede, *The Messianic Secret,* trans. J. C. G. Greig (London: James Clarke, 1971).

8. The very difficult questions about the meaning of the designation "Son of man" and its origin have occasioned an enormous literature and little unanimity of opinion. Among the more useful treatments are: H. E. Tödt, *The Son of Man in the Synoptic Tradition* (Philadelphia: Westminster Press, 1965); C. Colpe's article on Son of man in Kittel's *Theological Dictionary of the New Testament,* trans. G. Bromiley (Grand Rapids: Eerdmans, 1972), vol. 8, 400-77.

9. The hypothesis is even more attractive in light of Papias' own use of I Pet. 5:13 to establish the link between Mark and Peter. (See Eusebius, *History of the Church,* pp. 88-89.)

Chapter 9

1. Martin Dibelius, *Studies in the Acts of the Apostles,* ed. H. Greeven (London: SCM Press 1956), p. 146. The claim has been disputed by other scholars.

2. The transition from Luke 24 to Acts 1 involves several problems. According to the Gospel of Luke, Jesus' appearances to his followers are confined to Easter Day ("that very day," 24:13), and it is on the same day that Jesus departs from his followers (v. 51). According to Acts, Jesus appeared to his followers for a period of forty days after his resurrection (Acts 1:3). According to Luke, Jesus departs at Bethany; in Acts, the place is identified as the Mount of Olives (Luke 24:60; Acts 1:12). The various explanations offered for the differences are considered in E. Haenchen, *The Acts of the Apostles,* trans. B. Noble and G. Shinn (Oxford: Blackwell, 1971).

3. Pentecost, from the Greek word for fiftieth, was an ancient Jewish harvest festival celebrated, by the first century C.E., on the fiftieth day after Passover. On the festival in Jewish life, see T. Gaster, *Festivals of the Jewish Year* (New York: Morrow, 1952–53). At some point in the history of postbiblical Judaism this festival came to be a celebration of the season in which the Law was given on Sinai. (Exod. 19:1: "On the third new moon after the people of Israel had gone forth out of the land of Egypt, on that day they came into the wilderness of Sinai.") Traditions about the miraculous translation of the Torah into all the languages of the earth came to be associated with the festival, which would make an interesting background for the story of Pentecost narrated in Acts. Unfortunately there is no way to ascertain whether Pentecost was celebrated as the festival of the giving of the

Torah as early as the first century C.E. Extant evidence seems to suggest that it was not, making it improbable that Luke's narrative is in any special way related to traditions about the giving of the Torah. For further reference, see the article on Pentecost by E. Lohse in *Theological Dictionary of the New Testament,* 10 vols. Edited by Gerhard Kittel and Gerhard Friedrich, trans. G. Bromiley (Grand Rapids: Eerdmans, 1968), VI, 46-53.

4. The quotation from Deut. 18 in Acts 3 follows neither the Hebrew nor the Greek text. In fact, the quote seems to be a conflation of two texts:

"The LORD your God will raise up for you a prophet like me from among you, from your brethren—him you shall heed." (Deut. 18:15)
"And whoever will not give heed to my words which he shall speak in my name, I myself will require it of him." (Deut. 18:19)
"For whoever is not afflicted on this same day shall be cut off from his people." (Lev. 23:29)

5. Matthew is also interested in fulfillment of prophecy, but not in the context of a history of promise and fulfillment. In a manner more similar to methods of interpretation practiced at Qumran, Matthew employs the biblical text as code book, the secret interpretation of which has been revealed. It is not the history of promise to which it points and of which it is a part but the meaning of the particular prophetic passage that is important for Matthew. Continuity between past and present is not historical in the sense that two events belong to the same story. Scripture is viewed almost ahistorically as a repository of secrets that have now been revealed in present events.

6. There seems to be some tension between Paul's characterization of Peter as the one entrusted with the "gospel to the circumcised" in Gal. 2:7-8, and the portrait of Peter in Acts as the first apostle to the Gentiles. Even in Acts, Peter's introduction in chap. 9 is somewhat unexpected. One learns later that both the Hellenists (Acts 11:19-21) and Paul (chap. 13) preach to Gentiles. But the story of those driven off after Stephen's persecution and the story of Paul's career are broken off to narrate Peter's visit to Cornelius. The placement of scenes is of obvious importance to the author.

7. According to Jacob Jervell, *Luke and the People of God* (Minneapolis: Augsburg, 1972), pp. 51-52, the "fallen tent of David" refers to the Jewish people: a righteous remnant has been erected. According to Ernst Haenchen, *The Acts of the Apostles: A Commentary,* on 15:16, the expression refers to Jesus, particularly to his resurrection. Support for this interpretation can be found in the Qumran Scrolls, where the passage from Amos is interpreted as a reference to the coming Messiah (4QFlorilegium).

8. Real tensions exist between the portrait of Paul in Acts and the self-portrait sketched by Paul in his letters.

9. H. Cadbury, *The Making of Luke-Acts* (London: S.P.C.K., 1961), pp. 219-20 and the articles there cited.

10. Some of the evidence is cited by Cadbury, *ibid.,* p. 118. His detailed proofs are to be found in the articles cited.

11. Perhaps the most striking event mentioned in both Paul's letters and in Acts is Paul's escape from Damascus via a basket lowered over the wall (Acts 9:24-25; II Cor. 11:32-33).

12. On some of the differences between the Paul of the letters and the Paul of Acts, see Phillip Vielhauer, "On the 'Paulinism' of Acts," *Studies in Luke-Acts,* ed. by Leander Keck and J. Louis Martyn (Nashville: Abingdon, 1966), pp. 33-50.

Chapter 10

1. The pattern, "You have heard that it was said. . . . But I say," is found also in rabbinic writings, suggesting perhaps that it is not as revolutionary as it might first appear. See Daube, *New Testament and Rabbinic Judaism,* pp. 55-62.

2. See, for example, Davies, *Setting of the Sermon on the Mount,* pp. 14-25; and P. Feine, J. Behm, and W. G. Kümmel, *Introduction to the New Testament,* trans. A. J. Mattil, Jr. (Nashville: Abingdon, 1966), p. 75.

3. The parable is from *Shabbath* 153a, *Babylonian Talmud,* trans. and ed. by I. Epstein (London, 1938), vol. 2, part 2, pp. 781-782. See Jeremias, *Parables of Jesus,* pp. 187-88.

4. The saying is paralleled with a statement attributed to R. Halafta ben Dosa in the Mishnah: "If ten men sit together and occupy themselves in the Law, the Divine Presence [the Shekinah] rests among them" (*Aboth* 3, 6; translation from H. Danby, *The Mishnah* [Oxford: University Press, 1933], p. 450).

5. Eusebius, *History of the Church,* p. 152.

6. For a summary of opinions, see Kümmel, *Introduction,* pp. 43-44, 85.

7. J. Kürzinger, "Das Papiaszeugnis," pp. 19-38. He justifies his translation by appeal to the whole context of the comments about Mark and Matthew and to the use in the quote of what he believes are literary terms.

8. The strongest advocate of such a position is K. Stendahl, *The School of St. Matthew* (Philadelphia: Fortress, 1968). G. D. Kilpatrick, *The Origins of the Gospel According to St. Matthew* (Oxford: Clarendon, 1946), believes that the Gospel was written principally for use in public worship. Most agree, however, that Matthew was composed to be of use to a clearly defined community.

9. According to Davies, *Setting of the Sermon on the Mount,* Matthew was composed as a reply to the new Pharisaic institution at Jabneh.

10. On this topic, see esp. Stendahl, *The School of St. Matthew.*

11. *Ibid.*

Chapter 11

1. According to the Synoptic Gospels, Jesus' last supper with his followers occurs on the first day of Passover; the last supper is thus a celebration of Passover (Mark 14:12; Matt. 26:17; Luke 22:7). The meal is to be eaten in the evening, after the new day has begun (i.e., after sunset). The crucifixion, therefore, is dated also on Passover, since Jesus' trial and execution were completed before sunset on the following day. According to John 13:1, the last supper occurs before the first day of the festival. Consequently Jesus' trial and execution are also dated on the "day of Preparation for the Passover" (19:14).

2. For a thorough consideration of the evidence for various editions of John, see R. Brown, *The Gospel According to John,* 2 vols., The Anchor Bible (Garden City, N. Y.: Doubleday, 1966), pp. xxiv-xl.

3. The hymn to Zeus by Cleanthes can be found in C. K. Barrett, *The New Testament Background: Selected Documents* (London: SPCK, 1956).

4. For a discussion of the relation of the prologue to the Gospel, see Brown, *John,* pp. 18-21.

5. A concise summary of the wisdom speculation is provided by Brown, *ibid,* pp. cxii-cxxv. Already in the book of Proverbs, wisdom has been personified and has been related in particular ways to creation. The far-reaching speculation has clearly been of importance for the author of the Fourth Gospel in his search for categories appropriate to the figure of Jesus.

In the past, there has been considerable disagreement among commentators about the milieu out of which the Gospel of John arose. Some have argued that the use of the term *Logos* (Word) suggests roots in Greek philosophy or at least in a Jewish philosopher like Philo who had by the time of John's Gospel produced several works attempting a synthesis of Jewish and Greek thought. Other scholars, notably Rudolf Bultmann, have argued that the background of the Fourth Gospel must be sought in so-called Gnostic speculation. The issue is thoroughly discussed in Raymond Brown's commentary (chap. 4 of the introduction).

Recent scholarship has become more convinced that direct dependence upon Greek philosophy or upon Philo seems unlikely, and there is a growing concensus that Gnosticism as a full-blown religious system did not predate the New Testament. It seems more likely that various forms of Hellenistic Judaism provided the setting out of which the Gospel of John arose.

6. "Beloved are Israel, for to them was given the precious instrument [Torah]; still greater was the love, in that it was made known to them that to them was given the precious instrument by which the world was created." (Mishnah, *Aboth,* 3:15)

[Comment on Genesis 1:1]
The Torah declares: "I was the working tool of the Holy One, blessed be He." In human practice, when a mortal king builds a palace, he builds it not with his own skill but with the skill of an architect. The architect moreover does not build it to arrange the chambers and the wicket doors. Thus God consulted the Torah and created the world, while the Torah declares, "In the beginning God created . . . ," "beginning" referring to the Torah, as in the verse, "The Lord made me as the beginning of His way" (Prov. 8:22). From *Midrash Rabbah: Genesis,* trans. H. Freedman (London, 1939), vol. 1, part 1.

7. The question whether to translate the Greek verb as transitive or intransitive is discussed in Meeks, *Prophet-King,* pp. 73-76.

8. According to Mishnah, *Pesahim* 1:5-6, preparation for Passover must begin on the sixth hour of the day preceding the feast with the burning of all leavened grain products.

9. The ancient hymn, the Nismat, and its date are discussed briefly in Meeks, *Prophet-King,* pp. 77-78.

10. The first reference is attributed to R. Johanan bar Nappaha, a Palestinian teacher in the second to the third centuries C.E.

11. Iraenaeus, *Against Heresies,* III 1:1.

12. Brown, *John,* pp. lxxxvii-civ.

13. *Ibid.,* pp. lxxxii-lxxxiii.

14. Martyn, *History and Theology in the Fourth Gospel.*

15. The image of the Gospel of John as a trial is developed in Nils A. Dahl's essay "The Johannine Church and History" in *Memory of the Early Church,* pp. 99-119.

Chapter 12

1. William Doty, *Letters in Primitive Christianity,* Guides to Biblical Scholarship (Philadelphia: Fortress Press, 1973), chap. 1, esp. pp. 8-11.

2. *Ibid.,* pp. 10-16.

3. The term used by Doty, *ibid.,* pp. 7-8, is "discursive letter."

4. *Ibid.,* pp. 13.

5. G. Milligan, *Here and There Among the Papyri* (London: Hodder & Stoughton, 1922), p. 35.

6. There is still considerable debate among scholars about the reliability of the information Acts provides about Paul, particularly in regard to Paul's attitude toward the Jewish Law and the focus of his missionary activity. Because reliability of Acts is disputed, we will restrict ourselves in this chapter to information Paul provides about himself in his letters.

7. For concise account of pseudepigraphical practices in antiquity and their possible bearing on New Testament writings, see B. M. Metzger, "Literary Forgeries and Canonical Pseudepigrapha," *Journal of Biblical Literature,* 1972, pp. 3-24.

8. The Greek verb *parakalo* is unfortunately translated with several English terms even in the same English version—suggesting that it has not always been viewed as an epistolary convention.

9. Studies of other features of Pauline letters are cited in Doty, *Letters,* chap. 2.

10. I owe much of this to John Hawkins, "The Opponents of Paul in Galatia" (Ph.D. diss., Yale, 1971).

11. Mark 12:29-31; see also Matt. 7:12. Hillel's famous summary of Torah ("What thou hatest for thyself, do not to thy neighbor: this is the whole law, the rest is commentary") is recorded in Babylonian Talmud *Shabbat* 31a. The summary of R. Akiba also approximates Paul's: "'Thou shalt love thy neighbor as thyself'; this is the greatest general principle in the Torah" (*Sifra* on Leviticus 19:18).

12. Walter Schmithals, *Gnosticism in Corinth,* trans. John Steely (Nashville: Abingdon, 1971).

13. Nils A. Dahl, "Paul and the Church at Corinth According to I Cor. 1:10–4:21," *Christian History and Interpretation* (Cambridge: Cambridge University Press, 1967).

14. The attractiveness of this proposal is its simpliciy and its ability to explain the four slogans. There is no evidence that Peter (Cephas) ever visited Corinth, and the "Christ party" does not easily fit into a schema, often proposed, according to which the parties form around leaders in the Corinthian church who baptized them.

15. Plato, *Symposium,* Loeb Classical Library Series (London, 1921–66), 5, pp. 59-61.

16. Variant readings in the Greek manuscripts in v. 4 make the structure less clear than the English translations suggest.

Chapter 13

1. G. B. Caird, *A Commentary on the Revelation of St. John the Divine* (New York: Harper, 1966), pp. 22-58.

2. Other apocalyptic works include I Enoch, II Enoch, IV Ezra, II and III Baruch. They can be found in Charles, *Apocrypha and Pseudepigrapha,* vol. 2.

3. Paul Hanson, *The Dawn of Apocalyptic* (Philadelphia: Fortress Press, 1975).

4. E. Stauffer, *Christ and the Caesars,* trans. K. and R. G. Smith (London: SCM Press, 1955), pp. 147-191, esp. 155.

5. In Hebrew and Greek, letters of the alphabet also served as numerals, each letter having a numerical value. The numerical total of the Hebrew letters in the words "Nero Caesar" equals 666. A variant spelling in the name Nero in Hebrew also explains a variant reading in several Greek manuscripts according to which the number of the beast is 616. This would suggest some type of Hebrew or Aramaic precursor to Revelation, perhaps in the form of traditions; yet it still seems to be the most plausible explanation of the mysterious number, which the author presumes his readers will be able to interpret.

6. See the chart comparing several outlines of Revelation in John Wick Bowman, "The Revelation to John: Its Dramatic Structures," *Interpretation,* 1955, p. 44.

7. Kenneth R. R. Gros Louis, "Revelation," in *Literary Interpretations of Biblical Narratives,* pp. 330-45.

ANNOTATED BIBLIOGRAPHY

Translations of the New Testament

Good News Bible. New York: American Bible Society, 1977.
Recent completion of *Good News for Modern Man* (the New Testament in Today's English Version) first published in 1966. Very helpful translation into American idiomatic English, designed for the unsophisticated reader. It remains essentially faithful to original texts, but the purposely limited vocabulary (*ca.* 600 words) restricts its usefulness for students. Includes a glossary of troublesome terms. Paperback.

The Jerusalem Bible. Garden City, N. Y.: Doubleday, 1966.
The English translation of the original French version by the Dominican Biblical School in Jerusalem. Very good critical notes to the text and helpful introductory essays to each book. Extremely well written from literary standpoint, carefully reflecting prose and poetry of original texts. Paperback.

The Living Bible. Wheaton, Ill.: Tyndale House, 1971.
This interpretive paraphrase of the Old and New Testaments by Kenneth Taylor is the completion of work begun in *Living Letters* (1962). Not intended to be a translation, *The Living Bible* is a restatement of biblical thought in conversational American English. The storytelling style modernizes particularly Old Testament narratives, shortens sentences, and reduces to prose many poetic forms. It is written from a self-consciously "rigid evangelical position," resolves most ambiguities in the text in favor of that stance, and makes theological judgments reflecting extremely conservative thought. The marginal notes often constitute a running commentary. A very readable book, helpful for illuminating what theological issues are at stake in interpretation, but potentially endangers a true reading of the text if used as a translation. Paperback.

Phillips, J. B. *The New Testament in Modern English.* New York: Macmillan, 1960.
Phillips' paraphrase, from a slightly less thoroughgoing conservative position than Taylor's, is its equivalent in conversational British English. The same advantages and liabilities of that paraphrase apply here. Helpful for occasional comparative reference. Paperback.

Introduction to the New Testament

Behm, Johannes, P. Feine, and W. G. Kümmel. *Introduction to the New Testament.* Translated by A. J. Mattill, Jr. Nashville: Abingdon, 1966.
In terse fashion, the critical details of current scholarly investigations have

been added to an outstanding and popular New Testament introduction. Complete with lengthy bibliographies at the beginning of each chapter, this book is highly recommended as a resource book for the teacher.

Davies, William D. *Invitation to the New Testament.* New York: Doubleday, 1969.
Designed for the beginning student, this book seeks to provide a comprehensive description of the major books of the New Testament (excluding Revelation) and a clear rundown of various scholarly approaches and interpretations. Popularly written, but most responsible in content. Paperback.

Kee, Howard C.; Young, F. W.; and Froehlich, K. *Understanding the New Testament.* Englewood Cliffs, N. J.: Prentice-Hall, 1965.
Probably the most complete modern introductory text. Companion volume to Anderson's *Understanding the Old Testament.* Good introduction to the Synoptic problem, survey of New Testament history, and discussion of each book in its context within the early church.

Price, James L. *Interpreting the New Testament.* New York: Holt, Rinehart and Winston, 1961.
A very competent introduction to New Testament literature and religion. Good introductory discussion of methodology and helpful reconstruction of early Christianity, with reference to each book. Particularly good general exposition of Pauline thought and outlines of the Epistles.

Sandmel, Samuel. *A Jewish Understanding of the New Testament.* Cincinnati: Hebrew Union College Press, 1957.
Written by a leading Jewish scholar, this book takes full advantage of modern liberal scholarship while preserving a well-handled sensitivity of treatment for the more volatile issues. An especially useful book for the teacher who wishes to become familiar with a Jewish approach to the New Testament.

Background to the New Testament

Barrett, Charles K. *The New Testament Background: Selected Documents.* London: S.P.C.K., 1956.
A helpful collection of nonbiblical texts contemporary with the New Testament, illuminating the historical and cultural backgrounds of the Roman world and the Hellenized Near East. Paperback.

Bickerman, Elias. *From Ezra to the Last of the Maccabees.* New York: Schocken Books, 1962.
A two-hundred page description of the history and thought of the Jewish community that returned from the Babylonian exile, describing how Judaism interacted with Hellenistic culture and thought. Outlines the eventual parting of Judeo-Christianity from rabbinic Judaism.

Bultmann, Rudolph. *Primitive Christianity.* New York: Meridian, 1960.
An interpretive account of the historical forces that led to the birth of Christianity as a religion and a philosophy of life. Contains an especially good account of the influence of Hellenism but is somewhat narrow in its assessment of Judaism and Old Testament heritage. Paperback.

Cornfeld, Gaalyaha. *Daniel to Paul: Jews in Conflict with Graeco-Roman Civilization.* New York: Macmillan, 1962.
This book provides an excellent background—both historical and religious— to the Hasmoneans, Dead Sea Scrolls, New Testament world, early Christianity, and the Bar Kochbah revolt. A companion volume to *From Adam to Daniel.* Richly illustrated. Good for classroom reference.

Daube, David. *The New Testament and Rabbinic Judaism.* New York: Arno Press, 1956.
A very impressive scholarly work that sets forth the thought, life, ethos, and literature of early rabbinic Judaism and their influence on the New Testament. Examines rabbinic styles of biblical interpretation used by New Testament writers and suggests some heretofore unheralded backgrounds of Christian thought in Jewish tradition. Detailed table of contents and index of biblical, rabbinic, and classical sources cited.

Glatzer, Nahum N. *Hillel the Elder.* Washington: B'nai B'rith Hillel Foundation, 1959.
Essential for an understanding of the milieu in which Jesus' ministry took place, this brief (ninety pages) volume outlines the story of a major figure in first-century Judaism. Paperback.

Hengel, Martin. *Judaism and Hellenism.* Philadelphia: Fortress Press, 1974.
One of the finest works on the intertestamental period, this recent volume operates with the assumption that Palestinian Judaism of the first century was thoroughly Hellenistic. The standard survey of political and religious sources of the time from historical, archaeological, and literary perspectives. Highly recommended.

Herford, Robert T. *The Pharisees.* New York: Macmillan, 1924.
The author's purpose is to remove Pharisaism from the polemical atmosphere of the New Testament and provide the reader with a fair and unbiased description of the history of theory of Pharisaism, its role in pre-Christian Judaism and its ongoing importance in rabbinic Judaism and Christianity; for the intermediate to advanced student of the Bible.

Kee, Howard C. *The Origins of Christianity: Sources and Documents.* Englewood Cliffs, N. J.: Prentice-Hall, 1973.
An invaluable selection of texts illuminating the political history of Judaism, its relationship to the Roman Empire, the religious atmosphere of the intertestamental period, and representative early Gnostic thought, with critical notes and interpretation.

Jeremias, Joachim. *Jerusalem in the Time of Jesus.* Philadelphia: Fortress Press, 1969.
A very detailed and annotated study of the economic, social, religious, cultural, and political conditions in Jerusalem during the century immediately prior to and following the time of the apostolic church. Complete index of biblical and rabbinic works cited. Highly recommended for reference use.

Jonas, Hans, *The Gnostic Religion.* Boston: Beacon Press, 1958.
The most authoritative work on early Gnosticism. The first section deals with basic Gnostic thought, imagery, and language; the second elucidates five representative Gnostic systems both from western and eastern branches of the movement. The third section traces the growth and development of Gnostic thought, its sources, and its influence on later movements. An essential text for serious students.

Reicke, Bo Ivan. *The New Testament Era.* Philadelphia: Fortress Press, 1968.
An extremely readable outline of the history of the political, religious, cultural, and literary situations in Palestine between 539 B.C.E. and the end of the first century C.E. Well documented with an eye to New Testament understanding.

Schürer, Emil. *The History of the Jewish People in the Age of Jesus Christ.* Revised and translated by Geza Vermes and F. Millar. Edinburgh: T. & T. Clark, 1973.

This recent translation and revision makes Schürer's classic work from the late nineteenth century still more valuable. The updated bibliography and information from the Qumran documents contribute to the most helpful history of the Jews of the intertestamental period.

Stendahl, Krister, ed. *The Scrolls and the New Testament.* New York: Harper, 1957.

This anthology includes treatments of the relationship between the Dead Sea Scrolls and Paul, John the Baptist, the Lord's Supper, the Sermon on the Mount, Acts, the Gospel of John, and others. The introduction provides an excellent understanding of the perspective necessary to an investigation of the scrolls. Though some of the studies are now dated, it is still a useful volume. Paperback.

Vermes, Geza. *The Dead Sea Scrolls in English.* Baltimore: Penguin Books, 1962.

The most accessible translation of the scrolls. Excellent glosses and introductions included in the paperback edition.

————. *Scripture and Tradition in Judaism.* Leiden: E. J. Brill, 1961.

Excellent essays on the development of Jewish tradition and its relationship to biblical interpretation within orthodox and sectarian Judaism and Christianiy. Recommended for the advanced student.

Resources for New Testament Study

The Anchor Bible. Edited by David N. Freedman and W. F. Albright. Garden City, N. Y.: Doubleday, 1964–

A series of translations, critical notes, and introductions to every book in the Bible that will comprise forty volumes when complete. As with every commentary series, some volumes are more helpful than others, but the Anchor series is fairly consistently responsible, and some volumes are excellent. Scholars are representative of ecumenical and international positions.

Black, Matthew, and Rowley, H. H., eds. *Peake's Commentary on the Bible.* Camden, N. J.: Thomas Nelson, 1962.

An excellent example of liberal Protestant scholarship, with 285 pages of helpful introductory articles on archeology, history, form criticism, Near Eastern culture, languages, the Bible as literature, and so forth, and 780 pages of finely done verse-by-verse commentary on the biblical text. Recommended for school library.

Brown, Raymond E.; Fitzmyer, J. A.; and Murphy, R. E., eds. *The Jerome Biblical Commentary.* Englewood Cliffs, N. J.: Prentice-Hall, 1968.

A monumental work, representing liberal Roman Catholic scholarship, with one thousand pages of excellent verse-by-verse commentary and almost five hundred pages of introductory articles. The slight overemphasis on New Testament thought and the strong theological concern do not undermine the value of this book for the teacher of literature. Recommended for school library.

Bultmann, Rudolph. *Theology of the New Testament.* New York: Scribner's, 1951.

A massive, frequently difficult, but consistently rewarding work that gives the central meaning and message of the New Testament as seen by this leading German scholar. A classic in New Testament study, now available in a one-volume paperback.

Dodd, Charles H. *The Old Testament in the New.* Philadelphia: Fortress Press, 1963.
   A sensitive interpretation of the relationship between the two Testaments and a plea for the necessity of understanding this relationship for New Testament study. Paperback.
Ellison, John W. *Nelson's Complete Concordance of the Revised Standard Version Bible.*
Fuller, Reginald H. *The New Testament in Current Study.* New York: Scribner's, 1962.
   A brief, lucid presentation of the main problems facing New Testament scholars, including the major alternative positions taken. Paperback.
International Critical Commentary. New York: Scribner's, 1908–51.
   Under the editorial supervision of S. R. Driver and A. Plummer, this series of translations, introductions, and critical notes of the Bible was produced to aid exegesis with linguistic, historical, archaeological, and theological data. The volumes vary in usefulness, but are generally reliable, insofar as early twentieth-century scholarship permits. A new series is in the process of replacing some volumes and supplementing others.
McKnight, Edgar V. *What Is Form Criticism?* Philadelphia: Fortress Press, 1969.
   One in a series of short paperbacks dealing with new techniques of biblical criticism as applied to the New Testament. Form criticism begins with the findings of source criticism and proceeds to break down gospel narratives into component units that then may be evaluated with an eye toward modifications of the earlier tradition by the church. Contains a short glossary and annotated bibliograph.
Perrin, Norman. *What Is Redaction Criticism?* Philadelphia: Fortress Press, 1969.
   This volume deals with the most recent of the disciplines of New Testament criticism, investigating the relationship between an inherited tradition and a later interpretive point of view. A short, cogent overview that includes an annotated bibliography and a good introduction that traces the historical origins of the discipline.
Neill, Stephen. *The Interpretation of the New Testament 1861-1961.* London: Oxford University Press, 1964.
   Traces the major notions governing New Testament scholarship in the past century and surveys representative schools of biblical interpretation and their leading proponents. A very helpful volume for the teacher who wishes to understand the presuppositions governing various scholars' work.
Taylor, Vincent. *The Formation of the Gospel Tradition.* New York: Macmillan, 1953.
   Early in the development of form critical research, this book was written to suggest the consequences of the discipline on study of the Gospels in their formative stage. The author takes a somewhat critical stance toward form criticism and gives therefore a helpful balance to discussion.
Throckmorton, Burton H., ed. *Gospel Parallels.* Camden, N. J.: Thomas Nelson, 1957.
   An especially useful synopsis of the Synoptic Gospels printed in parallel columns that allows a clear comparison of the sources. Extensive footnotes giving noncanonical parallels. Highly recommended for the student.
Young, Robert. *Analytical Concordance to the Bible.* New York: Funk & Wagnalls, 1920.

Jesus: His Life and Teachings

Beare, Frank W. *The Earliest Records of Jesus.* Oxford: B. H. Blackwell, 1962.
Originally designed as a companion volume and commentary to Huck's *Synopsis of the First Three Gospels,* it is equally appropriate for use with Throckmorton's *Gospel Parallels.* The author's outlines and format are especially useful for the teacher in need of quick and competent source for the fruits of scholarship.

Bornkamm, Günther. *Jesus of Nazareth.* Translated by I. & F. McLuskey with J. M. Robinson. New York: Harper, 1960.
A first-rate scholarly treatment of the message and history of Jesus. The author is optimistic about the possibility of reaching an historical understanding of the traditions about Jesus through the use of historical-critical method, while remaining realistic about its limitations.

Dibelius, Martin. *From Tradition to Gospel.* New York: Scribner's, 1965.
The pioneer work of form criticism on the origin and intent of the early traditions about Jesus by an important German scholar. Highly recommended. Paperback.

Hunter, Archibald M. *The Work and Words of Jesus.* Philadelphia: Westminster Press, 1951.
With full awareness of the problems of other lives of Jesus, the author attempts to write one nevertheless. This "life of Jesus" uses the tools of historical-critical scholarship.

Jeremias, Joachim. *The Parables of Jesus.* Translated by S. H. Hooke. New York: Scribner's, 1963.
An exhaustive critical analysis of the parables by an important scholar. The author attempts to recover the original intent and significance of the parables as they were spoken by Jesus, with the tools of form critical research. Paperback.

Kee, Howard C. *Jesus in History.* New York: Harcourt Brace and World, 1970.
The aim of this book is to provide the student with an understanding of the various ways in which Jesus was perceived by segments of the primitive church. Through its discussion of the special aims of the gospel writers and their different views of history, it acquaints the reader with the "new quest of the historical Jesus." Included are fine treatments of the historical importance of the Qumran scrolls and such apocryphal works as the Gospel of Thomas. Paperback.

Klausner, Joseph. *Jesus of Nazareth.* New York: Macmillan, 1959.
Originally in Hebrew by a leading Jewish scholar, this volume is valuable to the non-Jew not so much because of its analysis of the teachings and ministry of Jesus (which is a bit biased despite the author's intentions) but for the material concerning the cultural and historical environment of the time.

The Synoptic Gospels

Bultmann, Rudolph. *Form Criticism.* Torchbooks; New York: Harper, 1962.
The author applies form critical theory to the Gospels to show what the full application of such a method can be. Paperback.

Cadbury, Henry J. *The Making of Luke-Acts.* London: S.P.C.K., 1961.
Originally published in 1926, this book offers a dated but still extremely useful examination of the author of Luke-Acts, the importance of his work, as well as a comprehensive and realistic description of the literary process that led to the writing of the Gospel.

Flender, Helmut. *St. Luke: Theologian of Redemptive History.* Philadelphia: Fortress Press, 1967.
Written as a contribution to the discussion of the relationship between theology and history, this exegetical research of Luke-Acts reveals the potentials of redaction criticism.

Jervell, Jacob. *Luke and the People of God: A New Look at Luke-Acts.* Minneapolis: Augsburg, 1972.
An excellent group of essays discussing themes in Luke-Acts and a reconstruction of primitive Christianity and the development of Christian theology. Recommended for student use.

Nineham, Dennis. *The Gospel of St. Mark.* Baltimore: Penguin Books, 1963.
A verse-by-verse commentary on the Gospel intended to reveal the evangelist's original meaning. Of special interest is the brief historical introduction to the Gospels.

Schweizer, Eduard. *The Good News According to Mark.* Translated by D. H. Madvig. Richmond: John Knox Press, 1970.
Using Today's English Version (Good News), this verse-by-verse commentary takes into account all current theories about Mark's purpose and theology and suggests a fresh use of them. Good treatment of the additional endings to the Gospel.

Stendahl, Krister. *The School of St. Matthew.* Philadelphia: Fortress Press, 1968.
An excellent study of the uses of the Old Testament in Matthew to support the contention the Gospel is a product of a Christian rabbinic school of biblical interpretation. Very careful scholarship, for the advanced student having working knowledge of the biblical languages, although some sections are accessible to informed readers. Extensive bibliography and index.

Paul

Bornkamm, Günther. *Paul.* Translated by D. M. G. Stalker. New York: Harper, 1969.
Sensitive and responsible treatment of Paul the missionary pastor and apostle, his thought, and suggested sources and interpretations of his theology. Recommended for student use.

Dibelius, Martin, and Kümmel, Werner G. *Paul.* Translated by F. Clarke. Philadelphia: Westminster, 1966.
A brilliant and well-written book that exhibits first rate scholarship and sensitivity to issues of Pauline research. Highly recommended for the beginning student.

Francis, Fred O. and J. Paul Sampley. *Pauline Parallels.* Philadelphia: Fortress Press, 1975.
Sets forth the entire Pauline corpus sequentially with suggested parallel passages based on similarity of language, thought, images, letter structure and form. Based on the RSV, it is similar in layout to Throckmorton's *Gospel Parallels.* A very helpful resource for the student.

Knox, John. *Chapters in a Life of Paul.* Nashville: Abingdon, 1950.
A good basic text for the student beginning an investigation of Paul. The author uses and explains techniques of textual criticism necessary to understand Paul's life, religious experience, and role in early Christianity. Paperback.

Nock, Arthur D. *St. Paul.* New York: Harper, 1938.
A very helpful and readable introduction to the life and writings of the apostle Paul. Recommended for the beginning student. Paperback.

John

Barrett, Charles K. *The Gospel According to St. John.* London: S.P.C.K., 1956.
An exhaustive technical commentary on the Fourth Gospel. Includes an excellent comprehensive introduction, with sections on the relationship between John the evangelist and the writer of the Johannine epistles.

Bultmann, Rudolph. *The Gospel of John.* Translated by G. R. Beasley-Murray, R. W. N. Hoare, J. K. Riches. Philadelphia: Westminster, 1971.
This major commentary dwells heavily on reflections of first-century Gnosticism on the Fourth Gospel. The excellent critical notes are particularly helpful. Bultmann's analysis of the sources of John have been rejected by most scholars, but his brilliant insights are still challenging.

Brown, Raymond E. *The Gospel According to John.* 2 vols. Garden City, N. Y.: Doubleday, 1966.
Volume 29 in the Anchor Bible series, this responsible translation of the text, with introduction and critical notes is written by a leading Catholic scholar. Particularly good section on questions of dating, authorship, and relationship with Johannine epistles and Revelation. Recommended for student use.

Martyn, J. Louis. *History and Theology in the Fourth Gospel.* New York: Harper, 1968.
A most creative reconstruction, based on internal evidence, of the Johannine community, its history and theology. Suggests John's Gospel is a "two-level drama," at once the story of Jesus and the experience of the Johannine church. Reads like a detective story. A good secondary work.

Later New Testament Writings

Beker, J. Christiaan. *The Church Faces the World.* Philadelphia: Westminster Press, 1960.
A very good overview of late New Testament writings: the Pastoral Epistles, Hebrews, James, the Catholic Epistles, and Revelation, from the perspective of their place in the life of the church as it entered the second century. Recommended for student use.

Caird, G. B. *A Commentary to the Revelation of John.* London: A. and C. Black, 1966.
Very good verse-by-verse critical commentary, with a particularly helpful introduction on the nature of apocalyptic. Recommended for teachers' reference use.

Rowley, H. H. *The Revelance of Apocalyptic.* Woking, Surry: Lutterworth Press, 1944.
A good introduction for the beginning student, dealing with intertestamental and Christian apocalyptic writings. Good notes on dating,

authorship, and structure of various texts, particularly one on the synoptic "little apocalypse" (Mark 13 and parallels).

Russell, D. S. *The Method and Message of Jewish Apocalyptic.* Philadelphia: Westminster Press, 1964.

A volume in the Old Testament Library, this book examines the milieu of Jewish apocalyptic literature between 200 B.C.E. and 100 C.E., its place in the history of Jewish and Christian tradition, and elements of the apocayptic message. One of the finest recent works, highly recommended for teacher use. Contains an excellent bibliography.

APPENDIX

I. The Political History of Palestine: 175 B.C.E.–135 C.E.

175-164	Antiochus IV Epiphanes, king of Syria; Onias III, high priest in Jerusalem
170-169	Antiochus marches against Jerusalem
168	Pagan sacrifices offered in Jerusalem Temple
168-143	Era of the Maccabees
165	Reconsecration of the Temple under Judas Maccabeus
153	Jonathan, brother of Judas, becomes high priest
139	Roman Senate recognizes independence of Judea
135-105	John Hyrcanus, son of Simon Maccabeus, Hasmonean high priest and ruler
104-63	Period of internecine rivalry among Hasmoneans
63	Pompey enters Jerusalem; rise to power of Antipater of Idumea
47	Antipater becomes procurator of Judea; his son Herod becomes governor of Galilee
44	Julius Caesar assassinated
42	Brutus and Cassius defeated at Philippi by Antony and Octavian;
40	Invasion of Syria and Palestine by the Parthians; in Rome, Herod designated king of Judea
39-38	Parthians driven out of the country; Herod lands in Palestine to claim his throne
37 B.C.E.-4 C.E.	Reign of Herod the Great
30 B.C.E.-14 C.E.	Augustus Caesar (Octavian), Roman emperor
4 B.C.E.-6 C.E.	Archelaus, son of Herod, ethnarch of Judea, Samaria, and Idumea
4 B.C.E.–39 C.E.	Herod Antipas, son of Herod, tetrarch of Galilee and Perea
4 B.C.E.-34 C.E.	Philip, son of Herod, tetrarch of Batanea, Trachonitis, and Auranitis
6-41 C.E.	Judea, Samaria, and Idumea, as Roman province of Palestine, governed by procurators residing in Caesarea.
6	Census of the population taken by Quirinius, Roman legate of Syria

14-37	Tiberius Caesar, Roman emperor
26-36	Pontius Pilate, Roman procurator of Judea
30 (?)	Crucifixion of Jesus
37-44	Herod Agrippa I, grandson of Herod the Great, granted the tetrarchy of Philip; from 41 C.E., reigned as king over the former realm of Herod the Great
37-41	Caligula, Roman emperor
38	Anti-Jewish riots in Alexandria
40	Embassy of Alexandrian Jews (headed by Philo) to Caligula
41-54	Claudius, Roman emperor
44-66	The Roman procurators
	44-? Cuspius Fadus
	?-48 Tiberius Alexander, nephew of Philo
	52-60 Antonius Felix
	60-66 Porcius Festus, Albinus, Gessius Florus
51-60	Rise of Zealots and Sicarii; imprisonment of apostle Paul at Caesarea
54-68	Nero, Roman emperor
66	Outbreak of revolutionary movement against Rome
67	Vespasian arrives; war in Galilee
67-68	Civil war in Jerusalem between the Zealots, led by John of Gischala, and the men of order, led by high priest Ananus; flight of the Christian community from Jerusalem to Pella
68	Death of Nero; suspension of war operations
69	Murder of Galba, successor of Nero; Vespasian proclaimed emperor; Jewish war committed to his son Titus
70	Fall and destruction of Jerusalem
71	Titus and Vespasian celebrate triumph in Rome
73	The fortress of Masada, defended by Eleasar ben Jair, conquered by Flavius Silva
69-79	Vespasian, Roman emperor
79-81	Titus, Roman emperor
81-96	Domitian, Roman emperor
96-98	Nerva, Roman emperor
98-117	Trajan, Roman emperor
100	Palestine incorporated into the province of Syria
115-117	Jewish rebellions in Egypt, Cyrene, Cyprus, and Mesopotamia; Lusius Quietus appointed governor of Palestine
117-138	Hadrian, Roman emperor
132-135	The great rebellion under Hadrian; Bar Kochbah, Jewish leader, proclaimed Messiah by Rabbi

	Akiba b. Joseph; Julius Severus, Roman general
135	Fall of rebel fortress of Beth-ther; Jerusalem converted into a Roman colony (Aelia Capitolina)

II. Pauline Chronology

Dating Paul's letters and travels is difficult for several reasons. During the first century of the common era there was no common calendar. Events were dated by correlation with more important occurrences or with the career of an important official (see Luke 3:1). In Paul's letters, there are regrettably few references to public events or persons datable by comparison with secular sources. For plotting dates we are almost wholly dependent upon Acts, whose reliability is not universally accepted. And even for those who generally accept the reliability of Acts, correlation with Paul's accounts of his travels is difficult.

The most significant piece of information for dating is the reference in Acts 18:12 to Gallio, the proconsul of Achaia before whom Paul appeared. On the basis of an inscription found in Delphi it is possible to date Gallio's short tenure of office with high probability from 51-52 C.E. With this as a fixed point, it is possible to sketch a rough outline of Paul's career from the bits and pieces he provides in his letters (see esp. Gal. 1–2). There is generally more agreement among scholars about dates prior to 51-52 than about later stages of Paul's career. Those wishing to study the problem of dating in more depth are invited to consult standard introductions like those of Kuemmel or Kee. Dates are given only for the undisputed letters.

32-34	Conversion (I Cor. 15:3-8; Gal. 1; Phil. 3:4-11; Acts 9)
35 (36)	First visit to Jerusalem (Gal. 1:18-19)
35 (36)-48	Work in Syria and Cilicia (Gal. 1:20-24)
48 (49)	Second visit to Jerusalem (apostolic conference) (Gal. 2:1-10; Acts 15)
48-56 (49-58)	Travels in Asia Minor and Greece
50 (51)	First Letter to the Thessalonians
54 (53-55)	Letter to the Galatians
55 (54)	First Letter to the Corinthians
56 (55)	Second Letter to the Corinthians
57 (55-56)	Letter to the Romans
56 or 62	Letter to the Philippians
56 or 62	Letter to Philemon
58 (56-57)	Arrest in Jerusalem
unknown	Martyrdom in Rome

INDEX OF SCRIPTURE